Advanced praise for Broadcast Rites and Sites:

"Joe Castiglione is an integral part of the spirit of the Red Sox and Broadcast Rites and Sites reflects that spirit. Every fan will enjoy this thoughtful look into life in Red Sox Nation, both at Fenway Park and around the American League."

— **Theo Epstein**, General Manager, Boston Red Sox

"You don't have to be a diehard Red Sox fan to enjoy what Joe Castiglione has entertainingly written. My wife's a Yankee fan to the core, and I had to pry Joe's wide-ranging book away from her. Castiglione might not have been able to play ball as a kid—that's what he says in the book—but he's cleared the Green Monster with this one."

— **Bill Christine**, author of a Roberto Clemente biography and sportswriter for the *Los Angeles Times*

"Shakespeare wrote of 'Nature's nobleman.' This book is by and about a baseball nobleman. Joe Castiglione is a truly fine big-league announcer— and an even better person. *Broadcast Rites and Sites* etches ballparks, colleagues, the Red Sox's bewitching lure, and the peripatetic life of a radio baseball man. A wonderful read—and life."

— **Curt Smith**, author of *Voices of the Game*, *The Storytellers*, and *What Baseball Means to Me*

"Having arrived in Boston the same year as Joe, I have always been impressed by his preparation and attention to detail. The latter is just one of the things that stands out in this book, which clearly shows Joe hasn't wasted a lot of his time in the 21 years we've known each other. A great read!"

— **Mike Shalin**, *Boston Herald* and author of *Out by a Step*

"This book is for you if you have ever dreamed of being a sports broadcaster. From the parks to the players, from Spring Training to the postseason, Joe Castiglione tells his personal stories about what being a major league baseball announcer is really like. Don't 'wait 'til next year'—read it now, and let Joe teach you about the baseball life in the same way that he taught and inspired me."

> — **The Rev. Leslie K. Sterling**, the first female public
> address announcer in the American League,
> Fenway Park, 1994–1996

"*Broadcast Rites and Sites* is a readily readable discourse by one of America's leading baseball broadcasters, Joe Castiglione, the voice of the Boston Red Sox and Red Sox Nation. For those with a passion for baseball, it is chock full of perceptive discussions of the past two decades of the game, the Red Sox, and Joe's observations about leading Bosox players. Baseball fans and those who are just plain interested in life itself will not be able to put down this page turner of a book."

> — **Bill Gould**, Stanford law professor and
> Boston Red Sox fan since 1946

Broadcast Rites and Sites

Broadcast Rites and Sites

I Saw It on the Radio with the Boston Red Sox

Joe Castiglione
with Douglas B. Lyons

TAYLOR TRADE PUBLISHING
Lanham • New York • Dallas • Boulder • Toronto • Oxford

Published by Taylor Trade Publishing
An imprint of The Rowman & Littlefield Publishing Group, Inc.
4501 Forbes Boulevard, Suite 200
Lanham, Maryland 20706

Distributed by National Book Network

Library of Congress Cataloging-in-Publication Data

Castiglione, Joe.
  Broadcast rites and sites : I saw it on the radio with the Boston Red Sox /
Joe Castiglione with Douglas B. Lyons.—1st Taylor Trade Pub. ed.
    p. cm.
  ISBN 1-58979-081-2 (hardcover : alk. paper)
  1. Radio and baseball. 2. Castiglione, Joe. 3. Sportscasters—United States.
4. Boston Red Sox (Baseball team) I. Lyons, Douglas B. II. Title.
GV880.C37 2004
070.4'49796'092—dc23   2003027672

⊗™ The paper used in this publication meets the minimum requirements
of American National Standard for Information Sciences—Permanence of
Paper for Printed Library Materials, ANSI/NISO Z39.48–1992.
Manufactured in the United States of America.

This book is dedicated to family.

My father Frank and my mother Pam.

Dad taught me to read the baseball box scores before my ABCs.

He also hit the best pop-up fungoes. He really created a monster.

It is also for Jan, the love of my life, for letting me pursue my dream,

and for our children, Duke, Tom, and Kate, who have lived the baseball life.

Contents

PART III
Along the Way

Acknowledgments

The authors wish to thank Dick Bresciani of the Boston Red Sox, Terry Cashman for use of his title "I Saw It on the Radio" from his song and recording *Play-by-Play (I Saw It on the Radio)*, words by Terry Cashman, James Austin, and Warner Fuselle, music by Terry Cashman, Copyright © 1990 Metrostar Music (ASCAP), www.MetrostarRecords.com; our editor Jill Langford, and our agents Alfred Geller, Michael Kane, Lori Pope, and Sam Lockhart.

Special thanks too for Red Sox photographer Julie Cordeiro, Tim Samway (unofficial broadcast booth photographer), and our official scanner Ken Dubrowski.

Foreword

Pedro Martinez

In my six years in Boston, I have seen that Joe Castiglione is very disciplined and attentive to his work—and has the experience to do his work. He has the respect of all the reporters and announcers because he is a good human being.

It's a daily adventure, seeing and reporting games. It's very difficult—traveling so much, being away from your family. Only a person with discipline and a respect for the work can do it. I can understand what he says and his ability to analyze a game, not only for baseball fanatics who listen, but the emotion he puts into it is admirable because he's so creative.

With the years he's had, he has the experience to describe the game wonderfully. I've learned much, but he's seen many more games than I have. He's seen things no one else has seen—people simply see things better from the outside—what we do, before, during, and after games and during travel. I couldn't do that sort of work; I don't have the patience for it.

Joe has the ability to observe and report not only what goes on in the game, but insights into what happens before and after the games—

how we live, what we do, how we cope with all the travel and time away from our families. He broadcasts not only for the fanatics who follow the game, but also for people who can enjoy the emotion he conveys into his descriptions and insights.

I can't imagine ever having the discipline and patience to do what he does.

Preface

Since 1983, I have been blessed with the opportunity to bring Boston Red Sox baseball to the greatest fans in the world—the fans of New England and to the citizens of Red Sox Nation throughout the country. I have been able to describe the fortunes of a baseball club that has competed for championships in almost all of those seasons from the best seat in the house, which John Updike called "that quaint, little bandbox of a ballpark" known as Fenway Park. I have dealt with marvelous athletes, coaches, managers, scouts, umpires, writers, executives, and all that comprise the unique family of baseball. As my good friend Ernie Harwell wrote in his wonderful essay, "Baseball—the Game for All America," baseball is "just a game as simple as a ball and bat, yet as complex as the American spirit it represents."

Baseball has given me many opportunities: to see World Series and the game's classic events, to visit the White House, to meet people from all walks of life—the famous and the not so famous—and to form many lasting friendships. Baseball has made it possible for me and my family to escape part of the winter and view life through rose-colored glasses at Spring Training and to see the great attractions of this country. Baseball has also given me the chance to bring entertainment and light to the shut-ins, the lonely, and the elderly, to help in the fight against cancer through the Jimmy Fund, and to stay in tune with the youth of America by teaching sports broadcasting to college students.

I have had many priceless experiences and want to share them with those who love the game of baseball as much as I do. I hope this book will help those fans who travel to different ports around the nation following their favorite team and who want to get some feeling of the baseball lifestyle. The secret of the charmed life of a baseball broadcaster cannot be kept a secret.

Special thanks to the Boston Red Sox, to my coauthor Douglas Lyons, and to all who assisted in the production of this book—especially to my friend Pedro Martinez, who provided the foreword, to my family for living the baseball life with me, and to the loyal listeners of Red Sox baseball.

Joe Castiglione
Boston, February 2004

Introduction

Douglas B. Lyons

Joe Castiglione was my brother Jeffrey's good friend long before I met him. Of course, Jeffrey has been a Red Sox fan for the last 50 years or so, and I have only been a baseball fan for the last 24 years.

Jeff has been to Boston to visit with Joe, Joe's wife Jan, and Joe and Jan's children, Duke, Tom, and Kate, many times.

Jeff invited me to lunch with Joe in New York a few times when the Red Sox were in town. Then came 1999. The All-Star game was in Boston, and *Out of Left Field*, our first book of baseball history and trivia, had just been published. Jeff and I drove to Boston—about a four-hour drive from New York, where we live.

We checked into the hotel, then met Jan and Joe for lunch at Five North Star, a fabulous Italian restaurant right near Paul Revere's house. (This was portentous—Joe showing his expertise not only on baseball, but also on restaurants—particularly Italian ones—and historic places of interest.)

That night, we went to the All-Star game, my first. It was my first time at Fenway Park, too. Our seats were in the press annex section, atop the leftfield roof, which means we looked down at the Green Monster. It also meant that when military jets did a flyover—coming from behind us—it seemed as though we were all about to get new haircuts.

In 2000, Jan and Joe invited Jeff and me to stay at their home outside of Boston. We went to two Red Sox-Yankee games at Fenway, and walked around the entire park while the teams worked out on the field. There were about 15 people in the stands.

I saw Joe again in New York City in January 2001 at the Baseball Assistance Team (B.A.T.) dinner. Two months later, we were again Jan and Joe's guests in Fort Myers, Florida, when Jeff and I went to Spring Training—a first for both of us.

It was during this trip that the idea for this book took shape. Joe had so many stories to tell, and in such detail, that we all persuaded him to write his autobiography, and I offered to help.

Joe and I have spent time together working on this book in Massachusetts, New York, and Florida, and we also met at Jacobs Field in Cleveland. We have made generous use of the phone and e-mails.

When we started work on the book, I recalled the many baseball biographies and autobiographies I had read by players, managers, and broadcasters. I was not particularly interested in working on a book that simply recited all the games and players Joe had seen, although those are integral parts of any baseball autobiography. But Joe is much more than a broadcaster (and he's excellent at that).

I hope that this book is a little different. First, there's the behind-the-scenes look at what it's like to be a broadcaster: how Joe prepares for each season and each game; how he gets along with players, managers, front office staff, and opposing players while maintaining credibility.

Also included are the adventures Joe and his family have had throughout major league baseball—from being held up in Kansas City to talking baseball with the president of the United States in the White House, to calling seven no-hitters.

And, finally, there are Joe's favorite places to visit in every city in the American League, and in several cities in the National League, too. The places he has enjoyed biking, kayaking, shopping, walking—and, of course, eating.

My guess is that some big league broadcasters go from the airport to the hotel to the ballpark to the hotel to the airport, with just a few side trips to restaurants. As you will see, this is not the case with Joe

Castiglione. While, as a baseball broadcaster, he does not have much free time when he travels with the team, he does have some—on an occasional off day or during the day before a night game. And he puts that time to good use, whether visiting San Simeon, Laguna Beach, Harry Truman's birthplace, or the Bronx Zoo. So, in addition to being a baseball book, this book is also something of a travelogue.

I must say that Joe's memory for details is absolutely incredible. He's written from his memory that there were about 13,000 people at a particular game. To me, that is a challenge. When I can get the specific details, I try to do so. In one game I checked, Joe's estimate of the crowd was wrong. He was off by 400. In other instances, Joe has recalled a particular hit in the third inning, with one out and two men on. I have checked the box score and the written play-by-play, and—although I am no longer surprised—Joe had recollected just the way the play happened: third inning, one out, two men on. (Of course, Joe also probably has remembered the baserunner's wife's name—and the names of their children, too!)

Although my career as a baseball researcher and writer has been relatively short, I have met a number of extremely knowledgeable and experienced baseball experts—broadcasters, sportswriters, researchers, and other authors. But I have never met anybody with the easy and accurate recall of so many facts, dates, and events as Joe Castiglione. That is not to say that Joe is a walking encyclopedia of baseball. I know some people who are, and they are usually boring, one-dimensional people. If the subject under discussion is not baseball, talking with them is like talking to a wall. But you can talk with Joe for hours (as I have done) without mentioning baseball, because his interests are so wide-ranging—the Kennedy assassination, presidential monuments, kayaking, biking, and the Jimmy Fund, to name just a few.

During the course of my collaboration with Joe on this book, I occasionally met people in baseball and mentioned that I was working with Joe on his book. Without exception, their faces lit up. I have never met anyone who had anything other than nice things to say about Joe. There's a reason for that.

I hope you enjoy reading Joe's book as much as I have enjoyed working on it with him.

PART I

Behind the Mike— My Career in Broadcasting

Family, Fungo"casts," and Rock and Roll

I was born in New Haven, Connecticut, on March 2, 1947, at St. Raphael's hospital. My father, Frank, born in 1915, was a doctor on the staff at St. Raphael's from 1940 to 2000, when he retired.

We lived in New Haven and moved to Hamden, the adjacent town, when I was about four. I was very close to my Aunt Mary, an elementary school teacher and my Uncle Charlie, a World War II hero, and my grandparents, Guiseppe and Francesa Castiglione, who came from Messina, Sicily, and met and married in New Haven in the late 1890s. We called them Nonno and Nonna—Italian for grandfather and grandmother.

My mother Pamela is a native of New Haven. She grew up in the Westville section of New Haven, near the Yale Bowl. My parents both went to the same high school—Hillhouse High in New Haven—and Mom studied at the Yale School of Music. She played the organ at churches around the New Haven area.

◆ ● ◆

I am the oldest of eight children—three boys and five girls. We have been a typically close Italian family. In fact, I studied Italian in junior high school and high school. I knew the formal Florentine Italian, which my

Uncle Sal and his wife, my Aunt Pierina, spoke. He founded the Italian School at Middlebury College in Vermont. When I was about 14, I went to Florence to visit them.

I tried to teach Italian kids how to play baseball with a tennis ball and a broom. A few times when I didn't hit a fungo properly, the ball went into the Arno River, which is muddier than the Mississippi.

The ability to talk sports runs in the family. My father went to Yale on a full scholarship and walked to campus from home every day, graduating in 1936. Then he applied to Yale Medical School, but his application was lost. So he applied late to New York Medical School and didn't think he was going to be admitted. (I didn't hear this story until some years later.) He thought he'd have to go to Rome for medical school. But when he was called in to New York Medical School for an interview, all the interviewer wanted to talk about was football—particularly the Yale-Princeton football game. (Yale was quite a football power at the time. Larry Kelley, the second man to win the Heisman Trophy, and Clint Frank, the third man to win it, both played for Yale.)

The next day, he was admitted. He studied at Flower-Fifth Avenue Hospital and later spent time as an army doctor in Japan. A few years later, when he decided that he wanted to specialize in dermatology, he took the train from New Haven into New York City twice a week. I went with him sometimes.

My father, who passed away in November 2003 at the age of 88, knew everybody in New Haven.

One of the first things he taught me to read was the box scores in the newspaper. I think I got my interest in sports, and in baseball in particular, from him. He created a monster!

My father's family was all Yankee fans. First, New York was much closer than Boston. Also, the Yankees had a number of Italian players.

Mel Allen, the "Voice of the Yankees," was my idol—my favorite broadcaster. I made a few trips to Yankee Stadium where I saw my first heroes, Jerry Coleman and Gil McDougald, and eventually Mickey Mantle. But, all along, the guy I would mimic was Mel Allen.

As Ernie Harwell used to say, I wanted to be a ballplayer in the worst way, and that's the way I played.

I used to think that my father was the greatest fungo hitter of all time. He used to take me out and hit high pop-up after high pop-up with a tennis ball. He was also a very accurate football passer.

As a little kid, I was not bad, but I could not run, because I had a short Achilles' tendon in my left leg. Although I was pretty good as a Little Leaguer, I reached the peak of my athletic prowess at about age ten. When I was 12, I thought I was going to be a real star. Our team, Botwinik Brothers factory, went to the city championship. There were about 3,000 people at the opening game at Bassett Field in Hamden, right up the street from our house. I was the shortstop as our opponent loaded the bases. The ball was hit hard to me and went right through my legs—all the way to the wall. Three runs scored. One of the most embarrassing moments of my life, before the entire town. Then, when I came to bat in the first inning, I tried to bunt. And I laid down a beauty, but I ran so slowly I was thrown out at first. That was pretty much the end of my baseball career.

After that, I played mostly Whiffleball and announced the games. I loved to hit fungoes. I would mimic the stances of various players and I'd announce the games. I was a switch hitter, at least for fungoing. In my games, no Yankee ever made an out. They always batted around. They played against any team in the league. I was a baseball card collector and a good card flipper, too.

Once, I traded a big green eraser (worth about 10 cents) for a Phil Rizzuto card. My parents were quite upset.

I "broadcast" my fungo games almost every day. Some of our friends and neighbors thought I was crazy. I also played dice baseball by the hour and keep statistical records of the games.

I knew I could not make the baseball team at Hamden High School, so I tried out for the swimming team, because I had heard that they didn't cut anybody. I made the team, but I was very slow. I wound up becoming the team manager and the announcer, doing the public address work for the team—my first actual announcing job with a microphone. There I'd be in my sweatsuit, occasionally announcing myself, then I'd get in the pool, unofficially in the outside lane, where I finished last.

My father was very demanding when it came to my grades. Bs were not good enough. I had to get As. We all did. School came first for all eight of us. His favorite expression was "Good, better, best—never let it rest, 'til your good is better and your better best."

My first summer job was bagging groceries at Pegnataro's grocery store. I also worked as a lifeguard in a swimming pool in a downtown apartment building.

A few years later, my father's friend Art Barbieri, New Haven's Democratic Party boss, got me a job delivering mail for the post office. When I started college, I started working in radio.

When I started thinking about colleges, my father wanted me to go to Yale because he had gone there. My grades were good, but I was rejected. So I opted to go to Colgate, largely because I had seen the Raider football team play at the Yale Bowl and because I liked the campus radio station.

WRCU-AM 640, the Colgate radio station, was carried throughout the campus on the phone lines. So if the dormitory or fraternity was too far from the street, there was no reception.

I walked into the station as a freshman and got my own Saturday night rock and roll show. Colgate and Brown were two of the rare schools in those years that played rock and roll on their radio stations. Most played just classical music. I was "Joey C, The Big Cheese!"

Then I got a 7 to 9 AM show two days a week and got the chance to call the Colgate football games, mainly because the upperclassmen had lost interest in broadcasting them. I started with the second game of the 1964 season, a win over Cornell. We had a good team that year, finishing at 7-2.

When the basketball season started, I did those games, too. I started out working with a senior, but he soon lost interest, so I wound up doing the games with Al Robbins, also a freshman who was from my hometown and a very close friend. We did the football and basketball games together for the rest of our college days. Al later earned a Ph.D. in educational research. I did selected road games and every home game.

◆ ● ◆

My first job was when I was 18, as a public address announcer for the Wonderettes of New Haven, a woman's softball team sponsored by Wonderbread.

They were archrivals of the famous Raybestos Brakettes and played at Quigley Stadium in West Haven, later home of the West Haven Yankees and West Haven Whitecaps (the Athletics' AA club of the Eastern League). I got that job through Carl Grande, whose brother George is now with the Reds and was the first anchor ever on ESPN. George and I are both from Hamden, Connecticut, and we've been friends for nearly 40 years. So when our paths cross, particularly in Spring Training, we always get together. Carl was a great broadcaster on New Haven radio and TV and later owned a number of radio stations in New Haven and Westerly, Rhode Island. The Grande brothers' late father, Carlo Grande Sr., was the truant officer at Hamden High School, but I never had to be disciplined by him.

Our football team played ten games, and eight were on the road. I did every game. Every week—a free trip! Colgate had good teams in those years. In 1965, we upset Army. We were down 28-6, then rallied in the fourth quarter to win 29-28.

In 1966, we were 8-1-1 in football. Our basketball teams had very little talent, and we were lucky to have records like 9-18 and 10-16. Bob Duffy was our basketball coach. An All-American at Colgate, he was just 24. Duffy had played in the NBA for the St. Louis Hawks and the Detroit Pistons.

We did not broadcast Colgate's baseball games. College baseball games are long and dull, and we had no electricity at the field, so no power to plug into for broadcast equipment.

I got my first job in commercial radio while I was at Colgate, working for WRUN in Utica, New York. WRUN has broadcast Colgate football games since 1952. Starting in my sophomore year, I started working there with their great announcer Lloyd Walsh. I still see him. We occasionally traveled together. He'd let me come over and do the third quarter of his Saturday broadcasts, and then he'd come over and do the third quarter on the college station. I didn't get paid for my work at WRUN, but I had something to put on my resume. Lloyd is one of the most giving people I have ever known. In November 2003, I had the opportunity to introduce Lloyd, who got a special award from the Colgate Hall of Honor for his 37 years of broadcasting Colgate football.

During the summer of 1965, I worked doing news at WELI, then as now the number one radio station in New Haven. (As it happens, I never listened to WELI, because they never played rock and roll—just "middle of the road" music—Sinatra, Montovanni, Jerry Vale, Perry Como, and the Ray Coniff Singers.)

I announced the players as they came to bat, and played music between innings. What a great job for an 18-year-old! Most of them were very good athletes.

In the summer of 1966, I got a job at WADS (Ansonia, Derby, Shelton) in Connecticut's Naugatuck Valley. I was hired to do a morning show, and I was known as "Joe Anthony," because it seemed less cumbersome for a disc jockey than my real name. I wound up doing weekends. I played mostly rock and roll.

In 1967, one of my high-school friends, a very talented broadcaster named John Whitten, known as "the Chief," now deceased, helped me get a job at WDEW in Westfield, Massachusetts, where he had a morning show. I did news from 6 to 10, then from 12 to 5. I also did a talk show, and then more news—a very long day. As for my talk show, I was replacing a popular guy who talked about UFO sightings. I talked about politics and other current events, but I didn't get any calls, so I just did the news.

WELI wanted me to come back to do evening news. So I went to quit my job at WDEW. I was making $90 per week for 48 hours work. I thought I would work at WELI and make the same money for three hours per day.

So I spoke to John Wallace Spencer, the station manager at WDEW, and told him that I was going to quit. He called me every name in the book but wound up asking me what I wanted to stay. I said, "Give me $110 per week, and get rid of this split shift." "$110? You're *killing me!*" he replied. I wound up getting the $110 and working only 6 AM to 3 PM in Westfield, Connecticut. Then I'd get in my car and drive 70 miles to New Haven, and be on the air on WELI from 6 to 9 PM. At 9:30, I went to sleep, only to wake up again at 4:30 to drive to Westfield. I had no days off. On Saturdays, I worked only in New Haven, and on Sundays only in Westfield. I put a lot of miles on a new 1967 Chevrolet Impala and I got a lot of experience.

My first experience following the Red Sox was also in 1967—the year of their memorable American League Championship "Impossible Dream." Even though our Westfield station carried Yankee games, we were only 90 miles from Boston.

I listened to the Red Sox games during many long drives. Their broadcasters that year were Mel Parnell, Ken Coleman, and Ned Martin. I also went with my friends to Fenway Park for the first time in late August and stood in the centerfield bleachers as the Red Sox lost to the Washington Senators on a double by Hank Allen, Dick's older brother.

During the school year, I worked at WRCN in Norwich, New York, and when I didn't feel like taking the bus, I hitchhiked down Route 12b, about 23 miles to the station.

I'd do the news and the Montovanni Hour on Sundays. We did not have cartridges, let alone CDs, so I had to play the commercials on ancient reel-to-reel tape machines.

I knew nothing about classical music, even though my mother and my brother Frank, who majored in music at Yale, are classical pianists.

But one day, I backtimed some classical music selection. That is, I started it late so that it would finish at the top of the hour. In other words, I cut off the music in the middle of the selections. Bill Hall, who was both the station's owner and the station manager, had been listening, and he called me up and reamed me out. I thought I was going to be fired.

The news was mostly rip and read at the time. That is, I'd literally rip the paper out of the Associated Press or United Press tickers, and read the wire service stories—unedited and unrewritten—right on the air. I didn't know any other way.

I had known since the end of my productive athletic career at age ten that what I wanted to do was be a sportscaster—and a baseball broadcaster at that. So all the jobs in radio I held—the paying ones and the ones I took just for the experience—were for the purpose of advancing my sportscasting career. The only other career I ever thought about was being a full-time rock and roll disc jockey, but I found that doing that every day got boring. It was pretty much the same every day. To be sure, the mid-1960s was a great time to be a rock and roll disc jockey—the Beach Boys, the Beatles, the Rolling Stones, the Byrds, the Dave Clark Five, the Kinks, the Animals, and a hundred more, plus my favorites, Motown Sounds.

But every baseball game is completely different—different pitchers, different lineups, different opposing pitchers, different ballparks every few days, new rookies, new managers. The game refreshes itself whenever the umpire says, "Play ball!"

◆ ● ◆

I got as much out of Colgate as I could. I learned as much about broadcasting as I could from the school's radio station. I was also one of the leaders of my fraternity, Alpha Delta Phi. We were a liberal house in terms of membership and acceptance. As I mentioned, Colgate was an all-male school at the time, and we had some good parties on weekends, with girls from Skidmore, Wells, Cazenovia Junior College, Manhattanville, and others. I majored in history, because the subject fascinated me.

I still see my college roommate Bob Straetz. He became a sportswriter in Poughkeepsie, New York, and is now with the Federal Trade Commission in Washington. Bob and I always shared a love for baseball and roomed together for three years. Bob has always been a fan of Willie Mays and of the Baltimore Orioles.

Unlike Notre Dame or Ohio State, not that many people went to Colgate, so when I see a fellow grad, we seem to have a special bond.

In 1968, I got a job at WMMW, a 1,000-watt daytime radio station in Meriden, Connecticut. I did high-school games, and at night I taped the play-by-play for the games of the Meriden Shamrocks, a semipro

as I hired him and paid him myself. I was only making $15 per game, so I didn't think there was room in my budget for me to hire my own color man.

Ron Jaworski, later a Super Bowl quarterback with the Philadelphia Eagles, was the star in 1970 but Youngstown State had a terrible year, finishing the season 0-9. The season ended when a last-play pass that would have won the game was caught but out of the end zone. Incomplete, and the Penguins were 0-9.

Dike Bedee was the coach at Youngstown State. His wife invented the penalty flag. Shortly after he retired in 1972, he drowned when he fell into a creek on his farm in Lisbon, Ohio. His former players searched for him and recovered his body from the creek.

I covered the Pittsburgh Pirate team while I was in Youngstown. Youngstown was about midway between Cleveland and Pittsburgh. Bill Guilfoile, public relations director of the Pirates, was very kind to me, and helped me a great deal. I went to the first game of the 1971 World Series to see Pittsburgh in Baltimore. Unfortunately, Game Two was rained out, and to this day I remember baseball commissioner Bowie Kuhn carrying an umbrella, walking in the outfield to test the ground.

I called the general manager at the station to see if I could stay overnight to watch the game the next day. He told me sure, but Mickey Krumpak, my colleague, had to be back. So I had to drive him five hours back to Youngstown. I was very disappointed that I had to miss the second game of the series.

In Game Four, the first night game in World Series history, Bruce Kison hit two batters, including Frank Robinson. Milt May had the game-winning hit and Nelson Briles pitched a shutout in Game Five.

I did the Ohio high-school basketball tournament in Columbus on radio—60 tables at courtside, each with a broadcaster accompanied either by an engineer or a color commentator. One day we did four games, some involving teams not from the Youngstown area. Hey, we were paid by the game! Except for the Saturday night TV show, I received no overtime pay, because as station sports director, I was considered "management," and not a member of the union.

Another $15 twice a week went a long way for each game. Friday night, Saturday afternoon, and Saturday night, football and basketball—all on live radio. Pretty good!

During those days, there was just one event that I hated covering, and we covered it live—the Soapbox Derby.

My friend Al Robbins, also from Hamden, Connecticut, was my color man at WRCU at Colgate. He was at my apartment in Youngstown watching our live telecast of the Soapbox Derby. I was told to interview a boy of about ten who had broken both his arms in a practice run and could not compete. So I asked him some pretty standard questions: "What is your name?" His answer: "I don't know." I moved on to "Where do you live?" Again, he answered, "I don't know." "What grade are you in?" I pressed on. His answer was the same: "I don't know." I tried one more question: "How did you get interested in soapbox racing?" The kid's answer was the same, "I don't know."

Finally, I had had enough. I patted the kid's head, and said that apparently he had hurt more than his arms in his crash. It seems to have affected his thinking process. Just an honest, spontaneous remark, which I knew immediately that I should *not* have made. "Do you know what you said to that kid?" Al Robbins asked. I choked when I watched the tape with Al back at my apartment. I did not hear from the boy's parents. Maybe they did not remember his name, either.

◆ ● ◆

The station was very cheap, and I was always sending out audition tapes, looking for a better job. But in November 1970, I met Jan—who did not like me at first—at a ski club function. (I don't ski.) The nighttime switchboard operator introduced us. Jan and I were married November 27, 1971, the greatest day of my life. Jan was teaching second grade at the time, and had her own classroom by the age of 19. Youngstown State had a program with the Catholic diocese of Youngstown. If a student agreed to become a teacher in the Catholic school system upon graduation, the church would pay his or her tuition. At St. Patrick's, she started out teaching eighth grade, where some of her students were not much younger than she was. I would take some of the kids for gym, and we played baseball or kickball. But quite a few were hard to handle, and when they did get out of hand, I just called for Jan. She knew what to do. Still does.

◆ ● ◆

I learned a great deal on the air in Youngstown, every day at 6 and 11 PM. I did interviews with everybody who came to town. We did studio interviews, specials, all kinds of hands-on experience, which I could not have gotten as the third man on the team in Syracuse. But, as I said, the general manager of our station was very cheap, and I kept looking for something better.

In 1970, there was an opening for a sports reporter at KDKA radio in Pittsburgh to do sports updates and news. I was thrilled that they were interested. KDKA was the Pirates's flagship station and broadcast the first baseball game ever in 1921 with Harold Arlin, a Westinghouse engineer, at the mike. They had a slogan, "KDKA Pittsburgh, listen to what we started." I had an interview, and I thought I had the job—quite a step up from Youngstown. Pittsburgh had major league teams in football (the Steelers), baseball (the Pirates), hockey (the Penguins), and basketball (the Condors of the American Basketball Association).

But they never filled the position at KDKA. They got a talk show host instead, and I did not get that job. Of course, had I taken the job in Pittsburgh, I would not have met Jan.

Two years later, KDKA TV came back to me and asked me to fill in for two weekends. I made the mistake of going to Mitch Stanley, the station manager in Youngstown, to ask his permission to work two weekends in Pittsburgh. He refused. He was afraid they'd hire me for a permanent position.

I have never been so embittered and resentful in my life. I was trying to better myself, but Stanley was trying to hold me back. His attitude strengthened my resolve to get out of Youngstown—which I did.

Two months later, in August of 1972, I got a job with WKYC-TV, Channel 3, in Cleveland, a station owned and operated by NBC, as weekend sports anchor.

I was so happy to tell Mitch Stanley that I was leaving. I offered to stay on until he found a replacement, but I didn't even get that satisfaction.

He told me just to serve out the two weeks of my notice, then I could leave. I did.

But I made great friends in Youngstown, and, of course, that's where I met Jan and her family, the Lowrys, and where I got married.

We moved to Cleveland in September 1972. I was doing just weekend sports, making $150 for two days work—the same amount I made for five and a half days a week in Youngstown.

Since going to Cleveland in 1972, I have been a member of AFTRA and am vested. My health benefits and pension come from AFTRA. My station pays 10 percent of my salary in benefits to AFTRA Pension and Welfare to cover these costs. AFTRA is not a strong union in terms of job security but it has good benefits and retirement and it goes with you if you change jobs as long as you remain at an AFTRA station.

Right down the street from our apartment in Broadview, a Cleveland suburb, where our rent was $150 per month, was WJW, a radio station owned by Storer Broadcasting. I filled in on weekends—all day Saturday while anchoring weekend sports at WKYC-TV, the NBC-owned station.

More work developed, both in radio and TV. When I started in Cleveland, I was doing both. Director Roy Wetzel, who hired me for TV news, later became an election specialist for NBC News. He said that he liked me because I didn't shout. I still don't (except when the Red Sox win).

I stayed in Cleveland for nearly 11 years. I filled in at the news desk, listening to police and fire radios and answering the phone in the newsroom, occasionally dispatching a network camera crew to a breaking story. One night, I saw that the *Edmund Fitzgerald* has been lost on Lake Superior and I called out a news crew to cover the story. Gordon Lightfoot wrote a song about the ship. WKYC was one of the five NBC O & Os—owned and operated by NBC itself—so we were responsible for providing coverage for any news story in our region of the country. Quite a step up from Youngstown. Youngstown's population at the time was about 200,000. Cleveland had a market of 2.5 million, the sixth largest market in the country at the time.

Working all night (11 PM to 7 AM) was not a great way to live but we still managed to become parents and to buy our first home in Mentor-on-the-Lake, Ohio. Our first child, Joe Jr., whom we have always called Duke, was born in 1973.

In 1977, I was offered the job as public address announcer for the Cleveland Indians. I had to decline the not-very-generous offer ($15 per game) because it would have conflicted with my TV broadcast job.

My crazy schedule of night work and weekends continued for about three years, until we got a new news director at the station. At that point, I was demoted and lost my TV anchoring slot and just did news producing. First, the new news director treated me well. Our veteran sports director was a wonderful, classy guy named Jim Graner, who did color on the Browns football broadcasts on the radio. Jim took ill with a brain tumor and passed away in 1976.

I also worked with reporter Dick Hammer, longtime voice of Lafayette basketball and football in Easton, Pennsylvania. He did both local and network sports. Dick taught me how to do "packages"— putting video and film and audio together. At the time, it was mostly film. He went to New York to work for the network for about two years, then went back to Lafayette. Although Dick works alone, whenever the Leopards play in New England, I sit in with him in the broadcast booth and do color commentary. His wife Millie is Dick's radio statistician for both the Lafayette football and basketball games.

So Jim Graner died and Dick Hammer was let go. Instead of promoting me to take their places, management brought in somebody from outside the station for the weekday broadcasts. Football Hall of Famer Paul Warfield took my job. I was asked to stay on as Paul's producer. It was quite a demotion from an on-air job, but I did it. We needed the money.

Paul is a very nice guy who did everything he could to make my job easier. Paul never relaxed on the TV set. He was much better doing analysis on television football. Eventually, Paul left the station, and in 1978, I was back on the air.

In the interim, I did news producing at WKYC-TV in Cleveland and rock and roll news. It was with WGAR in Cleveland, 50,000 watts for $5 per hour in 1976. Lots of fun, in 1976, including July 4, the day of the Bicentennial.

I also covered events for NBC—$33 per report (pretty good money at the time). NBC producer Fred Farrar was a big Ohio State fan. I got him a pass to the Ohio State-Michigan football game, always a great game. He was so happy that he let me cover any game I wanted to cover. For example, I covered the Cleveland Cavaliers, who were playing the Indiana Pacers on a Thursday night. Although there was not much national interest in this game, I managed to do six reports. Four live updates during the game, and another two wraparound reports after the game. Six spots at $33 each was pretty good money for one night's work in 1976. $198 was a big payday. I made a lot of money that year—the station didn't always know how much network work I was doing because I had to get most of it directly from NBC in New York, rather than through the station.

In 1979, Paul Warfield and I were doing a series called "Superstars to Superstars" for Channel 3, WKYC-TV in Cleveland. I was paid by the hour, at about $10 per hour.

The day before we left Cleveland for Miami, I was interviewed by Bill Flynn, general manager of Channel 8 in Cleveland, owned by Storer Broadcasting. I had applied for the job of TV broadcaster for the Cleveland Indians. Flynn had worked at Channel 38 in Boston in 1975 and took over the Red Sox TV package. He tripled the station's coverage from 40 games on TV to 120 games.

Then Flynn came to Cleveland and decided to make a change on the Indians's telecasts in 1979. That year proved to be one of the most eventful years of my life.

Bill answered his own phone—which was rare. Most station executives don't do it, to protect themselves from jobseekers like me.

He asked me why I wanted the job, and I told him that it had been my lifelong ambition to broadcast baseball games. I gave him an audio tape of some of my work. He asked whether I was really willing to give up my regular job to do 40 games for the Indians—the last year of their contract with WJKW TV-8. The interview was on a Monday. Flynn said, "Call me on Wednesday at 2 PM, and I will have a decision."

Warfield and I were scheduled to interview Don Shula, Don Carter, and Roger Staubach in Miami for "Superstars to Superstars." Warfield's wife Beverly was part of the series in an effort to boost ratings during sweeps week.

Don Shula's wife didn't want to do the interview, so we interviewed Garo Yepremian instead on Tuesday, our first day in Miami.

The next day, we went to suburban Miami to see Don Carter at the "Don Carter Bowling Alley." We were to interview his wife Paula, too. She was a beautiful blond who was also a top bowler.

At 2 PM on Valentine's Day 1979, I had to call Bill Flynn. He was very precise and a man of his word. In fact, he was one of the most honest people I have ever met in broadcasting. I called and he told me that I had the job broadcasting Indians games. He said that he would make the official announcement in an hour. I told him that I needed some time to resign from WKYC. His response: "We're announcing it at three o'clock. Do what you have to do." Bill told me that I'd be working with Fred McLeod. He was 26. I was 32.

"Aren't you going to ask me about the money?" asked Bill. My salary was going to be $300 per game. Times 40 games, that's $12,000 per season. I couldn't wait to call Jan, my parents, and the rest of my family.

I wanted to go home, to celebrate with Jan in person, and to prepare for my new job, but we still had to do the Roger Staubach interview in Dallas.

When I eventually got home to Solon, a southeast suburb of Cleveland, the response to my being named the new Indians broadcaster was overwhelming. There were more than 100 letters and notes (no e-mails in those days) from people in our business—from my peers and friends in Cleveland. Everyone who knew me knew that what I really wanted to do was broadcast baseball.

I was still serving out my notice at Channel 3. Tom Ryther, our sports director, and news director Bill Peterson told me that I could continue to broadcast weekend sports for them, even though I'd be doing Indians games for Channel 8. It's amazing how much more valuable you become when somebody else wants you.

So I told Bill Flynn, and he checked with news director Virgil Dominick, who had been an anchor at Channel 3, and was considered so good that he occasionally filled in for Frank Blair on the *Today Show*.

Virgil worked without a teleprompter—he *memorized* his news script. I never saw any other newscaster do this. But Virgil was now the news director at Channel 8, and he told me "you are ours now—we're not going to help them." He also told me that he'd "take care of me"— that is, make up the salary I was losing at Channel 3. And, a man of his word, he did. He found other work for me.

◆ ● ◆

I went to Spring Training with the Indians—my first as a team broadcaster—in Tucson, but the Indians never broadcast any games from there. They thought it was too expensive and the station did not want to preempt lucrative network broadcasts.

I was there for two weeks with my family. Jan was pregnant with our daughter Kate, and I'm glad we could all be together. The station paid all our expenses.

I flew to New Haven just before Opening Day to see my Aunt Mary, who was ill with cancer. The day before the opener, I took the train from New Haven to Boston. That morning, the *New Haven Journal Courier* ran a story about me by Vinny Carbone—a friend of my father—saying that I was now a big leaguer.

I did my first game on TV at Fenway Park in Boston, Tuesday, April 5, 1979.

Rick Wise was the Indians starter that day, and Dennis Eckersley started for the Red Sox. Four years later, Eckersley also started my first game as a Red Sox broadcaster. (Eckersley won the first game 7-1, and lost the latter.) Bobby Bonds misplayed a few fly balls in his Cleveland debut. Dwight Evans hit the first home run I ever called at Fenway.

My partner in the booth that year with the Indians was Fred MacLeod, who was the weekend anchor at WJKW-TV. We had a great location in the broadcast booth at the old stadium, only about 70 feet from home plate—a perfect angle. The booth was great though old and with many spiders.

The Indians manager was Jeff Torborg, whom I still consider a good friend.

Neither Fred nor I knew that Bill Flynn was in the back of the booth listening to us for a while. He told us later that we did a good job.

After the game, we were in the bar at the back of the press room. My father and my Uncle Charlie were there for my first game, as they were for so many events in my career.

They met our general manager, Phil Seghi, and Gabe Paul, the president of the team, and they thought he was the most charming man in the world.

Then we flew home to Cleveland. Our plane was hit by lightening as we were ready to land. The plane shook but was not damaged, though it was a scary experience that left at least one player in tears.

Our home opener was not televised. We were shut out by Steve Comer of the Rangers in Texas in our next televised game, and got off to a bad start, as far as the games that were on TV were concerned, including a ten-game losing streak in June. The losing streak, including a three-game sweep in New York, ended in Baltimore.

Traveling with the Indians through the American League in 1979 took me to many places I had never visited before. In late May, our broadcast schedule changed. After a series against the White Sox in Chicago, we were scheduled to fly to Anaheim to do a game there. Channel 8 was a CBS affiliate, but because of the network's schedule, our games in California would not be broadcast. Our June 1 broadcast was changed to a later date. Lucky for me, because I got word that Jan had gone into labor with Kate.

I was present at the birth of our first two children, Joe Jr. and Tommy, and frankly, I was hoping for a daughter. I wanted to be there. After the game, I learned that our neighbor had taken Jan to the hospital where her brother, Chris Lowry, met her. United Airlines was on strike, and it was hard to find a flight to Cleveland. But I got to the hospital a little after 11 AM. Mary Katherine—Kate—arrived at 3:35 PM.

Instead of talking to Jan during her long labor, the obstetrician was only interested in talking to me about the Indians. Once again, it always comes back to baseball.

I rejoined the club in Seattle, where Sid Monge saved a game for us. He handed me the baseball, on which he had written, "This is in honor of your new daughter. To Katie. May she live to be 101." She still has the ball.

Sid and I became quite good friends over the years, even as he moved around the majors to several clubs including Detroit, San Diego, and Pittsburgh. He later lived in the Boston area.

Also on that 1979 Indians team was Andre Thornton, one of my favorite players.

The Indians were lucky in 1979, because we had a rainout. That missed game, which we never made up, enabled us to finish with a winning season, but just barely—the team was 81-80. And that was the first time the Indians had finished over .500 since 1968!

In late August or early September, it was announced that Channel 8 had been awarded the Indians contract for another three years. But Indians president Gabe Paul and Bill Flynn had a disagreement about money, among other things, and the day after the season ended it was announced that Channel 8 would no longer be carrying Indians games.

Obviously, this was terrible news for many people at the station who worked the games with me—cameramen, engineers, producers, and the like—but it also hurt me, because broadcasting Indians games was virtually all I did at Channel 8 during the season. After the station lost the Indians contract, they found other work for me.

I went to see Bill Flynn at the end of the season, hoping that the dispute between the station and the Indians was just a negotiating ploy—not a farfetched idea. "No," said Flynn, "This was no ploy. I don't do business this way. I pulled the plug, and the Cleveland Indians will never be on Channel 8."

Before Opening Day in 1980, the Indians had to scramble for a flagship TV station, and they wound up on Channel 43, WUAB, an independent station. The stations wanted their own broadcasters, and they got them, Joe Tait from radio and Bruce Drennan.

I stayed at Channel 8 through early 1982 as a freelancer (actually making more than I would have as a full-time employee, a position I turned down), anchoring sports and reporting on sports.

In 1980, the only baseball I broadcast was when I did radio play-by-play for the first time during two Indians-White Sox games with the late Ned Chandler. (Herb Score, the regular Indians broadcaster, had to go to a funeral.) Ned and I had been friends for many years, even though we were technically rivals at competing Cleveland stations. Whenever we met during those years, we'd commiserate about the way sports was treated on television—camera crews, time on the air, etc.

The two games I did were well received, but I still could not get regular big league play-by-play work. I had never worked for a minor league team. Before going to the Indians in 1977, I was considered for a job broadcasting for the Columbus Clippers in the International League, where I was interviewed by the general manager George Sisler Jr. Like me, he was a graduate of Colgate. But my friend John Gordon got the job, and I stayed in Cleveland. John went on to broadcast for the Twins.

In 1981, I tried to get the main broadcast TV play-by-play job with the Milwaukee Brewers. It went down to the wire, but I did not get the job. Steve Shannon, who had broadcast for the Angels, was hired instead, and he later became a good friend. But Bill Haig, the Brewers's director of broadcasting, did not forget me. That year, the Brewers broadcast a number of games on SelecTV pay cable TV—with a box on top of your set. If you were not wired for cable—and at the time, the city of Milwaukee was not wired—and you wanted the 20 games we did, you had to get a separate box. We were on in the city and some of the suburbs. Bill recommended me for the job there, and I got a call on March 17, 1981, St. Patrick's Day, from Tom Spertell, their executive producer. He offered to pay me at the going rate of $300 per game, plus $30 a day meal money. That was decent money at the time. They offered to fly me back and forth, and to put me up whenever I had to be in Milwaukee. I was ecstatic. He told me that my partner would be Tom Collins, who came to Milwaukee in 1959, and worked for the Braves in 1963, 1964, and 1965 before they left for Atlanta. Tom was the original voice of the Brewers in 1970 with Merle Harmon. He was also the main buyer of airtime for Schlitz Brewing for the Brewers and Kansas City.

In those days, the agencies or the breweries that sponsored the broadcasts controlled the broadcasts and hired the broadcasters. Oftentimes, if the broadcast changed brewery sponsors, the old broadcaster, closely identified with the old brewery, was out.

When I got the job, I didn't know much about either Milwaukee or the Brewers, so I went to the library in Cleveland to find out as much as I could. I had done this when I was hired to work with the Indians, too. This was well before the days of the Internet, when reams of information about visiting teams are available online. At the time, I had only been to Milwaukee twice to broadcast Indians games in 1979, and I really knew very little about the city or the team.

By the time I was hired, it was too late to go to Spring Training. We were scheduled to do the second game of the season. I flew to Milwaukee and met Tom Collins for dinner the night before Opening Day. We hit it off instantly. "The Ol' Redhead," Tom Collins was one of the funniest and nicest people I've ever met.

In fact, all the Milwaukee people were nice to me. Even though I was an outsider, they never treated me like one. They treated me as if they had known me for years. Tom Spertell, our executive producer, Glenn Clark, our general manager, Mary Horst, our producer—everybody. We'd all go out to dinner together after night games, frequently to a place under a viaduct called "The Fourth Base." It was sort of a dive, but it was a fun sports bar.

SelecTV put me up at their executive condo in Waukesha, Wisconsin, just west of County Stadium, but I usually stayed on Tom Collins' couch and flew out of Milwaukee the next day.

Because of the baseball players' strike, we only did ten Brewers games that year.

After the Brewers clinched the second half title and a playoff spot, we celebrated at Ray Jackson's, a neighborhood sports restaurant that had become a hangout for the Brewers. Tom and I stayed a long time. He had tried to do some postgame interviews with the ecstatic Brewers, but his mike was not working. So unless you were able to read lips, you could not hear any of them. Their victory was the first of any significance for the Brewers, who came into existence in 1970, when the Seattle Pilots moved to Milwaukee, brought there by team owner Allan "Bud" Selig.

I had a great experience in Milwaukee. Bill Haig, the Brewers director of broadcasting, was a big supporter of mine and my mentor in Milwaukee, and he was later instrumental in my being hired by the Red Sox. He gave me a glowing recommendation. I'm still friends with Bill, who is now retired.

When the season ended, I was still working at Channel 8 in Cleveland, anchoring and doing weekend sports. I had just commuted to Milwaukee for the ten home games we actually did.

I enjoyed being a field reporter. In addition to covering sports, I did lots of feature stories, personal profiles, and interviews.

We walked in to lots of city schools to profile star athletes or teams and kids would shout at our crew "Take my picture, mister! I want to talk on camera."

We had fun doing these features. I was still working as a freelancer, making about $36,000 a year from Channel 8 in 1981, plus $300 per game in Milwaukee (ten games, $3,000). Virgil Dominic, the station's news director, offered me a full-time position, but my goal was to get back to play-by-play. A new regional sports cable enterprise in Cleveland, called "The Sports Exchange," was being launched and I was the first person hired by its owner Ted Stepien. He was very active in trying to promote professional softball. He owned a little bar called "The Competitors' Club." Even when I was not working for him, I interviewed him frequently, and he gave me a scoop in 1980 that he was going to buy the Cleveland Cavaliers in the NBA. I didn't believe him, but I did put the story on the air—and he did buy the team.

Ted offered me $60,000 per year to sign with his new regional cable network. I told him, "Ted, look what you paid James Edwards and Scott Wedman, and all these other basketball players on the Cavaliers who helped you finish in last place. I want $5,000 more." Ted was easy to negotiate with, and I got it. And a car, too. He told me to pick one out. We were based out of the Richfield Coliseum, where the Cavaliers played.

We went on the air with the Indians in Spring Training. Most of the cable companies picked up our broadcasts, because the Spring Training games were free. They'd give us channel space and we got free programming.

My broadcast partner was Bob Feller, then as now a legend in Cleveland. I knew he was a star, and the stories I had heard about him gave me some trepidation, but Bob was wonderful to work with. We had a great time together. My family came to Tucson that year, and we stayed at the Sheraton Pueblo, or as Feller called it, the "Old Pwee-ebblo."

When the season started, we were on the air with a number of sporting events, including a local wrestling show. We did a sports news show called "The Sports Exchange" at 6 and 11. We hired Jack Corrigan, who later went on to do Indians TV for many years and now Colorado Rockies' baseball, and Denny Shriner who had worked on the pro bowling tour (and still does).

Our cameramen were Dirk Smith and Eric Schultz. Jeff Kuiper, brother of Indians second baseman Duane Kuiper, was our producer. He was a quality guy who learned TV very well. Duane became a Giants broadcaster after his playing career, and Jeff became the producer of the San Francisco Giants cable broadcasts, Giantsvision. We were glad to have helped him break into broadcasting.

In September, we went off the air. Ted was paying the Indians about $20,000 per game in rights fees, and we could only get the cable system in Ravenna, Ohio, to take the broadcasts on a paid basis. So we went dark. Ted had to lay off everybody except the program director Dick Fraser and me. (I had a contract and I think he was afraid of bad publicity.) Despite having nothing to do, we all got together at the Coliseum every day, in case Ted's girlfriend Janis called. She was a 22-year-old beauty. Ted was 56. Janis was a part-time anchor. Ted was concerned about her career.

I used the dead time in the office to look for another job. We also played lots of basketball in the Cavaliers's practice gym. Our games often lasted over two hours. That was our workday. I like to think that I was being paid to play basketball! And in an NBA facility!

As the winter of 1982–1983 wore on, we worried about whether we would ever get back on the air.

Ted hired Harry Weltman, who had been with the Spirit of St. Louis basketball team in the ABA and with Warner Communication, as the new general manager of the Cavaliers. Ted thought that if he hired Harry, we'd have an in with Warner's cable system. But Weltman could not deliver Warner, so he was not a very happy guy. Weltman brought in Tom Nissalke as the new coach of the Cavaliers. Tom was a world-class racquetball player who had a reputation of bringing teams up to respectability. While he did that with the Cavs, he never got them to the championship level.

I broadcasted Cavalier pay-TV games the previous season when Stepien had three coaches. The first coach of the 1981–1982 season was Bill Musselman, then Chuck Daly—hired on December 1, fired on February 1. Daly went on to coach the Detroit Pistons to consecutive NBA championships in 1989 and 1990, and became a Basketball Hall of Famer. After Daley came Don Delaney, who coached Ted's softball team.

The Cavaliers lurched from one disaster to another.

Amid all this turmoil, I still needed a new job. I had shown Casey Coleman all about TV and television production, and he was doing special features at Channel 8. I'm not claiming credit for his success—he was very good on his own. I just opened the door for him.

Casey told me that his father Ken Coleman, the number one Red Sox broadcaster, was looking for a new partner. Jon Miller was leaving the Red Sox after three years to go to Baltimore. I also learned that Campbell Sports Network of Plymouth, Massachusetts, was the new rights-holder for Red Sox broadcasts. I had met Ken a few times in Spring Training in the mid-1970s when he was doing TV broadcasts for the Cincinnati Reds, and we had met a few times at Ohio State during football games, which he also broadcast.

I first heard Ken in 1957. WTIC in Hartford, Connecticut, carried Cleveland Browns football games, which Ken also did. That was Jim Brown's rookie season, and the Browns won the NFL Eastern Division championship, only to lose the title game to the Detroit Lions. Ken did those Browns games with Jimmy Dudley, who went on to win the Ford C. Frick Award at the Baseball Hall of Fame for his service with the Cleveland Indians from 1948 to 1967. (Dudley was also the "Voice of the Seattle Pilots," though I'm not sure that he'd want to be remembered for his affiliation with that abysmal team.)

So I had been following Ken's career, so to speak, for some time, and had a lot of respect for him as a baseball broadcaster. Ken was in his second stint with the Red Sox, sandwiched around his five years with the Reds. I sent one of my audition tapes to Ken, and he sent it on to the Red Sox. (At the time, I had only done two games on the radio.) I also sent a tape to Jack Campbell, who ran WPLM, the Campbell Sports Network, but they had no idea what the situation was.

I was told that Jack Campbell wanted to talk to me, so I flew into Boston (paying for my own flight) in January 1983, the night of the Boston baseball writers' dinner. It was a Thursday night, and I spent the night at a Howard Johnson's in Kingston. In fact, I had stayed there once about eight years before, when Jan and I decided to drive to Cape Cod without any motel reservations. Everything was full, so at 3 AM, we convinced the manager to put us up in a conference room at the Howard Johnson's, where we slept on a couch. But we slept.

As it turned out, I wound up living very close by where I stayed that night.

I went to dinner at Mama Mia's in Kingston, which has become a family favorite.

The next morning, I drove down to Plymouth, about three miles, to a little radio station on top of a hill. WPLM, the new flagship station of the Red Sox. There was quite a bit of resentment in Boston about the rights to the Red Sox games going to a little FM station few had ever heard of 50 miles out of town. But they had a powerful signal, 50,000 watts at 99.1 in the middle of the dial.

◆ ● ◆

Jack Campbell had a lot of foresight, and predicted the future growth of FM radio. His station started in a sub shop in downtown Plymouth as a 500-watt daytime station. He was a political contributor and fundraiser for the Kennedys, and through his political connections he was able to persuade the FCC to grant him a license for a powerful station in the middle of the FM dial. Although the station was hard to pick up in parts of Boston, he added WHDH as a Boston affiliate, and he eventually signed about 70 affiliate stations.

Jack's station had been the flagship broadcaster for the Boston Bruins of the National Hockey League for a year, but this would be his first year with a major league baseball team. With the Bruins, he provided the production and the network stations, but the Bruins provided the announcers and sales. With the Red Sox, Jack would be in charge of everything.

Jack and Paul Mooney, the president of the Bruins, interviewed me. Jack asked me about my background. Jack had never hired a sports announcer before, and I don't think he even listened to my tape. When his station started doing Bruins games, he inherited the Bruins announcers Bob Wilson and Hockey Hall of Famer Johnny Bucyk from the hockey team. But the Red Sox and Ken Coleman had recommended me.

For some reason, Jack took a liking to me. He was impressed by the fact that my father was a doctor. Jack was leery and insecure around the Boston establishment. He was very strong-willed and well connected. Not a guy you would want for an enemy.

Jack asked me what salary I was seeking, and I knew how to answer because Ken Coleman had coached me for this question. I knew that there would not be a lot of money. I had been making $65,000 in Cleveland, and Ken thought that I might make about $40,000 in Boston, but I decided to aim high and I asked for "40 to 45" thousand. Jack thought that sounded pretty good.

I met his wife Jane Day, a wonderful lady who had been Boston's first TV weather girl (that's what they were called then) in the 1950s. She had been with Jack for many years. For some reason, she also seemed to take a liking to me.

Jane was the executive producer of our Red Sox network. Jack told me that he would let me know their decision over the weekend. On Saturday morning Jack called me at Ken Coleman's house where I was staying. He told me that I got the job "if it doesn't get out. If you tell anybody, and it gets out, I may have to do something else. It will be announced Monday morning. Go to Boston Garden, meet Paul Mooney, and you'll be introduced."

I called Jan to tell her. I was still supposed to do Indians games with Bob Feller. In fact, I was supposed to bring the donuts to a meeting with Ted Stepien on Monday morning.

After I was introduced as the new Red Sox broadcaster at the press conference, I called Ted. It was about noon on Monday, and I was calling to resign. His secretary Joanie told me that he would not take the call. He didn't want to talk with me. "You missed the meeting, and you didn't bring the donuts. Ted had no donuts at the meeting!" I told her, "Joanie, he's going to like this. Tell him I'm resigning." She agreed to pass the message on to Ted. A minute later, he came on the line, and asked me, "Where were you? You didn't bring the donuts!" I told him that I was going to be the Red Sox broadcaster. He responded that he was sorry to lose me. He told friends later that I had run out on him, but I think he was really relieved. Now, he didn't have to pay me any more.

Ken Coleman drove me to the Garden to meet Paul Mooney, then to the press conference at Fenway Park. Jack Campbell was not there. I was going to be introduced (along with Tony Torchia, the new manager of the Red Sox AAA affiliate in Pawtucket, Rhode Island) during a Monday morning coffee on January 31, 1983. A few writers asked me a few questions, then I was put on the phone with Jim Baker of the *Boston Herald* and I spoke with Jack Craig, probably the nation's first newspaper critic for sports broadcasting. He also wrote for *The Sporting News*. I stayed in the Red Sox office for a while, as Jack McCarthy and Dick Bresciani, the media relations people for the Red Sox, called up various media outlets to make me available. Although the Boston papers had brief items about me, it was not a big story. Some mentioned that I had only done 70 games on TV, and two on the radio before coming to Boston.

I flew home that night, got ready to sell our house and go to Spring Training in Winter Haven, Florida. Duke was ten, Tommy was eight, and Kate was four.

I went to Spring Training on a Saturday night and stayed at the Holiday Inn in Winter Haven. I had been there before when I was freelancing with NBC radio. All of sudden, I realized that besides Ken Coleman and his wife, I didn't know anybody on the Red Sox or in Winter Haven. I did not know the players and they did not know me. It was a lonely and scary feeling. Opening Day was just six weeks away.

The next day, I got to the Red Sox clubhouse at Chain O'Lakes Park and spoke to Ralph Houk, the manager. We had met briefly when he was with the Tigers. I still held Ralph in awe because of his career managing the Yankees to three pennants in his first three years.

I met Larry Whiteside, the baseball writer for the *Boston Globe* and Mike Shalin of the *Boston Herald*, and they invited me to dinner. Larry was the first African American beat writer for a major daily newspaper, first with the *Milwaukee Journal*. He took me under his wing.

The first game we did was at Joker Marchant Stadium, in Lakeland, Florida, against our Polk County rivals, the Detroit Tigers. I don't remember much about that game, except that I was nervous. Ken Coleman worked with me and congratulated me on the job I did broadcasting that game. Of course, my family was still in Cleveland so they could not hear the game.

We did 20 games in Spring Training, and I got to know most of the players. But there are so many players and reporters in Spring Training that the players did not really get to know me until the start of the regular season, when the minor leaguers are gone, the major league team roster is cut down to 25, and we all traveled together.

I met Johnny Pesky, who treated me very well. At the time, Pesky was a coach. Ned Martin was very nice to me, too. I got to know Jack Rogers, the traveling secretary, who really added a lot of class to the Red Sox organization during his long tenure. Dick Bresciani and George Sullivan, public relations directors for the team, were also very warm and welcoming to me.

I felt better about things as we approached Opening Day. Jan and the kids were able to spend some time with me in Spring Training. Tommy was eight, and made his First Communion at the Pool Mass at the Holiday Inn in Winter Haven, on Saturday at 5 PM. It was very crowded, and for many years afterwards, people would tell me that they were there, and that they remembered it very well.

We had not yet sold our house in Cleveland, so at the end of Spring Training, Jan and the kids went back to Cleveland and school, and I went to Boston with the team. I spent the first few nights with Ken Coleman at his home in Cohasset.

◆ ● ◆

On Opening Day, April 4, 1983, we hosted the Blue Jays. Dennis Eckersley for the Red Sox against Dave Steib for Toronto. Eckersley had pitched for the Sox against the Indians in 1979—the first game I ever broadcast. And just as before, my team lost. We were pounded 7-1. Rance Mulliniks planted an Eckersley pitch in the bullpen. I don't think Mulliniks took it well when, some time earlier, Eckersley was quoted as asking, "What is a Rance Mulliniks?" That year, the Blue Jays platooned Mulliniks with Garth Iorg, perhaps the most unusual names for a pair of platooned players ever.

The day after Opening Day was an off day, and I used it to move to the Susse Chalet. My room was $26 a night. The manager, a guy from Haiti named Al, and I struck a deal. When I was in Boston, I had my room at $26 per night. When I was on the road, I packed up my foot-locker and Al stored it in the basement. Saving $26 a night was a great deal for me at the time.

For our second game, we beat Toronto in an afternoon game. The Sox usually played weekday afternoon games in April, because it was too cold in Boston for night games.

My father came to that game along with our good friend Joe Rossomando, a former assistant baseball coach at Yale, where he coached George Bush, captain of the 1947 team.

Then it was off on my first road trip with the Sox. We took a commercial flight to Texas, where we lost two out of three.

The reaction to me was pretty good. Ken Coleman was very support-ive and newspaper comments were mixed. Jack Craig praised me for the way I did a game, but in June, he ripped me for precisely the same things he had previously praised me for. Jack, though, was generally supportive.

The season progressed on a relatively even keel until June, when there was a reunion of the 1967 Red Sox team—the "Impossible Dream" team that had defied all odds and overcome all obstacles to win the American League pennant, only to lose the World Series to the St. Louis Cardinals.

Tony Conigliaro was in a coma as the result of a heart attack. Although he had made it back to the majors after being struck in the face by a pitch, he never totally recovered, and he was working as a TV anchor in San Francisco. He had suffered a heart attack in his brother Billy's car while he was in Boston to apply for a job as a TV broadcaster in 1982.

The 1967 reunion was to be a benefit for Tony C, and included a concert at Symphony Hall with Frank Sinatra. Ted Williams was a featured star at the concert. I was at Fenway on June 5, 1983, for a very strange scene. The 1967 team was gathered in the dining room when Buddy Leroux, who ran the team with Haywood Sullivan, entered the room and announced the coup—the "coup Leroux," as it came to be called. (Although Leroux and Sullivan were partners, Mrs. Jean Yawkey had a controlling interest in the team.)

Leroux said he had enough of the limited partners support and was taking over the team himself. Leroux had been the team trainer, and started a number of nursing rehabilitation centers. That gave him the capital to move into an ownership position.

Former catcher Haywood Sullivan was out as general manager and Dick O'Connell (who was fired by Mrs. Yawkey after the 1977 season) would be back as general manager.

This announcement, in the presence of the legendary 1967 team, certainly made that night's game seem secondary. The coup was real news. That game against Detroit was also the Monday night nationally televised game of the week with Howard Cosell and Don Drysdale calling the game for ABC-TV.

The timing of the Leroux announcement—upstaging the 1967 team's celebration, and upstaging the benefit for Tony Conigliaro, who was still a beloved figure in Boston—hurt the Leroux cause. Mrs. Yawkey, who bought the team after her husband, Hall of Famer Tom Yawkey, died in 1976 and Sullivan went to court to reclaim ownership and control of the team, and prevailed. Leroux was out.

But the proceedings dragged on in court, and the team could not really make any roster moves while the team's ownership was in dispute.

Due in part to the turmoil in the front office, the 1983 Sox wound up with their first losing season since 1966.

Meanwhile, our Cleveland house had been on the market for eight months, and still was not selling. Every time we had an off day, I flew home to Cleveland to see my family. On a few occasions, I spent the night in a writer's hotel room, or sleeping at the airport. But it was really harder on Jan. One time, she drove the kids to meet me in Toronto, so we could spend some time together. Jan also met me in Detroit, where a cab driver took her on a wild and scary ride through the worst parts of town.

When we played in Cleveland, I stayed at home.

Jan also drove to meet me in Connecticut, and we went to New York the next day, July 4, 1983, the day before the All-Star break, when Dave Righetti of the Yankees pitched a no-hitter against the Red Sox. It was almost 100 degrees, as Righetti struck out Wade Boggs for the final out.

The next day, we drove to Plymouth. Jane Day put us up at a great hotel by the beach, the Pilgrim Sands, and took us to see the Mayflower II, Plimouth Plantation, and took us to lunch and dinner. The next day, we all went back to the Susse Chalet, where I got us a second room. At the time, I had no car. (I had to surrender my Ted Stepien car when I left that job in Cleveland.) Jan had our only car, and I was taking the bus or the subway from the Susse Chalet to Fenway Park. Sometimes I got a ride back with Ned Martin, and other times I took the subway.

Duke spent some time with me in Boston that year. He was ten. The old broadcast booth at Fenway Park was so small that we didn't have room for Duke to sit. The visiting clubhouse guy offered to put Duke to work there. He shined shoes for George Brett and Robin Yount, both of whom he loved. Once, a group of Brewers sent him to the Boston Garden to buy wrestling tickets for that night. Don Sutton took a liking to Duke.

Duke also helped set up and serve the postgame meal, and he earned a few tips, but he wasn't doing it for the money. He thought it was important, he had fun doing it, and he remembers it to this day. Today, Duke is a sportscaster for WCBS-TV in New York City. I try to watch it on my computer at home. Otherwise, Duke sends me the tapes. Duke's resume says that he got to serve Billy Martin not only his postgame meal, but also his postgame drink!

Boston Bound

My first year with the Red Sox, 1983, was also Carl Yastrzemski's last year. I was very happy that I had the chance to spend a year with this great Hall of Famer. Yaz announced early in the season that this would be his final year. There were farewell tributes in every city we visited.

Carl was well respected around the league. The tributes, usually in the form of a team gift, were usually conducted on our last game in whatever city we were playing in.

I remember Yaz getting a double down the rightfield line into the corner to beat Toronto on August 22, 1983, his 44th birthday. Yaz had a real hot stretch that season, and could really turn on the fastball, although he hit only .266.

Carl really treated me well that year. We had met while I was still with the Indians, and I had interviewed him in Cleveland. He was courteous, but not particularly outgoing or forthcoming. But he accepted me when I went to the Red Sox and because I worked with Ken Coleman, whom he really respected.

I remember sitting on a bus with Yaz, stuck in traffic as we left Exhibition Stadium in Toronto. We were sitting right in the front—there was only one team bus in those days—right across from the manager Ralph Houk and the traveling secretary, Jack Rogers. Yaz and I discussed young hitters coming up through the Red Sox farm system.

On October 1 and 2, the Red Sox had scheduled "Yaz Weekend," to mark his retirement. Nobody knew quite how he would react. He didn't particularly enjoy speaking to large crowds, and didn't really enjoy mixing very much with people. But the weekend came off very well. Some of it was planned, and some was spontaneous. The ceremonies were scheduled for a Saturday afternoon, with the next day held as a rain date, because the game would not be made up. The entire weekend at Fenway was sold out. My son Duke managed to get on camera, because he was working on the field and was in charge of setting up folding chairs. In fact, he brought out the chair for Mrs. Yawkey. Duke was ten. I still have the tape.

Yaz Weekend came off beautifully. Gifts were presented to him, and he made a fine speech. At the end of the ceremonies, Yaz ran around the perimeter of the field, and touched hands with hundreds of fans who could reach over the fence. His final words were, "New England, I love you."

He did that again on Sunday, October 2—the last game of the year. We were hoping that he would get a hit in the final at bat of his career (number 11,988), but he didn't. He started his final game in leftfield, the position he had played so well for so many years at Fenway before moving to first base later in his career, and made a fine Yaz-type play off the wall.

His final at bat was in the eighth inning to face reliever Dan Spillner of the Indians. Spillner had been a good friend of mine during my years in Cleveland.

I was prepared to turn the microphone over to Ken, out of deference and respect for him. After all, he had broadcast Carl Yastrzemski's games since 1966. But it was his inning anyway.

Spillner was doing everything he could to throw a strike, but the count got to 3-0. The last thing he wanted to do was walk Yastrzemski. The next pitch was very high, but Yaz didn't want to walk either, so he chased it, and hit a pop-up to Jack Perconte at second base. The Red Sox were ahead 3-1 as the ninth inning began, with Al Nipper on the mound for the Sox. Jim Rice hit his 39th homer of the season in that game. In the ninth, manager Ralph Houk sent Chico Walker out to leftfield to replace Yaz, and he got another tremendous round of applause from the fans as he ran off the field for the last time, in his 3,308th game.

Yaz Weekend was also an important weekend for me personally, and not just because Duke had been working in the Sox clubhouse and had appeared on TV. That weekend, the *Boston Herald* ran a story reporting that unnamed sources said I would not be back in 1984 as the Red Sox broadcaster. Sure, it was just one writer's opinion, but it really stung, especially since that was the weekend we were moving into our new house. It was also Jan's 34th birthday.

Other reporters asked Jack Campbell about the rumor, and he said, "Do you really think I'd let a guy move into a new home if I weren't going to hire him again?" Jack was very supportive, but the story was still disconcerting.

In fact, that was the only year I had a written contract with Jack Campbell, and that one was signed in July. In the other years, I had a handshake with Jack, and I asked, "Jack, what am I going to make this year?" And he'd tell me. I usually got a $5,000 raise each year, so in 1984, I was making $50,000.

So, in 1983, we moved into the new house, about 55 minutes from Fenway Park. On October 2, the kids started their new school. All of a sudden, it was the offseason for me, and I was able to be home to help unpack and get us settled. Money was tight, because I had taken a substantial pay cut when I came to Boston to do the Red Sox games. I paid my own moving expenses. I should have asked the radio station to pay them, but I didn't. Jack had never moved anybody before. The only break I got was at tax time. My income was down, and I had so many expenses associated with the move from Cleveland.

Jan and I spent much of the fall and winter driving around New England, trying to get to know our new neighborhood. Duke and Tommy were in school, and Kate was four, so she frequently came with us.

In January 1984, Jack Campbell called me. He told me that he was now Campbell Sports all by himself. He had assumed sole ownership and management of the company. No more Paul Mooney and no more Connors Advertising Agency, both of whom had been in the original Campbell partnership. Jack needed somebody to contact the affiliated stations, renew their contracts to carry the Red Sox games, and to collect the rights fees from them for the previous season, which had not been paid.

I was not entrusted with contacting the larger affiliate stations like Boston, Providence, or Worcester, just the smaller ones like Norway and Calais, Maine, and Keene, New Hampshire.

The work was welcome, and gave me an extra paycheck, which I needed, because I didn't have any offseason work.

As the start of the 1984 season, my second with the Red Sox, drew near, we decided that the kids would not go to Spring Training with me because it was their first year in a new school. Jan came by herself while a babysitter watched the kids. That was the year I went to the wrong airport to meet her.

Spring Training was a lot easier in 1984 because I felt that I knew the team, and the team knew me. I was no longer "the new guy," and players opened up to me a little more. I knew my way around, and I knew how the Red Sox did things. I also knew where things were in Winter Haven.

1984 was the year of the Detroit Tigers in the American League. They started the season 35-5, under the leadership of Sparky Anderson, and led the league from wire-to-wire. They went on to beat the Padres in the World Series in five games. The Red Sox had a pretty good year, finishing 18 games behind the Tigers. (The team closest to the Tigers that year was the Blue Jays, 15 games back.) Tony Armas led the league with 43 home runs and Dwight Evans had an excellent season, too. The Sox had five players that season with 600 at bats (Jim Rice, Dwight Evans, Wade Boggs, Tony Armas, and Mike Easler). The team's lineup was pretty much the same every day.

Ralph Houk retired at the end of the 1984 season, and I was sorry to see him go. He was always nice to me, and that helped me a great deal. Having no relationship or having a bad relationship with a manager can be terrible for a broadcaster.

John McNamara succeeded Houk as Red Sox manager in 1985. The Sox opened the season at home with a three-game sweep of their traditional rivals, the New York Yankees. Oil Can Boyd pitched well in the opener and wound up with a win. But that was the highlight. The Sox finished at .500, 18½ games behind the Toronto Blue Jays in the American League East—a very disappointing season.

So when the 1986 season began, expectations for the Red Sox were not very high. Roger Clemens had just had arm surgery and did not have a stellar Spring Training. The Sox made a big trade during Spring Training, getting Don Baylor from the Yankees for Mike Easler. This turned out to be a good trade for the Sox, because, particularly in the first half of the season, Baylor had some big hits and turned into a real clubhouse leader, a very positive guy who just wanted to win.

Dwight Evans hit the first pitch on Opening Day for a home run off Jack Morris of the Tigers, but the Sox lost. Evans said that he had decided in the middle of the winter to swing at the first pitch of the season. Ever since then, when I meet a rookie, I ask him what he intends to do with the first pitch. Most say that they hadn't thought about it. I suggest, "Why don't you hit it out? You'll never have another chance to do it!"

Roger Clemens didn't start a game until the fourth game of the season in Chicago. He won.

I'll never forget watching Clemens pitch on April 29, 1986, when he struck out 20 Mariners (including eight in a row) without a single walk. It was one of the most memorable days I've ever seen. The temperature was in the mid-50s on a cold misty night. There were only 13,414 people in the stands. Many of the media people in Boston were at the Boston Garden watching the Celtics in the NBA playoffs.

I knew from the first pitch that something special was going to happen because the Mariners hit very few foul balls. There were lots of called strikes and swings and misses. But who could have predicted that Clemens would set the major league record, which he later tied himself, by striking out 20 batters in a nine-inning game?

In the middle innings he struck out eight in a row.

In the ninth inning, with Vic Voltaggio umpiring behind the plate, Clemens struck out Spike Owen (19), and Phil Bradley looking (20). The last batter was Ken Phelps, and I thought Roger might strike him out again, too, for number 21. But Phelps grounded out to the shortstop, and the game was over. Twenty strikeouts!

Clemens really did get an extra chance during the game, because Don Baylor was playing first base for the Sox—quite a rarity. He dropped a foul ball hit by Gorman Thomas, who was given an extra life. But Clemens struck him out.

After the game, Clemens came over to his wife Debbie, who was seated behind home plate, and hugged her. He was so thrilled by his own accomplishment. Roger was gracious enough to be on our postgame show.

Another reason I'll never forget that game was that early in the game, perhaps in the third inning or so, Ken Coleman was reading from the Red Sox Yearbook, which had just been published. It mentioned the players' favorites—foods, actors, movies, singers, etc. Ken read that Roger Clemens' favorite singer was "Steve Nicks." I told him, "Ken, I think that's Stevie Nicks, not Steve." Ken replied, "I know him well, and I call him Steve." The next day, somebody sent us a poster of Stevie, so all of us in the broadcast booth could look at her.

Except for the last two games of the season, 1986 was a magical year. The Red Sox moved into first place in the American League East on May 15. The team won some games in unusual ways, such as the bases-loaded walk to Mike Stenhouse in a game against the Blue Jays. In another game, Marc Sullivan was hit by a pitch right in the backside, forcing in the winning run. In a July 10 game, the Sox seemed to be out of it, but the game went into extra innings. Don Baylor hit a pop-up against the California Angels with two out and the tying run on third base. Former Red Sox Rick Burleson was playing third base for the Angels, and he dropped the ball. The tying run scored, and the Sox went on to win the game in the 12th inning, when Todd Fischer balked home the winning run.

September 28, 1986, was the date the Red Sox could win the American League East pennant. The Sox beat Toronto that afternoon on Oil Can Boyd's win, and went on to beat the Angels in a memorable American League Championship Series (ALCS), which saw the Sox in a comeback win and Dave Henderson's home run in Game Five. Then came the New York Mets.

◆ ● ◆

My first ambition has always been to broadcast a World Series and here we were in my fourth season with the Red Sox opening the 1986 World Series at Shea Stadium. The Mets, who had beaten Houston in a tough National League Championship Series, had won 108 games curing the regular season and were heavy favorites to beat the Red Sox. The Mets had a great party the night before the opener, which included a boat trip on the Hudson River. However, the Red Sox's pre- and postgame parties were the best, featuring a raw bar and all one could eat and drink.

In Game One, Bruce Hurst spun a beauty and won 1-0, beating Ron Darling on an error by Tim Teufel. Game Two was the anticipated pitchers' duel started by Roger Clemens for Boston and Dwight Gooden for New York. Neither made it to the sixth inning and the Red Sox won easily, 9-3. So it was back to Fenway with a 2-0 lead in games. However, Lenny Dykstra led off Game Three with a home run, the Mets got four runs in the first and beat Oil Can Boyd 7-1. New York evened the series the next night behind the strong pitching of Darling and two home runs by Gary Carter. But in Game Five, Hurst went the distance and the Red Sox again pounded Gooden in a 4-2 win that gave Boston a 3-2 lead in the series. Then came Game Six.

◆ ● ◆

Every Red Sox fan knows where he or she was and what they were doing on Saturday night, October 25, 1986. The Red Sox had a 3-2 lead behind Roger Clemens through seven innings. Then Clemens left with a blister, a very controversial decision in Red Sox history. The Mets tied it against Calvin Schiraldi in the eighth inning and the game went to extra innings.

I will never forget being at the microphone in the tenth inning when Dave Henderson led off with a home run off the *Newsday* sign in left to put the Red Sox ahead. I waited an extra beat on the call to make sure the ball was gone. Marty Barrett then singled home Boggs and the Red Sox were on the cusp of their first World Championship since 1918 with a two-run lead in the last of the tenth inning.

During the mid-inning break, I asked Ken Coleman if he wanted me to continue play-by-play in the last of the tenth of go down to the club-house to cover the postgame celebration. Ken, gracious as always, left the decision up to me. Well, I thought Ken deserved to call the last out because of his many years with the Red Sox—and I also wanted to be there to get soaked with champagne, do the interviews, and experience the euphoria. So I ran down from the top of Shea Stadium to the base-ment where the clubhouses are located. By the time I arrived, Schiraldi had retired the first two Met batters. I watched as champagne was brought into the Red Sox clubhouse. I could see the players' lockers cov-ered with plastic sheets to protect their clothes from what would be the free-flowing bubbly. A security guard waiting with me had a radio.

Then I heard the hits by Carter and Kevin Mitchell—who had already taken off his uniform and was hardly dressed when called upon to pinch hit. The single by Ray Knight made it 5-4 Boston. Then, with Bob Stanley pitching and the tying run on third, I heard Mets Hall of Fame broadcaster Bob Murphy say as Stanley delivered a pitch to Mookie Wilson, "It gets awaaaaaay . . . and here comes the tying run." At that point, workers began to remove the champagne from the Red Sox clubhouse and I started to run back to the booth to broadcast the eleventh inning. However, there would be no eleventh inning. While on the ramp headed for the broadcast booth, I heard the crowd roar and knew the Mets had won but did not know how. Ken soon informed me but I never did see the ball go through Buckner's legs until TV replay hours later at the hotel. Somehow, it seemed like I was spared from witnessing that awful moment as it happened, though that did not decrease the pain at all. I still think the result might have been different had Stanley, who according to bullpen coach Joe Morgan, had nasty stuff in the bullpen, started the last of the tenth instead of Schiraldi. In later years, Stanley told me that the word from the dugout in the top of the tenth was, "You're in the game." Well, that decision was reversed and the sad history remains.

Still, the series was not over. Game Seven was rained out Sunday night and Jan and I had dinner with the Morgans at a restaurant owned by former Met Rusty Staub, who came by our table. Game Seven was played on Monday night, October 27. The Red Sox jumped out to a 3-0 lead on home runs by Evans and Geldman, but the pivotal inning was the sixth. Hurst had been breezing but the Mets loaded the bases with two outs and with Keith Hernandez at the plate. I was doing play-by-play and thought, "If Hurst gets him out, the Red Sox win; if Hernandez gets a hit, the Mets win." Well, Hernandez lined a two-run single to left center and the Mets quickly tied it at 3-3. That was it for Hurst and when Schiraldi gave up a home run to Ray Knight leading off the seventh, the Mets were ahead to stay.

The final score was 8-5. Ken and I did the sad wrap-up and went down to the clubhouse to await the bus to the airport. Outside the clubhouse, we saw Mets pitcher Bobby Ojeda, who had pitched so well in the series, in tears as he hugged his former Red Sox teammates. It was a very emotional scene. Then, as we headed to the bus to go to the airport, the Red Sox traveling secretary, Jack Rogers, was hit by a glass bottle thrown by someone in the upper deck. Jack suffered a deep gash and was leading profusely but, as always, he remained very stoic. He was stitched up in the clubhouse and was there to shepherd us to the nearby La Guardia Airport for the short—but in many ways long—trip home . . . a trip that would be repeated on another sad October night in New York some 17 years later.

◆ ● ◆

The 1987 season started with great expectations—the Sox were the defending American League champions—but the year turned out to be a major disappointment. It usually is a year after you come close. Repeating is very difficult. The Red Sox have not repeated as pennant winners (or even division winners) since they won back-to-back World Series in 1915 and 1916. They have not won the World Series since 1918. They were in the American League Division Series in 1998 and 1999, both times as the wildcard.

The wildcard is a necessity to keep interest up late in the season in different cities now that there are 30 teams.

Spring Training in 1987 was tough. Rich Gedman, the Sox regular catcher, held out because of the collusion of the team owners. He could have signed with another team, but if he resigned with the Red Sox, he couldn't play until May 1. Roger Clemens also held out, and didn't resign with the Sox until late in Spring Training. When the Sox broke camp, Clemens pitched a game in Winter Haven, Florida, against Harvard at a minor league field. After his late start in Spring Training, Roger started the season 0-2, but went on to finish 20-9, with an ERA of 2.97, and won the Cy Young Award for the second consecutive year (one of only six pitchers to do so; the others are Sandy Koufax, Jim Palmer, Randy Johnson, Greg Maddux, and Pedro Martinez).

Despite Clemens's success, the Sox had a terrible first half of the 1987 season, and were out of the race early, as Detroit and Toronto battled for the American League East crown. Detroit won the AL East pennant, winning 98 games, with Toronto two games back. The Red Sox finished a dismal fifth, 20 games back.

Todd Benzinger also came up in 1987 and showed a great deal of promise, as did Mike Greenwell. In just 125 games, Greenwell drove in 89 runs and smacked 19 home runs. John Marzano came up late in the season and hit five homers. Ellis Burks made the biggest splash as a rookie with 20 home runs and 20 stolen bases—a Red Sox rarity.

Expectations were high again for the 1988 season, but the team struggled in the early months. The fight at the team's hotel in Cleveland and the Wade Boggs/Margo Adams story blew up that year, too.

There were also some tough plays in 1988. In early July, Rich Gedman hit a home run in Kansas City which hit the foul pole in right field. Umpire Dale Scott mistakenly called it a foul ball and the Sox lost. At the All-Star break, the Sox were one game over .500. After that game in Chicago, I was on the team bus with the manager, John McNamara, going from Comiskey to the airport. McNamara told the reporters that, considering all the injuries and setbacks that had hit the team in the last few months, being one game over .500 wasn't that bad. That was about the last thing he ever said as the Red Sox manager, because he was fired the day the second half of the season resumed at Fenway, replaced by Joe Morgan.

The Sox finished the 1988 season in first place, just a game ahead of the Tigers—thanks to the "Morgan Magic." The Boston media started using that phrase because Morgan won his first 12 games as manager (a major league record), 19 out of 20, and a club record of 24 straight at home.

Unfortunately, the Sox were swept by the Oakland A's in the American League Championship Series.

There were not a lot of highlights for the Red Sox in 1989; they finished 87-75, six games behind the Blue Jays.

But 1989 was memorable for other reasons. That was the year that the new press box and broadcast facilities at Fenway were opened, and the team built the "600 Club," with theater-type seats.

Our old broadcast booth was cramped, hot, cold, and hard to get to. The new broadcast booth was five stories up, bigger, more comfortable, and more climate controlled.

It was also the last year I worked with Ken Coleman. Ken had missed some time in 1988 when he was out with the flu. Johnny Pesky filled in for him. In February 1989, Ken suffered a heart blockage. Although it was not considered major, he missed part of Spring Training. He came back to work a few innings of a game against the Dodgers, then, after three innings, he had to rest. The game went 15 innings. (Eddie Romero won the game for the Sox with a homer.)

At the end of the season, Jack Campbell's contract as the rights holder for Red Sox games was up, and there was some question as to whether he would retain the rights. If not, Ken Coleman and I might be out of work.

When I walked into general manager Lou Gorman's office for our daily pregame show, I knew that the rights had been awarded that day, and I knew that Lou knew what had happened, but Lou was on the phone. He saw me and gave me a sign—thumbs down. That meant that Campbell had lost the rights to the Red Sox broadcasts. The new rights holder was Atlantic Ventures, owned by Steve Dodge.

◆ ● ◆

Dodge, a Yale graduate, grew up in Hamden, Connecticut, a mile from where I grew up, but we traveled in different circles. He went to Hotchkiss and I went to Hamden High. Steve later worked for the Bank of Boston and later in the cable television business. After he sold his cable interests, he bought WRKO Radio.

Steve loved the Red Sox and seemed to like me. He listened to many of our games on the radio, and he liked the way I described the games.

This was a great blessing for me, and probably saved my job. Frequently, when the company that owns the broadcast rights to a team's games changes, so do the broadcasters.

I was very concerned when the rights changed hands, but in late July 1989, I got a call from Joe Winn, who said, "I really can't tell you the details, but don't worry. We'll meet after the season. We just wanted to touch base with you and let you know that we are thinking about you."

Joe was the chief financial officer for Atlantic Ventures, which changed its name to American Radio when they expanded some years later. (American Radio owned about 100 stations before they sold to CBS, which then sold to Entercom, our current employer, the owners of WEEI Radio.)

Steve Dodge's favorite player as a kid was Gary Geiger, a journeyman outfielder who had once been sidelined with a collapsed lung—the first time I had ever heard that term. Geiger was with the Red Sox from 1959 to 1965. Only a real fan would pick Gary Geiger as his favorite player.

On the next to last day of the season, I was in the player's parking lot at Fenway, on my way home, and I saw John Harrington. He smiled and greeted me and said, "I guess you know how things are going to turn out," which I hoped meant what I thought it meant—that I would be back in 1990. But I did not know about Ken.

That morning, the Tuesday after the season ended in early October 1989, I had a 9 AM meeting at the radio station, which was on Brookline Avenue around the corner from Fenway Park. I had been up most of the night worrying about it.

At that time, I had been with the Red Sox for seven years. We had a house in the suburbs, and our children were 16, 14, and 10 years old. I did *not* want to be told that I didn't have a job for the next season.

When I got to the meeting, I was told that I would be back, but that Ken would not be returning. We negotiated for a new salary. My 1989 salary, even including modest annual raises, was well below the standard level for experienced major league broadcasters. They offered me a raise. I negotiated with Joe Winn and Eric Schultz, the general manager of WRKO. Eric was a Harvard graduate who went on to become the author of several children's books. I asked for a somewhat larger raise—and I got it!

There was no talk about me being the lead broadcaster. I knew that Ken was not coming back, and, in fact, he came in a little later that day to announce his retirement.

It was a trying day—I was very happy to keep working in Boston, particularly with a hefty raise, but I was sad to see Ken go.

In any event, I was told that I would have a new partner.

I went to see Ken that afternoon. He was, as always, gracious. He told me that he had been worried about me, not himself. He was very happy for me. Ken said that he was not sure what he would do day to day, but that he would continue his consulting work for the Jimmy Fund.

Steve Dodge called me to congratulate me, and told me how descriptive I was on the air—that he could visualize the game while listening to me. I knew when he said that that he listened closely to each pitch.

Steve also told me that he had been considering three broadcasters to replace me. The finalists included former New England Patriots broadcaster Bob Starr, who was anchoring Channel 4.

Dodge asked me which of those three I thought would be best. It was awkward, because I felt like telling him that I thought *I* should be the lead broadcaster. The lead broadcaster usually does more innings and also is usually paid more than his partner.

But I was very happy with my new salary, whether or not I was the lead broadcaster. I talked over the situation with my great friend Mark Holtz, the voice of the Texas Rangers, who unfortunately passed away from cancer in 1997 at the age of 52, about my age. Mark was a wonderful man, and I appreciated his advice. Mark thought that Bob Starr would be a comfortable fit. I didn't know Bob, although he'd been doing Angels games. I had seen him on TV, and he'd been in New England before, too. I told Steve Dodge that I thought Bob would be right for the job. And Bob was hired.

I called Bob and we hit it off right from the start. We wound up working together for three years and had a wonderful time.

We started to work together during Spring Training in 1990. Bob and his wife Brenda were there and we bonded instantly. It was always fun to be with him.

So we went to Florida at the end of February 1990, ready to broadcast the Red Sox Spring Training games. But the clubs locked out the players and the season started late after only four Spring Training games.

Because I was not broadcasting games during the lockout, I had time to do other things, such as relax and hang out. (Of course, Florida in March is somewhat warmer than Boston.) One day, Jan, the kids, and I went to the Strawberry Festival in Plant City, the strawberry capital of Florida. It was dirty and dusty, but apparently a treat for those who work in the strawberry fields.

Joe Morgan was the manager in 1990, and the Sox played well with some surprising performances. The Sox battled the Toronto Blue Jays all season.

Lefthander Tom Bolton came out of nowhere and went 10-5. Dana Kiecker, a longtime minor leaguer, won eight games, including some big ones. Jeff Gray, an unknown, came in out of the bullpen to get some key saves. In July 1991, Jeff had a stroke right in the clubhouse. He was 28. Unfortunately, he never recovered well enough to pitch again. A middle reliever, he had great command of his pitches.

Dennis Lamp also pitched effectively in 1990.

The Red Sox won the American League East Division that year with an 88-74 record, two games ahead of the Blue Jays, their closest rivals.

Roger Clemens pitched well and had a good year, going 21-6 but he missed some time with tendonitis in his shoulder. And there was more Morgan Magic. Morgan put Jeff Stone in to pinch-hit against Toronto with first place at stake on September 28 at Fenway. Stone, a longtime minor leaguer, hit a single in the gap off Tom Henke, the Blue Jays hard-throwing closer, to drive in Wade Boggs with the winning run. Red Sox 7, Blue Jays 6.

The next day, Clemens came off the disabled list and pitched brilliantly for seven innings. Tom Brunansky hit three home runs in the game, and the Red Sox won the series.

The season ended on a Wednesday, with the Red Sox holding a half-game lead over Toronto. They needed either a win or a Toronto loss.

The Red Sox were playing Jeff Torborg's White Sox, which had had a surprisingly good year. The Red Sox had a lead in the ninth inning, with Jeff Reardon on the mound. Then the White Sox put the tying run on with two outs. Ozzie Guillen was at bat, but I went down to the clubhouse to get the postgame interviews, and I was standing near the box seats of Joe Morgan's wife Dorothy. Guillen, who never pulled the ball, hit a line drive down the rightfield line. Tom Brunansky came out of nowhere to make a sliding catch to end the game and give the Red Sox the American League East title. But nobody had seen the catch. Certainly not Bob Starr in the broadcast booth by himself. There's a blind spot on the field, and that's right where Brunansky made the catch in the corner. I couldn't see the catch from my spot in the stands, and the catch could not be seen from the dugout. Umpire Tim McClelland did not give a definitive sign, and while I did see a tape later in which he gave the "fair ball" sign, to this day I have not seen him give the "out" sign.

But the Sox won, and the celebration started.

The players ran right by me with my wireless microphone, and I had to go into the clubhouse to get the interviews. This was the Red Sox's second division crown in three years. They were swept again in the League Championship Series by the Oakland A's in four games.

My second year working with Bob Starr was 1991. I really enjoyed that, but it was a very disappointing year for the team. I recall that the team was swept in a three-game series in Kansas City. They were about eight games under .500, August was beginning, and there were rumors that Joe Morgan's job was in jeopardy.

The Sox swept a four-game series in Toronto, including two 1-0 wins, one by Roger Clemens. The Red Sox got back in the race. On a Sunday afternoon in late September, the Sox were half a game out of first place, with a chance to take over the lead. With two out in the ninth inning, against the Yankees at Fenway, I had one of the most crushing moments I ever experienced. Roberto Kelly was up with an 0-2 count. Jeff Reardon hung one and Kelly hit it over the wall to tie the game. In the tenth inning, Bernie Williams, just up from the minor leagues, hit a three-run double to win the game. The Red Sox fell to a game and a half back. The Red Sox went into Baltimore, where Clemens won the first game of an afternoon doubleheader on September 26. In the second game, Greg Harris walked in the winning run with the bases loaded. The man he walked was Dwight Evans. (After 19 seasons in Boston, Evans finished his career with one season in Baltimore.)

That was pretty much the end of the season for the Red Sox. Joe Morgan tried to take some of the blame for the loss, saying that he should not have left Harris in the game.

The Red Sox finished the season in second place at 84-78, seven games behind the eventual American League East Champion Toronto Blue Jays. Two days after the season ended, I went out to get my lawnmower fixed, and when I returned, I got a call from my son Duke's hitting instructor, Arthur Hartung, telling me that Butch Hobson was the new manager of the Boston Red Sox. Joe Morgan had been fired.

Morgan's final words to Red Sox management when he was fired were "Your team is not as good as you think it is." As happened more often then not, he was correct. The 1992 Red Sox finished 73-89 under new manager Butch Hobson—dead last in the American League East, 23 games behind the Blue Jays, who went on to win the World Series again. That was the first time the Red Sox had finished last in 60 years, since 1932.

1992 was a miserable season for a dreadful team. No speed, no power, lots of injuries, no scoring, plus Wade Boggs, who had hit .332 the previous year, had the worst season of his career, hitting only .259, a career low. His contract was up, and he was pressing. I kept track of how many times he hit the Green Monster. In a typical year for Boggs, he'd hit the wall 20 to 25 times. In 1992, he did not hit the wall at all after May 22.

It was also the third and last year I worked with Bob Starr. WRKO management tried to cut expenses by having us make our own travel arrangements. I thought this was just cheap, but I tried to look on the bright side—lots of frequent flier miles. I used them to take my family with me. My kids have traveled with me to every city in the American League, and Jan has been to every stadium but Texas, where she thinks it's just too hot.

But Bob pointed out that we'd be making early morning or late night flights, making our own arrangements to get to and from the hotel from the airport, and he hated it. Bob was unhappy, but he didn't say anything about it to me. But he did talk with the Angels. The last trip of the season, he told me that he was through with the Red Sox—he was going back to the Angels even though he had a year to go on his Boston contract. The next day, he told everybody. I got a call from Steve Dodge, who said that I was to be the lead broadcaster. Probably.

Sadly, upon being informed that he was leaving, the station in Boston tried to withhold Bob's pay. He had already done the work for them. Bob had our union take the station to arbitration, and he won—as he should have. The station's move was nothing more than vindictive.

After his announcement, Bob did the last three games of the season with me. As the last pitch of the 1992 season was delivered, Bob was on his way to the airport to head west. The minute the game was over, he shook hands with me and left, as I prepared for the postgame show. I finished up and did a brief season wrap-up.

As we headed into the offseason, I took what Steve Dodge had told me—that I was going to be the lead broadcaster—and I thought that perhaps I should try to renegotiate my contract and demand more money. I did demand a raise. Of course, the station insisted that I was bound by our contract. This went back and forth for a while.

In January, with Spring Training approaching, there was some news—I had inherited Bob Starr's car—the Burly Bobmobile—which the station provided.

By this time, I had hired Jeffrey Kline to be my agent. I wanted him to do two things for me. First, I needed help negotiating my contract with the radio station. But I was also interested in offseason work. Eventually, we agreed on a contract for a $500 raise and a car. Klein has been representing me ever since. He is the agent for Dave Winfield and Jeff Kent but primarily works as a corporate lawyer for a major New York firm.

Luke Griffith, our executive producer, and I listened to many audition tapes as we tried to help select my new broadcast partner. Luke asked for my input, but the station's management never did. A number of broadcasters called me about the position. One of the tapes I listened to was from Jerry Trupiano. I thought it was very good. I told Luke that Jerry Trupiano's tape was the one I liked best.

◆ ● ◆

Trup was hired, and we went to Spring Training for the start of the 1993 season. Although Jerry was new to the Red Sox, he had plenty of experience as a major league broadcaster: He did Astros games in 1985–1986 and broadcast for the Expos in 1989–1990. He had been to some of the American League ballparks and knew many of the people around the league. The 1993 Spring Training season marked two big changes.

My first year with Trup was 1993. He was the first partner I had worked with who was from my own generation. I'm only seven months older than Jerry. We shared similar interests, too, besides baseball. Our families (Jerry has two sons, Michael and Brian), and rock and roll. So we had lots to talk about.

After 27 years in Winter Haven, the Red Sox had moved, and this was their first year in Fort Myers and their beautiful new stadium at City of Palms.

I remember a 15-inning game against the Cleveland Indians. Jeff "Whitey" Richardson won the game with an extra-inning double on a cold spring night.

Trup and I were traveling on our own as the season started to save the station money. I remember having to wait in Oakland for a late-night flight back to Boston. With the evening free, I went to see the Giants and the Mets play at Candlestick Park—the only game I ever saw there. I visited with my old friends, Mets manager Jeff Torborg and Tommy McCraw.

The 1993 season was another disappointment for the Red Sox. They had no offense—they were slow and they couldn't hit. Roger Clemens, victimized by arm woes and bad relief pitching, finished the season at 11-14, the first under-.500 season of his career.

Jeff Russell, the team's closer, gave up a number of walk-off home runs, which are always demoralizing and deflating.

1993 was also Lou Gorman's last year as general manager. After the season, he was bumped upstairs to another position. Haywood Sullivan sold out to John Harrington, and he took over the club for the Yawkey estate. (Mrs. Yawkey died in 1992.)

During Butch Hobson's second year as manager, 1993, the team finished under .500 with an 80-82 record, in fifth place, 15 games behind the Toronto Blue Jays.

Best Seat in the House

What started as a promising year became a disaster because of the strike. In 1994, the Red Sox wound up their Spring Training exhibition season with two games against the Yankees at the Superdome in New Orleans. That was an unusual experience. There were two temporary fences that were short. The crowds were small, only about 20,000. This was my first visit to New Orleans, but we arrived at noon on a Friday, played Friday night and Saturday afternoon, and then left. Unfortunately, all I had time to do in New Orleans was walk around the French Quarter.

Like some other teams, the Red Sox used to squeeze in a few exhibition games between the end of Spring Training and Opening Day. The Sox played two games at RFK Stadium in Washington, D.C. In 1984, they played a game in San Diego and a game in Denver and in 1999, there were two games in Denver. In 2000, Boston played two games in Phoenix. In 2001, we were in Houston and Milwaukee for one game in each city. In 2002, Boston played two games in Houston.

The 1994 Red Sox had little power, little speed, and weak pitching. Not a formidable combination as the season started. Roger Clemens had little run support (9-7, only 170 innings pitched).

The team had a family trip to Minneapolis and Baltimore in early August. I took Tom and Kate with me. Tom was 19 and Kate was 15.

The flight was fun, and we had a good time in Minnesota, including going to a casino and the Jesse James Museum in Northfield. After the Sox played a three-game series in Minneapolis, the team flew to Baltimore to take on the Orioles.

The strike deadline was midnight, August 11. We went to the ballpark at Camden Yards under threatening skies. The game was held up and then cancelled when the strike deadline was reached. I thought how fitting it was that the last game before the strike ended with a rainout. The strike was on, and players had to scramble to get home—no more team bus, no more team plane, no more team travel arrangements. I rented a car, and Tom, Kate, and I drove to see my sister, Pam Potolocchio, and her family in Bethesda, Maryland. We spent an extra night there, hoping that the strike would be a short one. But it wasn't, so we made arrangements to go home. Nobody knew what was going to happen or how long the strike would last. I had a clause in my contract with WRKO, which provided that my salary would be docked if more than ten games were missed because of a work stoppage.

When I got home, the station called and asked Trup and me to do a daily talk show. So for two weeks, we were on the air from 10 AM to 2 PM. This really worked out well, because we were paid the same as if we had been broadcasting the games. The format was a talk show, not a sports show. Actually, the station was waiting for a new host of the talk show, and we were glad to fill in, as the strike was on everybody's mind. But four hours was a long time to do a talk show, particularly when we were not flooded with calls. Occasionally, the phones just didn't ring, so we were glad to have some of our baseball friends call in. Jeffrey Lyons, for example, called in and talked for an hour about movies.

Our studio show ended in late August. I went to see the Red Sox top minor league affiliate, the Pawtucket Red Sox known as the PawSox. My son Duke was working out in the bullpen with Bill Fischer, the former Red Sox pitching coach who was then the Richmond Braves pitching coach. We also saw the New Haven Ravens play, which actually turned out well for Duke, because he got an internship position in the front office there for 1995. (He did a little play-by-play on the radio, too.) But soon the minor league season was over, too.

Without baseball, September 1994 seemed very strange, very long, and very boring. I watched Stonehill College's fall baseball practice and a football game at Colgate and another at Holy Cross, where Tom was a sophomore.

My father had heart bypass surgery in September, so we spent a lot of time at the hospital in New Haven. I was happy to have the time to be with my father, but was still shocked when then-acting commissioner Bud Selig made the announcement on September 14 that the World Series of 1994 would be cancelled—the first fall without a World Series since 1904. It was very distressing.

That fall, I played some golf, something I rarely do.

On October 15 that year, a date I will never forget, I came home from playing golf and found messages from Trup and from the station telling me that my paycheck would be severely reduced by the number of games we missed. This was two months after the strike started.

We are paid by our station for the entire 12-month year. But the CFO of American Radio told me that my salary would be pro-rated for the games missed because of the strike minus the two weeks we did for the studio call-in show. I was appalled. Virtually all the television and radio broadcasters were being paid in full, although a few were probably paid half of their regular salaries. The radio station decided to save about $25,000 to $30,000 on me! Why were Trup and I being treated differently? *We* weren't on strike. We were ready to work, and we wanted to work. Of course, the stations all got their rights fees back from the teams, and they broadcast other programs and commercials during the strike. So the stations recouped their losses. The Red Sox TV broadcasters, like most broadcasters throughout baseball, were paid in full. At the time, I was paying about $55,000 to $60,000 a year in college tuition for both Duke (at Stonehill) and Tom (Holy Cross). A $30,000 instant pay cut was quite a hit, and while American Radio treated me rather well over the years they carried the Red Sox, I still resent the unfair way they treated us during the strike. After much begging and pleading, we were eventually paid for rained out games.

The 1995 season approached with the same uncertainty. The owners announced that they would start the season with "replacement" players. Some were playing in the independent league, and saw this union-busting opportunity as their only chance to be able to say to their grandchildren, "I played in the major leagues! I played for the Red Sox!" Most replacement players had some previous professional experience.

Because the Major League Players Association is such a strong union, we knew that the use of replacement players would do nothing but sow ill will among teammates and between such players and the fans. The owners tried to put a pretty face on the plan, but what if the Orioles, for example, had played a regular season game with a team stocked only by replacement players. Would that have counted as an official "game" played without Cal Ripken Jr.? To avoid having to answer this particular question, Peter Angelos, the owner of the Orioles, and a powerful labor lawyer, declared that his team would not employ replacement players.

Mixed into this bag of replacement players were a few familiar names trying for a comeback such as Randy Kutcher, who had a five-year, 244-game career with the Red Sox and the Giants.

So, as Spring Training for 1995 began in Fort Myers, we were faced with the prospect of an entirely new ballclub, made up of players nobody had ever heard of. The Sox also had a new manager, Kevin Kennedy, and for the most part an entirely new coaching staff, which included Tim Johnson, Herm Starrette, John Cumberland, and Dave Oliver.

Red Sox general manager Dan Duquette sat with us in the broadcast booth for one game early in the Spring Training season, and as we spoke, he saw Don Barbara, a slow-footed first baseman running to first base on a grounder. Duquette said that he looked like Fred Flintstone trying to start his car.

Those Spring Training games seemed like they were played in slow motion. Even in a minor league game, you can see an occasional excellent play, but most of the time, the game is obviously not played on a par with a major league game. But these replacement players just didn't have the talent. The pitchers were as much as ten miles an hour slower than real major league pitchers. Runners were not nearly as fast. Batters had very little power.

The games were played quickly, but they were boring. The talent just wasn't there. There were no flashes of brilliance, such as you would occasionally see in a good minor league game.

Aubrey Waggoner was another replacement player I remember. Waggoner had about 100 at bats that spring. He had been in the White Sox minor league system, but never even had a cup of coffee in the majors. Jerry Remy called him "The Jeep."

As Spring Training wound down, and Opening Day approached, we prepared to open the season in Minnesota. Then, a few days before we left camp, Federal District Court Judge Sonia Sotomayor in New York issued an injunction ending the strike. The regular players would be back, and the teams would have a second Spring Training to let them get into shape.

We went home for a few weeks and planned to return to Florida when exhibition games started about two weeks later. It was so rare for me to be home in April, and I took advantage of my being there. Duke was a junior at Stonehill College in Easton, Massachusetts, and I had the chance to go to some of Duke's games.

One advantage of the second Spring Training was that by April, when the exhibition games started, Jan had a week off from school. She was teaching second grade. So she was able to go with me. Because of the screwy schedule, there were very few fans at the four or five exhibition games that we broadcast. And the Sox had acquired José Canseco. Management thought that he would provide the extra power the team needed. It was good to have the regular players back.

The 1995 season opener was at home against the Twins on April 26. Because of the delayed opening of the season, the game against the Twins was not part of a series—just one game. One welcome difference in 1995 was that we broadcasters were paid for the games that had been missed.

The Sox got off to a good start that year, going 20-11 through May. In a May 15 game against the Yankees, catcher Mike Macfarlane came up to bat in the bottom of the ninth inning in a tie game with one out against Steve Howe and homered into the bleachers to end the game. This was a "walk-off home run." In fact, I first heard that term from

Macfarlane, who may have coined it, or been among the first to use it. I use the phrase now whenever it is appropriate, because it is both short and very descriptive. A walk-off home run is the most exciting play in baseball—the other team walks off the field slowly and dejectedly as the hero circles the bases.

The next day, we had a big rally by the leftfield wall. Baseball was trying to lure the fans back to the game after the long and bitter strike that had alienated so many. The rally drew a very large crowd of fans and quite a few players, too. Mo Vaughn and José Canseco were there, the team was hot, and everything was going well for the Sox. The team moved into first place early that season and stayed there just about all season. And they were able to stay in first without Roger Clemens for most of the early part of the season. The story then was knuckleballer Tim Wakefield. He had been given a look-see in Fort Myers. Phil Niekro, who, along with Hoyt Wilhelm, was one of the greatest knuckleballers of all time, and a 300-game winner, gave him a look. Niekro had been hired as a consultant by the Red Sox to work with Tim. Wakefield had been with the Pittsburgh Pirates, and had been successful for them in the 1992 postseason, but had a terrible year in 1994 at Buffalo. When the Pirates eventually cut him, the Red Sox invited Wakefield to work out for them in Anaheim. When the team went to Oakland, he won a game for the Sox, then won another on just one day's rest. He got off to a tremendous 14-1 start in 1995, and Wakefield was the main reason the Sox moved into first place, and he was the main reason they stayed in first place for most of the season.

Mo Vaughn had a monster season, and wound up winning the American League Most Valuable Player Award in 1995. He tied Albert Belle for the RBI crown (126), too. Vaughn also led the league in strikeouts with 150. José Canseco also had a good year in 1995—24 home runs, 81 RBI.

Roger Clemens had a sore shoulder when the strike ended and when he came back in 1995, he was just good, not great, going 10-5.

The Red Sox decided during the season that the one missing piece to put them over the top was a first rate closer, so they made a trade for Rick Aguilera. In fact, Aguilera was warming up in the Twins' bullpen in early July at the Metrodome in a game against the Red Sox when the trade was made. He simply switched uniforms the next day.

After the Sox clinched the American League East title at home, Trup and I were invited to a get-together at "The Diamond Club," a fancy party room that was created at Fenway when the park was renovated in 1989.

Then the Sox had to play the Cleveland Indians in the best-of-five series that started on October 3 in Cleveland. The Indians had not been in postseason play since the 1954 World Series.

There was much speculation as to who would start the first game— Roger Clemens, still considered the ace of the staff, or Tim Wakefield, who had a terrific season. (He started the season at 14-1, but struggled down the stretch and finished 16-8.) Clemens got the nod from Kevin Kennedy for the first game, and pitched well. But the Red Sox could barely score. By the ninth, the score was tied at three. Tim Naehring homered in the 11th inning to put the Red Sox ahead, but Sox reliever Rick Aguilera gave up a bomb to Albert Belle to tie the game in the bottom of the inning. Aguilera had pulled a muscle or a hamstring and was taken out of the game, replaced by Mike Maddux and then Zane Smith, the seventh Red Sox pitcher of the game. That was the end of Aguilera's career with the Red Sox. He never pitched for the Sox again. By the next season, he was back in Minnesota. Tony Peña's walk-off homer off Smith ended it.

In the second game, the next day, the Sox were shut out 4-0. Game Three turned out to be the only game of the series played in Boston. Charles Nagy shut down the Red Sox, and Tim Wakefield gave up six runs. Just as in the second game, the Sox had no homers in Game Three, and fell to Cleveland 8-2, as the Indians swept the series. José Canseco went 0 for 13 in the series, and Mo Vaughn was 0 for 14. As a team, the Red Sox hit .184 during the series.

After the final game, we did a wrap-up, and I read a passage from Bart Giamatti's book, *Green Fields of the Mind*. The station played highlights from our calls during the season, and we left. We went to Artu's Ristorante in the North End to commiserate. The next day, the players came in to the Fenway clubhouse to clean out their lockers, and the season was officially over.

The Indians's sweep of the Red Sox in the Division Series was, frankly, a surprising end to the 1995 season. The Red Sox had been in first place virtually all season long, and won the division crown without much of a challenge.

◆ ● ◆

The Red Sox opened the 1996 season in Texas, where they were swept in three games by the Rangers. Then they went to Kansas City, where they lost two more. They finally won a game behind Jamie Moyer, and were off to a 1-5 start. Things didn't improve much, and they went to 3-15. Clemens had a tough year until the last month or so of the season. Kevin Mitchell, José Canseco, and Dwayne Hosey—not much of an outfield. The team had quite a few power hitters, such as Canseco, Mo Vaughn, and John Valentin, but was not a well-rounded ballclub. The team improved somewhat as the season progressed until September 18, a cool night in Detroit. The Tigers were well out of the pennant chase, and the Sox had only a remote chance at the wild card. Roger Clemens had had a sub-.500 season up to that point. But he struck out 20 Tigers, tying his own major league record. Our broadcast booth was rather close to home plate—closer than the pitcher, in fact—and I could hear the ball popping catcher Bill Haselman's mitt, the swish of a swing and a miss, and some of the home plate arguments. Clemens's last strike out victim that game was Travis Fryman.

In my opinion, that 20-strikeout game led to Clemens's departure from the Red Sox, because he thought it gave him more negotiating power at the bargaining table. His contract demands for 1997 were high, and the Red Sox offer was below what Clemens thought was fair, so he moved on to the Toronto Blue Jays in 1997. Clemens's salary with the Red Sox in 1996 was reported as $5.15 million. When he jumped to the Blue Jays, his salary jumped too, to a reported $8.4 million, making him the third highest paid player in the game at the time, behind Albert Belle of the White Sox ($10 million) and Cecil Fielder of the Yankees ($9.23 million).

The 1996 season was marked by discord at the end. Even as late as the last week of the season, the Sox still had a chance at the wild card. Mike Greenwell went to the front office to find out what plans the Red

Sox had for him for the following season and for the future, and was told that he was not seen as a full-time player. Greenwell was not happy with that news, and he came into the clubhouse and started emptying his locker. This was an act of defiance. Kevin Kennedy, the manager, was hurt in the eyes of the front office, and the team continued its skid. Next season, Kennedy was gone. José Canseco was gone. Greenwell was playing in Japan, but quit after one or two games. And Roger Clemens was gone. We were surprised that Roger signed with the Blue Jays, because he had stated that he wanted to be closer to his home in Texas, and many thought he would sign with the Rangers or the Astros.

In the offseason, the Sox tried to sign Jim Leyland as their new manager, but finally settled on Jimy Williams, who turned out to be one of the best managers in the history of the team.

◆ ● ◆

The 1997 Red Sox did not really have an ace. Nobody replaced Roger Clemens. Mo Vaughn and a few other players had good years, and Nomar Garciaparra was the American League Rookie of the Year, setting the record with 209 hits as a leadoff hitter. But the team just couldn't put it together. Tim Naehring was hurt in June and never played again. That was really tough. Jimy tried to keep the team above water but the club was never really in the race, finishing 20 games out.

The team approached the 1998 season knowing that they needed one more player—an ace of the staff—to be competitive, so they made a deal with the Montreal Expos to obtain Pedro Martinez. I had not seen Martinez pitch before, but he was indeed one of the best pitchers in the game.

There was also much speculation about Mo Vaughn's future with the team—would he stay, or would he go? One of the highlights of the 1998 season was the Sox home opener against the Mariners. The Sox were behind the entire game, but rallied to get the tying and winning runs on as they loaded the bases in the ninth inning. With lefty Paul Spoljaric on the mound, up came Mo Vaughn who lined a shot past Pesky's Pole in rightfield for a game-winning walk-off grand slam. The team had a good year in 1998, battling New York all season long. But they came up short, finishing 92-70, 22 games behind the Yankees (114-48). But the Red Sox were the wild card team in the American League in 1998 and faced the Cleveland Indians in the Division Series, the winner to go to the League Championship Series. Despite a stint on the disabled list, Pedro Martinez had an excellent year in 1998 (19-7, with an ERA of 2.89, 251 strikeouts, and just 67 walks). Tom Gordon also had a good year, setting a Red Sox record for saves with 46. Gordon had Tommy John surgery in 1999, and managed only 11 saves. But he did appear in a Stephen King book, *The Girl Who Loved Tom Gordon.*

Mo Vaughn had two home runs and seven RBI in the first game of the Division Series and Martinez won the game, as the Sox clobbered the Indians 11-3 in Cleveland.

The second game turned when the Red Sox had a rally going in the first inning when starting pitcher Doc Gooden argued a play at the plate and umpire Joe Brinkman ejected him. Dave Burba relieved Gooden, and gave up three runs, giving the Indians a chance to stay in the game. The Sox battled back but the Indians won 9-5.

The Sox came close in Game Three, scoring two runs in the bottom of the ninth inning, but the Indians held on to win 4-3.

The question for Game Four was whether to bring Pedro Martinez back on short rest, as the team faced elimination in the best of five series, or start the lefty Pete Shourek. Jimy decided to go with Shourek, and I think Pedro's later years showed that Jimy made the right decision.

Shourek kept the Sox in the game, but David Justice had a big hit in the eighth inning off Tom Gordon, and the 1998 season was over. After the season, Mo Vaughn left the team and signed with the only team that made him an offer—the Anaheim Angels.

◆ ● ◆

The Sox had a surprising team in 1999. Nomar Garciaparra continued to improve, and won his first batting championship, hitting .357. The Sox were the American League wild card again in 1999, but the highlight of the season was the All-Star game played in Fenway Park. It was a marvelous scene to see Ted Williams mobbed on the pitcher's mound by the current All-Stars and by the members of the All-Century team, such greats as Carl Yastrzemski, Willie Mays, Carlton Fisk, Stan Musial, Hank Aaron, Tony Gwynn, Mark McGwire, and the other current All-Stars. Williams asked, "Where's my kid? Where's my kid?"—meaning Nomar. Williams liked Garciaparra as a player, and said that Garciaparra reminded him of Joe DiMaggio.

All of the other players on the All-Century team had walked onto the field from the centerfield gate, but Ted had suffered a number of strokes, and he didn't walk very well. So he came onto the field in a golf cart driven by Al Forrester, a member of the grounds crew who had been at Fenway when Ted was a player—more than 50 years at Fenway.

Ted threw out the ceremonial first pitch of the game to Carlton Fisk behind the plate. Pedro Martinez took over on the mound and struck out five of the six National League batters he faced. Pedro was voted the Most Valuable Player of the game, which the American League won 4-1. After the game, Pedro went up to the owner's suite where he met Ted and discussed pitching.

The 1999 Red Sox were trying to survive the loss of Mo Vaughn. (Vaughn was also trying to survive. In his debut with the Anaheim Angels, he fell down the dugout steps trying to catch a foul pop-up and played hurt all season.) Brian Daubach emerged as a rookie, and hit 21 home runs. Mike Stanley also had a good year, and Jimy Williams found new ways to win games. The Yankees had a few injuries, and showed some vulnerability, but they still came out on top, with the Red Sox finishing 94-68, four games behind them.

The 1998 and 1999 seasons were the first time the Red Sox had played in the postseason in consecutive years since their World Championship seasons of 1915 and 1916. The 94 wins were the most by the Red Sox since 1986. These years also marked the first time the Sox had back-to-back 90-win seasons since 1977, 1978, and 1979. The Sox led the American League in ERA in 1999 (4.00) for the first time since 1914, primarily because of Pedro Martinez's brilliant season—one of the best ever by a pitcher. He won the Cy Young Award that year, going 23-4 with an ERA of 2.07, 313 strikeouts (a Red Sox record), and just 37 walks. Boston also set a team attendance record that year with 2.4 million.

The pitching staff led the league with 12 shutouts. The Sox tied their club and major league record of nine players with at least 100 hits.

The Red Sox victory on September 29 in the first game of a double-header in Chicago clinched the wild card spot in the playoffs. Once again, the Red Sox met the Indians in the Division Series.

Al Reyes of the Orioles hit Nomar Garciaparra on the wrist late in the season, and he was doubtful for the series. But he started and hit well. Pedro Martinez had to leave Game One in the fifth inning with the Red Sox leading 1-0 because of a pulled muscle in his upper back, and the Red Sox lost the first two games to the Indians. The team returned to Fenway Park needing a victory to stay alive. They won Game Three, 9-3, and Game Four, 23-7, with a postseason record of 24 hits.

Then we all went back to Cleveland for Game Five—one of the most dramatic games in Red Sox history. The Sox took the lead on a Nomar Garciaparra home run. They then fell behind on a Jim Thome home run, and by the bottom of the second were behind 5-2. The Sox came back on Troy O'Leary's grand slam. The Indians tied the game again on another Jim Thome home run. In the fourth inning, a hush came over the Jacobs Field crowd as Pedro Martinez got up in the bullpen to warm up. The Indians had a great fear of Pedro, who had dominated the Indians all season. With his injured back, he was not supposed to pitch any more, but he came in to relieve Derek Lowe, who followed starter Bret Saberhagen.

Although his pitches were clocked at about 91 miles per hour—well below his usual speed—Pedro pitched brilliantly and no-hit the Indians for six innings. That was one of the most heroic performances I've ever seen.

In the seventh inning, for the second time in the game, the Indians intentionally walked Nomar Garciaparra to pitch to Troy O'Leary, who had hit a grand slam on the first pitch he saw in the third inning. O'Leary smacked a three-run home run, also on the first pitch, off Paul Shuey, as the Sox went on to win the game 12-8, and the Series, 3-2.

In the other Division Series, the Yankees had swept the Texas Rangers in three games, so they were well rested. The Red Sox started off the American League Championship Series by losing two one-run games to the Yankees in New York. The first game ended in a walk-off home run by Bernie Williams in the tenth inning off Rod Beck. Those games saw a few bad calls that went against the Red Sox. Game Three was scheduled to be a pitching matchup for the ages—Pedro Martinez against Roger Clemens. But the pitching duel did not live up to expectations, as Clemens was hit hard. José Offerman opened the first with a triple and scored. John Valentin homered, and Clemens was gone by the second inning. Pedro held the Yankees scoreless through the first seven innings, and the Red Sox won 13-1. But the Yankees won Games Four and Five, and Boston's season was over.

With a few breaks in the League Championship Series, Boston might have prevailed, but the Yankees went on to sweep the Atlanta Braves in the World Series.

Overall, 1999 was a very good year for the Red Sox. It was a likeable team, including Jason Varitek, Tom Gordon, Nomar Garciaparra, Pedro Martinez, Lou Merloni, and Derek Lowe, to name just a few. When Tim Wakefield did well—he had 15 saves in 1999—the Red Sox did well. John Valentin continued to do well particularly as a big-game player.

Hopes were therefore high for the Red Sox in 2000.

◆ ● ◆

The Red Sox got off to a good start in 2000, battling the Yankees. One of the most exciting games of the season was on May 28, a Sunday night game at Yankee Stadium. Roger Clemens, in his second season as a Yankee, faced Pedro Martinez. In the seventh inning, Trot Nixon tripled and slid into third with Clemens hovering over him. They were real adversaries, probably because Nixon always hit Clemens well. In the ninth inning, Nixon came up with a runner on base and banged a two-run homer into the right centerfield bleachers—the most exciting moment of the entire 2000 season. The Yankees loaded the bases in the bottom of the ninth inning against Martinez, but he got out of the jam and the Red Sox won 2-0.

But the Red Sox did not have enough to stay with the Yankees, and they finished in second place for the third straight season, two and a half games behind the Yankees.

Carl Everett homered in his home opener for the Red Sox, after getting lost on his way to Fenway Park, and had a wonderful first half. But things went downhill in a hurry after he had a confrontation with home plate umpire Ron Kulpa, about where Everett was standing in the batter's box. Bobby Valentine, who had managed Everett with the Mets, knew how to get to Everett, and he made an issue about where he was standing—too close to the plate, and out of the batter's box, according to Valentine. Everett lost it when Kulpa made him stand in the box, and Everett bumped him. Everett was suspended and had a tough time the rest of the season.

The Sox faded down the stretch, and had a particularly tough time with two day-night doubleheaders at home against Cleveland, September 20 and 21. Everett was nursing an injury and was late getting to the park for treatment. Jimy Williams thought he was okay and wrote his name into the lineup. This all happened after Williams had a confrontation with Everett in August at Fenway, which was heard by teammates and writers in the clubhouse. Everett said he couldn't play and Darren Lewis who replaced him in centerfield confronted Everett and they had a major argument. Things pretty much fell apart after that. Even though the Sox finished second in the American League East for the third year in a row, they were not the American League wild card in 2000.

During Spring Training of 2001, the Red Sox played a game against the Boston College team. They told me that Carl Everett had been very helpful to their team. He had a great first half of the season. I got along fine with him. When he was going great, we did many postgame interviews, and he always gave me what I needed. I didn't really have occasion to do any postgame interviews with him in the second half of the season because he had such a bad second half. His confrontations with

Kulpa, with Jimy Williams, and with his teammates made many feel that he had let the team down.

◆ ● ◆

The 2001 season was similar to the 2000 season—the Sox did not get to the postseason. Jimy—he spells his name that way just to be different—Williams started the season on the hot seat. Management had backed Everett the past September at Jimy's expense. Jimy didn't get a whole lot of backing from the front office.

The Sox got off to a decent start. There was a stormy clubhouse meeting in Oakland in early May after Tomo Ohka kicked a water cooler after being removed from a game. Everett spoke out during the meeting.

The Sox lost a few close games to the Yankees in late May and early June, but were in first place for some time, and even when out of first, they were well within striking distance. But Everett had a tough time. The second day of Spring Training was the toughest day of the season for the Sox. Nomar Garciaparra injured his wrist. He had surgery on Opening Day when the Sox lost to the Orioles in ten innings. Nomar didn't return to the lineup until late July. He homered in a game against the White Sox and looked like he was back to stay, but the tendonitis in his wrist came back in August, and he played only 21 or so games before being shut down the rest of the season.

Pedro Martinez got off to another very good start. In a makeup game in New York on June 4, Pedro had a four-run lead. He gave up two runs in the sixth and left the game with a 4-3 lead. The bullpen blew the lead, but Manny Ramirez tied the game with a dramatic home run in the top of the ninth inning off Mariano Rivera. The Sox lost the game in the last of the ninth. There was some second-guessing of Jimy Williams by the front office on the question of whether Pedro should have been taken out of the game. You could tell something was wrong with Pedro in his next start against the Phillies on June 9 when he gave up a lot of hits and took the loss. He tried to come back a few times, but Williams was proven right when Pedro went on the disabled list shortly thereafter.

Manny Ramirez had a great first half in 2001, hitting a home run in his first Fenway Park at bat as a member of the Red Sox. Williams kept the team in contention with smoke and mirrors. Mike Lansing filled in OK at shortstop while Nomar was still recovering from wrist surgery and the club stayed competitive and overachieved for most of the season. There was some more controversy on the team about who was getting enough playing time, a controversy that included Lansing and veteran Dante Bichette. They wanted to get their numbers up because they were in the final years of their contracts, and they needed big numbers to demand more money. I could see things slipping for the team even as they remained within three games of the wild card on August 16, when Jimy Williams was fired. General manager Dan Duquette said that he was hoping for some "Morgan Magic," and pitching coach Joe Kerrigan became the manager.

Kerrigan had been the pitching coach since 1997. One of the first things Kerrigan said after being named manager was that under his leadership, the team would have a set lineup, so day after day, the players would know where they were playing, and when they would be batting. Williams had been criticized for using a new batting order virtually every day, and Kerrigan apparently thought that this had deprived the team of a consistent attack. But in Kerrigan's first 24 games as manager, he used 24 different batting orders himself.

Unfortunately for the team, there was no "Morgan Magic," and no Kerrigan Magic, either. The team was 17-26 under Kerrigan, and the team fell apart at the end of the season. Manny Ramirez had been hit in the hand by a pitch in Detroit and he didn't play the last week. He said he couldn't swing a bat. Dante Bichette said he had a sore elbow and played very sparingly. Carl Everett, who had hurt his knee in June in Tampa didn't play regularly and was sent home early. Pedro Martinez tried to come back a few times but had to shut it down and he went home.

◆ ● ◆

We had a Blo Hards [die-hard Red Sox fans] meeting on September 10, 2001, in New York. I was the emcee. Our guest was Allen McDill, a lefthanded pitcher who had a brief stint with the Red Sox. After that, I took the subway to Yankee Stadium, but the game was rained out. We left LaGuardia Airport for Tampa Bay. We didn't get to bed until about 4:30 AM. The next morning, Jerry Trupiano called early and woke me up to tell me that he had spoken with his wife Donna. The Twin Towers of the World Trade Center had been hit and we were under attack. I turned on the TV in the hotel room and saw the second plane hit.

The toughest thing, at a time of crisis like September 11, is being away from home. Also, I had a son and daughter-in-law who lived in midtown Manhattan. I called Duke and Kiki immediately and was able to get through, although phone lines were very busy especially into and out of New York. They were both fine. Jan was in school with her second grade class. Tommy was at medical school and Kate had just started a new job with a Boston advertising firm.

Ballgames, which suddenly seemed a little less important, were postponed for a week. All commercial flights were grounded. We were at the Renaissance Vinoy in St. Petersburg and stayed there for three days.

On Thursday, September 13, the team chartered a bus from St. Petersburg to Sanford, Florida, where the team and all of its equipment boarded the Auto Train at about 3 PM. At 10 the next morning, we arrived in Lorton, Virginia, where we boarded a bus to Baltimore-Washington International Airport, and boarded a charter flight to Providence, Rhode Island. Our plane was the first to leave Baltimore after the 11th, and the first to land in Providence. We then had a surreal two-hour bus ride through Boston traffic before arriving at Fenway about 4 pm.

While the Red Sox worked out that weekend, Pedro Martinez and Carl Everett separately reportedly got into shouting matches with manager Joe Kerrigan.

The rest of the 2001 season was all downhill for the Red Sox. The only highlight was the Red Sox beating the Baltimore Orioles in what turned out to be the final game of Cal Ripken Jr.'s career. The season ended with Ripken waiting in the on-deck circle as Brady Anderson (in his last game for the Orioles, too) swung at a 3-2 pitch that should have been ball four. Anderson struck out on a high pitch by Ugueth Urbina.

I'm always sad to see the baseball season end, but 2001 was one of the only seasons I can recall when I was glad to see the season end. During the offseason, the Boston papers were full of stories about the sale of the Red Sox. The sale by the Yawkey Trust was not complete until December 20 when it was announced that the John Henry/Tom Werner group had purchased the club for $660 million, a record price for a baseball team, doubling the previous record.

The 2002 team would have done well, I think, in either a five- or a seven-game series. But there was very little depth, especially among middle relievers. Rich Garces, for example, who had done such a good job for years, just lost it and when he refused a minor league assignment, he was released. There was nobody left to fill that spot in the bullpen.

Derek Lowe pitched a no-hitter on April 27, 2002—one of the team's high points. On May 11, in a Saturday night game in Seattle, Manny Ramirez went down with a broken finger—surely one of the low points. But just before the All-Star break, the Sox lost two out of three games at home to a bad Detroit team and I thought that was a bad omen for the remainder of the season. Then they lost three out of four games to the Blue Jays and two very tough games in New York. On Friday night, Martinez beat the Yankees 4-2. Then on Saturday, they came from behind to take the lead then lost it 9-8 in the 11th inning when Wayne Gomes fell apart. On Sunday, the Sox had an 8-7 lead going into the ninth inning. Ugueth Urbina couldn't hold it as Jason Giambi's soft hit sparked a rally, and the Yankees won by the same 9-8 score when Urbina walked Jorge Posada with the bases loaded.

Things did not go well the rest of the season, despite Manny Ramirez winning the batting championship with a .349 average. Nomar Garciaparra came back somewhat frustrated. He told me that he never felt comfortable, though he played the entire season. Nevertheless, he drove in 120 runs, scored 101, and hit 24 homers—not bad for a guy who had missed virtually all of the previous season with a career-threatening wrist injury and subsequent surgery.

The Red Sox finished the 2002 season 93-69, second in the American League East, 10½ games behind the Yankees.

◆ ● ◆

I do not believe in the "curse of the Bambino," but being a broadcaster for the Boston Red Sox has been something of a 20-year rollercoaster ride, full of ups and downs.

The Red Sox have come close but have not won the World Championship since 1918 because each year they are just a little short in some areas—usually pitching or defense. In most of my years in Boston, they did not really have a strong defensive club. Great individual defensive players like Dwight Evans, Tony Peña, Nomar Garciaparra, sure, but there were times when the defense gave the opposition extra outs, putting more pressure on the pitchers. Catching the ball, turning double plays, and not giving the opposing team extra outs are essential.

The other factor that was always lacking for the Sox was speed. As Trup said, "Those Red Sox uniforms were heavy." We are not talking about stolen bases—they are overrated—but speed on defense and running the bases, going from first to third base, and scoring from second.

The team never had quite enough pitching even in the very good years. Yes, they had fine individual pitchers, like Roger Clemens, Oil Can Boyd, Pedro Martinez, Bruce Hurst, Mike Boddicker, Derek Lowe, and Bob Stanley, but the pitching rotation was always in need of one or two more solid starters. Also, the Yankees always had more bench strength.

I believe that the Red Sox had the better team in 1986, and should have won the World Series, especially after the way the Sox persevered in the American League Championship Series. That was unreal.

So I take a wait and see attitude each Spring Training, and I try never to get down.

Spring Training is a great mirage. The season, 162 games from April (or, more recently, March) through October is a marathon. Injuries, depth, additions, late-season callups, cohesiveness as a team, all are critical.

Red Sox fans should realize, though, that since 1967, with the exception of the 1992 through 1994 seasons, the Red Sox have had a legitimate chance to win every year and they have been competitive year after year. After that, you need depth, breaks, and timing.

A Fight to the Finish

It breaks your heart. It is designed to break your heart. The game begins in the spring, when everything else begins again, and it blossoms in the summer, filling the afternoons and evenings, and then as soon as the chill rains come, it stops and leaves you to face the fall alone. You count on it, rely on it to buffer the passage of time, to keep the memory of sunshine and high skies alive, and then just when the days are all twilight, when you need it most, it stops . . . and summer is gone.

　　　　　—A. Bartlett Giamatti, *The Green Fields of the Mind*

In a tradition started by my mentor and former partner, the late Ken Coleman, I close the final broadcast on the last day of every season with this passage, written by Bart Giamatti, the late commissioner of baseball. Bart had been a Red Sox fan, and never were his words more appropriate than in the early morning hours of October 17, 2003, following Game Seven of the American League Championship Series.

The Red Sox, who had a three-run lead with five outs to go to get to the World Series, suffered one of the most crushing losses in their history to the hated New York Yankees. The loss ended what had seemed like a magical season.

Despite the bitter loss, the 2003 Red Sox were the most entertaining team I have seen in my 21 years of play-by-play broadcasting for the club. With their powerful attack, the best in baseball, the Red Sox were never out of any game. Nearly one-quarter of their wins came in their last at bat. By the same token, few Red Sox leads ever seemed totally secure, primarily because of a bullpen that was shaky at least until the postseason. The first two games set the tone for the entire season. Opening Night, March 31, Pedro Martinez left after seven innings with a 4-1 lead over the lowly Tampa Bay Devil Rays. However, in the bottom of the ninth, the D-Rays scored five times with Carl Crawford hitting a walk-off three-run home run off Chad Fox for a 6-4 Tampa Bay win that stunned the Red Sox.

The very next night, though, the Red Sox showed the resiliency that would be their trademark as they put the bitter loss behind them and beat the Devil Rays 9-8 on a 16th-inning home run by Kevin Millar. That trend continued throughout the season. With new and refreshing personalities like Millar, David Ortiz, and Bill Mueller added to the clubhouse mix, not to mention their big bats, the Red Sox refused to brood over heartbreaking losses and when they happened, they were shaken off quickly, at least until mid-October. "Cowboy Up," an expression popularized by Millar and reliever Mike Timlin in particular, became the slogan . . . the theme being if you are thrown down or off the horse, get right back up and ride again. And what a ride it was.

The Red Sox had an excellent opening month going 18-9 in April while averaging nearly six runs a game. They staged one of their great comebacks on April 20, Easter Sunday. Down 5-0 in the sixth to Toronto, the Red Sox rallied to beat the Blue Jays on Nomar Garciaparra's ninth inning walk-off home run into the Monster seats. On April 27 at Anaheim, the bullpen blew a win for Pedro but Ortiz, pinch-hitting in the 14th inning, smacked his first Red Sox home run for the win.

May would be the only losing month as the Red Sox went 13-14 but continued to mash the ball. Bill Mueller, who would go on to win the American League batting championship, hit .418 and his emergence made it possible for Theo Epstein to trade Shea Hillenbrand to Arizona on May 29 for Byung-Hyun Kim. Though he began in the rotation, Kim was moved to the closer's role, which helped the bullpen take shape with the relievers moving into more defined roles.

The Red Sox and the Yankees, who would face each other a record 26 times during the season, hooked up for the first time in late May, splitting six games with the Red Sox beating Roger Clemens on Memorial Day in his first attempt at his 300th win. However, two nights later, Jorge Posada, who would be in the spotlight in October, took a borderline pitch from Brandon Lyon with the bases loaded and two out in the ninth inning to force home the deciding run. The Red Sox howled to umpire Joe West who made the call on the walk-off walk.

Then after a terrible series in Toronto where the Red Sox lost three of four, they got rolling again as interleague play began. Trailing at Milwaukee 10-4 on June 7, Kevin Millar sparked a huge comeback with a pinch-hit grand slam. Ninth-inning homers by Trot Nixon and Jason Varitek gave the Red Sox a 10-9 win.

There were more crushing losses, though, including one to St. Louis on June 12 on a 13th inning home run by the Cardinals' Jim Edmonds off the disappointing Ramiro Mendoza. The Red Sox bounced back to sweep Jimy Williams's Houston Astros, taking the series finale in 14 innings.

But then came one of the worst losses at Philadelphia on June 21 as the bullpen blew another would-be Pedro win. Twice Jim Thome homered to tie the score and then in the 13th, after the Red Sox had taken a two-run lead, reserve catcher Todd Pratt hit a three-run game-ending home run off the soon to be departing Rudy Seanez.

The Sox hit .315 as a team in June and led the majors in runs, home runs, and just about every other power stat. They made history on June 27 at Fenway by scoring 10 runs before making an out and 14 runs in the first inning. Johnny Damon had three hits in the inning to tie the record set by Boston outfielder Gene Stephens 50 years before. The game ended with a 25-8 drubbing of the Florida Marlins.

However, the next night they blew a 9-2 lead to the Marlins in the last two innings and lost on Mike Lowell's two-out, three-run, ninth-inning home run off Lyon. Still who would have thought they were playing the eventual 2003 World Champs?

The Red Sox would set a club record with 238 home runs and what a power display they put on at Yankee Stadium July 4 and 5—seven home runs, the most ever against the Yankees, on July 4, and three more the next day. Ortiz had two in each game (becoming the first visiting player ever to hit two home runs in consecutive games at Yankee Stadium) but the Yanks split the four-game series, winning the finale on Todd Walker's error in the ninth. At the All-Star break, the Red Sox trailed the Bronx Bombers by two games.

Later in the month, the Yanks came to Fenway and won the opener of the three-game series but Ortiz beat them the next afternoon with a two-out pinch double off the wall.

The following night, Sunday, July 27, the Red Sox, down 3-0 in the seventh, got a dramatic three-run homer from Jason Varitek to tie it and went on to score six in the seventh to win, moving within a game and a half of the Yanks.

Varitek was such a force during the season, not only with his outstanding defense and key hits but also with his presence. A tower of strength, Jason was, to my way of thinking, the Red Sox's most indispensable player.

That night was especially memorable because I brought Ken Coleman to Fenway for what proved to be his last visit. Ken had a chance to visit with a lot of old friends including Jon Miller and Joe Morgan of ESPN and to watch from our booth. He had a marvelous evening and was in great spirits but he became ill a week later and passed away on August 21. Our radio booth is now dedicated to Ken. His picture hangs by the entrance. I was honored to do a script reading at Ken's funeral.

The Red Sox went on to set a major league slugging record, breaking the old mark of the legendary 1927 Yankees—and what slugging they got from Mueller on July 29 at Texas. The switch-hitting third baseman, a very polite and truly humble and team-oriented guy, hit three home runs including grand slams in consecutive innings: one left-handed and one right-handed. He is the first major leaguer to hit grand slams from both sides of the plate in the same game. But the Rangers won the series when Alex Rodriguez hit a walk-off grand slam in the 11th off Todd Jones.

The Red Sox then lost five of seven to Baltimore in early August and two straight in Oakland but earned a split of the four-game series with the A's. Manny Ramirez capped a ten-pitch at bat with a ninth-inning, game-tying home run off Keith Foulke, the league leader in saves, in the finale. Late in the month, the Red Sox made their surge for the wildcard by sweeping a four-game series at Fenway from Seattle, their prime challenger. That may have been the most critical series of the season. The Red Sox went into September one and a half games behind the Mariners in the wildcard and five and a half games behind the Yanks in the AL East.

September began with a bang. The Red Sox went into the ninth inning of the Labor Day makeup game at Philadelphia trailing the Phillies 9-7. But Trot Nixon, who had the best year of his career, capped a six-run ninth inning with a grand slam to give the Red Sox a 10-9 win . . . one of the season's most memorable. The next night, in Chicago, they got just two hits off Bartolo Colon but beat the White Sox anyway 2-1. They soon stretched the win streak to five with two wins in New York including an 11-0 romp over Roger Clemens to get to within one and a half games of the Yanks. But David Wells spun a beauty the next day and the Red Sox had to think wildcard.

After a horrendous 13-10 loss to Baltimore in which they made four errors the following night, the Red Sox got back on track and on the evening of September 23, staged perhaps their most dramatic comeback. Down to their final strike and trailing the Orioles 5-2, Todd Walker hit a 3-2 pitch off Jorge Julio into the visitors' bullpen to tie the score. "Can you believe it?" is what I said on the air. Yes, with this team, it was true.

Then in the tenth Ortiz hit a walk-off into the monster seats and two nights later in the final regular season home game, the Red Sox clinched the wildcard. Principle owner John Henry very graciously came to our booth in the eighth inning on that clinching night and thanked us for our efforts and everyone behind the scenes as well. When the game ended, a wild celebration began.

The players went from the field to the clubhouse and back to the field as thousands of fans stayed to watch. About an hour later, a half-dozen players, still in uniform, went to the nearby Baseball Tavern to celebrate with the fans. Our flight to Tampa Bay that night was a loud one. I think the celebration was in character with this club that really enjoyed playing the game, playing with each other, and playing in Boston.

It was the most together group we have had in my 21 years in Boston. No more 25 cabs for 25 players but a group of guys who had genuine feelings for one another, a spirit that doesn't happen every year.

So the Red Sox finished the season 95-67 with all kinds of offensive records as they went west to face the Oakland A's. The day before the best-of-five series began, I went with my former student Doug Greenwald, now the voice of the Fresno Grizzles of the Pacific Coast League to beautiful Pac Bell Park for Game One of the Florida-San Francisco series. Jason Schmidt of the Giants pitched a shutout beating Josh Beckett. Who knew that Beckett would be a World Series hero three and a half weeks later?

This was the fourth time the A's and the Red Sox had met in postseason play. The Red Sox swept the A's in the 1975 American League Championship Series and the A's swept the Red Sox in the American League Championship Series in both 1988 and 1990. The A's had won the American League West with great pitching and a low payroll.

Game One pitted the two best righthanders in the American League, Pedro Martinez and Tim Hudson. Todd Walker set the tone with a first-inning home run and Walker later homered in the seventh to give the Red Sox a 4-3 lead. Walker went on to set a Red Sox record with five roundtrippers in the postseason. The Red Sox could have padded their lead but through a series of maneuvers, ended up with Adrian Brown, who had spent most of the season at Pawtucket, pinch-hitting with a runner at third and one out in the eighth. He struck out and the Red Sox would not score again. But in the ninth, Kim walked one batter and hit another and then with two out, Alan Embree gave up a game-tying hit. It remained 4-4 in the 12th when the Red Sox, as they had done so often all year, failed to turn a double play. With the bases loaded, two out, and Derek Lowe pitching, catcher Ramon Hernandez put down a beautiful bunt for a hit that won it for the A's.

Game Two was Oakland all the way. The A's got five runs in the second as Manny Ramirez got burned for playing shallow when Eric Byrnes doubled over his head and Walker made an error that allowed two runs to score, victimizing Tim Wakefield. Barry Zito pitched well in a 5-1 A's win and Oakland needed just one more victory to win the series.

The A's stumbled and bumbled their way in Game Three, a pitchers' duel between Lowe and Ted Lilly. Thanks to a great block of the plate and a heads-up reaction by Jason Varitek, Eric Byrnes failed to touch home plate trying to score from third and was tagged out back near the screen. In the same inning, Miguel Tejada stopped running between third and home after obstruction had been called at third base. Tejada, who made the mistake of playing umpire, was tagged out by the alert Jason Varitek ending a wild sixth inning. The game was still tied 1-1 in the 11th when Trot Nixon, who didn't start because a lefty had been on the mound, batted for Gabe Kapler and hit a two-run, pinch-hit, walk-off home run into the centerfield seats, giving the Red Sox a 3-1 win and new life in the series.

Game Four looked like a mismatch with Hudson against 38-year-old John Burkett. But Hudson, pitching on three days' rest, left before the second inning with an injury. The A's tied the game at 2-2 in the sixth and then Burkett, who had been hit hard, was left in the game to face Jermaine Dye who smoked a two-run homer that gave Oakland a 4-2 lead. Walker homered but it was 4-3 A's with two on and two out in the eighth inning and Keith Foulke, their closer, on the mound. Somehow, it just seemed that there had to be a little more to this magical season . . . and there was. David Ortiz lined a double against the bullpen wall in right, two runs scored, and Scott Williamson got the win for the second day in a row as the Red Sox won 5-4 to even the series at 2-2.

That meant another cross-country flight for the fifth and deciding game. Pedro, with four days' rest and Zito working on three days' rest, were the starters. Zito was breezing with a 1-0 lead in the sixth, but we noted how he tends to get hit hard after throwing 90-plus pitches.

With his pitch count mounting, that is exactly what happened. Varitek homered to tie the game and with two out and two on, Manny hit a three-run bomb and pointed to the Boston dugout as he circled the bases. The Red Sox had a 4-1 lead but it was 4-3 entering the ninth when Williamson walked the first two batters. Lowe came out of the bullpen and after a sacrifice bunt, manager Ken Macha sent Adam Melhuse, a longtime minor leaguer, to pinch-hit for Dye. Lowe struck him out with a nasty sinker as the tying run remained at third and the winning run at second. The tension mounted as Chris Singleton walked to load the bases with two out. Trup had gone down to the clubhouse for the postgame celebration if the Red Sox hung on. But Lowe still had to get pinch hitter Terrence Long.

The tension was incredible. I recall Hank Greenwald, the former Giants announcer (now with Oakland) and his son Doug being in the booth with Trup and me, but otherwise I felt as close to what athletes call "being in the zone" as I have ever been—totally concentrating, on edge, and completely wrapped up in the scene on the field. Somehow the tension seems greater when it is your team trying to protect a lead with the bases loaded than when your team is at bat with the bases load. Anyway, Lowe got ahead 1-2 and then delivered the sinker of his life for called strike three. The Red Sox had won the series. My call: "Bring on the Yankees."

◆ ● ◆

The Red Sox barely needed wings for the flight from Oakland to New York. Game One matched Tim Wakefield, the Red Sox's senior member against Mike Mussina, and again David Ortiz victimized the Yankees. David, who had no hits in previous at bats against Mussina in his career, launched a two-run upper deck bomb and the Red Sox were ahead to stay. Ortiz had become a fan favorite with his big smile, deep voice, and outgoing manner. In fact, he made himself an American League MVP candidate. Walker later homered by the foul pole in right, a ball that first was called foul by the rightfield umpire and then fair by the home plate ump. Williamson earned the save for the Red Sox, winning 5–2.

Andy Pettitte was too much in Game Two. The Red Sox could have broken it open in the first two innings but squandered two chances. They couldn't score despite three hits and a walk in the first because of a caught-stealing-strikeout double play. They saw a second-inning rally fizzle because of another double play. Nick Johnson homered off Lowe to put the Yanks ahead to stay in the second and the Yanks won 6-2 to even the series.

Game Three at Fenway—a Pedro vs. Clemens matchup. It would turn out to be Pedro vs. Zimmer, Manny vs. Clemens, and the Yankee bullpen vs. grounds crewmember Paul Williams. Clemens fell behind 2-0 in the first but Derek Jeter's home run tied it in the third, and in the fourth, Hideki Matsui doubled to put the Yanks ahead. With first base open and men on second and third, Pedro threw high and tight to Karim Garcia and hit him in the upper back. Words were exchanged but Pedro escaped the jam. Then Manny, leading off the last of the fourth, overreacted and charged the mound after a high pitch from Clemens that was almost in the strike zone. While the benches emptied, Yankee bench coach 72-year-old Don Zimmer made a beeline for Pedro Martinez near the Red Sox dugout. Pedro tried to grab and hang on to Zim but pushed him down to the ground. Pedro told me he was trying to hold on to Zim but had to push him away when he saw Zimmer's fist headed for his face. Pedro said the incident was embarrassing and regrettable. Zimmer broke down in tears in front of the media while apologizing the next day.

Mariano Rivera, the biggest difference between the Yanks and Red Sox, pitched two perfect innings to preserve a 4-3 Yankee win. There was a delay in the ninth inning when the grounds crew member assigned to the Yankee bullpen had a scuffle with reliever Jeff Nelson and right-fielder Karim Garcia, who charged across the outfield and jumped into the bullpen to join the fray.

The Red Sox got a break when Game Four was rained out Sunday night giving them the chance to pitch Wakefield against Mussina again on Monday. Walker and Nixon homered and the hustling Varitek beat out a potential inning-ending double play ball for the decisive RBI as the Red Sox won 3-2 to even the series at 2-2.

In Game Five Lowe pitched well except for the second inning when the Yanks scored three times, which proved to be enough in a 4-2 win. Again Rivera went two innings to save the win for Wells and the Yanks had a 3-2 lead in games.

It was back to New York for Game Six and what seemed like a mismatch. Burkett vs. Pettitte. Burkett was knocked out in the fourth and Pettitte struggled but left after five with the lead. In the seventh, the Red Sox got to José Contreras. The Cuban righthander was the subject of a recruiting war between the Yanks and Red Sox during the winter but the Red Sox got the last laugh by scoring three to take the lead. Trot Nixon's two-run homer in the ninth made it more comfortable as the Red Sox won 9-6, setting up a seventh-game showdown.

Game Seven was billed as the matchup of the century . . . the 21st century at least. Pedro vs. Roger for the pennant in the Bronx. It was soon evident Clemens didn't have it when his nemesis Trot Nixon homered in a three-run Red Sox second. Joe Torre removed Clemens with the Sox up 4-0 in the fourth but Mussina escaped a first and third jam that would prove critical. With two out in the seventh, Jason Giambi hit his second home run of the game off Pedro and the next two batters got hits. But with a 4-2 lead, Pedro fanned Soriano and left the mound with a 4-2 lead and pointed skyward and hugged his teammates, two signs his night was over.

Ortiz homered off Wells in the eighth to make it 5-2 Boston and, to the surprise of many, Pedro came out to start the eighth. He retired Nick Johnson on one pitch but then Jeter doubled on an 0-2 pitch and Bernie Williams singled on a 1-2 pitch to make it 5-3. At that point Grady Little jogged to the mound to talk to Pedro. Normally when Grady jogs out, his does not replace the pitcher. Alan Embree and Mike Timlin, who had allowed just one baserunner in the entire postseason were ready but Little stuck with his ace even though the batter Matsui had doubled off Pedro in both Game Three and earlier in Game Seven. Pedro got ahead 0-2 but Matsui lined a double down the rightfield line, fair by inches. The tying runs were in scoring position and up came Posada who exchanged words with Pedro in the Game Three excitement.

Again Pedro got ahead 1-2 but Posada hit a blooper over second. At first I thought it might be catchable but it carried into shallow center and fell for a two-run hit that tied the game. I called the play but was stunned. The Red Sox, so close to going to the World Series, had blown the lead. I tried not to sound like Herb Morrison, who broadcast the infamous explosion of the *Hindenburg*, but I felt awful. Could this really be happening after all the wonderful events of this season? Finally, Little removed Pedro and the game went into extra innings, but with Rivera pitching, I felt almost resigned to the fact that nothing would happen with him still in the game. Rivera went three innings and would not have pitched another but there was no need because Aaron Boone led off the 11th with a walk-off home run off Tim Wakefield on the first pitch of the inning. I knew the ball was crushed but tried to wish it foul. "Home run and the Yankees win the pennant"—the toughest words I have ever had to say on the radio.

I tried to stay professional but it was devastating. A wonderful season had ended and we were going home to stay out of instead of play in the World Series for the first time in 17 years. Pedro tried to take the blame for the loss but most of the fan anger was directed toward Grady Little. The venom was the worst I can ever remember—far worse than Bill Buckner, Calvin Schiraldi, or John McNamara got in 1986. The Red Sox decided not to pick up Grady's option to manage in 2004 though they praised his abilities to handle so many personalities and stated that Game Seven was not a factor in the decision. In my case I felt mostly great sadness—sad because this team deserved better, sad because I really felt the Red Sox were better overall than the Yankees (with the exception of Mariano Rivera), and sad because when it really matters, the Yanks have always beaten the Red Sox.

It was a very quiet, almost eerie plane trip home. It reminded me so much of a similar plane ride from La Guardia to Boston 17 years before, after Game Seven of the 1986 World Series. It's tough to say which is the greater hurt—being one strike away in 1986 or losing a game that was so winnable against the archrivals for the pennant. I don't think a curse had anything to do with either, but we will never get over either.

A few days later, I got a call from someone who could really feel our pain, my old friend Pat Hughes, the radio voice of the Chicago Cubs. Pat said, "Can you believe, we both had three-run leads in the eighth inning with one out and nobody on and both of us lost the pennant?"

Still, it was a most entertaining season and a wild ride right to the end. Much credit should go to general manger Theo Epstein who did a marvelous job of making roster adjustments during the course of the season. He rebuilt the bullpen after the initial struggles and did a great job of bringing character people into the clubhouse with the additions of people like Millar, Mueller, and Ortiz. He built one of the strongest attacks in baseball history and handled tough situations and the media with grace. It was a pleasure to do his daily pregame show, on which he is always thoughtful and insightful. The future of the Red Sox seems to be in good hands.

◆ ● ◆

During the winter of 2003, the Red Sox made big changes that eased the sting from Game Seven of the American League Championship Series—they acquired Curt Schilling from the Arizona Diamondbacks to bolster the starting rotation, signed Oakland's Keith Foulke as the closer, and Terry Francona was named to succeed Grady Little as manager for 2004. Despite the saga of Alex Rodriguez and his trade to the Yankees, I think that 2004 will be the year of the Red Sox. A-Rod can't pitch—and Theo Epstein and the rest of the Red Sox ownership did a great job of addressing the team's needs in pitching and defense. And as history has shown, pitching and defense are the most critical when it comes to crossing that final hurdle to a championship.

◆ ● ◆

My father passed away, peacefully and at home, on November 28, 2003, after a long series of illnesses. Dad had a full and meaningful life, practicing medicine until the age of 85. Mom did a wonderful job of caring for him, making it possible for Dad to spend his final days at home surrounded by his family, which included 8 children and 22 grandchildren.

On Broadcasting and the Baseball Life

I've been a baseball fan since I was a kid. Although I follow other sports such as college basketball, college and pro football, baseball has been my passion for most of my life. I read a lot about baseball, because there is so much to read. So part of my style is to drop in interesting facts during our broadcasts, usually about the players and unusual aspects of their careers. I try to personalize the players. That's part of my style, too.

I am not a "gee-whiz" type of broadcaster, speaking as though every single play on the field that I describe is the most fascinating, most unusual, most interesting event in the history of baseball. Those broadcasters don't last long, particularly at the major league level.

"Wearability" is a phrase I like to use. I don't try to make plays more exciting than they are. Occasionally, people tuning in late to a game tell me that they can tell whether the Red Sox are ahead or behind in the game by the sound of my voice. I don't openly root for the Red Sox, but I want them to win. Of course I want them to win. I'd love to do another postseason game. Wouldn't any broadcaster like to broadcast for his team in the World Series? I can only imagine what it would be like to broadcast the first World Championship in the history of the Boston Red Sox in nearly a century. (We came as close as you can in

1986.) So yes, of course I want the Red Sox to win, but I try not to slant what I say on the air the Red Sox way. That is, if an opposing fielder makes a great play, I do not simply ignore it, or describe it in as few words as possible. If he makes a diving catch, gets up, sets, and throws the runner out at third, for example, I'll say he made a great diving catch, and a very powerful throw to nip the runner. A great play is a great play, even if by an opponent.

Likewise, if a Red Sox player boots a play, I might say just that, "He booted the play. That's a routine pop-up that he should have caught," or "Poor baserunning by *so-and-so*. He should have been standing on third base now. Instead, he had to retreat to first. He knows he made a mistake."

There's a great song by Terry Cashman called "I Saw It on the Radio," and that captures what I try to do—to describe for the radio listener what I see on the field.

◆ ● ◆

Generally, baseball broadcasters are the most genuine people in broadcasting. We have our own small fraternity and many are close friends: Ernie Harwell (in Detroit), Eric Nadel (Texas), the late Mark Holtz (Texas), Herb Carneal and John Gordon of the Twins, George Grande (Reds and ESPN), Bill King of Oakland, Paul Olden at Tampa Bay, Hank Greenwald of the Giants and the Yankees and now Oakland, Jon Miller (Baltimore, now San Francisco and ESPN). We are not rivals, vying for each other's jobs, or trying to outdo each other. Rather, we are comrades who share a unique job. Closeness depends on personal feelings and on how often we see each other.

◆ ● ◆

Typically, each of the 30 major league teams carries two main TV broadcasters, two main radio broadcasters, another two for cable, and perhaps two Spanish broadcasters. That's 8 per team, times 30 teams, so somewhere between 240 and 250 full-time professional major league broadcasters. (Some share cable and over-the-air TV.) There is a special bond among the broadcasters because, regardless of which team he broadcasts for, we all share the same problems and travails. No matter how many times we've all gone on road trips, the excitement of traveling across the country does wear off, and we all miss our families. Eating in media dining rooms every night is fun but, after a while, your favorite restaurant is your home. Laundry. Missing the kids' school shows, games, birthdays, and other family occasions. I know it comes with the job, but when I see other broadcasters (and one of the few benefits of interleague play is the time I get to see colleagues like Harry Kalas of the Phillies, or Bob Murphy of the Mets who was with the Red Sox from 1954 to 1959, or Pete Van Wieren in Atlanta), we talk about our shared experiences.

I became friends with some of the National League broadcasters when we played their teams in Spring Training. For example, I became acquainted with the Dodgers' Vin Scully when we played them in Chain O'Lakes Park in Winter Haven and we had him on the air.

In Spring Training 2002, we asked John Henry, the Red Sox new owner, to appear with us, and much to our delight, he appeared.

20002 was not the first time I had been with a team whose ownership changed while I was there. When I was with Cleveland, ownership seemed to change every year when the tax laws changed, the team depreciated, and they sold the team. But 2002 was the first time I had been with a team that had a complete sale.

◆ ● ◆

Most cities are blessed with fans who love their hometown teams. New Yorkers love the Mets and the Yankees (although, with apologies to Senator Clinton, very few are fans of both). Seattle fans love their Mariners. Houston fans love the Astros. In some cities with newer franchises, the attitude of many fans is that it's nice if the team wins, and too bad if they lose. But there seems to be something different about the relationship between the Boston, Massachusetts—indeed New England fans—and the Boston Red Sox. It's a passion, a caring. Pedro strikes out ten? Front page of the sports section, and the lead sports story on every news show. The Red Sox trade for a new catcher? Again, it's on the front page of every newspaper in town, and it's what everybody in town is talking about. And all the radio talk shows, too. New Englanders wear their passion for their team on their sleeves—either the euphoria of a win or the pain of a loss.

In my experience, East Coast fans—Boston, Baltimore, New York, Philadelphia—are the most knowledgeable and passionate about the sport.

◆ ● ◆

As a broadcaster, I have the opportunity to collect all kinds of memorabilia—hats, pennants, pins (I have a few pins), bobble head dolls, bats, miniature bats, and the like. But I don't. First, I'd have to carry all of these items with me on road trips, when I try to travel light. Second, I just don't have room for all of this stuff.

But I do collect a few things. I have lots of photographs, most of which show me interviewing a ballplayer. Tim Samway, the unofficial broadcast booth photographer, has taken almost all of the photos of me since I came to the Red Sox in 1983. Tim is an entrepreneur in the paper industry and a longtime BoSox Club member.

I do not collect autographs. But each season I get one ball autographed by a player who had a special season or someone who is special to me. I might have a player sign my scorecard, like Roger Clemens after his 20 strikeout games, or Mo Vaughn in his MVP year, Roger Clemens in 1986, Wade Boggs in 1993, Jimy Williams in 1998, and Pedro Martinez in 1999.

There is one souvenir that I wear every day: an American League champion ring from 1986. The Red Sox 1967 season was called "The Impossible Dream." The 1986 season didn't have a name like that, but it sure was memorable. It was just my fourth year with the team and they won the pennant and came within one strike of winning the World Series.

◆ ● ◆

As I have mentioned, I grew up as a devoted Yankee fan (until I saw the error of my ways) and stayed one all through college. In 1964, the Yankees lost the World Series to the St. Louis Cardinals and fell into the dreadful Horace Clarke Era (1965–1974), although it could just as well have been the Jake Gibbs, or Fred Talbot, or Arturo Lopez (the bank teller) era. One of the reasons for my love of the Yankees was that the Yankees of my youth had so many Italians. Even though my grandfather Guiseppe knew nothing about baseball, he knew which team Joe DiMaggio, Tony Lazzeri, Yogi Berra, Frankie Crosetti, and Mickey Mantelli played for.

In 1967, while pursuing a summer job as a radio newsman, I did my first baseball games in Westfield, Massachusetts—the Western Massachusetts championship and the state championship. I was in New England that year, the year of the Red Sox memorable "Impossible Dream."

◆ ● ◆

I was a Pirates fan when I lived in Youngstown. When I went to Cleveland, I became an Indians fan. When I worked for Milwaukee, I was a Brewers fan. But now I have been a Red Sox fan longer than I was a Yankee fan.

Growing up in New Haven, 75 miles from New York, 150 miles from Boston, I did not get any flack about being a Yankee fan. New Haven was part of the Yankees' territory. The Red Sox of the 1950s were terrible. I didn't know any Red Sox fans. Mostly Yankees, Giants, and Dodgers fans.

Now, the imaginary dividing line between Yankee fans and Red Sox fans is somewhere near Meriden or Hartford.

◆ ● ◆

I have missed very few games over the years, and when I did, it was always for important family events such as graduations and weddings.

I had laryngitis in Minnesota one night in 1985 or 1986. I went on the air anyway and croaked the lineups. Ken Coleman laughed because I sounded so bad and I couldn't do the game but I stayed in the booth and kept the scorebook and the out of town scoreboard. I did everything but talk.

I worked with Ken Coleman for seven years in Boston. He did play-by-play for the first, second, third, fourth, eighth, and ninth innings, while I did the fifth, sixth, and seventh. When I worked with Bob Starr (1990–1992) I did the middle three innings, and Bob did the first three and the last three.

My broadcast partner Jerry Trupiano came to the Red Sox in 1993, ten years after I did, and we have used pretty much the same formula since we started together. I do play-by-play for innings one, two, five, eight, and nine. Trup does the third, fourth, sixth, and seventh innings.

Trup used a desk microphone rather than a headset for years, but he recently switched. I've been using a headset for years, and that's the way I am comfortable.

Jerry really knows the game of baseball and works very hard. He's always prepared for the games. We like to kid each other about our respective diets. I don't eat beef, and Trup hates everything green, including vegetables and fruits. Trup is a very good partner and we have a lot of fun together.

◆ ● ◆

I am probably one of the few broadcasters who went from television to radio. My first games with the Indians and the Brewers were on television. In fact, except for two games when I filled in for Herb Score in Cleveland in 1980, I didn't do radio broadcasts until I came to Boston.

There is an obvious difference between broadcasting on television and on radio. On television, usually less talk is better—the viewer can see what happened. "Ground ball to short" Or "Garciaparra . . . Millar . . . one out." On the radio, the same play is "Ground ball to the shortstop, two steps to his left. He gloves it and fires to first—got him by a step."

◆ ● ◆

Over the years, we've had some interesting people sit in the booth with us for a few innings. Bart Giamatti, when he was National League president, was visiting with us when Ken was out sick. He was due to stay for half an inning but stayed for five.

Stephen King, a devoted Red Sox fan, is a regular visitor to the broadcast booth during spring training. Vice President Dan Quayle,

Speaker of the House Tip O'Neill, Robert B. Parker, Bobby Knight, rock singer Kay Hanley, Meatloaf, comedian Steven Wright, Jerry Vale, Robert Wuhl, Sonjii (the drummer for Hootie and the Blowfish), Mia Hamm, Jeffrey Lyons, Johnny Unitas, Morton Dean of ABC News, and Matt Damon have also sat in with us. Bill Belichek, coach of the New England Patriots, was on with us in 2002 after his team won the Super Bowl and seemed thrilled. "This is the first time I've been on a major league baseball broadcast," he said. Actor/stuntman Jackie Chan sat with us for one game, and said, "You guys have it easy—all you do is talk!"

◆ ● ◆

As broadcasters, we don't usually ride the team bus from the hotel to the stadium because we have to be there earlier to do pregame interviews and pregame shows. Except in New York, Chicago, Baltimore, and Toronto in the American League, where the hotel is close to or easily accessible to the stadium, Trup and I rent a car to get to the stadium early. On the last day of our stay in a city on the road, we turn in the car, take the team bus from the stadium to the airport, and ride with the team from the airport to the next city's hotel.

After a game, we do our wrap up and can leave much earlier than the team bus, which typically departs about one hour after the last out is recorded.

We fly with the team, and stay at the team hotel on the road. (I carry frequent guest cards from all hotel chains with me.) While I don't get frequent flier miles because I fly on the team charter, I do get points at the hotels where we stay. Jerry Remy gets on me when I am in front of him at a check-in line at a hotel, fumbling through my Marriott or Hyatt Rewards cards.

◆ ● ◆

My wife Jan doesn't go to very many games now because she teaches full time. But when Joe Morgan was the Red Sox manager, Jan went quite often because she was very close with Joe's wife Dorothy (whom everyone calls Dot). Dot was great at including the wives of coaches and broadcasters. Our families are still very close, and we see each other quite often. Joe still lives in his native Walpole, Massachusetts. We also see Joe and Dot in Fort Myers during Spring Training (when Joe tells the current players "hit that first #@#!!$* fastball") and Joe and I speak on the phone a few times each week. I think Jan's favorite time during my years with the Red Sox were when Joe was managing and she went to a lot of games with Dot. Although it's been more than 11 years since Joe managed the Red Sox, he is still respected and well received at Fenway Park and at Spring Training in Fort Myers.

Before Jan went back to work full time when the kids were old enough, we had a gigantic Christmas party every year. Ken Coleman, Ned Martin, Dick Bresciani, Joe Morgan, traveling secretary Jack Rogers, and their families came.

Jan used to know many of the players on the team and their wives, like Bob and Joan Stanley. They became close when our families stayed at the same hotel, the Holiday Inn in Winter Haven during Spring Training. Jan was also close with Jack Rogers's wife Ellie, Dick Bresciani's wife Joanne, and Ken Coleman's wife Ellen. Jan was included in their group when they went to games together in the 1980s and early 1990s.

But we're more spread out in Fort Myers now. Also, because she teaches, Jan only gets about four days with me in Spring Training, so she doesn't see much of the players. In recent years, we have hosted a St. Patrick's Day party at the condo we rent in Fort Myers, complete with Italian food.

◆ ● ◆

The phrase "baseball wife" applies to the wife of a baseball broadcaster as much as to the wife of a ballplayer. Despite the financial differences, there are many similarities, particularly with regard to the responsibilities of raising young children. While I was traveling with the team, staying in first-class hotels, eating in delicious restaurants, Jan was home with our children. She was always there. She was the disciplinarian, the one who drove to every Little League game and high-school practice. She went to all the parent-teacher conferences, rehearsals, plays, concerts—everything.

And whenever there was a crisis or a leaky roof, the baseball guy was somewhere like Kansas City.

◆ ● ◆

Duke had much more playing ability than his dad. I tried to groom him to be a player, not a broadcaster, and he went much farther than I did. He had some real ability, but pro ball was not in the genes.

Duke had lots of plastic bats and balls as an infant, as well as several baseball uniforms and baseball sleepers. When he started walking, he had a ball to throw. Right from the start, he had a tremendous ability to throw and catch a baseball. He had very large hands and could catch anything. His throwing arm was very strong. In fact, he threw such a heavy ball that it hurt my hand to have a catch with him.

Duke was always a star of his Little League team. He just couldn't run. I think it was in the genes. So I made him a catcher. One night, the Red Sox were playing at Tiger Stadium in June 1985, when Jan called the booth to tell me that Duke had smoked a three-run walk-off home run in the last inning to give his Little League team a great win. That same night, Dwight Evans hit a ninth-inning home run to win the game for the Red Sox. The next night, I told the story on the air.

Duke went on to play Babe Ruth ball, travel team baseball, American Legion Baseball, and high-school and college ball. He was the starting catcher of his high-school team for three years and cocaptain in his senior year. The next year, he played third base for a league championship team at Loomis-Chaffee in Connecticut. During the winter, Duke, Tom, and I went to a hitting facility in Boston where the kids and several minor leaguers worked with minor league hitting instructors Arthur Hartung and John Doherty, Cubs scout Ed DiRamio, and scouts Lenny Merullo and Tom Borque. We were there every Saturday and Sunday morning.

Then Duke went off to Ithaca College for a semester where he made the varsity as a third baseman because of his strong throwing arm. One night, he had a dream that Red Sox executive "Uncle" Lou Gorman, a graduate and great booster of Stonehill College in Easton, Massachusetts, had told him to transfer to Stonehill. So he did. At Stonehill, Duke became a catcher. In his sophomore season, he became a pitcher, and by his junior year, he was used exclusively as a pitcher, but on the mound, he was wild and finished his college career in the bullpen.

In retrospect, he should probably have stayed a catcher.

◆ ● ◆

When Duke and Tom traveled with me, they would often work out in the major league parks during early afternoon batting practice shagging flies and taking a few swings. They were not the only kids on the field: a number of ballplayers' sons also worked out on the field during early batting practice. Duke also worked out at Fenway Park with Tony Peña, who loved his arm.

Both Duke and Tom played football in high school. Duke was an offensive lineman and Tom was a starting center. Both were big and slow—perfectly suited to be offensive linemen.

Tom was a very good hitter in Little League, travel team, and high-school teams, where his best position was designated hitter.

Duke went on to a career in broadcasting, although I never pushed him into it. He broadcast games for the New Haven Ravens, the Colorado Rockies's affiliate in the Eastern League, while he was an intern with the club. Duke's roommate was a member of the team. When the Red Sox had an off day, I did a game with him. What a thrill!

After college, Duke worked sports at Media One on Cape Cod before moving to Channel 40 in Springfield, the third largest city in Massachusetts. We did a few games together for the University of Massachusetts basketball team in 1999. I did TV play-by-play, and Duke was the sideline reporter. The 11 PM news producer at Channel 40 was Kiki Yamer. She and Duke were married in 1999 in Springfield, Massachusetts.

In 2000, Duke became the host of his own hour-long evening sports show on NY1, a cable station in Manhattan. I have been on the air with him there several times. He moved to WCBS-TV, Channel 2, in New York City in April 2003.

My children have always been influenced by the Red Sox. In addition to making road trips with me and attending games, Duke, Tom, and Kate have all worked at Fenway. Duke was a vendor and a security guard. Tom was also a vendor, then an E.M.T. Kate worked at an ice cream stand. After her graduation from college, she worked in the public relations office.

Tom went to Holy Cross. He was recommended to Holy Cross by John Donovan, who was a Holy Cross graduate. John, an attorney, started with the Red Sox as a batboy in 1946 and went on to become vice president of administration. John was dying of cancer in March 1993, when he called me in the broadcast booth in Spring Training to tell me that Tom had been accepted at Holy Cross.

Tom loved Holy Cross, in Worcester, Massachusetts, and met his wife Rachel in a freshman math class there. They were married on campus in July 2000.

While he was working as an E.M.T. at Fenway, Tom became close with Red Sox physicians Arthur Pappas and internist Mike Foley. Dr. Foley is a graduate of the University of Massachusetts, and Dr. Pappas is one of the world's most renowned orthopedic surgeons. He is the director of the orthopedics department at the University of Massachusetts Medical Center.

With their help, Tom was accepted at the University of Massachusetts Medical School, and he became a doctor in June 2003.

As a premed student, Tom had to work much harder in college than Duke or Kate. He joins my father Frank, a dermatologist who practiced until his health forced him to retire at 85 in 2000, my brother, Frank Jr.— also a dermatologist, and my younger brother Charlie, a plastic surgeon in Harford. (Charlie played quarterback at Yale in 1976 and 1977, backing up NBC's Stone Phillips.) They are thrilled about Tom joining the medical side of my family.

Kate played varsity field hockey and basketball in high school. She was a good shooter, but gave up basketball after a year. She played four years of field hockey and we traveled all around the South Shore to see her games. To this day, after all these years, we still don't understand all the rules, or why there are so many whistles.

Kate had heard about Boston College all of her life from one of our closest family friends, former Red Sox manager Joe Morgan. With the encouragement of Red Sox CEO John Harrington, Kate was accepted and was graduated on the Dean's List in 2001.

As Dan Shaughnessy of the *Boston Globe* says, "Everything comes back to the Red Sox"—even my kids' college education.

After working briefly for the Red Sox at Fenway, Kate worked for an advertising firm specializing in direct mail. She now works with graphic artists for a production company that does sports videos including Red Sox videos and multimedia advertisements for clients and trade shows.

◆ ● ◆

I made a point of taking each of my three children individually on a road trip with me each year. They got to experience the lifestyle and share the amenities. It is a great way to bond—and even as young adults, they (and now their spouses) still make baseball trips with Dad.

The fact that Duke, Tom, and Kate have turned out so well is a tribute to Jan and the work she did with them while I was traveling for six months each year.

PART II

Places I Have Seen

Anaheim

naheim is about 40 miles southeast of Los Angeles. The Angels play at Angel Stadium of Anaheim, previously known as Anaheim Stadium—"The Big A"—and Edison International Field. I first visited there in 1979 with the Cleveland Indians. The first things I noticed were the cleanliness of the stadium and the politeness of the ushers and other service people around the ballpark. The ushers apparently went to a school that taught proper usher etiquette. One of the ushers was Eddie Hoffman, father of Red Sox shortstop, Glenn Hoffman. Eddie, who used to sing with big bands and sang the national anthem many times at the stadium in Anaheim, passed away a few years ago. He was a wonderful man.

When the stadium opened and through the 1970s, it was quite beautiful. There was no outfield seating—just a wide-open area in centerfield, where you could see the giant "A" in the parking lot.

The stadium was remodeled in the late 1970s to accommodate the Los Angeles Rams of the National Football League. They added seats but detracted from the stadium's beauty. In the late 1990s, the stadium was remodeled again. Seating was reduced, and rocks were added in left centerfield. And they set off fireworks, I guess to create a 21st-century effect. But the field is safe and sweet, and everybody is very courteous.

My most memorable game there was the American League Championship Series of 1986. The Red Sox and the Angels split the first two games of the best-of-seven series in Boston. The Red Sox then lost the first two games in Anaheim. Roger Clemens had a 3-0 lead going into the ninth inning in Game Four, then left the game still ahead 3-1 and was followed by Calvin Schiraldi, who hit Brian Downing on a 1-2 pitch in the last of the ninth with two outs to force in the tying run. Bobby Grich's one-out RBI single won the game 4-3 in the 11th. That loss might have been an omen for what was to come in the World Series against the Mets. So October 12 looked like the end of the line for the Red Sox, who were down three games to one. Game Five was close. Centerfielder Tony Armas had to leave the game with a sprained ankle. He was replaced by Dave Henderson. Then, in the sixth inning, Bobby Grich hit a ball to the fence in centerfield. Henderson went back to the fence and got his glove on the ball, but the ball bounced off the glove and over the fence for a home run. The Angels went to the ninth inning with a 5-2 lead. Bill Buckner started the rally with a single to center. Jim Rice and Dwight Evans made the first and second outs of the inning, around Don Baylor's two-run homer off Mike Witt to make the score 5-4.

By that time, police, state troopers, horses, and guard dogs were all on the field, before a crowd of 64,000 people, almost all of whom were screaming for an Angels victory. It was the loudest crowd I ever heard in Anaheim. The crowd was ready for an Angels win. Their manager, Gene Mauch, whose teams had the misfortune of blowing the big lead and the big game with the 1964 Phillies and the 1982 Angels, though a very innovative and brilliant baseball man, went out to the mound and brought in Gary Lucas, a left-hander to face Rich Gedman. Lucas threw one pitch, and hit Gedman—the only batter Lucas hit all year. Gedman, the tying run, went to first base. Lucas was then replaced by Donnie Moore, who faced Dave Henderson. To that point Henderson was 0-8 in the series, and he had just turned a catch into a two-run home run. The count on Henderson went to 1-2. Henderson fouled off three or four pitches. By this time, we were just about ready to pack it in for the season, ready for the desultory flight back to Boston and the beginning of the offseason. Donnie Moore got the sign from Angels catcher Bob Boone, then threw a split fingered fastball right down the middle of the plate. Henderson connected, and parked the ball over the fence in left centerfield for a two-run homer.

My broadcaster partner Ken Coleman was doing the play-by-play. That was the only time I have ever clapped in a broadcast booth. I felt a rush of adrenaline and excitement. We had been given up for dead, we were about to lose in the playoffs, nobody would remember what the team had accomplished during the season, and all seemed lost. Then, with one swing of the bat, suddenly the Sox were ahead 6-5.

In the bottom of the inning, Bob Stanley took over on the mound, and typical Stanley's tough luck, he gave up a few cheap ground ball hits. Joe Sambito took over for Stanley, and with the bases loaded, Rob Wilfong hit a ground ball single into rightfield, tying the score at six. With Dwight Evans' powerful arm in rightfield, the Angels would not take a chance of running. The call to the bullpen went to Steve Crawford, who allowed a single by Schofield and an intentional walk to Downing. He then faced Doug DeCinces who hit a pop fly into shallow rightfield. Evans reeled it in—far too shallow for the runner to score. Two outs. Bobby Grich was next and took the count to 2-0. We were thinking, what an anticlimactic way for the game, the series, and the Red Sox season to end: on a walk. On a 2-2 pitch, Crawford jammed Grich on an inside fastball, and he hits a soft liner right back to the mound. Crawford caught it, and the Sox are out of a jam. The game went to the tenth inning 6-6. By the bottom of the tenth, I was behind the mike. The Angels had a runner on with two outs. Gary Pettis hit a ball deep to leftfield. I didn't think the ball had enough on it to carry it over the fence, but I remember thinking, uh oh, the season's over. Jim Rice, who was playing deep, went back to the fence and made the catch.

In the 11th inning, Ken Coleman was back behind the mike for the play-by-play. The Red Sox loaded the bases and won the game on a sacrifice fly by Dave Henderson as Schiraldi retired the Angels in order in the bottom of the 11th. Red Sox 7, Angels 6.

We all went back to Anaheim Marriott Hotel for one of the greatest celebrations ever. We all felt an incredible high, even though the Sox were still down in the series 3-2. We knew that the win in Game Five had brought the Red Sox back from the brink of disaster, and there was no doubt that the Sox were going to win the last two games in Boston.

And they did, by a 10-4 score in Game Six, and by a score of 8-1 in the decisive Game Seven.

The Opening Day game in 1984 in Anaheim was also memorable for me. The Sox had finished Spring Training in Winter Haven on a Saturday morning, and flew to Denver, where they played an exhibition game that afternoon against the San Diego Padres at Mile High Stadium. (The Rockies did not come into existence as a major league team until 1993.) That night, after the game, the team flew to San Diego for another game against the Padres on Sunday afternoon. Then we took a bus from San Diego to Anaheim, about a 90-minute trip. On the way, I was listening to a tape of Marvin Gaye singing "I Heard It Through the Grapevine," from *The Big Chill* soundtrack—one of my favorite songs. Ken Coleman asked me what I was listening to. I told him I was listening to Marvin Gaye. Ken's musical knowledge ended with Guy Mitchell doing "Singin' in the Rain," in 1952 or so. Ken had never heard of Marvin Gaye.

We checked into the hotel in Anaheim, and Ken and I picked a time to meet for dinner. When I met him in the lobby, he said, "You're not going to believe this, but I just had the news on in my room. Marvin Gaye was shot and killed today by his father in a domestic dispute." That was Ken's introduction to Marvin Gaye. He first heard him an hour before, then learned that he had been murdered.

The next day, we opened the regular season with a night game in Anaheim. Bruce Hurst was spinning a beauty for Boston against Ken Forsch. The Sox led 1-0 into the bottom of the ninth. The Angels loaded the bases with two out when slow-footed Bob Boone came to bat. Boone hit a grounder to shortstop. Jackie Gutierrez bounced the throw to Dave Stapleton at first base. Both the tying and the winning runs scored— a crushing 2-1 defeat.

My sons Duke and Tommy occasionally made the trip with me to Anaheim, and we had the chance to work out on the field with Johnny Pesky. He hit fungoes to the boys.

On April 25, 1993, Roger Clemens faced Scott Sanderson in a 5 PM game at Anaheim. Clemens struck out nine in eight innings, and Sanderson struck out eight in seven innings. (Joe Grahe fanned two in two innings for the Angels.) The Angels went ahead on a home run in the fifth by journeyman Torey Lovullo and won it 2-1 on a Tim Salmon home run in the seventh inning.

Lovullo was one of those guys Sparky Anderson used to build up as the second coming of Al Kaline when Lovullo was with the Tigers. Torey Lovullo was no Al Kaline.

Up until 2001, we stayed at the Anaheim Marriott—the Disneyland Marriott—very close to the ballpark. That means lots of kids, lots of cameras, and Mickey Mouse everywhere.

The Jolly Roger Hotel has a very good coffee shop right across the street. We went there for breakfast many times. They gave menu items names like "The Gene Autry," or "The George Goodall," after Autry's publicist, "The Dave Garcia," after the team's manager. Jimmy Reese, longtime Angels coach and the best fungo-hitter in history, used to have breakfast there every day.

I've been to Disneyland a few times and I've gone to Los Angeles to see the sights, including Muscle Beach, Universal Studios, and the Improv. I went there in 1982, when I was with the Indians, to see a new comedian who was trying out some new material. This comedian was also from Cleveland: Arsenio Hall.

Most of the time we're in Anaheim, we don't go to Los Angeles. Even though Los Angeles is only 40 miles away, the traffic coming back can be brutal, and we can't risk being late for a night game.

It's much easier to go south from Anaheim, and I like the beaches.

Laguna Beach was a Red Sox radio and television tradition for many years. It started in 1967, when Red Sox manager Dick Williams, who had managed there, told Ken Coleman and Ned Martin about Crescent Beach and Laguna Beach, right off the Pacific Coast Highway. The scenery—magnificent million dollar homes overlooking the cliffs and the ocean—was spectacular. The warm water, complete with seals, was outstanding. The rest of the scenery was great, too. Some in our group called it "Hardbelly Beach." We went there almost every day when we had night games in Anaheim—Ken Coleman, Ned Martin, and me. One day, the clubhouse guy for the Red Sox saw us in the lobby of the hotel as we were leaving for the beach and said, "Look at this—two 60-year old guys and one 40-year old guy all dressed up with their towels and their bathing suits going to the beach. Can you believe it?"

We'd drive for about an hour to Laguna Beach, and stay there from 10 until 2 PM. Sometimes we stopped for lunch at a delicatessen along the highway. Ken and Ned liked it because Harriet Nelson (Ozzie's wife) used to eat there.

Laguna is an art colony and has quite a few art galleries. Jan and I found a place called the Surf and Sound Hotel just south of Laguna on the Pacific Coast Highway. It has a wonderful restaurant. Half of the open-air restaurant is at beach level, and you can see and hear the surf while eating.

We especially like Newport Beach, which is a little closer to Anaheim. Actually, we go to Balboa Island, which branches off to Newport Beach. There, we rent bikes on the beach off the main street, and we ride for miles on the beach boardwalk. We see the ocean, the cottages, and the beach. What a lovely way to get the surf, the sand, and the sun.

On the way to Newport Beach, we like to stop for cheap swordfish and crab legs at the Crab Cooker. The food is served on paper plates with plastic knives and forks. The red fish chowder is served from a bread bowl. The bread is outstanding, too. While the décor is sparse, the food is excellent.

I like to visit the St. Croix shop in the Newport Beach Fashion Mall.

The beach at San Clemente is somewhat further down the highway and San Diego's Delmar beach further still. The most beautiful racetrack I've ever been to is there, built by Bing Crosby and his brother in the 1930s.

I have visited Yorba Linda and Whittier, home of the Nixon Museum. He was my least favorite president but I visited the home in which he was born as well as his grave. What impressed me, shortly after his death, was the number of Chinese people visiting his grave.

Belisle's was a fun restaurant in Anaheim. The portions were huge (as were the prices), but the players really loved it. The portions were enough to feed a family. Sad to say, it's gone now.

Larry Parrish was born and grew up in Winter Haven, Florida, where the Red Sox trained for many years. In fact, Larry and his father had helped build Chain O'Lakes Park there. He spent most of his career with Montreal and Texas, but he played 52 games for the Red Sox in 1988 at the end of his career.

In a September 1, 1988, game, Parrish hit a two-run homer in the sixth inning to help give the Sox a 4-2 victory over Anaheim, a victory that put the Sox in first place, where they finished the season. Virtually everybody who was still in the stands when the game ended was a Red Sox fan—all the Angels fans had already left.

The press/media room bar at the stadium in Anaheim, which used to stay open after the game, was a dynamic place—so many interesting people!

The bartender at the Anaheim stadium press bar was a guy named Homer. What a name! He thought his offseason job was the best ever. He was the inside-the-locker-room security guard for the Los Angeles Rams cheerleaders. Homer said it was the greatest job in sports.

The price in that bar was right. Just leave a tip.

On April 30, 1985, the Red Sox played a 15-inning game in Anaheim. The team had decided to make Bobby Ojeda a relief pitcher, though he had been a starter virtually his entire career. I don't think it was a good decision. He came out of the bullpen in the 13th inning. In the 15th, with two outs, he proceeded to walk home the winning run on four pitches to give the Angels a 3-2 win.

By the end of the game, at about 3:20 AM Eastern time, Ken Coleman and I asked our listeners to send us mail—a letter or a postcard, as this was years before e-mail—to tell us where the listeners were, and what they were doing.

We got a letter (it was actually addressed to Ken Coleman) from a man in western Massachusetts. The letter was typed and seemed to be by a professional. The writer told us that he and his wife were loyal listeners, and had heard the entire game. But he was so depressed when Ojeda walked in the winning run that he rolled over and proceeded to take out his depression by making his wife and himself feel better by making love. One the best fan letters that any broadcaster has ever received.

Baltimore

Baltimore is one of the best baseball cities in the United States. The fans are very knowledgeable, and Camden Yards, which opened in 1992, is the best of the ballparks that has been built in recent years.

I remember the first time I went to Baltimore's old park, Memorial Stadium. It was for Game One of the 1971 World Series between the Orioles and the Pittsburgh Pirates. I was working in Youngstown and we covered the Pirates. Pittsburgh is only about 70 miles from Youngstown. That was the series in which Roberto Clemente's great talents were showcased, as the Pirates beat the Orioles in seven games.

I'll never forget coming up 33rd Street, a residential neighborhood in Baltimore filled with row houses and Eastern High School right across the street, and all of a sudden, here's the ballpark in the middle of the neighborhood. Memorial Stadium was completed in 1950 for the Orioles, who were then in the International League. When the St. Louis Browns moved to Baltimore in 1954 to become the American League's Baltimore Orioles, the stadium was expanded. It was very deep in centerfield—about 450 feet—and was a real pitcher's park. The fences were later moved in to 405 feet in centerfield. There was a lot of foul territory. It was always a good place to hit the ball down the line, because it was only 309 feet. Even though the seats were cramped and the ballpark lacked modern amenities, it was a good place to watch a game because of the franchise tradition established in Baltimore. At least up until 1984 or so, the Orioles always seemed to have a core of good pitchers and excellent defense. After that, they seemed to slip badly.

The broadcast booth at Memorial Stadium was the hottest in the league. A hot, humid day in Baltimore seems hotter and more humid than a 100 degree day in Texas or even in Kansas City, where the broadcast booth is air-conditioned. I had to duck to avoid hitting my head on steel beams as I entered the broadcast booth at Memorial Stadium. The booth was a little up the first base line, but was pretty good and had a homey, old stadium feel.

The broadcast booth at Camden Yards is small from side to side, but it's pretty good. The location of the booth is fine. Part of the rightfield corner is out of our line of sight, but I find that if I watch the fielder, I have a pretty good idea of where the ball is going. We have a TV monitor in the booth, so we can follow the play on video.

The pressroom at Memorial Stadium, while stark and barren, was well maintained and staffed by some sweet ladies who also worked at Camden Yards. The featured food, Maryland crab cakes, were available whenever we wanted them, whether before or during the game. Since the Orioles moved to Camden Yards, they decided to serve them only once a week. Either way, they are outstanding.

I remember watching Jim Palmer pitching to Carl Yastrzemski and Jim Rice in the old park. Each hit some home runs off him, but over the years, Palmer had a very good success rate against them.

The 1989 season opened on April 3 with Roger Clemens pitching for the Red Sox in Baltimore. President George Bush threw out the first pitch. Clemens gave up a three-run homer to Cal Ripken Jr., while Craig Worthington, a career minor leaguer, drove in the winning run for Baltimore with a soft bloop hit in the 11th inning. Orioles win, 5-4.

Memorial Stadium was the site of many spring and summer rain delays. One game was called at 6 o'clock. Lou Gorman, our general manager, and former farm director for the Orioles, came running into the booth, and said, "The game is off. Let's go!" And off we went to Vellegia's in Little Italy.

I remember Mo Vaughn's first major league home run, on June 30, 1991, in Baltimore, a tremendous shot down the rightfield line, which landed three rows from going out of the park. Frank Robinson was the only man to hit a ball out of Memorial Stadium (off Luis Tiant of the Indians), but Vaughn's ball came very close.

I remember a game the Red Sox played in Camden Yards. The Sox were down to their final out, and Mo Vaughn came to bat with two on and two out. He hit a tremendous blast off the back wall behind the centerfield fence, before ivy grew there—one of the longest home runs I've ever seen.

The outfield has plenty of nooks and crannies, as does Fenway Park. Outfielders can leap over the wall, which is only about five feet high to try to rob the batter of a home run. I've never seen it, but occasionally a home run hits the warehouse in rightfield and right center on the bounce.

The Red Sox have played well at Camden Yards and have hit quite a few homers there. Of course, the Oriole clubs they played were not very good over the last several years. The Orioles have not had a good club since 1997, when they were in the American League Championship Series, losing to the Cleveland Indians.

The area behind the rightfield fence is great because there are a lot of food stands there, including Boog Powell's Barbecued Ribs. Powell was the Orioles first baseman from 1961 to 1974, and was a real fan favorite. I've bought Powell's ribs a few times to surprise Trup. I love to see his hands and face after he's eaten the ribs. They are quite messy.

On April 2, 2001, Opening Day, Pedro Martinez was pitching for Boston at Camden Yards. He left the game in the seventh inning, with the score tied at one. Derek Lowe gave up the winning run in the ninth, setting the tone for a tough year for Lowe. He went 5-10.

I always felt that the real fans come out for the second game of the year because they just can't get tickets for the home opener.

April 3 was an off day. The day after Opening Day is almost always an off day so if it rains, the home opener can be played without ticket exchanges.

On April 4, the second game of the season, we saw Red Sox history. There were 35,602 fans at the park in Baltimore as Hideo Nomo made his Red Sox debut. Nomo struck out 11, walked only 3, and pitched a no-hitter, the first for the Sox since September 16, 1965, by Dave Morehead. But the clubhouse exuberance and media attention for Morehead was overshadowed by the news, released minutes after the game, that the Sox had fired general manager Mike "Pinky" Higgins.

When the excavation for what would become Camden Yards was being done, construction workers found dishes and some bottles from the saloon that Babe Ruth's father ran. Babe's father was killed in a brawl right outside the bar. There's a statue of Babe Ruth outside the park, and Ruth's birthplace, now a museum, is just a block or two away at 216 Emory Street off Pratt Street. Mike Gibbons, the curator, has done a wonderful job. The building is both a Ruth museum, restored to the way it looked in 1895, the year of Ruth's birth, and the Orioles Hall of Fame. I visit the museum every time I'm in Baltimore to see the new exhibits. The building was owned by the Schamburgs, Ruth's maternal grandparents. The bedroom where Ruth is said to have been born is upstairs and there's a theater downstairs, which shows a 1950s Mike Wallace feature on Ruth. There is also a wall of plaques for each of his 714 home runs. Each plaque notes the park where it was hit, and the pitcher who gave it up.

The museum also has photos of Ruth's grave, at Gate of Heaven cemetery in Hawthorne, New York, which I have visited. There's a large statue of Jesus with his hand on the head of a little baseball player. Fans have decorated the grave with hats, balls, gloves, even an occasional bottle of beer. By contrast, Lou Gehrig's grave in the Kensico Cemetery in Valhalla, New York, about a half a mile away, barely has a visible headstone. Ruth overshadowed Gehrig in death as in life.

Other exhibits at the Ruth birthplace include photos of Ruth at St. Mary's Industrial School, a letter from little Johnny Sylvester, the sick boy for whom the Babe promised to hit a home run. He later became a corporate president.

Rotating exhibits at the museum usually have an Orioles theme. One year, it was a salute to Cal Ripken Jr. Another exhibit included World Series highlights. The museum also honors the Baltimore Colts of the National Football League.

I wanted to see St. Mary's, the industrial school where the young Ruth was sent as an "incorrigible." The school, at Caton and Wilkins Avenues, no longer exists, (partially the result of a devastating 1919 fire) but on its site is Cardinal Gibbons High School, a real basketball power. Some of the old St. Mary's buildings are still standing, including the school's tower, and the building where Ruth learned the art of being a tailor. The ballfield where he learned to play baseball is also still there, but it has been turned around and home plate is now where centerfield used to be. Mike Gibbons took me there and introduced me to the current principal. Ruth's photo is on the wall, and his presence can be felt throughout the school.

Many Orioles who lived in Baltimore during their playing days stayed there when their playing careers ended. That tells you something about the quality of life in Baltimore.

During one of our visits to Baltimore, I went to Fort McHenry, where the "Star Spangled Banner" was written during the War of 1812. The fort is a wonderful place to walk by the outer harbor of the Chesapeake Bay. I got a real feel for the way the fort was dug into the ground. They've done an excellent job of preserving the fort, and it doesn't take much imagination to think what it must have been like with British warships firing on the fort and on American frigates, and how they withstood the rockets' red glare.

You can get from the Inner Harbor to Fort McHenry by taking a water taxi and then a bus. The water taxi is really a great way to get around parts of Baltimore. In addition to Fort McHenry, it can take you to Little Italy and Fells Point, an interesting area full of antique shops, fish markets, bars, and restaurants. There's a Charleston restaurant that I have enjoyed. The food court at the Inner Harbor is excellent.

An old factory near the Inner Harbor has been converted to an ESPN Zone sports restaurant. I've been there a few times to shoot baskets and to have a beer. The Barnes and Noble bookstore nearby is excellent.

The National Aquarium is at the Inner Harbor, not far away. It's one of the best I have ever visited.

Nightlife in Baltimore, once nothing to speak of, has grown to be very popular, particularly since the revival of downtown with the birth of the ballpark and the Inner Harbor.

But for me, the highlight of any trip to Baltimore is visiting Little Italy. Of all the Little Italys around the American League, Baltimore's is the most fun to visit.

First, and perhaps most important, you can walk there from our downtown hotel. There are about 20 Italian restaurants within walking distance. My favorite is Chipparelli's, which has a great chicken Sorrento—cooked in a white wine sauce covered with proscuitto, and a terrific salad. The Parmesan-based dressing makes the salad. There was a waitress named Rose, a 70-year-old Italian lady from the neighborhood who worked there. She was a big baseball fan, and loved to talk baseball with me. (She has since retired.) She knew all the Orioles who used to come in to her restaurant. Jim Palmer: "Oh, Jim Palmer, what a sweetheart. Love him in the underwear commercials. Brooks Robinson? What a sweet guy." But when Jim Gentile was mentioned, this little old Italian lady suddenly changed. I thought she was going to say, "Oh, Jim Gentile, what a great guy!" But instead she said, "Jim Gentile—he was a real $#@+@!#!!!" Not what you'd expect to hear from a 70-year-old lady.

Other good restaurants in Baltimore's Little Italy include Damimmo's, Vellegia's, and Sabatino's (which I like, despite the occasional slow service), because they serve food until about one in the morning. Vaccaro's is my favorite bakery in the entire American League. It serves the best lemon ices I have ever had. Lemon ice was a staple at my grandmother's house, my *nonna* in New Haven. Nothing better on a hot day.

Apicella's Osteria is a wonderful deli in Baltimore, where I get a grilled eggplant sandwich to take to the hotel, along with a Vacarro's lemon ice.

The Red Sox used to stay at the Cross Keys Hotel in Baltimore County, which had a lovely pool. That's where Billy Martin and Ed Whitson came to blows in the lobby. Martin got decked. Whitson got traded.

Recently, the Red Sox have stayed at the new Marriott in downtown Baltimore and now at the Renaissance Inner Harbor Hotel.

St. Leo's church in Little Italy in Baltimore is my favorite place to go to mass on the road. There is an Italian mass there, but it's usually too late for me. Father Mike Salerno, a Brooklyn native with 1968 side-burns, gives inspiring, often-humorous homilies. St. Leo's reminds me of St. Donato's in New Haven, where I was baptized.

Geppi's is a good place to get your hair cut in Baltimore. I go there occasionally, as does Orioles owner Peter Angelos. Geppi's, which was sold to new owners in 2003, is a very popular place with the players because of the attractive women who work there.

Hausner's was a terrific German restaurant on the east side of Baltimore. Unfortunately, it closed in 2000. Ernie Harwell took me to Hausner's. The desserts were big and wonderful. The highlight of Hausner's was the artwork. They had a huge display upstairs of paintings and sculpture, which was really museum quality.

Because of Baltimore's proximity to Washington, D.C., we have become friends with a number of people in the Secret Service. Tim Samway, an officer of the BoSox Club (the Red Sox fan club) is the brother of Terry Samway, the assistant deputy director of the Secret Service. Through Terry, we've had some special treats. On September 10, 1986, we were invited to visit the White House. Our group included Red Sox traveling secretary Jack Rogers and his wife Ellie, Ken and Ellen Coleman and their daughter Susan, plus a number of players including Don Baylor, Joe Sambito, Al Nipper, Mike Greenwell, and Roger Clemens. Clemens was pitching that night, but he likes to go out and do things during the day before he pitches in a night game. He says it helps him get his mind off pitching.

John Simpson, a native of Dorchester, Massachusetts, and a great Red Sox fan was the director of the Secret Service at the time. He brought us into the Roosevelt Room for a magnificent lunch. Vice President Bush came in to greet us and stayed for a brief visit. We thought, well, there's the highlight of the visit. A few minutes later, President Reagan walked in. We had been told not to bring our tape recorders, but Ken Coleman had his. Ken asked, "Mr. President, what was it like playing opposite Doris Day?" [in *The Winning Team*, in which Reagan portrayed Grover Cleveland Alexander.] "How did Doris Day get from the Astor hotel in Manhattan to Yankee Stadium with

Nate Pendleton driving the cab while you were walking in from the bullpen to the mound?" It was a fun interview.

Mr. Reagan told baseball stories and movie stories. He also recounted his days recreating Cubs games as a broadcaster for WHO in Des Moines. Reagan, known then as "Dutch," read the pitch-by-pitch account of the game off a wire ticker, and recreated the game for the Des Moines audience with a few sound effects like the crack of the bat and some crowd noises. He told of the game in which Billy Jurges was batting, when Curley, the man working the ticker tape machine, signaled frantically that the machine had stopped working. Reagan was still on the air, so he simply had Jurges hit foul ball after foul ball until the machine was fixed. Curley slipped him a note right off the wire: "Jurges popped up on the first pitch!"

Mr. Reagan seemed to be enjoying himself, but Simpson, and others, kept interrupting him to say, "Mr. President, you're due at a meeting— the national security advisor is waiting for you!" But President Reagan kept saying, "One more story! One more story!" Looking back now, I believe that the meeting we made him late for was about the Contras.

In addition to our private tour of the White House that day, we all got individual photos with the president and videotapes of our visit. I'll never forget it.

Our friends in the Secret Service have also taken us to Arlington National Cemetery, where we met the caretaker and saw the burial places of John and Jacqueline Kennedy. They've also given us private tours of the Capitol, including the House and the Senate.

Another highlight of our tours was in Beltsville, Maryland, to see the Secret Service training center. Like our day at the White House, this was a day that could not have been scripted. We went with my wife Jan, our daughter Kate, my partner Jerry Trupiano, and traveling secretary Steve August.

First, we got into the back seats of Mustangs driven at about 80 miles per hour in simulated chases in escape routes. Then we went to the firing range, where we fired Uzi submachine guns. The guns are very heavy, and my aim was not very good.

Next, they took us to the pool, where we watched agents practice water rescues.

Many Secret Service agents visit us at Camden Yards when the Red Sox visit Baltimore.

◆ ● ◆

I've been to the Vietnam Veterans Memorial in Washington, D.C., many times—always a sobering experience. Most of the 57,000 American war dead whose names are on the wall were about my age.

One of the newer sights to see in Washington is the Holocaust Museum. Usually there are very long lines, but our friends at the Secret Service knew we had only a limited time to see the museum before we had to get back to Baltimore for the game, so they walked us through the line. Terry Samway's beautiful daughter Lee gave us a private tour. It's very quiet inside with very little conversation. The experience is so powerful, so moving, most people are at a loss for words, especially when they see the bin full of children's shoes. The pictures and words in the exhibits lend the museum a prayerlike atmosphere.

The Red Sox played a few exhibition games in Washington at RFK Stadium—one against the Orioles and one against the Phillies. Two years in a row, the Sox wound up Spring Training in Washington, D.C.

The exhibition games were played at RFK in the hopes that this would help lure a major league team back to the capital, something that has not yet happened. Two different franchises have failed in Washington, and the prospects of a third seem slim. RFK is a terrible facility for baseball. It's hard to believe that it was built in 1962 for the Senators.

We had to share a broadcast booth with the Orioles crew, and our broadcasts bled into each other. We were separated by a wooden partition.

Being a JFK assassination buff, I have been fascinated on my visits to Ford's Theater in Washington, where Lincoln was shot. Across the street is Peterson House, where Lincoln was brought from the theater, and where he died.

◆ ● ◆

One time, Joe Morgan, John McNamara, and I took the hotel van to the big, beautiful cathedral outside of Baltimore. But the van driver forgot to pick us up. As we're standing outside the cathedral, Baltimore manager Joe Altobelli and his pitching coach Ray Miller drove by. Joe was nice enough to give us all a lift back to the hotel in time for the game.

Two weeks later, Altobelli was fired as the manager of the Orioles, to be succeeded by Earl Weaver.

Special Note: I am responsible for Brian Daubach meeting the love of his life in 2001. After having my haircut at Geppi's by a beautiful young woman named Chrissie Geppi, I told Brian that he should go there for a haircut. After having my haircut at Geppi's by a beautiful young woman named Chrissie Geppi, I told Brian he should go there for a haircut. I also told Chrissie about Brian and what a good guy he is and how he is Jan's favorite player. Brian did go for his haircut in April 2001, and hit two home runs that night, the same game in which Hideo Nomo pitched a no-hitter. However, Brian had no furthur contact with Chrissie until she cut his hair again on our last trip to Baltimore in early October. They talked on the phone during the winter and then began to date in Spring Training. They are very much in love and became engaged in late 2002. They were married in December 2003, and asked me to do a reading at the mass. They gave me the credit for bringing them together, even though I did not introduce them. I think it is my best scouting job. Chrissie is a wonderful young lady who resembles a young Sophia Loren, and she is very nice. On her first trip to Boston, Jan went to dinner with her and sat with her during a game, telling her about the ups and downs of the baseball lifestyle.

9

Boston

Fenway Park is among the greatest tourist attractions in Boston. The Red Sox give guided tours on a daily basis throughout the year. Even though I have broadcast over 1,700 games there, it is still a sacred and special place. Yes, a new ballpark with modern amenities that retains the charm of Fenway would be great, but what is now the oldest park in major league baseball, opened in 1912, the week the Titanic went down, is holding up pretty well.

The Green Monster seats, atop the leftfield wall, which were opened in 2003, fit in perfectly with the architecture and decor and look like they have been there since the wall was built. *Some* seats may not be the most comfortable and some don't face home plate but they are always filled. Also unique are the unusual outfield contours and dimensions of what Bart Giamatti called, "the eccentric angularities of Fenway." Pesky's Pole . . . the rightfield foul pole, only 302 feet from home plate . . . the triangle in deep right center, 420 feet away . . . and of course *The Wall*. The current ownership group has gone to great lengths to make the park more fan friendly by widening the concourses, adding a picnic area, and improving concessions.

For tourists and out-of-town fans attending a game or just visiting the city, public transportation is advised. Boston is a great walking city, from the Freedom Trail to the Back Bay over to Fenway. Driving is a nightmare—too many cars, too few parking spaces, and streets that were laid out by the colonists some 350 years ago. For visitors, filling the hours before and after the games is never a problem. There is plenty of history in Boston, from the State House to Symphony Hall, the JFK Library, Paul Revere's Old North Church, the Duck tours in and around the Charles River, and of course the many universities and colleges. The Museum of Fine Arts and the Gardner Museum are within walking distance of Fenway and the theater district and Boston Common are also close by.

As for cuisine, there is great variety but the most enticing to us has always been the North End featuring scores of Italian restaurants. Our favorites include Assagio, Artu's, Massimino's, Casa Italiano, and for pizza, the Pizzerina Regina. We really haven't found a bad restaurant yet in the North End but here's a word of advice: don't drive there. Parking is scarce and very overpriced.

New England and the Red Sox also have perhaps the best AAA franchise in baseball—the Pawtucket Red Sox of the International League, in Pawtucket, Rhode Island, just outside of Providence. Owned by Ben Mondor, a wonderful sportsman who took over a debt-ridden club in the mid-1970s, the Pawsox now set attendance records every year at McCoy Stadium. McCoy, built in 1942, was remodeled in the late 1990s and is now a state-of-the-art facility. Ben, President Mike Tamburro, and their staff provide the fans with real family entertainment, reasonably priced tickets, good and fairly priced concessions, and even free parking at the ballpark. So many of the Red Sox stars of the past 30 years have come through Pawtucket—from Jim Rice to Wade Boggs to Nomar Garciaparra.

If you're hungry, the Federal Hill section of Providence is only a few miles away. There are several outstanding Italian restaurants on Atwells Avenue in different prices ranges. Our favorites include Angelo's, where you can dine for less than $10 and where most pasta dishes are served with a side of French fries, Casa Christine on Spruce Street, where you have to bring your own wine, and Constantino's Venda Ravioli, a marvelous Italian deli and pasta shop for takeout. Closer to McCoy is Spumoni's, on the Massachusetts/Rhode Island line, a meeting and dining spot for scouts covering the game. For fine dining, there's

Luciano's on US Rt. 1 in Wrentham, Massachusetts, which we rank as the finest Italian restaurant in New England.

◆ ● ◆

The Red Sox have their AA and rookie league clubs in close proximity. In 2003, the Red Sox moved their AA affiliate to Portland, Maine. The Portland Sea Dogs of the Eastern League play to capacity crowds at Hadlock Field and the Lowell Spinners of the short season New York-Penn League have sold out LeLacheur Park in Lowell, Massachusetts, for the season—a complete sellout for the entire season!

Vermont has one franchise in organized ball, the Vermont Expos, also of the New York-Penn League. They play at Centennial Field in Burlington, which is even older than the name indicates, and is also used by the University of Vermont baseball team. The owner, Ray Pecor, who also owns the ferries that run from Burlington across Lake Champlain to New York State, runs a top-notch baseball operation and has assembled an outstanding young management team that he relies on heavily.

I had the pleasure of addressing their Hot Stove banquet in 2002. Burlington, by the way, is Vermont's largest city and a charming college town.

Organized baseball returns to New Hampshire in 2004 with the transfer of the New Haven franchise of the Eastern League to Manchester, where a new park will be built.

Connecticut has had three Eastern League clubs in recent years. The New Britain Rock Cats, the Minnesota Twins's AA affiliate who play in a new park, the Norwich Navigators, a Yankee affiliate until the Giants moved in 2002, and the New Haven Ravens, who have moved to Manchester. The Ravens, who had affiliations with Colorado, Seattle, St. Louis, and Toronto in their ten-year history, played at historic Yale Field, where a dying Babe Ruth once presented his memoirs to Yale University and its then-baseball captain, George Herbert Walker Bush. By the way, if you are going to New Haven, you really have to try the pizza for which New Haven is famous. The argument is Pepe's or Sally's . . . the two most popular pizza restaurants, both located on Wooster Street, though many of us, including Red Sox general manager Theo Epstein, a Yale grad, prefer Modern Pizza on State Street, where the lines are not as long and the pizza is just as good or better.

Independent professional clubs have also been successful in recent years: the Nashua (New Hampshire) Pride, managed by former Red Sox skipper Butch Hobson; the North Shore Spirit, located in Lynn, Massachusetts, and managed by former Red Sox utility infielder John Kennedy, and the Brockton Rox, owned by Mike Veeck, son of Bill Veeck, the Hall of Famer known as baseball's P. T. Barnum. The Rox play in a new park located in Brockton, Massachusetts, hometown of Rocky Marciano.

The Bridgeport (Connecticut) Bluefish play in a beautiful new park you can see from the train and from I-95.

As of 2004, the New Haven Cutters of the Independent Northeast League play at Yale Field in West Haven.

In addition to professional baseball, New England features the best collegiate summer league in the land, the Cape Cod League. The top players and coaches from all over the nation descend on the Cape each summer, as is proven by the long list of major leaguers who have matriculated there. After a day at the Cape's beautiful beaches, there is no better evening's entertainment than a night at the ballpark in Harwich, Hyannis, Orleans, Falmouth, Cotuit, Bourne, or Yarmouth.

In the mid-1990s the New England Collegiate League was formed. It also features top-caliber baseball, just a cut below the Cape League. The NECBL now has successful franchises from Newport, Rhode Island, to Keene, New Hampshire.

Yes, baseball thrives in New England and there is plenty to see.

10

Chicago

first went to a baseball game in Chicago in 1970 at the old Comiskey Park, the oldest park in the majors. It opened in 1910, two years before Tiger Stadium and Fenway Park. The Indians played the White Sox in a doubleheader. There was a nice view of the downtown Chicago skyline, and you had the feel that you were in a real old-time ballpark any time you were at old Comiskey. You could easily imagine Charlie Comiskey himself—the "Old Roman" as he was called, Luke Appling, and Minnie Minoso, a beloved White Sox player who was still at the ballpark. But for an old ballpark, old Comiskey did not have the kind of charm that Tiger Stadium, Wrigley Field, or Fenway Park had. It was big and it was old. That's about it.

Comiskey was on the south side of the city, and had a tiny and cramped clubhouse. I'm 5 foot 10 inches and I had to duck to go through some of the ancient doorways. The dugouts were also very small.

The old Comiskey was a pitcher's park—352 feet down the lines, later changed to 347. Centerfield was 415 feet from the plate. Some seasons, they moved it back to 430 feet. I recall some very long home runs there. In 1983, my first year with the Red Sox, Ralph Houk was the Boston manager.

Doug Bird, a relief pitcher through most of his career with the Royals, was pitching for the Red Sox on May 24 that year. He got a start because the Red Sox were always looking for a starter. He had a good sinker, but he got absolutely shelled. I remember the game well because he surrendered two rooftop home runs—one by Ron Kittle and one by Carlton Fisk. The White Sox scored early and often, and walloped the Red Sox 12-4. After the game, we were on the team bus going back to the hotel. Ralph Houk got on the bus last and, like virtually all managers, always sat in the front seat. But on this occasion Houk walked to the middle of the bus, and said, "Hey, everybody alright? Nobody got hurt, did they?" Then he looked right at Bird and said, "How you doin', Boom Boom?" and laughed. Then he said, "Get 'em tomorrow, guys!" While Ralph could laugh off a blowout like that game, he stewed after a one-run loss. You did not want to say anything to him after one of those.

The Red Sox were in Chicago on a Friday afternoon for the White Sox's home opener in 1985. The Red Sox had played an extra-inning game the night before in Kansas City and got to Comiskey Park after about two hours' sleep. That day, my friend Mike Easler was hit in the face by a Tim Lollar pitch. Later that year, Lollar was traded to the Red Sox for Reid Nichols. Easler had had a great year in 1984 (27 home runs, a .313 batting average, and 91 RBI) but getting hit in the face really ruined his 1985 season. He finished that year hitting just .262 with 16 homers and 74 RBI. Lollar turned out to be a better hitter than he was a pitcher. So much so that the Red Sox used him occasionally as a pinch-hitter in 1986—quite a rarity in the American League, especially after the designated hitter came into the league in 1973.

The Red Sox didn't do very well at Comiskey in those years, although the White Sox were not very good, except in 1983, when they won the American League West by 20 games. (They lost to the Baltimore Orioles in the American League Championship Series.)

I also recall a game on May 3, 1989, when the Red Sox played at old Comiskey Park. Joe Morgan, the Red Sox manager, had two catchers: Rick Cerone, a right-handed batter, and Rich Gedman, a lefty. Morgan platooned them. During a pregame show I did with Joe—as I did before every game—we discussed the White Sox starting pitcher, Shawn Hillegas, obtained by the White Sox from the Dodgers in September 1988. I noticed that Rick Cerone was in the lineup to face the right-handed Hillegas. Before we went on the air, I asked Morgan why

Cerone was catching instead of Gedman. He replied that Cerone was catching because Hillegas was a left-hander. But I told Joe that Hillegas was a *righty*. Morgan said, "Uh oh, I ***ed up." Gedman also wondered why he wasn't playing.

I did not want to embarrass Joe on the air by bringing up his mistake. He was a friend of mine, and always treated me well, both personally and professionally.

As it turned out, Rick Cerone hit a three-run home run off Hillegas to win the game for the Red Sox. After the game, as always, the sportswriters who covered the team came into the manager's office to ask Joe why he had started Cerone instead of Gedman. And Morgan, the most honest and direct man I know, said, "Because I screwed up. I thought Hillegas was a left-handed pitcher." The writers liked Morgan, and respected his honesty, and only a few ripped him for his mistake.

There were lots of cold nights and hot days at the old Comiskey Park. The broadcast booth was tiny, the smallest in the majors—barely large enough for two broadcasters to sit side by side. And it was up pretty high.

The Bard's Room was the press bar and restaurant at old Comiskey, open before and after the game. There was nothing like it, and there still isn't. They served hamburgers, cheeseburgers, hot dogs, and full meals. When Bill Veeck owned the White Sox, as he did during my first years with the Indians, you could stay in the Bard's Room all night. *He* certainly did, smoking cigarettes and putting away beer after beer. Veeck lost his right leg in World War II. He put the ashes from his cigarettes into an ashtray he bad built into his wooden leg.

The food in the Bard's Room was very good, as were the drinks and the company. Veeck loved the writers, and by extension, the broadcasters.

An old gentleman named Clarence, who had been at Comiskey since the 1930s, served hot dogs and other such fare to reporters and broadcasters in the press box.

I recall another game played on July 30, 1986, when the Red Sox played the White Sox at Comiskey, and Roger Clemens was thrown out of the game. The Red Sox were in first place, and we had had a tough road trip.

Clemens covered first base on a close play in the fifth inning and umpire Greg Kosc called the runner safe. He was clearly wrong and everybody knew Kosc had blown the call. Roger exploded, used the "magic words," and was immediately ejected. Clemens was 24-4 that year, but he lost two games to the White Sox. He also suffered a 1-0 loss to Jose DeLeon, a big right-hander, of the White Sox at Fenway. DeLeon beat Clemens twice in ten days that year, including a game that Clemens lost because of his own error.

In 1991, the White Sox moved to their new ballpark, the new Comiskey Park, right across from where the old one had been. We thought, well, this is new, this is nice, this is modern. The new park copied the dimensions of the old one, but we soon saw how poorly designed it was, particularly when we compared it to the Orioles new park at Camden Yards in Baltimore, which opened the next year. As Curt Smith, former speechwriter for Presidents Reagan and the first Bush, author of *Voices of the Game* and *The Storytellers*, wrote, the new Comiskey Park had "all the charm of a K-Mart." It's merely a big modern ballpark—just a slight improvement over the cookie-cutter parks in Cincinnati, Philadelphia, Pittsburgh, Atlanta's Fulton County Stadium, and others built in the 1960s and 1970s.

Many fans don't like the new park because the upper deck is slanted very steeply, to get in as many high-priced seats as possible. The upper deck is referred to as nosebleed country.

The broadcast area is not the greatest because during day games the booth bakes with the sun right in your eyes.

I remember the first series the Red Sox played at the new park, a three game series May 3, 4, and 5, 1991. Kevin Romine hit a grand slam in a rare win by Matt Young.

The first time I went to Wrigley Field was in 1970, to see the Astros play the Cubs. When the Cubs played a day game, and the White Sox played a night game, we could see a few innings at Wrigley and still get to Comiskey in time for the game. I like to take the subway or a cab to Wrigley, and walk around Wrigleyville, the neighborhood surrounding the old park. I usually take the subway to Comiskey Park, too, but it's hard to get a cab at Comiskey after the game to get back to the hotel.

I recall one trip to Comiskey in 2000, when my son Tommy was with me. After the game, we took a cab to Connie's, a great place not too far from Comiskey serving the kind of deep-dish pizza for which Chicago is famous. But when we were ready to leave, we could not find a cab to take us back to our downtown hotel. Connie's was about to close, and we noticed a number of pizza delivery trucks ready to go with the final deliveries of the night. So we asked for a ride, and Tommy and I rode in the front of the pizza truck all the way back to our hotel.

We love going to Carmen's Rosebud or Gino's on Rush Street in downtown Chicago, another great deep-dish pizza place, and Pizzeria Due. My favorite restaurant in Chicago is right on Rush Street and it's called the Lo Cal Zone. It features low calorie foods, including frozen yogurts: nine calories, no fat. Snickers, key lime, lots of wonderful flavors.

I also like to visit the Little Italy neighborhood of Chicago in and around Taylor Street.

When Jack Rogers was the Red Sox traveling secretary, he always took us to Eli's, The Place for Steak—which, surprisingly, is best known for its cheesecake. It's in downtown Chicago, not far from the lake. We used to go quite often when the Red Sox were picking up the tab. I don't go there much anymore, because I am not a steak eater, but when I did go, I'd have Lake Erie whitefish or perch, or occasionally walleye. Lou Gorman always recommended Eli's cottage fries. He'd say, "Gotta have 'em, gotta have 'em, gotta have 'em." Lou also loved the chocolate chip cheesecake. We went to Eli's once when Lou was not traveling with the team, and sent a chocolate chip cheesecake to Lou at his office.

Jerry Trupiano likes to go to Big Ed De Bevic's, a 1950s-style restaurant with ice cream sodas, greasy fries, and cheeseburgers. Johnny Rocket's on Rush Street is also fun.

One of the most fun nights I ever had on the road was in Miller's, an old-fashioned German pub in the Loop. I was there with some writers and a few scouts, including the late Howie Haak, a great scout and a great storyteller. Howie had us all in stitches with his great stories, only a few of which were off-color. The party was to honor Larry Whiteside, a baseball writer for the *Boston Globe*, who was taking a leave of absence to spend a year at Stanford University.

I've tried wading on the Lake Michigan beach in Chicago, but the water is always too cold. But there is a great walking path right by the lake, and an even better bicycle path. I've rented a bike from Bike Chicago and ridden along the lakefront to Navy Pier all the way north to Lincoln Park. You can also bike to Wrigleyville.

The shopping in Chicago is also first rate. I believe that the Water Tower shopping center was one of the first five-story indoor shopping malls in America.

The team stayed at the Westin on North Michigan Avenue in Chicago, a good location in downtown. In 1985, we waited there to see if there would be a strike—watching CNN in the days before we had the Internet. (There was a two-day strike on August 6 and 7, 1985.)

I like to visit the Broadcast Museum in the Loop. It has a great collection of both audio and video. I watched a kinescope there once of Don Caldwell's no-hitter on May 15, 1960, in his Cubs debut against the St. Louis Cardinals. The last out was a line drive to leftfield by Joe Cunningham. Walt "Moose" Moryn, a typical lumbering Cubs slugger, came in to make the catch for the final out of the game. The broadcaster was Jack Brickhouse.

The museum also has a videotape of Ernie Banks' 500th home run on May 12, 1970, and other great tapes.

Don McNeil's "Breakfast Club" tapes are there, and I like to walk by WGN's studio, which is also in downtown. There's a statue of Jack Brickhouse on the sidewalk. Chicago is a great city for walking.

Kate likes the "Untouchables" tour. It took us by Al Capone's old office building, the infamous garage that was the site of the Valentine's Day Massacre in 1929, and Holy Name Cathedral downtown, which is said still to have bullet holes from the shootout of Bugsy Moran and Bugsy Siegel.

Chicago is New York without the freak show.

Chicago fans are loyal to their teams, and don't boo a lot.

I like to visit the Italian Sports Hall of Fame, now being rebuilt on Taylor Street in the Italian neighborhood of Chicago. George Randazzo is the director. He picked up Joe Sambito and me at the hotel and took us to the hall to see, among other things, Sambito's locker from his days with the Houston Astros. They also have a uniform said to have belonged to Phil Cavaretta, but my friend Lenny Merullo, a longtime scout and Cubs shortstop, claimed that it was *his* uniform: Cavaretta was his roommate. Other exhibits include artifacts from, among others, Penn State football coach Joe Paterno and boxer Carmen Basilio.

The new Italian Hall of Fame will open on Taylor Street in 2004— called the Jerry Colangelo Center after the Diamondbacks and Phoenix Suns (NBA) owner, a Chicago native. It will have the Frank Sinatra Amphitheater, a TV studio, a cafe, and exhibits.

I have had the chance to emcee the local inductions into the New England Italian American Hall of Fame, which is held in Boston every year. In November 2003, Trup and I were inducted into the New England chapter.

I've driven two hours from Chicago to South Bend, Indiana, to visit the campus of the University of Notre Dame when they were playing Boston College. That's where I met Jill Langford, my future publisher and Notre Dame graduate. The Notre Dame campus is breathtaking. And the football stadium is magnificent. You really do wake up the echoes, although I usually do not root for Notre Dame.

Chicago is also home to the Second City comedy troupe in the Old Towne area on Wells Street. Old Towne is a great area of Chicago to walk around. Greek Town is another part of Chicago I like to visit. It's not far from downtown, and not far from the Italian neighborhood. I've been there several times and to the Museum of Science and Industry.

Cleveland

I s it the Mistake on the Lake or the Best Location in the Nation, as the Growth Association promoted it in the early 1970s?

I have a soft spot for Cleveland, having lived in the area from August 1972 until I came to the Red Sox in 1983. Cleveland was home. My three children were all born there. Duke was born in Parma in 1973, Tom in Willoughby in 1975, and Kate in Mayfield Heights in 1979.

They used to say that Cleveland was a nice place to live, but you wouldn't want to visit there—just about the opposite of New York City. The winters were brutal, with blizzards and subzero temperatures.

I have seen more games at Cleveland's old Municipal Stadium than at any other park except Fenway. I spent a lifetime in Cleveland Stadium. Even though Jacobs Field is newer, cleaner, and a great place to broadcast from—state of the art in every way—I still feel nostalgic about the old place.

I first went to Municipal Stadium in 1970 while I was working in Youngstown. The first time I was there was Opening Day, April 7, 1970, against the Baltimore Orioles. We did pregame interviews of Ted Uhlaender and manager Alvin Dark. Our seats were about a mile from home plate in the upper deck in rightfield. Boog Powell homered and the Orioles won, 8-2.

A few weeks later, I was back at Cleveland Stadium for a Senators game.

I interviewed Roy Foster, known as "Captain Easy," who at 25 was considered an elderly rookie. He had a good rookie season, hitting 25 homers and batting .268.

I was trying to work up the nerve to ask Ted Williams, the Senators manager, for an interview. I was 23 years old, and here's Teddy Ballgame. I knew about his reputation for disliking writers, and I assumed that he didn't like TV reporters, either. My roommate Mickey Krumpak was with me. He took photographs, and my cameraman shot film. Ted was on the bench, talking with one of his coaches and one of his players while the Senators were taking batting practice. I was still working up my courage to speak with him. I heard him speaking—bellowing, actually. He didn't just speak, he pontificated. He really was John Wayne. He was using language that I could not have used on the air. The language he was using helped break the ice, and I asked whether we could do the interview on the top of the dugout steps. He agreed, and we did the interview. But he never took his eyes off his players in the batting cage. One of my treasured photos was taken that day—a wall-sized picture of my interview with Ted Williams. He's not looking at me.

As the Senators manager and self-appointed batting coach, he made some bad hitters look pretty good. Ed Brinkman, who was a .210 hitter, wound up hitting .266 under Ted. I asked Williams about a catcher named Jim French, who was from Warren, Ohio, and lived in Andover, near Youngstown. Every time I ever met Williams, he was very positive about players, even scrubs like French.

I came to Cleveland in 1972. When I lived in New Haven, I had to plan well in advance if I wanted to go to New York for a game. What I loved about Cleveland was that when you lived right in the area—and I lived about 25 minutes from Cleveland Stadium—you could make up your mind half an hour before the game that you wanted to go. The team was always willing to give us tickets or credentials, and there were always plenty of seats. I was doing the 11 PM sports broadcast, so I could go to all the day games and sit in the press box. Sometimes I had a cameraman with me to shoot interviews.

I remember one game in particular. The date was August 26, 1973. Left-hander Jim Merritt was pitching for the Texas Rangers. He had been a 20-game winner in 1970 with the Reds. Merritt beat the Indians that day in the first game of a doubleheader, a 9-0 shutout. I went to the clubhouse between games, and he admitted that he had thrown a spitball during the game. The experience was great for me, because my interview was aired the next morning on the *Today Show*, my first appearance on the network.

On July 19, 1974, I was working in the WKYC-TV3 newsroom and I saw on the news wire that Indians pitcher Dick Bosman had a no-hitter going against Oakland. I asked Jim Graner, our sports director, whether he wanted me to go to the ballpark. He told me to grab a camera crew, and we got there as fast as we could. When we arrived, there was one out in the ninth inning. Bosman, a journeyman pitcher who was a sub-.500 pitcher, struck out Billy North to preserve his no hitter. I did an interview with Bosman after the game, and it was carried around the country on the NBC program service. I got a network fee of $33!

◆ ● ◆

In 1981, I did a talk show on 3WE (WWWE, now WTAM). I had no plans to be at the ballpark. But I got a call to fill in for Pete Franklin, the first prominent talk show host for sports. I remember it well. It was May 15, a cold, drizzly night. I was in the press box at Municipal Stadium because I had time to see the end of the game and then rush to the studio to do the talk show. That night, sitting in the press box, I saw Lenny Barker pitch a perfect game against the Toronto Blue Jays. Ernie Whitt hit a fly ball to centerfield to end the game.

Barker was a fun guy to be around. He had a great curveball, and threw in the mid-90s, but an elbow injury shortened his career.

I did my first major league game in Cleveland in 1979 and I have very fond memories of those Indians teams. The 1979 team featured Mike Hargrove (1974 American League Rookie of the Year), Bobby Bonds, Ron Hassey, Andre Thornton, Rick Manning, and Wayne Garland. They finished in sixth place at 81-80, 22 games behind the American League East champion Baltimore Orioles.

Opening Day 1979 was the only Opening Day start for centerfielder Horace Speed.

Another game I recall from 1979 was a home game against the Yankees. The game was supposed to start at 2 PM, but because of a rain delay, it started at 5:55 PM. Gabe Paul, the team's president, had sold 40,000 tickets to the General Electric plant as part of a promotion and he was not about to turn fans away. Why do I remember this game? Because we had to fill the entire 3 hours, 45 minutes of the rain delay. My broadcast partner that season was Fred McLeod. Gabe would not let us send it back to the TV studio during the delay. The station hated that, because they lost precious advertising. When people tune in for a game, either from the beginning or if they tune in late and all they see is rain-delay filler, most of them can't change the channel or turn the TV off fast enough.

During that rain delay, we had Gabe on the air. I asked him "Gabe, what do you hear, is it going to stop raining?" He answered, "It always has." We eventually got that game in, in less than two hours. Bobby Bonds led off the bottom of the first inning with a home run.

When I returned to the Indians in 1982, I did a lot of Spring Training games and some 25 regular season games. Bob Feller was my partner.

We went to the Metrodome for Twins games, and did some games from the West coast and some home games. We didn't do a lot of prime time games, because they were on the commercial station. We were on a cable network. When I was not working the games, I'd go to the games and sit in the stands. We had our own fraternity at the ballpark. Leonard Schur, an attorney who always brought his own kosher food to the games, had been a loyal Indians fan for many years. He shared the food with everybody. He had been a season ticket holder for many years, and sat in the first seat under the screen. He always counseled me about my job, and taught me the importance of the scouts. Leonard also counseled my kids about his ballpark rules. Leonard's rules included 1) Bring your own food; 2) One trip to the concession stand for one item; and 3) Nobody goes to the bathroom until the fifth inning.

Those were the rules for my children because they were the rules for Leonard's son Billy.

When my contract with Ted Stepien was offered, I negotiated it myself, because Ted was an easy mark, but I asked Leonard to read it over.

Leonard engineered the sale of our Cleveland house for us when I went to the Red Sox. Jan stayed in Cleveland with the kids when I went to Spring Training and to Boston. She was having trouble with the realtor. Leonard took care of everything, for which I will always be indebted.

I remember a party at Leonard's house. Leonard and his wife were dressed as vendors, as were the Ben and Angelo Bando, the parents of Sal and Chris. The menu was traditional ballpark food—kosher hot dogs, popcorn, peanuts, cotton candy, apple pie, and all the rest.

Leonard later retired and moved to Florida before Jacobs Field opened, and he never saw the Indians play in a World Series there. Leonard's wife called me the day he died, and we spoke for a while. Their daughter lived on a kibbutz in Tel Aviv.

Cleveland Stadium seated about 80,000. So even if 20,000 came to a game, it looked like about 2,000 in any other ballpark.

I recall the "Fog Game" of May 27, 1986, at Municipal Stadium. The Red Sox had the lead after five and a half innings of a night game. Mike Brown was the Red Sox pitcher. Steve Crawford relieved him with two on and no outs in the last of the sixth. Crawford fanned Joe Carter and Armas caught Mel Hall's drive at the centerfield fence.

When the fog rolled in off Lake Erie, Pat Tabler was up with a 1-0 count. The umpires halted the game. They wanted to see if the outfielders could see the ball. The fog was that thick. Indians coach Bobby Bonds grabbed a fungo bat and tried to hit balls to the outfielders, to see if they could pick up the ball. But he kept hitting balls over the fence. The game was delayed for an hour and 35 minutes. At 11:20 PM, the umpires decided that the fog was too thick and the game was called. The Red Sox had a five-inning 2-0 victory. After the game, Oil Can Boyd put it best: "Hey, that's what they get for building a ballpark on the ocean."

◆ ● ◆

On August 21, 1986, the Red Sox had a 12-run seventh inning in Cleveland and Spike Owen tied a record by scoring six himself. The Sox beat the Indians 24-5.

◆ ● ◆

Cleveland Stadium was built on a landfill, which always meant an uneven outfield and tricky bounces. The stadium was also filled with memorable characters. The head groundskeeper was Harold Bossard who worked with his brother Marshall, for example. Their father Emil had been the head groundskeeper, too. Another brother, Roger, was the groundskeeper at Comiskey Park. They were good storytellers, and did very good interviews.

Some of the most colorful people in the game are groundskeepers. Especially, Joe Mooney, Red Sox groundskeeper since 1970. I visit with Joe often. He is now in charge of maintaining the seats, while Dave Mellor takes care of the Fenway field itself. Joe has great stories about his days working in the minor leagues in Charlestown, West Virginia, where he also pitched batting practice and once threw at Gene Mauch's head . . . to his days in Washington at RFK Stadium, where he was very close to Sonny Jorgenson, Vince Lombardi, and Otto Graham of the Redskins and Frank Howard of the Senators. Joe is still very close to Don Zimmer, Joe Torre, and Jim Thome. He can tell you who the good guys are in baseball. Joe is a really colorful character and a great judge of character.

I had lots of friends who worked at the ballpark, including ushers and vendors, because I spent so much time at the ballpark when I wasn't doing games. Our Sports Exchange Cable Network only did 40 games. For almost all of the rest, even though I was not broadcasting, I was at the game, sitting in the stands.

Duke was born June 21, 1973, and we took him to his first game when he was three weeks old. We sat behind the screen under the press box. Bill O'Donnell, my great mentor and good friend who was an Oriole broadcaster, called me whenever he heard about a job opening. He came down from the press box to say hello and to meet Duke.

Opening Day 1975 was one of the most dramatic moments I have ever seen in baseball. I was covering for Channel 3 and also doing a piece, my first for NBC Nightly News. It was the debut of the first African American manager in the major leagues, Frank Robinson of the Indians. Frank was a player/manager that year, and in the last of the first inning, Frank came to the plate with a couple of runners on base. Doc Medich was pitching for the Yankees. Frank hit a line drive homer to leftfield in his first at bat, and the Indians went on to win the game. Boog Powell was the Indians first baseman at that time, and the team wore all-red uniforms. Boog said that, in those uniforms, "I looked like a giant blood clot."

We were still using film in 1975, just a year or so before the switch to videotape. Our cameraman filmed all the action and it all came out well, except for Robinson's homer. That part of the film was blank. It just didn't come out. But after a panic attack by network producers, we were able to rescue the shot from another source.

Frank Robinson really lives up to his name—he is incredibly frank. He likes the give and take of conversations and interviews, but he tests you a lot to see how you react. If you give it back to him, I think he respects you. I always enjoyed being with Frank.

While I was working in Cleveland, we lived first in a $150 a month apartment in Broadview Heights. That was September 1972. Duke was born in Parma in 1973. Then we moved to our first house in Mentor on the Lake, northeast of Cleveland, right in a bad snowbelt in the late summer of 1974. This was a two-bedroom brick ranch house, for which we paid $29,000. In the fall of 1978, we moved to Solon, which is where the kids went to school. They went to St. Rita's elementary school. Duke had a very influential third grade teacher there, Sister Seraphin. I always called her Sister Sledge, for the singing group that sang "We Are Family." When Tom's teacher was Sister Genevive, I called her Sister Genovese, after the crime family. Both nuns were baseball fans.

Among our neighbors in Solon were the Bandos—Ben, Angela, and Chris—who lived about a mile away.

I saw a lot of great football games at old Cleveland Stadium. Although I didn't do play-by-play for the Browns, I covered them for Channels 3 and 8. The coldest I've ever been was there—January 4, 1981, Browns vs. Oakland Raiders in the American Football Conference play-offs. It was −4 degrees at the one o'clock game time, with a windchill factor of −30 degrees. I was on the roof of Municipal Stadium with our cameraman. I put a cup of hot coffee down. Ten minutes later, it was frozen solid. The cold was unbelievable. In that game, the Browns were down 14-12, and were driving for a touchdown.

They could have had Don Cockroft kick a field goal, but they went for the touchdown. Mike Davis intercepted Brian Sipe's pass in the end zone.

Only rarely did the Indians draw large crowds. When they did, they were flash crowds—not much advance tickets, but lots of game-day sales. The stadium was not always prepared with enough hot dogs, beer, and soda for 70,000.

But they also drew well on July 3, when the Yankees came to town, and there was a fireworks show after the game. Those games usually drew about 70,000 fans.

I was invited to the final game at Municipal Stadium on October 3, 1993, when the Indians hosted the Chicago White Sox, but I was doing Red Sox games then, and I couldn't go.

Jacobs Field opened in 1994. It's a beautiful park with all the amenities. What I remember most clearly about that first year of Jacobs Field—the strike year—was a game in which Aaron Sele was pitching for the Red Sox against the Indians. As we were broadcasting the game, the monitor above us showed the Los Angeles police chasing O. J. Simpson in his white Bronco.

I was en route to the Jacobs Field booth on October 3, 1995, for the American League Division Series game when the jury returned its not guilty verdict.

Many years before, when he played for the Buffalo Bills, I had interviewed O. J. in the cramped clubhouse at Cleveland Stadium.

An older man named Joe was an usher in the press box at Municipal Stadium and now at Jacobs Field. He always kept me informed as to whether Bob Feller was going to be at that day's game. John Krepop, longtime press box assistant always provided us with statistics of biographical sheets, such as for recently acquired players. He started with the Indians as a teenager, and has been with the club for over 30 years.

Cy Buynak was the home clubhouse guy for the Indians for many years, and I considered him a friend. I interviewed him a few times on the air, too. I used to tease him about players he didn't care for. Cy also went through a lot of managers, as the Indians were always looking for the right guy. Cy is now the visiting clubhouse guy at Jacobs Field, so I see him whenever the Red Sox play in Cleveland. Cy's wife Mary is a good friend, too. She used to serve the meals in the press dining room at Municipal Stadium, which had very good food. She no longer does that, but she makes beautiful pastries for the visiting players.

◆ ● ◆

People in Cleveland never forget you. Even now, when I come to Cleveland with the Red Sox, I get to the ballpark early because there are so many old friends and people I want to see. People like public relations director Bob DiBiasio, and Dino Lucarelli, one of Bob's predecessors. I have maintained my friendship with Russ Schneider, sportswriter for the *Cleveland Plain Dealer*, one of the best reporters I've ever known. He is aggressive. Russ has written several books about the Indians. Sheldon Ocker of the *Akron Beacon Journal* is another sportswriter I like to visit whenever I'm back in Cleveland. So is Dan Coughlin, a colorful writer who traveled with me in 1979. Danny started every game story with one of his own poems.

I always like to visit with Kevin, the doorman at the team hotel in Cleveland. He's been there for years. We first saw him at the Embassy Suites hotels. Kevin remembers when I went to his old high school, Cleveland's JFK on the east side of town to do a TV story.

Jimy Williams used to tell me that Jacobs Field was his favorite of the new ballparks. I can see why. It's beautiful. Jacobs Field is a hitters' park. The balls really shoot out of there. The clubhouses—home and visitors—are very attractive and spacious. The cafeteria-style dining room for the nonplaying staff and the media is very good.

The broadcast booth has windows that face the field. We always open them just before the game, so we're not looking at the game through a window. There are large windows on the left and right of us, too, and I usually tape some stat sheets to the window so I don't have to go shuffling through a stack of papers to find them when I'm on the air. When I tape them up, all I have to do is turn my head, and the information I want is right there. I usually tape up the current standings, each team's won-loss records, and the league's leading hitters, RBI men, home run leaders, and the like. But in Cleveland, I taped my stats to the side of the window, which got rained on—rained on so much that the ink ran and the papers were illegible. Trup still kids me about it. But now I have figured out how to tape the papers on the inside of the window, the side that doesn't get rained on. (It takes me a long time to figure out such things.)

◆ ● ◆

I have some very strong memories of postseason games in Cleveland, some great and others not so great.

The Red Sox were at Jacobs Field for the American League Division Series starting on October 3, 1995. Roger Clemens started the game, which was tied at the end of nine.

Tony Peña, then with the Indians, one of my all-time favorite players, faced Zane Smith, a very soft thrower. With a 3-0 count, Smith threw a 78-miles-per-hour fastball. Peña either ignored or missed the take sign from Mike Hargrove, and hit the ball over the high scoreboard in leftfield to give the Indians the win. They swept the Red Sox in three games.

The Red Sox went back to Jacobs Field for the playoffs in 1998 and 1999.

Game Five of the 1999 American League Division Series was the most heroic performance I have ever seen. Pedro shut the Indians down in relief without a hit for six innings, in one of the most thrilling games I have ever broadcast. Trup had his ultimate "Way back" call on Troy O'Leary's three-run homer (after his previous grand slam).

I didn't get back to the clubhouse until about an hour after the game, and I got Pedro alone. I shook his hand and I said, "Pedro, that was the most heroic performance I've ever seen on a diamond." I knew he was hurting. He said "Thank you, señor." (He always calls me señor.)

◆ ● ◆

Jacobs Field does not get quite as cold as Municipal Stadium, which was right on Lake Erie. Jacobs Field is about a mile from the lake. Jacobs

Field was built on the site of an old Italian import store we used to go to, Gus Galucci, which sold great cheese.

In March 1981, we had an off day and drove to see the Pro Football Hall of Fame in Canton, Ohio. We had the radio on, and heard the news about President Reagan being shot.

I had been to Canton many times before, when I covered induction ceremonies at the Hall of Fame. I saw a lot of guys break down and cry—Lenny Moore, Roosevelt Brown, Jim Taylor.

William McKinley's grave is in Canton. His home was in Niles, Ohio, not far from Youngstown.

When I worked in Cleveland, I enjoyed covering the teams from Massillon and Canton-McKinley high schools—all great football powers. High-school football was and is very big in northeast Ohio. During the week before the game between the Masillon Tigers and the Canton-McKinley Bulldogs, Massillon has a real tiger on the sidelines.

I've been to the Rock and Roll Hall of Fame in Cleveland four times. It opened at about the same time as Jacobs Field. Trup doesn't care for it—he calls it a Hard Rock Café without the burgers. I like it because it lays out the history of rock and roll including many performers' costumes. One of my favorite displays is the wall featuring "One Hit Wonders," such as the Starland Vocal Band, which sang "Afternoon Delight." I saw it once with Jeffrey Lyons.

The second floor has an interactive exhibit that lets you listen to old disc jockeys. I heard Alan Freed there. He coined the term "rock and roll."

Freed started in Akron, at WAKR, then moved to WJW in Cleveland, where I once worked. I also got to hear one of my favorites, Dan Ingram, the afternoon at WABC in New York. I met one of my broadcasting heroes when Jeffrey Lyons arranged a memorable luncheon at Mickey Mantle's Restaurant in New York for Dan Ingram and me.

Murray Hill, on the east side of town, just past the campus of Case Western Reserve University, is an Italian neighborhood on Mayfield Road. I spent a lot of time there when I lived in Cleveland. Corbo's Golden Bowl and pastry shop is one of my favorite restaurants there. Guarino's, across the street, is another excellent place. The owner's husband, the late Dick Pischke, was my cameraman at Channel 3. I covered some of the Woody Hayes years at Ohio State with Dick, a very funny guy.

Mama Santa's has a great ravioli dinner for $5.

◆ ● ◆

One of the first hotels I stayed at in Cleveland was the old Hollenden House, site of a players' fight in June 1988. The Sox had a long day game in Baltimore on June 19, which they won. Then there was a long wait, about three or four hours in the Baltimore airport for a commercial flight to Cleveland. Some of the players had a few drinks while waiting for the flight. The airport was very hot. Somebody set off a stink bomb on the plane. The flight attendant was very upset at this low point in players' behavior. (They are usually very well behaved.) At the Cleveland airport, we all got on one bus to the hotel. The sounds on the bus were not normal bus sounds. They were loud and angry during the 20-minute ride. Ken Coleman was sitting next to me in the third row, in front of Ned Martin. I told Ken that this was strange—I thought there was going to be a fight. John McNamara, the manager, and Jack Rogers, the traveling secretary, were in the usual seats up front. When the bus got to the hotel, the reporters, broadcasters, coaches, and managers all got off the bus and went into the hotel to get their keys, but the players did not. They stayed on the bus. A few minutes later, Wade Boggs stormed through the lobby muttering something nasty, but there was nobody behind him. Ned, Ken, and I went up to our rooms, and came down a few minutes later to get our bags. We found out that there had been a fight near the elevators—a pushing match between two players. Oil Can Boyd tried to break it up and was bounced off the elevator walls for his trouble. Mike Greenwell gave us the blow by blow as we sat in the coffee shop with Joe Giuliotti of the *Boston Herald*.

Later that night, McNamara called the fighting players to his room to share a pizza, thinking he had mended some fences, but the story made the newspapers (Giuliotti was right there) and the team was greatly embarrassed. About ten days later, McNamara was fired and Joe Morgan took over as manager.

After the Hollenden House, we moved to the Bond Court Hotel in downtown Cleveland, which later became the Sheraton. It was run by Michael Burin, a devout Indians fan, and Jeffrey Lyons's cousin. I remember when the hotel was built. I was working in the overnight newsroom at WKYC. There was a fire at the construction site, and a crane fell through the roof. Now, the Red Sox stay at the Marriott Key Center, a lovely place.

If we have a day off, or a night game after a day game in Cleveland, I try to visit Jan's parents in Youngstown.

My favorite sports bar, the Golden Dawn, is in Youngstown. It was a sports bar before there were sports bars. Nothing fancy, just a neighborhood pub. I used to go there every night after anchoring the nightly sportscast when I was still single. I frequently met my good friend there, Dr. Tom Shipka, chairman of the philosophy department at Youngstown State University. Tom is a great sports fan who advised Ron Jaworski and many other football players. I'd have a schooner of beer in an iced glass, and my favorite sandwich, melted provolone and green peppers on Italian bread, made by Ralph and Carmen Naples. They have been working there since 1934, when their father ran the place. Carmen is 82 now. He was on Paul Brown's Big Ten championship and national championship team of 1942 at Ohio State. He was a guard, though he weighed less than 200 pounds. He and his brother Ralph, now 84, still work double shifts there. The place has changed very little over the years. It's a unique spot. Jan's parents go there for dinner, and you never heard four-letter words there. The food is good and the prices are low.

Alberini's, owned by Rich Alberini, was a restaurant where many sports-related press conferences were held. I remember covering Ernie Shavers's fight announcements there. Pitcher Dean Chance was a frequent patron. It's in the Italian section of Niles, and serves excellent Italian food.

Even though I have not been on television in Youngstown in 30 years, many people in Youngstown still remember me.

12

Detroit

When I'm in Detroit, I like to catch up on research, paper-work, and computer work. I spend a lot of time in the hotel. We stay at the Ritz Carlton Hotel in Dearborn, a somewhat stuffy but beautiful hotel. When I think of Detroit, I still think of Tiger Stadium, although the Tigers have played in Comerica Park since 2000. Going to Tiger Stadium really made you feel like you were in a different era—the 1940s or 1950s.

Tiger Stadium opened on April 20, 1912, the same day Fenway Park did, and was used up through 1999. There was so much history there. The dugouts were so small that when the major league rosters are expanded in September to 40 players, there was not enough room for all the players to sit in the dugout. The dugout roofs were so low that play-ers would bump their heads when they jumped out of their seats to see something exciting on the field. The clubhouse was dark and dingy, and the lockers were made of wire mesh. When you walked out the runway from the clubhouse to the dugout, you had to duck. When we had Baseball Chapel services at the old ballpark, the only room we could use was the shower room. No other room was available.

Nevertheless, the old park had a lot of character. All of the seats were originally green, I think. A broadcaster whose name I will not men-tion once went on the air to say that at Tiger Stadium, "All the seats at Tiger Stadium are blue . . . except for the orange ones."

I liked the overhang in rightfield. It was like the design of the old Polo Grounds. A fly ball would go out to rightfield. A fielder might be camped under it. It was 325 feet down the line. But if the ball grazed off the façade of the upper deck, or into the first row of the upper deck, which stuck out 8 to 10 feet above the lower deck, it was a home run. I remember walking around the outfield there and under the overhang just to see what it looked like from underneath.

Once when the Red Sox had an off day, I watched the Brewers play the Tigers from the upper deck in centerfield—a long way from home. Not a bad view. Centerfield at Tiger Stadium was the longest poke after Yankee Stadium was remodeled—440 feet to dead center. The flagpole was on the field in left centerfield. Like Fenway, it was a great hitter's park when the wind blew out. But when the wind blew in on a cold day, it was very tough to hit one out. But Tiger Stadium was probably the best home run park in the league because the ball really carried with the over-hang in right. It was 340 feet to left but only 365 feet to the power alley in left centerfield. If the batter hit a ball to left center, it carried rather well.

June 1983—my first year with the Red Sox—had two of the weird-est plays I have ever seen. I will never forget them.

The first involved Kirk Gibson. Gibson was a terror with a really mean-looking countenance. In fact, when my son Duke worked in the Red Sox visitors' clubhouse at Fenway Park, he loved Robin Yount and George Brett, but was terrified of Gibson. Gibson brought the same fero-cious approach to baseball that he had used as a football star at the University of Michigan.

Mike Brown was pitching for the Red Sox at Tiger Stadium on June 14, 1983, a Tuesday.

Kirk Gibson hit a tremendous home run in the fourth inning. I was on the air at the time, and although I had heard about balls going over the roof at Tiger Stadium—Ted Williams and Mickey Mantle had done it—I had never seen one hit over the roof, over the light tower, completely out of the park before. We found out later that the ball landed on the top of Brooks Lumber Company, across Trumble Avenue from the ballpark.

Lou Whitaker was on first base in the bottom of the sixth when Gibson hit a ball to deep centerfield, between the 400 and 440 feet signs.

Tony Armas went back and got a glove on the ball, but couldn't catch it. The ball rolled away. Whitaker had to hold up to see if the ball would be caught. When Armas lost it, Whitaker started around the bases. Gibson, a fast runner, was right behind him. The relay came in to Rich Gedman, the Red Sox catcher, at the plate. Whitaker tried to score but Gedman tagged him out. Right on his heels came Gibson. He barreled into Gedman and just kept going—flattening home plate umpire Larry Barnett. Barnett was injured and had to leave the game. Ken Kaiser, the first base umpire, called Gibson safe. But Gedman had the ball in his glove, and Gibson was really out. What happened was this: when Barnett went down, one of the balls he had in the pouch on the side of his belt had been jarred loose. That's the ball Kaiser saw. He thought Gedman had dropped it. But the Red Sox won 6-2.

I remember Opening Day, April 7, 1986. Dwight Evans had made up his mind over the winter that he would try to hit the first pitch of the season for a home run, but he didn't tell anyone. He did just that on a Jack Morris fastball. We had a 1:30 start, the earliest for any team, and Evans was the lead off batter for the Red Sox. One pitch, one hit, one home run into the leftfield seats, but the Tigers won, 6-5.

Two days later, in the second game of the season, the Red Sox lost again 6-5 in a snow flurry.

August 4 to 7, 1988, the Sox played a wrap around series (Friday, a Saturday twi-night doubleheader, Sunday, Monday) in Detroit against the first-place Tigers and lost the first three games. Then came a touch of "Morgan Magic," when Joe said, "Don't worry, [Bruce] Hurst will spin a beauty." And he did. The game was a scoreless tie through nine innings. In the tenth, Todd Benzinger singled in the winning run, and Hurst had a complete game 3-0 win. The Red Sox got back to a tie for first place in the American League East, and went on to win the division.

◆ ● ◆

Most big league stadiums, and those in Spring Training too, have some kind of press dining rooms, where the media covering the game, including the broadcasters, can have a sandwich or dinner before or even during the game. In addition to the reporters, I usually run into lots of old friends in these rooms. I've mentioned the Bard's Room at old Comiskey Park, where Bill Veeck held court. The Tigers's Den at Tiger Stadium in Detroit was another. The food was good and you could go there after the game while waiting for the team bus to go back to the hotel. I always saw lots of people such as Jim Campbell, the former Tigers general manager, and Hall of Famers Rick Ferrell, George Kell, and Al Kaline.

I would also run into former managers and general managers, as well as many scouts who were still with the teams but perhaps not in positions as visible as they had been. The food runs the gamut from fair to pretty good, but most of us go for the company.

But whenever I think of Tiger Stadium, I think most of all of my great friend Ernie Harwell. He began his career as a teenage sportswriter for the *Sporting News*, and for his hometown paper in Atlanta. Harwell was a sportscaster for Atlanta's WSB starting in 1940. He became the broadcaster for the Atlanta Crackers in the Southern Association. In 1948, he became the only broadcaster traded for a player when Branch Rickey, the general manager of the Dodgers, traded Cliff Dapper for Harwell. (Rickey needed another broadcaster in the Dodgers's booth because Red Barber was ill.)

After two years with the Dodgers, Ernie moved to the Giants, and did the final game of the unforgettable 1951 National League playoffs on television. While Russ Hodges's immortal "The Giants win the pennant! The Giants win the pennant!" has been heard by most baseball fans, Ernie jokes that the only person who heard his call of Bobby Thomson's game-winning home run off Ralph Branca was Mrs. Harwell. This was years before videotape, and no recording is known to exist of Harwell's call of the game.

After broadcasting for the Giants, Harwell became the voice of the Orioles in 1954. In 1960, Ernie made the best move of his life—to Detroit, to become the voice of the Tigers.

Ernie Harwell is a wonderful Christian gentleman who has always gone out of his way to help young broadcasters, such as me. I met him when I started broadcasting in Cleveland. He counseled me but always in a very gentle, unpushy way. He's been a speaker at Baseball Chapel, and is the author of a number of books. Ernie's a real family man and is a prince of a person.

Ernie's partner for many years was Paul Carey. I called him "Mr. Pipes," and Ernie said that when you hear the voice of God, it will sound like Paul Carey. What a voice! But I always felt a little sorry for Paul because he had to be his own engineer in the booth. There is enough to worry about when broadcasting a major league game to millions of people without having to worry about electronic technicalities. He carried the equipment, set it up, checked the phone lines and set them up, then broadcast a game.

I had lunch with Ernie Harwell at his suburban Detroit home. Ernie asked me to introduce him to Pedro Martinez in 1999. Pedro, a real student of the game, knew all about Ernie and was very gracious during their chat.

As Ernie used to say, Tigers Stadium was located at the corner of Michigan and Trumble. The streets surrounding that corner were full of potholes, and there was very little parking available near the stadium. Detroit is a city where, at least until Comerica Park opened in 2000, redevelopment had been just a rumor. The opening of Ford Field, the Detroit Lions new football stadium, in 2002 has also helped. It's too bad that all the heavy industry in Detroit has not invested in the revitalization of downtown.

Sparky Anderson managed the Tigers from 1979 through 1995, after managing the Cincinnati Reds from 1970 to 1978.

The Tigers trained in Lakeland, Florida, about 15 miles from Winter Haven, so we saw them quite often in Florida. It was always fun to spend time with Sparky. He is the master of hyperbole. In 1988, the year of the "Morgan Magic," Sparky was doing a live TV spot with Joe Morgan, the Red Sox manager. The Red Sox were in a hot streak, and Sparky said, "Joe, one of these years, a team is going to get hot, and it's going to get really hot, and it's going to stay hot, and it's going to be hot all year and it's going to go 162-0!"

Sparky built up mediocre players into the second coming of Ty Cobb. Each spring he seemed to have a phenom. One year it was Chris

Pittaro (three seasons, .221), and another year it was Torey Lovullo (eight seasons, seven teams, .224). There was also Barbaro Garbey, an outfielder whom Sparky predicted would be the next Roberto Clemente. They were going to be Hall of Famers. They ended up as utility players at best. But Sparky meant well, and he was a good judge of talent. Sparky loved to philosophize about the game of baseball and the game of life. He always had a good coaching staff in Detroit, and I liked to spend time with Alex Grammas, the former Cardinal and Red shortstop. He had earlier managed the Brewers.

In Detroit, I also liked to visit with Hall of Famer George Kell, who became an excellent broadcaster with a great set of pipes and a charming Swifton, Arkansas, drawl. It was always delightful to see George in Detroit or when he came to Boston. And I always enjoyed his partner, Hall of Famer Al Kaline.

The broadcast booth at Tiger Stadium was the closest to home plate of any stadium in the league—closer than the pitcher was. We could hear the batter and the pitcher. When a left-handed batter was up, you took your life in your hands because we were only about 55 feet from home plate. The Tigers broadcasters, up the first base line, worked with a protective screen. It's hard to get used to a screen when you only do six games a season in that ballpark, so we didn't have one. But lefty batters would foul balls back into the booth. I remember one foul ball that I thought was going to hit me in the mouth. I got out of the way just in time. The ball just missed the left side of my face. On a few occasions, we wore baseball gloves in the booth at Tigers Stadium, but I don't know if I could have put the glove up fast enough to protect my face.

Another time in 1995 or 1996, the ball bounced off the back wall of the booth, near where the engineer sits, and hit Jerry Trupiano in the head. He was OK.

The Tigers had some very good guys on their teams over the years. One of my favorites was Alan Trammell, the Tigers's shortstop from 1977 through 1996. His first year of eligibility for the Hall of Fame was 2002, and while he was not elected that year, I think he has a chance for election. Trammell was a real gentleman. He was named the Tigers's manager for 2003.

I always enjoyed watching Jack Morris pitch. I think he too belongs in the Hall of Fame. Big winner. Big game winner. Workhorse.

The Tigers moved into Comerica Park in 2000. It's very pretty from the outside, with all the tigers and the statues of great Tigers in left centerfield—Ty Cobb, Charlie Gehringer, Al Kaline, Hank Greenberg, Willie Horton, Hal Newhouser, and Ernie Harwell.

The field is pretty, with very bright green grass, which occasionally makes it hard to find the ball in the bright sunlight of an afternoon game.

The broadcast booth is spacious, and the pressroom cafeteria is OK.

Although the park is virtually brand new, some little things could be fixed up. The visiting clubhouse, for example, is rather small. Unlike Tiger Stadium, the dugouts are very big—and very deep, too. Sometimes, you have to stand to see the action on the field.

Greek Town was a part of Detroit we used to frequent when we stayed downtown at the Renaissance Center. We haven't been there very often since the Red Sox started staying in Dearborn, near the Fairlawn Mall.

Greenfield Village is not far from Dearborn. It is a village built by Henry Ford, and there's a good museum of old cars, including the car in which President Kennedy was shot.

I like to visit the University of Michigan campus in Ann Arbor. Ace Adams, the former Red Sox batting practice pitcher was the assistant baseball coach there. I like to have lunch at the Cottage Inn in Ann Arbor, and to visit my friend Ben Lyons, who was a student there. I've covered the Ohio State-Michigan football game at Michigan Stadium a few times. These games are played in the third or fourth week of November, when it's usually very cold, and occasionally snowing. The Big Ten title is frequently at stake. The crowds at Michigan are about 111,000, to a mere 100,000 at Columbus.

Schembechler Hall on campus houses the football trophies and Michigan's Football Hall of Fame.

For me, the highlight of any visit to Detroit is a visit to the Motown recording studios where Berry Gordy first recorded Motown music. The Motown Hall of Fame is on West Grand Avenue on Detroit's west side.

It's an old house that Gordy owned and lived in. It's interesting to me to see how primitive the old equipment and studios were. Recordings were made on just two tracks. Boom microphones and music stands are there. Marvin Gaye, Tammy Tyrelle, the Temptations, Diana Ross and the Supremes, Martha Reeves and the Vandellas—all the great Motown performers seem to have started here. I guess my favorite music is the Motown sound. So to go to Detroit and see the old photographs and costumes is always a delight. I've taken many people there, including Larry Whiteside of the *Boston Globe*, as well as some players and partners. The museum is not far from Henry Ford Hospital, where the Tigers's team physician was located. I always thought the team doctor had a great name: Dr. Clarence Livingood. Another interesting thing about Dr. Livingood—unfortunately now the late Dr. Livingood—is that he was a dermatologist, which peaked my interest because my father Frank and my brother Frank are both dermatologists.

The London Chop House is a good, fancy restaurant in downtown Detroit. If you come in without a tie, they give you one. Mario's on the east side was pretty good, too. In the Fairlawn Mall, we go to TGIF or the Big Fish—which has surprisingly good seafood.

Right across the Detroit River in Windsor, Ontario, are a number of casinos. I've been to these a few times, but like most casinos, they are very smoky. I first learned about Windsor when I listened to their great radio station CKLW at 800 on the dial—a great 1960s rock and roll station.

13

Kansas City

O nce, during Trup's first year with the Red Sox, I tried to get to Kansas City, Missouri, from the airport, took the wrong bridge over the Missouri River, and wound up in Kansas City—*Kansas*. Trup never lets me forget it.

Kansas City, Missouri, is a very underrated city. The place is beautiful, the food is good, and the people are friendly. But it sure gets hot in the summer—very hot.

We played the Royals on Sunday, August 2, 1987. It was 132 degrees on the artificial turf. Royals's rookie third baseman Kevin Seitzer went six for six. I always called Kauffman Stadium the "House of Horrors." The Kauffman Stadium broadcasters' facilities are wonderful. In fact, everything about the stadium, built just for baseball, is wonderful. But the Red Sox had a terrible record there for years. Only recently has our record improved to 40 percent, up from 33 percent—almost unheard of in major league circles.

The Royals were a turf team, a fast team, with good pitching. The Red Sox with their lumbering sluggers didn't cope very well.

We lost games in horrendous ways. I remember a game where we had Rob Murphy and Jeff Reardon in relief of Roger Clemens in 1990. Murphy allowed a home run by Bo Jackson in the eighth inning. Reardon allowed the tying run in the ninth on a pinch hit double by Mike MacFarlane and then lost the game in the tenth when the immortal Rey Palacios hit a two-out grand slam. The Red Sox lost lots of games there like that.

We were rarely swept in Kansas City, but we lost the series 1-2, 1-3. In a typical year, we went 2-4 or 1-5 in Kansas City. And the Royals were good. They had great pitching, including Dennis Leonard, Paul Splittorff, Bret Saberhagen, Larry Gura, and Dan Quisenberry (we never touched him). We just could not cope with the Royals style of baseball.

In fact, it goes back to my days with the Cleveland Indians in 1979. The Royals ran wild against the Indians that year. Willie Wilson and Frank White and company were stealing bases. The Indians had a catcher named Gary Alexander who threw three or four balls into centerfield in one game.

Joe Hall, a Kansas City native and Red Sox fan, has seen every game the Red Sox have played in Kauffman Stadium but one, and 98 percent of the games the Red Sox played in Municipal stadium in Kansas City against the Kansas City A's. Joe, who grew up in Kansas City, is an investor and a very cultured gentleman who speaks fluent Italian and was a student of my uncle Sal Castiglione at the Georgetown School of Foreign Service in the mid-1950s. Joe lived in a large home on 55th Street in Kansas City for many years and then moved to Leawood, Kansas.

He watched the Kansas City Blues as a youngster. Joe became a fan of a young Johnny Pesky, then with Louisville, who became his hero for life. Now he socializes with him, and sees Pesky when we're in Kansas City.

Joe also visits Fenway at least once a year and has been there for many memorable events including Game Six of the 1975 World Series, the 1978 Bucky Dent playoff fame, and the 1986 World Series.

Joe and I usually have a postmortem following Red Sox games in Kansas City, most of which were spent lamenting a tough defeat. After one such postmortem, shared by Jan, we had a terrifying experience.

On July 31, 1997, Jan was with us on the trip, and we were staying at the Ritz Carlton Hotel at Country Club Plaza. The plaza is a beautiful place, built in 1923 as part of the first shopping center in the country.

The hotel bar was a cigar bar, and we were not interested in that, so we went across the street to the Raphael Bar, where the menu features chicken and veal "Castiglione."

We had a few drinks, then left the bar and walked by a statue of Winston Churchill and his wife. (The players always joked that these were really statues of Lou Gorman, who was then the team's general manager, and Mrs. Yawkey.) The side door was closed, so we walked by the driveway. A small car pulled up, and the driver demanded Jan's money. It looked like he had a gun. She threw down her purse, then he pointed his gun at Joe and me. Jan ran into the Ritz Hotel lobby and tripped, screaming that we had been robbed and that they may have shot her husband.

Joe and I were standing behind a huge concrete flowerpot outside the hotel. It was dark, and I was wondering what being shot would feel like with that gun pointed at me. The gunman, however, never asked us for our wallets. He got back into the car and they drove away. Sean McDonough picked Jan up, and after we entered the hotel, we watched the incident on the hotel's security video. What an odd experience! I had just mentioned to Joe that we loved Kansas City, particularly because we always felt safe there. Thirty seconds later, this happened. We didn't get any sleep that night because we were still upset by the incident.

The next day, I called my answering machine at home in Massachusetts. There was a message from the police in Shawnee Mission, Kansas, right across the state line. They had found the contents of Jan's purse on somebody's lawn, and found our phone number. Everything was returned except our plane tickets, and I had to go to the airport to replace them. There was a story about it in the local newspaper. That afternoon, Dean Palmer hit two home runs to beat us.

That was the scariest moment we've ever had on the road, and to this day, Jan will not go back to Kansas City.

Kansas City is the home of great barbeque—Gates Barbeque, Arthur Bryant's Barbeque, and Masterpiece Barbeque are the most famous. Then there is Winsted's restaurant, which Bob Starr claimed was the home of the world's first cheeseburger. Louie's Lunch in my native New Haven claims to have originated the hamburger.

The Negro League Museum is in Kansas City, near 12th Street and Vine, and I've been there many times. It is a state-of-the-art facility. Buck O'Neil, the great Negro League player, and the man who helps keep the league's history so vibrant is usually there, and we try to spend time with him.

I have taken players including Darren Lewis and Troy O'Leary and general manager Theo Epstein there. The museum, which includes the International Jazz Hall of Fame, has helped to revitalize the inner city.

◆ ● ◆

Bob Feller, a living legend, grew up on a farm in tiny Van Meter, Iowa, now just off I-80 about 15 minutes from Des Moines. Just a few years ago, the Bob Feller Museum opened in his hometown. It is approximately a seven-hour drive from Kansas City to Minnesota, and in May 2003 we had an off day between visits to those cities so I decided to drive and visit my old partner's museum.

Leaving following a Wednesday afternoon game in Kansas City, I got to suburban Des Moines in time to first visit Winterset, Iowa, the birthplace of John Wayne. His house, a tiny one-floor structure built in the early 1900s, still stands in great condition though I arrived after visiting hours. While right in front of the house, I called New York movie critic, Jeffrey Lyons to tell him where I was. Within five miles of the Wayne homestead are the Bridges of Madison County, made famous in the novel and the Clint Eastwood-directed movie by the same name. How disappointing the bridges are. We have much more impressive covered bridges in Northern New England.

After spending the night in a motel near the Des Moines airport, I drove about 20 minutes to Van Meter the next morning. The Bob Feller Museum is a beautiful brick structure, designed by Bob's son Steve, an architect. It sits right in the small town, which features the Bob Feller baseball fields, a general store, some very neat old houses, and not much else. The Feller Museum contains his baseball cards, artifacts from his no-hitters and great games, his uniforms and other symbols of his excellent career. They also have a wall commemorating each of his 266 wins. Patrons and fans can buy individual plaques with their names engraved on them. I bought a plaque for win 141, a one-hitter vs. the Red Sox.

Bob, who lives in suburban Cleveland, visits the museum often, sometimes for autograph sessions with other Hall of Famers such as Rollie Fingers, Yogi Berra, and Steve Carlton.

The highlight for me, though, was the short ride to the Feller family farm, now owned by a doctor and his family. While the field Bob's father built for his amateur team is gone, the barn in which Bob pitched all winter is still standing. The museum people tell me that the holes are still in the barn door where Bob fired those blazing fastballs all winter while being taught by his dad. Also still standing is the beautiful home Bob built on the farm for his parents after he reached the major leagues. They grew corn, wheat, and soybeans on the farm in Bob's day and he always told me that his strength came from physical labor and that more athletes should do physical labor.

If you visit the Des Moines area, the Bob Feller Museum is well worth the stop.

I've been to the Truman Library in Independence, Missouri, 12 times. The first time was in 1979, and I went by the Truman house on Delaware Street. But I could not visit it that day, as Bess Truman was still living there. She had been a fan of the Kansas City A's—in fact, she was said to be a bigger baseball fan than Harry.

Bob Starr took us to Dixon's, where Truman used to go for chili. Bob grew up in Oklahoma, but was born in Kansas City. No beans, just ground beef and chili powder. I'm not a big chili fan, but Bob said it was great.

Also in Independence are an old-fashioned soda fountain and the jail where Frank James served time. He had a luxury cell, complete with a rug and a rocking chair. He'd get there at 8 AM, and leave at 5:00 in the afternoon—part of his plea bargain. The jail is now a museum.

I've been to Liberty, Missouri, north of Kansas City, where Jesse James held up his first bank. Five miles up the road is Kearney, Missouri, where he lived, and where the Pinkerton guards blew off his mother's arm when they firebombed the house. Jesse's half brother was killed there, and Jesse was buried in the backyard before he was moved to the local cemetery.

The history of Jesse and the entire James gang is on display in the museum there, an old farmhouse.

◆ ● ◆

In 1999, the Red Sox opened the season in Kansas City, and of course, we were off the next day, which is usually a rain date. I drove down Missouri Route 71 by myself to Commerce, Oklahoma, to see the home of Mickey

Mantle, my hero. Except to change planes, I had never even been in Oklahoma before.

I stopped in Lamar, Missouri, Harry Truman's birthplace, about 100 miles south of Kansas City. It's a historic site with only one person on duty. I'm a big Harry Truman fan. I continued on to the tri-state area, near where Missouri, Kansas, and Oklahoma meet.

I went to Baxter Springs, Kansas, where Mickey played for a youth team called the Whiz Kids, and was said to have hit a home run into the river. Baxter Springs is also famous as the place where Quantrill's Raiders, a Confederate guerrilla group, was formed. The sign out of town proclaims it be to the home of Hale Irwin, U.S. Open champ.

Next, I went to Joplin, Missouri, where Mickey played his only full year of minor league ball in 1950 in the Western League. In 137 games at shortstop, he managed 26 home runs and led the league with a .381 batting average.

The old ballpark was still there, now used by Missouri Southern University, who were practicing when I was there. The ballpark is only about 45 minutes from Commerce, which is on Route 66, part of which has been renamed Mickey Mantle Boulevard.

I saw the home in Commerce where Mickey grew up. It is a small building with a sign that said "MANTLE HOME UNDER REN-OVATION." Then I went to town hall. It happened to be Election Day. They were expecting a record turnout of 180 voters. Some Mantle memorabilia is displayed on the wall.

I introduced myself to the town clerk, and told her that I was with the Red Sox. She asked if I knew her brother-in-law, Steve Crawford, a Red Sox pitcher. He had won Game Two of the 1986 World Series (the game started by Roger Clemens and Dwight Gooden). She took my photo there, with the Mantle wall behind me. As Dan Shaugnessey, the *Boston Globe* columnist says, "Everything comes back to the Red Sox."

I went by the high school and saw the field where Mickey played football, and where he was kicked in the shin, an injury that led to osteomyelitis. The field has been named Mickey Mantle Field.

I saw Mutt Mantle Field, a girls' softball field that needs plenty of work. I have also been by the old ballpark in Kansas City, which was said to have had the best infield in baseball. A housing project is being built at Brooklyn Avenue and 22nd Street.

14

Milwaukee

I did the Brewer cable TV games in 1981. I really enjoyed the people in Milwaukee—some of the nicest people I ever met. Calm and laid-back, Milwaukee's streets are safe, and the city is really clean—"Milwaukee clean," they call it. There is no littering and there is little traffic. Milwaukee is one of the great restaurant towns in the United States. Our favorite is Giovanni's in the north end. One of the reasons I liked it was that they sent a car to the Pfister Hotel to pick us up. Trup loves their pork chops, and I love their chicken. We've been there with some scouts, and they seem to like it, too. The Pfister is more than 100 years old and retains its elegance. I always love to stay there.

Mader's, in downtown Milwaukee, is an outstanding German restaurant, the kind for which Milwaukee is rightly famous. Danny Carnevale, a scout for the Indians, told us that he tried to get in to Mader's one night, but was told that he needed a reservation. So he called back in 10 minutes and said, "This is Harry Fruehauf (president of Fruehauf trucking). We've heard lots of good things about your restaurant. Is 8 o'clock ok?" "Oh, yes, Mr. Fruehauf. 8 o'clock is excellent." So Harry went there at 8:00 with a group of scouts, and was given the royal treatment. He had a great meal, but Harry had to leave a big tip.

Karl Ratzsch's, near the hotel, is another excellent German place.

Milwaukee is a very livable city. There are two taverns on almost every corner. My broadcast partner on pay-TV in 1981 in Milwaukee was Tom Collins. "The Ol' Redhead" had also broadcast for the Milwaukee Braves in the 1960s before they moved to Atlanta, and then did the Brewers games with Merle Harmon.

Tom lives on 37th Street in Milwaukee. I've been to his home, and to his neighborhood pub that, like many in Milwaukee, has a fish fry. The food and the beers are reasonably priced.

Saz's is a chicken and ribs place past old County Stadium.

Milwaukee is right on Lake Michigan. My daughter Kate has roller-bladed along the lakefront in a park that stretches for several miles. One time she was going too fast down the sidewalk and scared the pants off me because she had lost control of her speed. Luckily, she had the brains to dive into the grass to avoid a serious injury.

Milwaukee holds numerous ethnic fests along the lakefront—German, Italian, Mexican to name just a few. Milwaukee also has a very underrated zoo. I took my son Tom there one Sunday morning before a late afternoon game. Next to the Bronx zoo, it's the best zoo I've ever been to.

The Milwaukee botanical gardens are beautifully maintained year-round.

County Stadium originally was built for the Milwaukee Braves. In April 1953, they played an exhibition game against the Red Sox, which opened the park. The stadium did not have many modern conveniences. The seats were very close together, and there was just one tiny elevator to the press box.

But Milwaukee County Stadium had great concessions—I remember particularly the bratwurst—and was therefore the best-smelling stadium I've ever been in. Good smells also came from the tailgaters. The Green Bay Packers of the NFL played a few games each year in Milwaukee, and their tailgaters were legendary.

We get to the ballpark about three hours before game time. In Milwaukee, the tailgaters are already set up with their grills, charcoal fires, and beer. When George Bamberger managed the Brewers in the 1970s and 1980s, after the game he'd go out to the parking lot and share a few beers and some bratwursts with the fans. The fans stayed in the parking lot for hours.

Night games in April and May, and then in September, were very cold at the old stadium. Unless you were a pull hitter, it was not an easy park to homer in—315 feet down the lines, and 392 in the power alleys, and 402 to dead centerfield.

Roger Clemens pitched some great games in Milwaukee, but I remember a game he lost there, 3-2, on a ninth-inning home run by Joey Meyer, a big, fat right-hand batting first baseman from Hawaii. The ball was lined down the rightfield line, just inside the 315 sign.

My most memorable broadcast there was at the end of the 1981 split season—split because of a players' strike. The Brewers were playing the Tigers on Saturday afternoon, October 3, the next to last day of the season. The game was tied 1-1 in the seventh inning when Gorman Thomas hit a sacrifice fly to put Milwaukee ahead 2-1, and in the ninth inning, Rollie Fingers struck out Lou Whittaker swinging. I had one of my famous calls: "The Brewers win the second half! The Brewers win the second half!" Not quite the same as Russ Hodges's "The Giants win the pennant!" but along the same lines. It's unlikely that any other broadcaster will ever make a similar call.

The Brewers lost the miniseries to the Yankees that year, but in 1982, after I had gone back to the Cleveland Indians, Milwaukee won the pennant. I went to the World Series for Games Three, Four, and Five but the Brewers lost the series in seven games to the St. Louis Cardinals.

The fans in Milwaukee are very supportive. In the 1950s, the Braves were outdrawing the Yankees 2-1.

The Brewers moved into Miller Park in 2001 and the Red Sox played a three-game series there in 2003. (The Red Sox played in Milwaukee more often before the Brewers switched to the National League in 1998.) The park is state of the art and the retractable roof is a necessity with the weather in Milwaukee. But with glass windows behind the outfield fences, you feel like you are in an airport terminal. Miller Park is another of the new parks that favors the hitters. Balls really carry there.

15

Minnesota

My first trip to the Twin Cities as a baseball broadcaster was in 1979 when I did television games for the Cleveland Indians. At that time, the Twins played in Metropolitan Stadium, "the Met," near the airport in Bloomington, Minnesota. It was a minor league ballpark that had been expanded for major league use when the Senators left Washington to move to Minnesota after the 1960 season.

The football Vikings played at the Met in the cold and the snow. I have never been to Minneapolis in the winter, but Bloomington was very cold in April, warm and pleasant in the spring and summer.

What made the Met a pleasure to visit was the pressroom—the best in baseball. The dining room was nicely decorated and both the service and the food were excellent. A wonderful sweet lady named Bea used to wait on all the visiting media people. Calvin Griffith owned the ballclub at the time and he spared no expense in wining and dining the media.

Sometime later, I found out that the Boston writers had set a dubious record: following a day game, they had stayed in the Met pressroom until 8 o'clock the following morning. After the service staff left, the writers were told to lock the door behind them.

The Twins moved to the Hubert Humphrey Metrodome in downtown Minneapolis (now at 34 Kirby Puckett Place) to start the 1982 season. The spot where home plate at the Met was is now marked with a plaque. It's in the amusement park area of the largest indoor shopping mall in the United States, the Mall of America.

The Metrodome is clean, climate controlled, and comfortable, but is not really a good facility. The dome is air-inflated, and what strikes you is the amount of force needed to open the doors, because of the air bubble. The place is built primarily for football—the Minnesota Vikings and the University of Minnesota—rather than baseball. Our sightlines from the visiting broadcast booth are good—we're right behind the plate. But the ballpark is antiseptic. When the Twins are not doing well, the place is nearly empty. When the Twins were good (1987–1988, 1991–1992, 2002), they packed them in.

The carpet at the Metrodome turns games there into carpet baseball, and a lot of strange things happen because of the rug. The Red Sox lost a number of games on bouncers that would have been outs on grass. I once saw an infield double on a high bouncing chopper, which took a funny bounce and then was misplayed. In day games, I've seen pop-ups lost (and therefore games lost) in the white roof. I've seen a number of walk-off home runs by Kent Hrbek and Kirby Puckett. I'll never forget a September 3, 1987, afternoon game. Calvin Schiraldi, making his first start with the Red Sox, pitched an outstanding game, striking out 11 in seven innings with no runs, no walks, and just three hits. The Sox had a 1-0 lead but lost it in the ninth inning and the game was tied. In the tenth inning, Wes Gardner pitched to Puckett. He hit the longest ball I have ever seen pulled. The ball went down the leftfield line into the second deck, a tremendous blast on a line drive. At Fenway, once a ball clears the Green Monster, you can't really see where it lands, but in Minnesota, you can see quite clearly. Twins 2, Red Sox 1.

That night, the Red Sox flew back to Boston on a commercial flight. I was sitting with Ken Coleman, a row in front of Wes Gardner. The plane hit some turbulence over Indiana, and it woke Gardner, who had been dozing. As his eyes opened, he asked, "What was that?" Ken said, "That was Kirby Puckett's home run flying by!"

It was always great to go to Minnesota to see my all-time favorite opposing player, Kirby Puckett. Kirby is a guy who just loves the game, and that's what I love most about him. He can't wait to be there. Even at home games, he was the first player out on the field, ready for early batting practice almost every day. He greeted almost everybody by name.

Kirby is the only person who calls ESPN's Peter Gammons "Petey." Kirby knows the names of all the opposing players, down to the 25th man. He treated clubhouse personnel the same way he treated superstars. Kirby always had a bounce in his step and a smile on his face. I always liked interviewing Kirby.

The first time I had him on the air was in a postgame interview in 1984. He had had a game-winning hit against the Red Sox. I barely knew him. Throughout the interview he kept referring to me as "Tony"—"Yes, Tony . . ." "Well, Tony . . ." I chuckled but I didn't correct him on the air. But for some time thereafter, our engineer Wayne Selly called me "Tony Castigliony."

When I saw Kirby the next day, I told him what had happened. He said, "I called you Tony? I'm sorry, Joe-Joe." I've been Joe-Joe ever since.

Some time after he retired because he had lost most of the vision in his right eye, I asked him about the glaucoma. He told me, "You will never see me down." Here's a kid who grew up in the toughest projects of Chicago, who was always told that at 5 foot 8 inches he was too small to play in the big leagues. He hit no home runs in 1984, his first year in the majors. In 1986, he hit 31. Now he's a Hall of Famer.

Puckett had some legal difficulties in 2003 but he was acquitted on all charges.

◆ ● ◆

Arquimedez Pozo, a nice little infielder from the Dominican Republic told me, in his limited English, that his family called him "Chimi." He had a grand slam at the Metrodome on July 28, 1996, but the Red Sox lost 9-8.

So we had him lined up to do the postgame show. Usually, Jerry and I stay in the broadcast booth after the game while we do the game recap and scoreboard reports. We pay the clubhouse attendant to hook up a microphone for whichever player we want for the postgame show. He gives the player a headset, and even though we can't see the player, we can talk with the player during a commercial before we go on the air.

We asked to interview Pozo, because of his grand slam and we were told he's ready. Once we went on the air, I said something like, "And here he is, Arquimedez Pozo, who hit the grand slam for the Red Sox." Then I hear, as our listeners all over New England did, "No, this is the clubhouse kid. Pozo says he doesn't speak English so he's not coming on." So we finished the postgame show without a postgame guest. After a big league career consisting of 26 games (one with the Mariners and 25 with the Red Sox), Pozo went to play in Japan.

◆ ● ◆

Roger Clemens recorded his first major league win in Bloomington on May 20, 1984.

On July 9, 1995, Tim Wakefield nearly pitched a no-hitter in Minnesota, but in the eighth inning, Jeff Reboulet broke it up with a grounder up the middle. Wakefield also flirted with another no-hitter in Tampa Bay on June 10, 2001. He pitched eight no-hit innings. Randy Winn broke it up leading off the ninth.

The ballpark is known as the "Homerdome," but it was hard to homer in parts of the park. Leftfield is long down the line, 343 feet. There was a Plexiglas barrier in left center that made homers very difficult until it was removed in the late 1990s. You could homer there more easily if you pulled the ball into the giant baggie in rightfield, which is now only 327 feet down the line.

When the Twins draw well, the fans can be extremely noisy, accentuated by the fact that you are indoors.

The Red Sox always seem to draw well when they visit the Twins, perhaps because the Minneapolis Millers used to be a Red Sox affiliate. Carl Yastrzemski played there. Gene Mauch was the manager. George Brophy, the general manager of the Millers and later a major league scout, became a good friend of mine. We used to enjoy going to the Metrodome to visit with Calvin Griffith's half brothers, Billy and Jimmy Robertson. When the Twins first moved to Minnesota, Jimmy helped promote the team by bringing copies of Macmillan's *Baseball Encyclopedia* to many sports bars around town to help settle bets and arguments.

The Twins became less family and more corporate after Calvin Griffith sold the team in 1984. But I still like going to the Twin Cities, and I especially like to spend time with my good friend, Herb Carneal, the "Voice of the Twins" since 1962, their second season in Minnesota. Herb worked in Syracuse, too, and we met in 1979.

His sign on "Hi, everybody, I'm Herb Carneal" is well known throughout the upper Midwest. Herb is from Virginia and still retains a southern twang to his voice.

When Herb was at WSYR in Syracuse, he was assigned to do a Bucknell-Colgate game, and arrived at the Colgate Inn in Hamilton, New York, on a Friday. He prepared his spotting charts in India ink. When he returned to Syracuse the next day, he realized that he had left his bottle of India ink at the Inn. The next year, he was assigned to do another game at Colgate and was given the same room. There, on the desk, right where he had left it, was his bottle of India ink. Not a lot of traffic flowing through Hamilton.

Herb and his late wife Kathy were engaged during the seventh inning stretch of a Springfield Cubs game he was broadcasting in 1951 in Springfield, Massachusetts. Herb gave Kathy an engagement ring during a commercial break.

Herb is a great storyteller. Kathy loved baseball and could remember every player who was with the Orioles when Herb did their games, and every player with the Twins. She traveled with Herb on most road trips, and always wore her Minnesota Twins jewelry. Nobody loved baseball more than Kathy Carneal. She was a great host, and when Jan traveled with me to Minnesota in 1998, she took Jan all around the city. Everybody loved her. When she passed away in 2000, Kirby Puckett was very consoling to Herb, as was the entire Twins family.

Herb has had a string of partners over the years including John Gordon, known for his long pregame shows, and for arriving at the ballpark about seven hours before game time. (I usually get there about three hours before game time.) John is a lot of fun. He loves to give the scores of minor league teams, such as the Fort Wayne Wizards, and the New Britain Rock Cats. John's home run call, "Touch 'em all, Kirby Puckett" or "Touch 'em all, Don Mattingly" became rather well known.

Peg has been with the Twins since they have been in Minnesota. She serves hotdogs and sausage to the broadcasters. She comes by our booth with ice water in the third inning, just when we need it.

When I'm in Minnesota, I like to visit with my friend Tom Ryther. I worked with Tom at Channel 3 in Cleveland for a few years. He was on the air in Minnesota for more than 20 years with two different stations, before he was fired in 1991. He filed an age discrimination suit and about eight years later he was awarded over a million dollars. I think it's a real landmark when a broadcaster can win an age discrimination suit.

Tom has taken me to such places as Lake Minnetonka, home of Hiawatha, just west of Minneapolis. Minnesota's nickname is "Land of 10,000 Lakes," but that's something of an understatement. There are more than 12,000 lakes in Minnesota larger than five acres. I love to see them. We go boating occasionally, and to a number of casinos, including one in Wisconsin.

Tom is a Jesse James historian, and he's driven with me to Northfield, Minnesota, to see the bank that the James Gang robbed on 1881. A skeleton, said to have belonged to one of the gang members, is on display. Some of the gang members were killed or wounded in the aftermath of that bank robbery. The town looks like an 1880s Western town.

I also like to visit Stillwater, Minnesota, where Cole Younger, a member of the James gang, was imprisoned. There are some great antique stores in the town, right across the St. Croix River from Hudson, Wisconsin, where the Riverside Restaurant serves excellent Walleye Pike, a Great Lakes fish that I really enjoy.

Stillwater is the home of the Lowell Inn, a beautiful old place that also serves excellent walleye.

We hire engineers in each city the team visits, and some have been with us for years.

Wayne Selly, one of our engineers, used to be a DJ. He was known as Wayne Anthony on the air. He has a deep voice and melodious tones. Wayne works as the engineer for some of the visiting radio broadcasters at the Metrodome. He connects our headphones and microphones to the soundboard that is fed via satellite to our flagship station, now WEEI in Boston, which also feeds our broadcast to the 60 or so stations on the Red Sox network throughout New England, such as WPRO in Providence and WTIC in Hartford. Wayne is employed by our network. In addition to being a real professional, he is fun to be with.

Wayne has taken us out on his boat, *The Radio Wave*, on the St. Croix, and docks it just south of St. Paul in Hastings, Minnesota, on a little inlet off the Mississippi. You can actually see the line of demarcation between the St. Croix and the Mississippi right in the water. The muddy Mississippi is joined by the clear St. Croix. It is very picturesque, probably the most beautiful river I've ever seen in the United States.

Another highlight of my trips to Minnesota was hearing the voice of Bob Casey, the public address announcer at Metropolitan Stadium and at the Metrodome. He is the only public address announcer in the majors who works at field level. He has a little booth right behind home plate. This, of course, is an open invitation to the players to play practical jokes on him, such as locking him in the booth or putting shaving cream on his headset.

Casey's first season was 1951, when he was with the Minneapolis Millers, the Giants's AAA affiliate in the American Association. Willie Mays started the season with the Millers that year before being called up to the Giants. (He was hitting .477 at the time, with 30 home runs in 35 games.) One of Bob's most memorable player introductions is for "Kirbyyyyyyyyyyyyyyyyyyyyyyyyyyyyyyyy Puckett." At each game, he also reminds fans that "There will be noooooooooooooooooooooooooo smoking in the Metrodome!" Players from every club in baseball love to imitate Bob's unique vocal stylings.

Bob used to work for Bob Short, who was involved in Minnesota sports for a long time. Short later owned the second Washington Senators franchise, which moved to Texas to become the Rangers. Short was the chairman of the Democratic National Committee. Bob Casey worked at hotels for Bob Short, including the Leamington Hotel in Minneapolis where I used to stay with the Indians. The hotel was noted for its cheese beer soup, which was excellent. The hotel once posted a sign which said: "For Your Convenience, There Are No Bellhops." I understood that there were no bellhops, but I still don't understand how that was for my convenience. The hotel has since been demolished.

In later years, the Red Sox stayed at the Hyatt, which was very nice, the Marriott, and then the Radisson, now the Grand Hotel, a beautiful boutique hotel with the best fitness club in the league.

We used to visit a restaurant near the Metrodome called "Scott's," owned by Ray Scott, the Voice of the Twins, the Super Bowl, and the Green Bay Packers games. He was known for his brevity on the air. Ken Coleman was, I think, the first to use a very economical style while doing football games. I met Scott in the restaurant one night after a game, and I said, "Ray, you got to do it for me please." So he did his famous call: "Starr . . . Dowler . . . touchdown!"

Former Red Sox manager Joe Morgan, one of the most colorful men I know, used to use the expression, "Catch you in St. Paul." Minneapolis had its minor league team, the Millers, and St. Paul had a team, the Saints, a Dodger affiliate in the American Association. Joe was with minor league teams in Louisville and Atlanta, and they would play in the Twin Cities. The players would take a cab from the hotel, and say, "Take me to the ballpark in Minneapolis." When they got to Nicollet Park, they would stiff the cabdriver and dash into the stadium, saying, "Catch you in St. Paul." That has been a Joe Morgan expression ever since.

Ciotti's is a terrific Italian restaurant in downtown Minneapolis. Murray's, an old-fashioned expensive steakhouse is also excellent, but my favorite restaurant in Minneapolis is Loon, near the Target Center, home of the Timberwolves in the NBA. Loon, a sports bar, is justly noted for its wild rice soup. That's one of the highlights of any trip to Minneapolis.

I am not a shopper, but we have a lot of time to kill on the road, so if there is a St. Croix store near our hotel, I make a point to visit it. Minneapolis has a good one. I buy my sweaters there, usually on our second trip of the season to Minneapolis. The sweaters are usually on sale then, sometimes at half price. The downtown store is run by a lovely woman named Karen. The factory is just a few hours south of Minneapolis.

St. Croix also opened a store in Boston, and since I actually wore their sweaters, I did a promotion for them in *Boston Magazine*. St. Croix gave me a nice clothing allowance for free sweaters. Because my job does not require a jacket and tie, which would be very uncomfortable for sitting and broadcasting for three hours a night, sweaters have become my clothing trademark, especially on the road. My fashion statement is the St. Croix sweater. They are beautiful and comfortable, though they can be somewhat pricey.

16

New York

The first game I ever saw at Yankee Stadium was September 13, 1953. My parents drove me down the Merritt Parkway from our home in Connecticut in the back of our 1953 blue Oldsmobile. We stopped at a Howard Johnson's, then got on the Major Deegan Expressway, which went directly to the stadium. It was the Yankees vs. the Cleveland Indians on Jerry Coleman Day. Jerry was my first baseball hero, followed by Gil McDougald, then Mickey Mantle.

The game was played on Coleman's first day back from service as a captain in the U.S. Marines in Korea. The Yankees won, but Coleman did not have a hit. Jerry is now a broadcaster for the San Diego Padres. Every time I see him in San Diego or in Boston, I remind him that he was my first hero, in the first game I ever saw. He still says that he should not have played in that game. His weight was down to 135 pounds and he felt terrible. "Casey Stengel made me play because it was my day, I went hitless and made an error." But the Yankees won 6-3 on their way to another World Championship.

I was a Yankee fan as a kid, and I saw many games at Yankee Stadium—"old" Yankee Stadium as it is still sometimes referred to. There is no "new" Yankee Stadium, as there is in Chicago, with old Comiskey Park and new Comiskey Park (now U.S. Cellular Field)—two different buildings. "Old" Yankee Stadium refers to the way the stadium was configured before 1974. During the 1974 and 1975 seasons, the stadium was completely refurbished, and the Yankees played their home games at Shea Stadium in Queens, home of the New York Mets. (Before "The Big A," the Angels home stadium opened in 1966, they played their games at Dodger Stadium for three years, but their broadcasters never called it that. They referred to it by its geographic name, Chavez Ravine.) The Yankees returned to Yankee Stadium in 1976, and proceeded to win the American League pennant. But, by then, the dimensions and ambiance of the place had changed. No more monuments on the field in center; no more façade all around the stadium; no more "Death Valley" in left centerfield, although it is still quite deep.

◆ ● ◆

I went to Yankee Stadium with my Little League team, the Botwinik Brothers (named for a factory that sponsored the team) and we sat in the mezzanine.

Then we went with Annie and Tony Iacobacci. Annie was my father's cousin. Tony was born on Mott Street, and they were both tremendous Yankee fans. They lived in a one-bedroom apartment on Dongan Place in upper Manhattan. My brother Frank and I would take the train from New Haven to 125th Street in Harlem, and Annie and Tony met us there. Then we took the subway to Yankee Stadium to watch the first game of a doubleheader. Frank and I wanted to stay for the second game, but Annie and Tony wanted to take us to dinner at a nice Italian restaurant, either to Mario's on Arthur Avenue in the heart of what is still the Italian neighborhood in the Bronx, or to Stella D'Oro, which became a favorite of mine, on Broadway between 237th and 238th Streets. That's where the Stella D'Oro cookie factory is.

We bought our tickets right at game time, for $1.30 each, and happily sat behind the rightfield foul pole in the third deck. We always hoped that Mickey Mantle would hit one there.

I also remember going to the Polo Grounds in 1955. The only time I saw the New York Giants play there, they were playing the Brooklyn Dodgers. I went with my uncles, Charlie and Bob Schwab. Jim "Junior" Gilliam led off the game with a home run, as the Dodgers won 8-5. The highlight was when Giants shortstop Alvin Dark fouled a ball into the upper deck and Uncle Bob, who later coached high-school baseball in Southbury, Connecticut, caught the ball against his belt buckle and gave me the ball—my first baseball souvenir. I still have it.

Later I went to the Polo Grounds when the Mets played there in 1962 to 1963. It had a unique shape, variously called bathtub or horseshoe. Never been another one like it. A fly ball would be hit down the line, the leftfielder would camp under it, then the ball would graze the overhang where the out-of-town scoreboard was—home run! The seats were uncomfortable, and the bathrooms were inadequate. Built in 1911, it was a relic of the 19th century, but retains a place in baseball history as the only stadium to be home of three major league teams: the Giants, the Yankees (who played there before Yankee Stadium was built), and the Mets.

I saw Mickey Mantle, my favorite, and Roger Maris play in 1961, and I recall Johnny Blanchard hit home runs in four straight at bats at Yankee Stadium in 1961.

By 1967, I was working in Westfield, Massachusetts, and I had shifted my loyalties. I was no longer a Yankee fan. In the year of the Red Sox "Impossible Dream," I became a Red Sox fan.

I attended a 20-inning game at Yankee Stadium on August 29, 1967, the second game of a doubleheader. By the end of the 19th inning, it was 1 or 2 in the morning. In the bottom of the 20th inning, with Boston and New York tied at 3, Horace Clarke singled in the winning run for the Yankees.

I never saw a World Series game at Yankee Stadium until 1996 when I went to Games One and Two of the Yankees-Braves Series.

The first time I came to Yankee Stadium as a broadcaster was in 1979 with the Indians. By then, the dimensions of the stadium had been changed. Left center still had that unique bulge, but it was not as pronounced as it had been before the renovations. The stadium looked beautiful. There were no more poles to block your view. My brother Charlie joined me at the stadium. Charlie had graduated from Yale in 1977. He was, at the time, the only Yale pitcher to beat Harvard two years in a row. Charlie was a first-year medical student at Columbia. He was on vacation, and also traveled with us to Baltimore. With the

Indians, he hooked up with manager Jeff Torborg. Even though he had not pitched in a year or so since college, he convinced Jeff that he could still get the ball over the plate, so he pitched some batting practice for the Indians.

He was assigned to pitch to the extra men, the nonregulars. The first batter he faced was Cliff Johnson, all 6 foot 4 inches and 224 pounds of him. Charlie's first pitch was right behind Johnson's head. At the time, I was standing on the steps of the Yankees dugout speaking with out-fielder Darryl Jones, a friend of mine who had a very brief cup of coffee (just 18 games) with the Yankees.

After a few more batters, Charlie settled down and started throwing strikes. The team started taking him deep. Indians coach Dave Garcia, who became the Indians manager later that year, said, "Hey, your brother throws good!" But Charlie was not invited to throw batting practice again. So Charlie went back to his medical studies at Columbia. He is now a plastic surgeon.

In the first game of that series, the Indians were down 1-0 in the top of the ninth with runners on first and third with nobody out. They could not score a run and lost 1-0. They were swept in the series.

I returned to Yankee Stadium as a Red Sox broadcaster in July 1983 for a four-game wrap-around series over the July 4 weekend, the last series before the All-Star break. It was sweltering—about 98 degrees. The Red Sox won on Saturday and had won two of the three games. The next day, my father went to the game with my sons, Tom and Duke, and my nephew, Tyler Peterson. They were going to give me a ride back to New Haven for the All-Star break. Before the game, I got to visit with Mel Allen, who was calling games for the Yankees on cable television. That was the first time I had met him. When I was a boy, he was my favorite sportscaster. John Tudor was pitching for Boston against Dave Righetti of the Yankees. There were no particularly difficult plays, except for Steve Kemp's grab of a foul ball in rightfield. The last Boston batter was Wade Boggs. Although he won his first batting championship that year with a .361 average, he couldn't get a hit that day against Righetti. Nobody else could, either, and Righetti had a no-hitter, the first Yankee no-hitter since Don Larsen's perfect game in the 1956 World Series.

In May 1986, the Red Sox had a three-game series with the Yankees in New York. In the final game of that series, Don Baylor hit a gap shot to left center to put Boston ahead in the eighth inning. The Sox went on to win, as they swept the series. I knew it would be a good year for the team. Don was our guest on the postgame show, and he was very happy not only to win, but to beat the Yankees. He had been with the Yankees the previous three years, and didn't think he had been treated fairly by George Steinbrenner, the team's principal owner. So he had some scores to settle now that he was playing for the Red Sox.

◆ ● ◆

On June 26, 1987, with Roger Clemens pitching for Boston at New York, the Sox had a 9-0 lead in the third inning and lost the game. That was one of the low moments at Yankee Stadium.

I recall another game in New York, on September 23, 1988, during the "Morgan Magic" spell. The Sox were down 9-5 after six innings but they kept chipping away, with Dennis Lamp pitching well in relief. Finally, pinch hitter Spike Owen hit a bounding ball, a two-hopper up the middle. Willie Randolph, the Yankee second baseman, and shortstop Wayne Tolleson crossed, the ball went between them. Two runners scored, and the Red Sox hung on for a great 10-9 comeback win.

The next day, the Sox thought they were going to pull off another win. The game was tied at four in the ninth when the Yankees had the winning run at third. With two out, Willie Randolph hit the ball to Jody Reed at short, but the ball hit him in the chest and knocked him down. Claudell Washington scored from third, game over. Yankees win.

The Red Sox won the American League East championship that year to cap the Morgan Miracle, leaving the Yankees three and a half games back.

In 1991, the Red Sox had a 5-0 lead on Memorial Day at Yankee Stadium. Danny Darwin, a good pitcher, was on the mound. That day he gave up three solo homers. Jeff Reardon started the ninth inning, With the score 5-3, Hensley Meulens and Kevin Maas singled and Mel Hall, who had already homered, hit a 2-2 pitch for a game-winning three-run homer.

I didn't know Hall, but I didn't like his body language. He strutted to home plate. A one-dimensional hitter, but dangerous nonetheless. Reardon hung a curveball and Hall smacked it down the rightfield line for a three-run, walk-off home run. Yankees 6, Red Sox 5.

◆ ● ◆

Bob Starr, who was broadcasting Red Sox games with me at the time, looked over at me, and said, "This was a tough loss for the Red Sox, but especially for my partner, who looks like he's just been harpooned." That's exactly what I looked like, and what I felt like. It was a very tough loss to swallow.

After the game, a friend offered me a ride back to the hotel in Manhattan, swearing that his car was air-conditioned. I went with him. His car was not air-conditioned, as I found out while we were stuck in traffic. But it did indeed have a little air vent. It was a miserable day.

◆ ● ◆

The angriest I have ever been in New York was on September 18, 1993. Jan was at the game with my cousin Annie Iacobacci, who was in her 70s at the time, and our friends Jeffrey Lyons and his daughter Hannah. Greg Harris was pitching in relief with a 3-1 lead, two outs, and a runner on first. Mike Stanley was at the plate for the Yankees. Harris set and just as he released the ball, a fan ran out on the field in foul territory. Third base umpire Tim Welke held up his hands to call time. Stanley hit a fly ball to leftfield, and Greenwell made the catch. Everybody thought that the game was over and that the Red Sox had won 3-1. But no. The game was *not* over because "time" had been called. The at bat continued. Stanley singled on the next pitch and three batters later, Harris surrendered a 2-RBI hit to Don Mattingly. Yankees won 4-3.

I don't remember ever being as angry as I was at the kid who had run on the field and cost the Red Sox that win.

In 1995, the Red Sox played well against the Yankees as they won the Eastern Division crown by seven games.

It always hurts to lose a game at Yankee Stadium, especially late, whether by a walk-off home run or otherwise. The public address system

plays Frank Sinatra singing "New York, New York" four or five times
while fans are leaving and I'm trying to do a wrap-up and postgame show.

◆ ● ◆

I love the Museum of Radio and TV in New York. I sat there one day
and listened to Mel Allen's call of Game Seven of the 1952 World Series
in which the Yankees beat the Dodgers. I've taken part in seminars there,
too. One was a seminar with author Curt Smith, Harry Kalas, the
Phillies broadcaster, John Sterling, who broadcasts Yankees games, Gary
Cohen of the Mets, Bob Wolff, who did the Senators games in
Washington, then cable sports for a Long Island TV station, and is in the
Hall of Fame, and me. That was a lot of fun.

I've really enjoyed the Ellis Island tour in New York harbor. I found
my grandfather Guiseppe Castiglione's name there. My sister-in-law
Linda had paid the fee to have his name inscribed there. He came to
America through Ellis Island in 1894 from Messina, Sicily. My grandmother came over a year or two later. She was also from Messina, but
she met my grandfather in New Haven, and they married there.

Pino's restaurant was one of my favorites in New York. It was on
34th Street between Park and Lexington Avenues, walking distance from
the Grand Hyatt, where the Red Sox used to stay in New York. Pino's was
owned by former Red Sox pitcher Jerry Casale. Whenever you were in
Pino's for more than ten minutes, Jerry would play you the tape (originally
made on a wire recorder) of Phil Rizzuto calling his home run (one of four
in his career) off Bob Turley of the Yankees on September 7, 1959—one
of three homers in that inning. Jerry's homer was a tremendous blast
over the light tower in left centerfield. In 1959, Jerry won 13 games as a
rookie, which is still the Red Sox record.

We went to Pino's with Al Nipper one day in 1984, the year he beat the
Yankees four times. That was particularly satisfying to Nipper, who always
remembered what Phil Rizzuto said about him on the air: "Who is this
guy? He couldn't break a pane of glass with his fastball." Roger Clemens
has been to Pino's as have former managers Joe Morgan, Jimy Williams,
and Grady Little, and former general manager Dan Duquette. My photograph was on the wall. Pino's closed in December 2003.

Pirates catcher Manny Sanguillen talks to Joe at Forbes Field in Pittsburgh, May 1970. *Photo by Mickey Krumpak*

Joe interviews Julius Erving at the NBA All-Star Game, Richfield Coliseum, February 1981.

Joe, Kate, Duke, Tom, and sister-in-law Pat in Tucson, Arizona, 1982.

Joe and Bob Feller, TV partner, Hi Corbett Field, Tucson, Arizona, 1982.

Joe, Andre and Gail Thornton, and Jan at Joe's Red Sox send-off party in Solon, Ohio, February 1983.

Duke, Jan, Tom, and Kate at the Holiday Inn, Winter Haven, Florida, during their first Spring Training with the Red Sox.

In the old booth at Fenway, 1986. *Photo by Tim Samway*

Joe and Ken Coleman, Fenway booth, circa 1986.

To Joe Castiglione
With best wishes,

Ronald Reagan

Joe meets President Ronald Reagan during Red Sox visit to the White House,
September 10, 1986.

With rookie Mark McGwire at the Oakland Coliseum, 1987. *Photo by Tim Samway*

Joe and Carl Yastrzemski on Yaz Day in Fenway booth, 1989. *Photo by Tim Samway*

Joe Morgan and Joe tape a manager's show at Fenway in 1990. *Photo by Tim Samway*

Joe and partner Bob Starr, 1990.

With daughter Kate (then 12), counting pitches in Fenway booth, 1992.

Joe and Kate, Father-Son-Daughter Game, 1992.

At Fenway with Roger Clemens, 1997.

Joe at Red Sox Fantasy Camp, Fort Myers, Florida, 1998.

Joe interviews Jimy Williams at Fenway in 1998.

Jerry Coleman (Joe's first hero) and Joe at Jacobs Field, Cleveland, 1999. Then-Cleveland general manager John Hart in background.

Joe with the original Jimmy of the Jimmy Fund—Mr. and Mrs. Einar Gustafson, 1999.

Joe and George Grande, Cincinnati Reds broadcaster—two natives of Hamden, Connecticut.

At Commerce (Oklahoma) City Hall on Mickey Mantle pilgrimage, April 2000.

Three Italian broadcasters—Jerry Trupiano, Joe Garagiola, and Joe in Fenway booth, 2001. *Photo by Tim Samway*

Joe and Jerry Trupiano at Fenway. *Photo by Tim Samway*

Joe's hero, Hall of Fame broadcaster, Mel Allen, and Joe at Yankee Stadium. *Photo by Tim Samway*

Baltimore Oriole scout Deacon Jones and Joe at Fenway in 2002. *Photo by Tim Samway*

Chrissie Geppi and Brian Daubach (Joe's best scouting job) were married in December 2003.

With another Hall of Famer, Carlton Fisk, at Fenway.

Joe and Uri Berenguer—Jimmy Fund patient, now Red Sox Spanish broadcaster—at Fenway.

Red Sox TV broadcaster, Don Orsillo, Joe's former student at Northeastern and former radio booth intern, capsized his kayak in Lake Union in Seattle in August 2002. *Photo by Michael Narracci*

Jerry won 17 and 19 games at AAA in 1955–1956 and expected to be called up to the Red Sox. He was probably better than any pitcher the Sox had at that time, about 1957. But he told me that general manager Joe Cronin and manager Pinky Higgins called him into their office one day to tell him that he was being sent to the San Francisco Seals because they have a lot of Italians there.

Jerry finally came up to the Red Sox in late 1958 after almost two years in military service. Those two years he spent in the military did not count as major league service, and to this day, he is 35 days short of qualifying for a big league pension.

We also like Bricco's on West 56th Street, near my son Duke's house, for great Italian food. Jeff Lyons likes to take us to Trattoria Del'Arte on 7th Avenue near 57th Street, across from Carnegie Hall. Fifty-seventh Street and 7th Avenue is the center of the universe for Jeffrey. He lives there. Seeing Jeffrey is always a highlight of our visits to New York. He's the entertainment critic for WNBC-TV, and a lifelong Red Sox fan. We have gone to a number of movie screenings with him. Jeff has been with us in the broadcast booth at Yankee Stadium, at Jacobs Field in Cleveland, at Comiskey Park in Chicago, and at Fenway, too, and it's always fun to see him. He passes us interesting notes during the games.

The visitors' broadcast booth at Yankee Stadium, remodeled in 1976, is not the greatest. It's a three-tiered booth with very little room. In fact, there is barely room for Jerry and me in the front row. Our engineer, Carl Infantino, one of the best, sits behind us, and there are two seats behind him. Usually it's Jeffrey and my daughter-in-law Kiki who sit there. We're off to the side, slightly up the third base side, not behind the plate. So we occasionally cannot see the balls hit into the leftfield corner.

I enjoy going to Monument Park at Yankee Stadium, to see the plaques and monuments to my heroes when I was a kid.

I played in a few media games at Yankee Stadium and I was thrilled to run out to leftfield.

During one of those games, I hit a bounding ball up the middle—one of those 89 hoppers that sneaked through the infield, and I was able to drive in a run.

Those games involved mostly writers, with a few of us electronic types thrown in. We used to have home and home media games at Fenway and Yankee Stadium, and I also played in media games at the Kingdome in Seattle, and Cheney Stadium in Tacoma, Washington. I never realized how big the outfield at Yankee Stadium is until I had to run in and out.

The people we see regularly at Yankee Stadium, like clubhouse guys Lou Cucuzza and Lou Jr., are always very nice to us. I always feel the presence of baseball ghosts and traditions at Yankee Stadium—Babe Ruth, Joe DiMaggio, Mickey Mantle. Of course, Yankee Stadium is not the most convenient or comfortable place to get to. I usually take the subway, but occasionally I take the team bus. When we get to the stadium, there is a group of fans behind police wooden horses. They're like caged animals yelling at the visiting players. One night after a game when I was with Cleveland, as our bus approached the stadium, a fan lay down in front of the bus and we could not move. He had to be carried off.

On another occasion in 2000, a fan dived out of the seats onto the screen behind home plate. He stayed there, inert, as though he were dead or at least unconscious. Everyone was going wild. We were upset and nervous, expressing our sympathy on the air. Stadium security people were trying to find a way to remove the body from the screen, which was not designed to support such a weight. All of a sudden, the guy got up. He was neither dead nor unconscious—just trying to get attention. His dangerous stunt had disrupted the game. You never know when a fan is going to interfere with the game at Yankee Stadium.

In 1986, we took our children to New York. We got up and looked out the window of the Grand Hyatt Hotel. The kids were impressed by the huge number of taxis lined up by the hotel. We had an off day and we went to dinner at Asti's, near city hall. The singing waiters recited the menu as though it were an opera. After the food was served, the waiters put on a show dressed as animals. As they paraded around the restaurant, they dressed up the kids in animal costumes, and they joined the parade. They had a great time.

I enjoy delis in New York, particular the neighborhood delis. Our hangout has become Foley's (named for veteran sportswriter Red Foley) on West 33rd Street. The owner, Shaun Clancy, is from Ireland but knows more baseball than almost any American. Shaun is a Yankee fan and a close friend of Duke's. Shaun has been to nearly every ballpark in the major leagues. Shaun has seen Red Sox series in Kansas City, Oakland, Chicago, Boston, and New York, and even went to St. Petersburg for a Tampa Bay game.

We used to stay at the old Sheraton Hotel on 7th Avenue between 56th and 57th Streets. When I was with the Indians and Dave Garcia was the manager, he didn't like it because the hotel had only one chair in the lobby. Dave was one of the great lobby sitters of all time. He used to get up early, have breakfast, then by nine o'clock he'd sit in the lobby until it was time to go to the ballpark, usually about noon.

Later we moved to the Grand Hyatt. The bar and the restaurant in the hotel are very expensive. Now, we stay at the Westin Times Square, a good location.

We also like Rolf's between 21st and 22nd Streets and Third Avenue. Rolf's is German, and Jan likes German food. The restaurant is decorated in various themes—Christmas, autumn, even a Madonna theme. The prices and the ambiance are good.

Yolanda's is also a favorite restaurant. Jeffrey and Douglas Lyons went there with us before a game in the 2000 Yankees-Mets World Series. It's near the Grand Concourse on 149th Street in the Bronx. The eggplant is excellent. The owner, Aniello Calisi (called Neil), caters the Yankee clubhouse with Italian food. He occasionally arranges a car to take us from the restaurant to the stadium. Jeff Idelson, former public relations director for the Yankees, told me about Yolanda's. He used to go there with Yankee executive Arthur Richman for lunch. When Jeff, who is now a vice president of the Hall of Fame, is in New York, he still eats there. Sometimes he stops on the way back to Cooperstown to bring an Italian dinner home for his family. Neil Calisi is a very good friend and we socialize with him and his wife Maria, who, like Neil, hails from Ponza, an island off the Italian west coast.

We also love to visit Greenwich Village and Monte's at Bleecker and McDougal Streets. It is a wonderful Italian restaurant frequented by Yankee executives. We had several large dinner parties there. The food is great and the owner, Giovanni, makes it special. Giovanni kisses just about everybody—when they enter the restaurant and when they leave—male or female. Giovanni, who is from Milan, has even parked our car for us when we have driven to Monte's—no small feat on the narrow streets of the Village. He is his own valet service.

Jeffrey Lyons has taken us to Mickey Mantle's a number of times. I've seen some well-known people there. Of course if you're in New York City on a Tuesday afternoon between May and August, you can see Jeff play softball in Central Park in the New York Show Business League. The way to Jeffrey's heart is to watch him play softball. I remember Al Bumbry watched him play once. Al had Broadway tickets whenever he wanted them after that. Jeff was grateful. Jeff is able to get Broadway tickets for Jan and me when we're in New York. Of course now that Duke and Kiki live in Manhattan, we visit more often, especially during the offseason.

Jan loves the theater. She finds Yankee Stadium exciting, but she'll usually go to one game during a series in New York, and try to see a few shows. Jeff was able to get us tickets for many big hits including "42nd Street." Jan had a ticket to see Judd Hirsch in "A Thousand Clowns" on a Wednesday afternoon. Jan was going by herself because I was doing the game. There was rain in the forecast, but it was not raining. The Yankees must have been short of pitching or else there was just a small gate that day, because the game was called off at about 11:30. I called Jeffrey, and he was able to get me another ticket. After the show, Jeff took us to the ESPN Zone in Times Square.

I love to walk around New York City—it's a great walking town. Times Square, 42nd Street, Fifth Avenue, Madison Avenue. I've walked many times from the Grand Hyatt to Jeff and Duke's neighborhood near Carnegie Hall on West 57th Street. I used to want to work in New York but I never had the opportunity to do so. Now Duke works in New York and has done so since he was 26.

Let me add a word about the Blohards, the Benevolent and Honorable Ancient Honorable Order of Red Sox Diehards—a group of Red Sox fans in New York. They have luncheon meetings and a player or front office executive attends and speaks. The lunches can be fun but some of the Blohards are irreverent.

17

Oakland and San Francisco

I've broadcast over 100 games from the Oakland Alameda County Coliseum, now known as Network Associates Coliseum. I first went there in 1979 when I was with the Indians. To this day, I still carry an umpire's indicator with me because of my experiences in Oakland. Charley Finley owned the A's at the time, and the team was drawing crowds of about 1,000. They had Dixieland bands to entertain the fans, but at some games, the members of the band outnumbered the paid admissions. The scoreboard didn't always work, so I could not see balls and strikes or outs. That's when I got my own indicator to keep the stats accurate.

The A's had a very bad club that year, finishing dead last in the American League West with a 54-108 record. They won just one third of their games, finishing 34 games behind the Angels.

The only bright spot on the team was Rickey Henderson's arrival from the minor leagues. The A's did manage to sweep the Indians in a three game series. Mike Norris pitched a beauty for Oakland.

When the Walter Haas family bought the A's from Finley in 1980, the Coliseum was refurbished. They were still in charge when I went to Oakland with the Red Sox in 1983. In the 1980s, the A's were dominant at home against the Red Sox. The most memorable games were the playoffs of 1988 and 1990. The A's swept the Red Sox in both American League Championship Series 4-0.

What I remember about the final two games of the 1988 series in Oakland was that we didn't broadcast from our regular booth high behind the plate. We were assigned to do the game from directly behind the screen. We were on a makeshift platform. But we were closer to home plate than the pitcher's 60 foot 6 inches. Oakland leads the world in foul territory down the baselines, but there's not much foul ground behind the plate.

In 1988 after Bruce Hurst had lost Game Four of the Oakland Series, Bruce got off the plane and walked away, taking another flight home. He never wore a Boston uniform again, leaving as a free agent for San Diego.

I have a photograph of Mark McGwire and me on the field at Oakland in 1987—when he and José Canseco formed the "Bash Brothers." It's amazing how slim McGwire was. McGwire was a very impressive rookie. I thought that the A's with Sandy Alderson and the Walter Haas group made it a pleasant place to work. The Coliseum was a pleasant place to play—not as cold as at Candlestick Park on the other side of the Bay. Also, I noticed that late in the games, Boston fans frequently outnumbered Oakland fans, because Oakland fans tend to leave the park early.

For many years, the Red Sox stayed at the Oakland Hyatt Hotel by the airport. The area around the airport was a very quiet, almost desolate area—an industrial park. But over the years, it became a wild place with a lot of undesirables hanging around. The hotel was closed down and eventually demolished. The team moved to the Oakland Hilton, even closer to the airport. Later the Sox stayed at the Park 55 Hotel in San Francisco and later still at the San Francisco Marriott and the St. Francis Westin.

I don't find much to do in Oakland, but I love San Francisco, just across the bay. The restaurants in San Francisco are excellent, especially on Fisherman's Wharf. One of my favorites is Scoma's, which has long lines and high prices. But it's worth it. My old partner Bob Starr told me that if you mention Joe Torre's name, you get in quickly.

I also like Dante's New Tower of Pisa in North Beach. It has the best minestrone I've ever had. They bring a large bowl, and you can help yourself to two or three servings. The vegetables are wonderful, too. A lunch or dinner special consisting of minestrone, salad, and an entrée costs less than $11.

I was there once with Jan when a group of Hell's Angels came in. They told us that they wanted our table. I think they were trying to scare us. They did. But they were joking! Unfortunately, Dante's closed in 2003 but may reopen. However, its sister restaurant, Cappy's, in the same neighborhood has the same minestrone and a similar cuisine.

Dante's is named for its owner, Dante Benedetto, who coached the University of San Francisco baseball team for $1 a year for many years. Dante is a very interesting character who grew up in North Beach with Dominic and Joe DiMaggio. Dante told me that when they were kids, Dom and Joe's parents wanted their boys to forget about baseball—they should get *real* jobs. But when Joe came home to San Francisco after the 1936 season, his first year with the Yankees, he used his salary and his World Series winner's share to buy his parents a new home in the Marina section of San Francisco. After that, every kid in the neighborhood had a bat, a glove, and a ball under the Christmas tree.

North Beach was a haven for young, Italian ballplayers such as Dario Lodigiani and Tony Lazzeri.

Moose's is another excellent North Beach restaurant featuring fish and steak. I went there with Hank Greenwald, the longtime Yankees and Giants broadcaster, now with the A's. Moose's is right across from St. Peter and Paul's Church where Joe DiMaggio's funeral was held. Hank also took me to Perry's, a sports restaurant on Union Street.

North Beach is also home to a number of great pastry and coffee shops.

Kuleto's, on Powell Street downtown, has excellent appetizers and antipasto.

I've taken a number of players on the Alcatraz tour. We take the ferry over and see the old prison. There's a concrete ballfield on the prison grounds, with a short porch in left. Anyone with pull power to the left could have parked one in the bay.

I also like to visit the Haight-Ashbury neighborhood of San Francisco, home of "flower power" in the 1960s. It is not far from Golden Gate Park with its beautiful Japanese gardens. Kezar Stadium, where the '49ers played for many years, was nearby, too.

I like to cross the Golden Gate Bridge, or take the ferry to Sausalito, a lovely little seaside port. We stayed in Sausalito one year during the All-Star break at the Alta Mira—35 rooms and a great view of the Sausalito harbor, the San Francisco Bay, and the San Francisco skyline.

Jack Rogers was the traveling secretary for the Red Sox from 1969 to 1990. He was the best traveling secretary in baseball. He was also a terrific guy. As traveling secretary, he made sure that the hotel rooms were reserved, that the plane was waiting for us, that the buses from the airport to the hotel and from the hotel to the ballpark were all ready. His job was also to make sure that the players were at the ballpark on time and he helped them if trouble found them.

◆ ● ◆

Jan went to Sausalito in 1988 when we had an off day during the ALCS. Jack took the players' and broadcasters' wives to the Alta Mira for lunch.

The Casa Madrona restaurant, also in a hotel overlooking the Sausalito harbor, is another of my favorites.

The Spinnaker is a water view restaurant with excellent seafood.

There's an excellent sports art gallery in downtown Sausalito, the Mark Reuben Gallery. A beautiful woman named Lynn works there, and she knows more about sports than just about any businesswoman I've ever met. Lynn tells me that a number of ballplayers visit her gallery to purchase some of their great photographs of athletes. I bought photographs of Josh Gibson, Babe Ruth, and Mel Allen there and have them in my family room.

Right across the bay from Sausalito is the town of Tiburon, which has a lovely waterfront and interesting shops. We've taken the ferry from Tiburon to Angel Island, where we rented bikes to ride around the island. Angel Island is virtually uninhabited, and there is no auto traffic on the bike path.

The wine country north and east of San Francisco is truly delightful. I love the climate. We've toured both the large and the small vineyards. We rented bikes in Calestoga and rode through some of the smaller vineyards.

Once, we took the Napa Valley wine train, about 12 miles each way. The three-hour trip stops at a number of wineries and they serve a gourmet meal. The excursion is rather expensive, but it was an unforgettable experience.

South of San Francisco, I visited Stanford University in Palo Alto. A great Red Sox fan lives there—the Jeffrey Lyons of the West Coast. Bill Gould is a professor of law at Stanford Law School, and has served as an arbiter in a number of baseball arbitration cases. Bill served a six-year term as chairman of the National Labor Relations Board under President Clinton. Bill once passed up a speaking engagement so he could watch Marty Pattin pitch for the Red Sox. Bill has seen the Sox play all over the country, and he has timed a number of lectures in various cities after consulting the Red Sox travel schedule. We've seen Bill in Boston, Detroit, Anaheim, Seattle, Pittsburgh, and Cleveland, as well as in Oakland. Once, he flew back from a lecture in Milan so he could be back in Oakland for the Red Sox series there.

Bill Gould really knows the game, the players, and the history of the franchise. And Stanford is the most beautiful college campus I have ever seen. Even prettier than Colgate's. If you see it, you'll want to go there. The baseball field has a sunken diamond—top shelf.

◆ ● ◆

The Santa Cruz and Carmel areas are really beautiful. I've been there during a few All-Star breaks. There's a lovely inn in Carmel Highlands called The Tickled Pink. Wine and cheese before dinner, hot tubs nestled amongst the rooms that are built right into the hillside overlooking the ocean. The rooms also come with diaries to record your experiences. It's so romantic. It has one of the most beautiful views I've ever seen, overlooking the Pacific. It can be chilly, but it's gorgeous. It's about two hours from San Francisco. Mark Holtz, the late broadcaster for the Texas Rangers, went there with his wife Alice, and they told us about it.

The Pacific Coast Highway is beautiful as we drove down to Big Sur on the rocky coast. Just don't take your eyes off the road—and don't go over 30 miles an hour.

One time, we drove north from Los Angeles to San Francisco, and the highlight of the trip was stopping at San Simeon, the home of William Randolph Hearst, just north of Santa Barbara. We had to park quite a distance from the castle, then took a bus up the rocky cliff to the house. It's simply unbelievable. The swimming pool is one of the largest private pools ever built, and the view is spectacular.

One year, the Red Sox stayed at the Waterfront Plaza Hotel on Jack London Square in Oakland. I was having dinner there one night with Lou Gorman and Joe Giulliotti of the *Boston Herald*. We had a wonderful meal, and Lou was his usual, ebullient self. As usual, when we ate with Lou, who was then the Red Sox general manager, he picked up the tab. Suddenly, Lou was silent as we were about to leave. Reggie Jackson had just entered with a beautiful young woman. Reggie had just retired as an active player. Lou invited them to sit at our table and they did. Reggie never stopped talking, and we stayed during his entire meal. He told us the entire story of his career, paying virtually no attention to the young woman he was with, and virtually silencing Lou Gorman. A broadcaster, a reporter, and a general manager silenced by Reggie Jackson.

One of the highlights of our trips to Oakland is hearing the public address announcer at the Coliseum, Roy Steele. He has a great set of pipes. I understand Roy is a former minister. He announces play-by-play of the dot races on the scoreboard between innings. Trup, the engineer, and I would each put down a dollar and select the color we thought was going to win in each race. Trup accused me of knowing the winner in advance, but I never did.

When the Haas family ran the team, the concession stands at the stadium were very good. The Oakland Coliseum was one of the first stadiums to go beyond the usual ballpark fare of hotdogs, popcorn, peanuts, Cracker Jacks, and cotton candy.

When Finley owned the team, the press box food was Kentucky Fried Chicken almost every night. I got tired of it in a hurry, and would get something from the public stands.

The broadcast booths used to be down the third base side. Now, they are deep and pretty far from the plate, but we have a good view of the field.

18

Seattle

S eattle is one of the most underrated cities in the United States. It is one of my favorite spots in the American League. Both the mountains and Puget Sound are very accessible from the city. The whole place is beautiful, and it's so different from anywhere else. Different from New England, from California, and even from other parts of the Pacific Northwest.

It does rain a lot in Seattle, but the rain seems to hold up somewhat during the baseball season, particularly during Red Sox games. Despite the usually good weather when we're in Seattle, the roof at Safeco is a must, as was the case at the old Kingdome. The Kingdome, which opened in 1977, was a good place to broadcast a game. Our booth was right behind home plate and about four stories up. The press box was nice but the elevator service was not very good. The Kingdome had good seats and the clubhouse was decent.

I recall the night game Boston played at the Kingdome on April 22, 1993, when the first two Red Sox baserunners reached on walks issued by Chris Bosio. Mike Greenwell, as usual, swung at the first pitch and grounded into a double play. That was it. The Red Sox did not have another baserunner the entire game as Bosio pitched a no-hitter. The game ended when Ernest Riles, pinch-hitting for Boston, hit a ground ball up the middle to shortstop Omar Vizquel. He barehanded the ball near second base and threw Riles out at first. Vizquel probably didn't have to barehand it, but how can you argue with Vizquel's Gold Gloves?

Another night I remember was probably the biggest blow with a fist I ever saw in a ballgame. Al Nipper was pitching for the Red Sox against the Mariners in Seattle on May 7, 1986. Nipper hit Phil Bradley of the Seattle Mariners with a pitch in the fifth inning, and Bradley charged the mound. Nipper held his ground, dropped the glove off his left hand, and decked Bradley with the best left hook I've ever seen in a baseball game. One punch and Bradley went down and out. Nipper kept his cool and did not risk injury to his right hand. Of course, Bradley was ejected. Rich Gedman was also ejected for arguing with home plate umpire Greg Kosc that the pitch had not, in fact, hit Bradley. Nipper pitched 6.1 innings and got an 11-5 win.

In those days, it really hurt to lose to the Mariners, but the Red Sox always had a tough time winning in the Kingdome. The Kingdome was a good home run park. I shagged balls in the outfield there with my sons, Duke and Tom. When Joe Morgan was the Red Sox manager, in his early 60s, he stood in at the plate during early batting practice, and tried to hit one over the 23-foot fence in rightfield, 312 feet away. Joe had warning track power. He didn't hit it over the wall, but he bounced one into the seats. Pretty good for 61.

The best media game I ever played in pitted the Red Sox media against the Mariners media. The Kingdome was unavailable so we played at Cheney Stadium in Tacoma, then home of the Tacoma Tigers, the Oakland AAA farm club. The game was played in 1989 or 1990. During the game, I made the play of my life. Playing second base, I made a diving stab of a hard hit ball up the middle, and from flat on my back made the flip to the shortstop covering the bag for a force out.

Safeco Field is beautiful. The forest green really works there, and you can see the lovely Seattle skyline from the ballpark. Safeco is more of a pitcher's park than was the Kingdome. One of the unique features of Safeco Field is that tracks for the Union Pacific Railroad run about 18 inches behind the rightfield grandstand. You hear the train whistles blow quite loudly about three times an hour.

The broadcast booth and facilities at Safeco are fine, but the press-room is quite small. There are usually long lines, too. But Seattle has a number of outstanding restaurants—especially seafood places—so we try to eat before we get to the ballpark.

One of the most memorable games I saw in Seattle was a 19-inning game on August 1, 2000. In the bottom of the 19th inning, Jeff Fassero took over in relief for the Red Sox. Fassero had been moaning about being demoted from the starting rotation to the bullpen. The first man he faced was Mike Cameron who parked Fassero's pitch just outside the rightfield foul pole by a few inches. The next pitch was just *inside* the rightfield foul pole—a walk-off, opposite field home run. It was about 3:42 in the morning in Boston when the game ended.

By the time we got to the 17th inning, we asked our listeners to e-mail us to tell us where they were and what they were doing. We had responses from all over the world, including the United States, the Near East, the Far East, and an island off Borneo.

Jan was with me at that game. For some reason, she has a talent for picking games that will go into extra innings.

In 1984, my second year with the Red Sox, I went with Mike Easler, Reid Nichols, and Dave Stapleton to the town of Spanaway, south of Tacoma. Reid, the driving force behind the trip, was speaking there to a church group. A retired soldier named Matt Cunningham picked us up. Matt was a Connecticut native. His friend Lee had a private plane that took off at a very small airstrip in Spanaway (or occasionally at Boeing Field near Seattle). We flew over Mt. St. Helen's, which erupted on May 18, 1980. The view was sensational. The only really scary moment I had in the plane was when Lee turned the controls over to Bobby Ojeda, who—at least during his years with the Red Sox—was not known for his control. He was a very good lefthander who beat the Red Sox in the 1986 World Series.

Over the years, we were able to see the area around the mountain and nearby Spirit Lake come back to life. Even some of the nearby towns started to regenerate. The devastation was spectacular, but so was the rebirth, especially as seen from the air. Fortunately, I was able to bring Jan and all of our children with us at one time or another to see this incredible view from the air.

Also in the mid-1980s, we visited Snoqualmie Falls. A shot of the falls was used in the opening of the TV show *Twin Peaks*. The falls, about 40 minutes east of Seattle in the Cascades, are more beautiful than Niagara, I think. The mountains are very green and the view is spectacular. You can walk or drive up to the peak. Dave Sax, Rick Miller, and Marc Sullivan went there with us. The highlight of our visits to the falls was having breakfast at the Inn at Snoqualmie Falls. This was not just breakfast. This was a 12-course meal—the biggest breakfast I've ever seen. Fruit, juice, pancakes, oatmeal, quiche, omelets, bacon, and eggs—everything for $18.95. The players absolutely loved it. It was a little too much for me, but I did manage to sample just about everything. Unfortunately, in later years the lodge went from a backwoods-type place to a luxury hotel. Cal Ripken Jr. used to stay there when the Orioles visited Seattle. The food was still very good, but it had changed to a gourmet restaurant and lost its rustic charm.

I always found plenty to do in and around Seattle, Puget Sound, and Elliott Bay right in downtown Seattle. I remember a rainy off day when we took the ferry to Bremerton, a big naval yard. At the time, the *Missouri* was docked there, and I wanted to see where the Japanese surrendered to end World War II. I couldn't believe how narrow the passageways and how low the ceilings were.

The Elliott Bay area has lots of shops featuring Asian imports, and cut glass made from ash deposited by the volcano at Mt. St. Helen's, plus a great view of Mt. Rainier. On a clear day, you can see this beautiful snow-covered mountain from downtown Seattle. But it's a four-hour drive. We've flown around it on one of our Mt. St. Helen's trips, but I have never driven to see it.

Across the bay, you can see the majestic Olympia Mountains, which are snow-capped almost all year long. The Cascades to the east, Mt. Rainier to the south, the Olympia Mountains to the west. What a beautiful site!

We've taken the Seattle harbor tour by boat. We saw Puget Sound, the container factory, Safeco Field, the Space Needle, and the imploded remains of the Kingdome. Seattle is built on a series of hills. Not quite as steep as San Francisco, but still hills. Seattle is also the city that coined the phrase "Skid Row." In the 1880s to 1900, they greased the hills, then brought timber from the Cascades and slid them down the hills directly to the ships on Puget Sound. Hence the name.

The Seattle underground tour in Pioneer Square is a comedic look at the way Seattle looked in the old days. Just north of downtown Seattle is the Space Needle, built for the 1962 World's Fair. You can take the monorail for about three quarters of a mile to get there from downtown. The view from the restaurant is wonderful, but only on a clear day. The food is just ok.

The Thirteen Coins near the *Seattle Post-Intelligencer* building, north of downtown, is one of my favorite restaurants in Seattle, partly because it's open 24 hours a day. We went there after the 19-inning game. The prices are good, and the seating is arranged so that you can face each other while sitting at the counter.

I also like McCormick's on Fourth Street. They feature about 40 kinds of fresh fish.

F. X. McCrory's, not far from Safeco, is another good bet for seafood and almost any kind of beer.

Leomelina's, near the Pike Place Market, has Italian cuisine. The market is worth visiting. It has the biggest salmon I've ever seen. Fresh fish, meat, and fruit. It stretches for about three blocks. It's a tourist spot overlooking the sound, but it's fun to see the giant salmon there.

The Seneca Deli, near the Holiday Inn in downtown Seattle, where the Red Sox used to stay, is a good place for breakfast. The specialties are oatmeal with Washington apples.

The local beer, Rainier Beer, is a nice treat.

The islands across Elliott Bay, west of Seattle, are worth a visit. You can get there by taking a ferry from Seattle, or driving around the peninsula through Tacoma. I took the Tacoma route in 2002 so I could stop at Cheney Stadium and watch my first Pacific Coast League game. The Tacoma Rainiers, the Mariners' AAA club played the New Orleans Zephyrs, Houston's top farm team. I stayed for three innings, then toured the Kitsap Peninsula, which includes the towns of Winslow, Gig Harbor, and Poulsbro (home of Aaron Sele), beautiful little seaside villages with gift shops and quaint restaurants. I stopped at Bainbridge

Island on the west side of Elliott Bay, where I kayaked in the harbor then took the ferry back to Seattle.

Jan and I have taken the trip to Vancouver Island by ferry. We did that in 1991 with Joe and Dot Morgan and our daughter Kate. It's about a three-hour trip to the city of Victoria, British Columbia. When you get off the ferry, you think you're in London. We went to the Butchart Gardens—the most beautiful gardens I've ever seen. Fifty acres of gorgeous flowers in a walking garden.

By the time we took the ferry back to Seattle, the seas had become rough, and it was a tough ride.

Northwest of downtown Seattle is the Hiram Chittendam Locks, where Puget Sound meets Lake Union. You can watch the boats being raised and lowered by the locks. Anthony's Portside is an enjoyable seafood restaurant with a fabulous view of Puget Sound just before the locks. On Lake Union, you can watch seaplanes land, or you can rent a kayak. That's what Jan and I did. Duke's is another good fish place on Lake Union. Chandler's is also on Lake Union. Lake Union connects to Lake Washington. The University of Washington is right there on the lake. You can tailgate on a boat before a Huskies's game.

There is a wonderful bike path that goes through the campus, by the stadium, and along the lake. We rented bikes there. Another time, Jan and I biked on the Seattle waterfront through the shipyards and locks. It was about eight miles. Jan thought it was too strenuous.

One of the worst things you can do is fly when you need a root canal. But I did it, flying from Orange County airport to Seattle in 1991 with Bob Starr. The pain was intense. I wound up going to a dentist who had been a basketball star at Baylor. The dentist's office was owned by the late Dr. Jack Nichols, who had played for the Boston Celtics. You never forget pain like that.

One night in Seattle, after a late night game at the Kingdome, I shared a cab back to the hotel with Joe Giuliotti of the *Boston Herald*. Our route to the hotel took us past a fleabag hotel where we saw an elderly man, who looked homeless, being pushed down by two thugs. We told the driver to stop. Just as we exited the taxi, the assailants fled. We picked up the man from the sidewalk. He was shaken up and his glasses had been knocked off, but he didn't appear badly hurt. We flagged down a police car and set off after the thugs. We thought they had boarded a city bus, so we had the police officers stop the bus. We searched it, but we didn't see them on the bus. If they had boarded it, they must have gotten off before the bus was stopped.

We felt good that we had saved the victim from what might have been a serious beating. Joe wrote a story about the incident and Bob Starr made a big deal of it on the air during our next broadcast. A Sons of Italy group in New Hampshire learned of our actions and sent us a letter commending Joe and me for our actions.

In Seattle, we had a chance to visit with Hugh Millen, former quarterback for the New England Patriots, and his wife Michelle. He lives on the east side of Lake Washington. Hugh is a very classy guy who does radio and TV work in Seattle. Hugh and I were in his boat, set for a ride on the lake with Sean McDonough, who does Red Sox games on TV.

Just as we launched his boat from the dock, the engine caught on a metal basket of some kind and was ruined. Meanwhile, we were stuck out on the lake with no power. Luckily, a guy in a rowboat came to our rescue and threw us a rope. He towed us to shore. We made it to the start of that night's game in plenty of time.

There are a lot of Red Sox fans in Seattle. They cheer loud and stay late.

I also took my former student, Don Orsillo, who now does Red Sox games on television for NESN (New England Sports Network), when we went kayaking on Lake Union in 2001. When we went again in 2002, we nearly lost Don on Lake Union. Just after we paddled past the famous houseboat that was used in the film *Sleepless in Seattle*, a little motorboat created a wake near Don's kayak. He lost control and overboard he went. His TV director, Mike Narracci, was nearby in his own kayak. Instead of pulling Don to shore, Mike grabbed his digital camera and took photographs of his capsized announcer. That made for great TV that night! Fortunately, Don was safe, though very wet and cold as we dragged him onto the dock. I doubt he will ever kayak again.

19

Tampa Bay

went to Tampa Bay long before there was a major league team there. The first time was for spring training with the Mets and the Cardinals, at Al Lang Field in 1976.

The Yankees had trained in St. Petersburg since Babe Ruth's time but moved to Fort Lauderdale in 1962. Now they are back in the area and train in Tampa.

The first time I went to St. Petersburg, I saw the ballpark—an old-fashioned wooden one with chicken wire around the screen to protect the older fans.

In Game Seven of the 1986 World Series, Darryl Strawberry of the Mets hit a home run and took forever to circle the bases. The Red Sox pitcher, Al Nipper, thought that Strawberry was trying to show him up, and determined to get him the next time he faced Strawberry.

That opportunity didn't come until Spring Training in 1987, when the Red Sox played the Mets at Al Lang Field. Bart Giamatti, a family friend, then National League president, was sitting with us in the broadcast booth. Nobody was surprised when Nipper hit Strawberry. Ballplayers have long memories, and don't like to be shown up.

Now, with the Red Sox, when we play Tampa Bay—the only major league team that does not play in the city it's named for—we stay at the Renaissance Vinoy Resort, a beautiful hotel in St. Petersburg. It was an old resort from the 1920s, a pink building that fell into disrepair. Street people were living there before it was renovated. It's right on the bay, by the yacht club. It has a beautiful pool and tennis courts. You can rent a bike and ride over to Snell Island. Biking is also outstanding at Fort DeSoto Park, overlooking the Skyway Bridge by the gulf. At Ft. Desoto Park, you can rent a bike and a kayak. I've been there with my family. There is a kayaking or canoe course mapped out, and you see manatees and flying fish in very shallow and clear water—an incredible thing to see. You used to be able to rent the kayaks right out of an old school bus. Somebody thought the school bus was an eyesore and it has been replaced with a stand.

Tropicana Field is only five minutes away, and there is little traffic, because nobody goes to the games. The team should be on the other side of Tampa or in Orlando.

St. Petersburg is in the far end, the southwest end—just on the wrong side of the bay.

The stadium was built some years ago in anticipation of the Chicago White Sox or the San Francisco Giants moving. In fact, the team's backers thought they had a deal with major league baseball and the White Sox for the team to move to St. Petersburg in the late 1980s. Then the White Sox completed a deal to build the new Comiskey Park, and the Sox stayed in Chicago.

Before the Tampa Bay Lightening of the National Hockey League moved to its new arena, the Ice Palace, they used to play in what is now Tropicana Field. So when Tampa Bay was awarded a major league franchise in 1998, they had to reconfigure the stadium for baseball, at a cost of millions of dollars.

The most famous game played at Tropicana Field was the NCAA basketball championship game of 1999, in which the University of Connecticut beat Duke.

In 1998, the Red Sox were only 4-9 against the Tampa Bay Devil Rays. In 2000, Pedro Martinez drilled Gerald Williams with a pitch. They had a history. Williams charged the mound and tried to punch Pedro. Both benches emptied.

Devil Rays general manager Chuck LaMar said that they had video-tape of Brian Daubach, our first baseman, throwing some cheap shots in the pile of players on the mound. They did not have any such tape. Daubach hyperextended his arm in that melee. The injury cost Daubach about 30 points on his batting average.

Roberto Hernandez joined the fight a little late, but still got in as many punches as he could.

In my view, the institution of the designated hitter in the American League in 1973 has increased the number of bench-clearing brawls. Before the DH, if you hit a home run, you could expect to get plunked the next time you came to bat. With Early Wynn, it was virtually automatic. You homered, you got plunked or dusted. Everybody knew it was going to happen, there was no personal animosity involved, it was part of the game, and the benches did not empty. This was just between the batter and the pitcher. You got hit, you dropped your bat and walked to first base.

Of course, your pitcher could plunk the opposing pitcher the next time he came to bat, too. But once the designated hitter came into the American League, the pitcher didn't come to bat, and there was no chance for a simple retaliatory tit for tat.

In recent years, the umpires have been instructed by the leagues to "police" pitchers intentionally throwing at batters, and to issue a warning after the first such incident in a game. A second pitch thrown intentionally (in the umpire's judgment) results in automatic ejection and a suspension. But having the umpires enforce this rule is ridiculous—unless a procedure is in place that lets them look into the head and heart of pitchers, to determine their actual intentions. Umpires may also eject pitchers without a warning.

It is rare for a pitcher to say anything other than "The ball got away from me. I was not trying to hit him." Or, "Hey, if I were trying to hit him, I would have hit him in the butt instead of in the shoulder!"

Ron Fairley, whom I came to know when he was a broadcaster with the Seattle Mariners, was with the Dodgers when he doubled off Bob Gibson of the Cardinals. The next time he came up to the plate, he looked at Cardinals catcher Tim McCarver, knowing that Gibson was going to plunk him, and said, "I'm not going to enjoy this." And of course, he got drilled.

Pedro Martinez had a near no-hitter at Tropicana Field, going into the ninth inning in that same brawl-marred game on August 29, 2000. But John Flaherty, a former Red Sox catcher, broke it up with a single to right centerfield in the ninth inning.

◆ ● ◆

We like to go over to the City of St. Petersburg Beach, to visit the Don Ce Sar Resort. Another beautiful, historic pink hotel, built in the 1920s, during the first Florida building boom. The resort is said to be haunted by the ghost of the builder. The outdoor restaurants are lovely—right on the beach. Uncle Andy's ice cream parlor with an old-fashioned soda fountain is my favorite spot in the hotel. We have also stayed at the Don during winter vacations.

Ray, a native of Woonsocket, Rhode Island, who runs Uncle Andy's, told us that Devil Rays rookie Rocco Baldelli would be an instant star. And he was right. I suppose it's just a coincidence that Baldelli, also from Rhode Island, is known as the "Woonsocket Rocket"!

◆ ● ◆

Clearwater Beach, near Tampa Bay, is lovely. I've been there with our children. The water is very warm and it is a great place for young adults.

Another good place to visit is the Ybor City section of Tampa—an old Spanish/Cuban neighborhood that has been revitalized with nightclubs and restaurants. Anchoring the area is the world famous Colombian Restaurant, which is more than 100 years old. The Spanish cuisine is excellent, though it is on the pricey side.

◆ ● ◆

Vince Naimoli, the Devil Rays's owner, has alienated many in the business and baseball community. I met him once and complimented him on having Italian lemon ices in the press box at Tropicana Field. Next year, it was gone.

◆ ● ◆

In Tampa, I enjoy the hospitality of Devil Rays broadcaster Paul Olden. Paul, who has a melodious, smooth style is a close friend. Paul has done play-by-play for the Yankees, the New York Jets, the Cleveland Indians, ESPN, the Anaheim Angels, and the Los Angeles Rams. He began his career in the Pacific Coast League. I believe Paul is the only African American who is not an ex-ballplayer broadcasting for a major league club.

In 1998, Paul took me to the Ted Williams Hitters Museum in Hernando, Florida, about 100 miles from St. Petersburg. It is very nicely done, with lockers, plaques, and uniforms of all the inductees. Ted lived about a mile away.

20

Texas

The Texas Rangers started life as the Washington Senators—the second Washington Senators. The first franchise known as the Senators left the capital in 1961 and became the Minnesota Twins. They were succeeded in Washington by the second Senators team in 1961. That team was managed by Ted Williams (1969–1971) and moved to Arlington, Texas, where they became the Rangers in 1972, Williams's last year as manager.

My first trip to Texas was in 1979 when I was doing television with the Cleveland Indians. Until 1994, the Rangers played at a converted minor-league ballpark called Turnpike Stadium, built for the Dallas-Ft. Worth club in the Texas League. The stadium was expanded several times for the Rangers, but it was still a minor league ballpark—not the best place to see a game. There were lots of seats in the outfield, but not many between the foul lines. Before the park was expanded, it was a tough park for a lefthanded batter, because the wind came off the prairie over the rightfield wall and would just knock the balls down. Ranger first baseman Pat Putnam was frequently victimized by the wind at Turnpike Stadium. But over the years, the team built advertising boards in rightfield and the winds just swirled around them. The balls carried well after that.

The Red Sox were up and down at Turnpike Stadium, although the Rangers did not have good ballclubs throughout most of the 1980s.

I recall specifically Roger Clemens's flirtation with a no-hitter in Texas on May 25, 1986. He had not allowed a hit through seven and one-third innings when Oddibe McDowell, the Rangers's left-hand batting centerfielder, hit a line drive to centerfield. Steve "Psycho" Lyons was playing centerfield for the Red Sox, and he had no chance to make a play on the ball. He fielded it on one hop, and the no-hitter was gone. Gino Petralli hit a home run in the ninth inning to break up the shut out. Clemens had to settle for a 7-1 two-hitter.

The Rangers had a number of walk-off home runs to beat the Red Sox. I remember a great game—Clemens against Nolan Ryan on April 30, 1989. The game ended on a walk-off home run by Texas's Rafael Palmeiro.

Geno Petralli always hurt the Red Sox, and probably hit Roger Clemens better than anybody else in the late 1980s.

Ellis Burks faced Nolan Ryan in a game, and Ryan buzzed him, nearly hitting Burks in the head. Burks shook his finger at Ryan, a pitcher who liked to intimidate batters, and smoked a base hit up the middle to beat the Rangers.

The walkway to the dugout at the old stadium was dreadful. Because of the heat—about 100 degrees at game time—it smelled awful. It was also a long way from the visiting clubhouse to the dugout. To get there, you had to walk under the stadium. We always expected to see snakes down there.

The new ballpark opened in 1994, the strike year. It's a little gaudy, but I like it. The Ballpark in Arlington tries to copy elements from many older parks. There's a mini Fenway Park scoreboard in leftfield, while rightfield mimics old Tigers Stadium. There are also some Ebbets Field features, and lots of nooks and crannies in the outfield.

The visiting radio broadcast booth is in a good location, but we always keep the windows closed until game time to keep the hot air out. I don't really complain about the heat, but I hate it when it's cold.

John Blake, a native of the Boston area, is the Rangers's public relations director. He does a great job and has always been gracious to us.

The Red Sox used to stay at the Hyatt in downtown Dallas near Reunion Arena, home of the Dallas Mavericks and the Stars. This was a rather desolate neighborhood, especially on the weekends. We could see the Texas Schoolbook Depository from the hotel. It was still being used for schoolbooks when I started going to Texas with the Red Sox.

Then the team moved to a different hotel about a quarter of a mile from the new ballpark. The hotel was a Marriott, then a Sheraton, and is now a Wyndham. The location is great.

◆ ● ◆

In the late 1980s, a museum was opened on the sixth floor of the School-Book Depository called the "Sixth Floor Museum." Part of the museum shows how the boxes of books were stacked when Lee Harvey Oswald is said to have fired the fatal shot from the building's window. The museum includes photographs, videotapes, audiotapes, maps, timelines, the Warren Commission report, and the reports of the 1978–1979 House of Representatives special committee, which investigated the assassination. The museum does not draw any conclusions about whether Oswald acted alone in killing JFK.

With the help of Steve August, former traveling secretary for the Sox, I've spent quite a bit of time visiting some of the sites in Dallas associated with President Kennedy's assassination. Steve has read all of the testimony before the Warren Commission, something I have not yet done. August met the late Harold Norman who worked as a guard a floor below Oswald at the Depository.

When we're in Arlington, a suburb of Dallas, we take what we have come to call the "assassination tour."

I've read a number of books about the assassination, and I've done quite a bit of research on the subject. I have also visited a number of the sites involved. In my view, there was indeed a conspiracy to kill President Kennedy, and I don't believe that Lee Harvey Oswald acted alone. That conspiracy may have involved the mafia, the CIA, and others. I don't really know, and I don't think we'll ever know.

After the School Book Depository visit, we follow the path Oswald took. He took a cab and a bus to his rooming house in the Oak Cliff section of Dallas. We go there by driving through the city, about four to five miles, to his rooming house at 1026 North Beckley Street. That's where he went right after the assassination, probably to change his shirt. The rooming house, part of a single-story home, is still in use in this rundown section of Dallas. From there, we proceed about a half mile to where officer J. D. Tippit was shot and killed. Then we go to the Texas Theater where Oswald was arrested while watching *Battle Cry*, a Van Heflin movie. There is still a big "Texas Theater" sign there, but the building is in disrepair. There's another rooming house in Dallas where Oswald lived before moving to North Beckley Street, which is where the infamous photograph of him holding a rifle was taken. (Of course, some people think that that photo was doctored, with Oswald's head superimposed on the body of another.)

The School Book Depository is adjacent to the grassy knoll, where many people believe that a second gunman stood. The concrete near the sewer is still scarred by what appears to be a stray bullet.

I used to see the late Larry Howard in Dallas. He had published some pamphlets about the conspiracy with information about the untimely deaths of so many people involved in the Kennedy assassination.

Over the years, I have taken a number of players and executives on parts of the JFK "tour." Darren Lewis, Andre Dawson, our Spanish broadcasters Uri Berenguer, J. P. Villaman, Juan Baez, and Bill Kulik, trainer Jim Rowe, Glenn Wilburn, Red Sox baseball information director, and others.

Roger Clemens's wife Debbie and her mother were both in Dealy Plaza November 22, 1963. His wife was an infant in her mother's arms.

There's another museum in the courthouse right around the corner from Dealey Plaza, but this place is a little too sensationalized for me.

In Dallas, I met Jean Hill, an eyewitness who wrote a book about the assassination. She was interested in one of the motorcycle police officers who was on duty in JFK's motorcade, which explains her presence so close to the event. She claims to have seen a shot fired from the grassy knoll. She is the woman in a red coat.

The JFK tour is probably the most interesting thing to do in Dallas. When I stay with the team, we stay in Arlington, about 20 miles west of Dallas. There are lots of amusement parks there. I took all of my kids to Six Flags over Texas. Of course, when it's 100 degrees out, the parks are very hot. Across the street is the "Wet 'n Wild" amusement park with lots of water slides, including one about six stories high. I did that once, but I don't know if I'd do it today. The winding "Lazy River" ride is also lots of fun.

When I have an off day in Arlington, I like to take a side trip to the stockyards in Fort Worth. Although there's not much cattle there any more, the Western stores selling expensive cowboy boots and hats are very good.

There's a great Lone Star Restaurant, a retro luncheonette, right in the stockyards, famous for its burgers and chicken-fried steak. When I go there, I have the chicken-fried chicken.

Near Lincoln Square in Arlington is a good restaurant called The Black-Eyed Pea, well known for its vegetables, including black-eyed peas and okra. The cornbread and grits are excellent, too. The restaurant specializes in southern-style cooking, so the fried chicken and chicken-fried steak are also good.

One year, we took another side trip from Dallas, and went to Austin to see the LBJ Library. The drive was about 200 miles south of Arlington—about a three and a half-hour trip, which we squeezed in on an off day.

Lyndon Johnson was not one of my favorite presidents, primarily because of his policies on Vietnam, but I wanted to see the library. From there, we went to the University of Texas, and saw Memorial Stadium, home of the Longhorns. We also saw the baseball field where Roger Clemens pitched during his college days. The field is old, but in good shape. There's also an excellent softball field for the women's team. We stopped in Roundrock, just north of Austin, to see Dell Diamond, the minor league stadium. It's probably the most beautiful I have ever seen. There's a pool in right center. The club is owned by Nolan Ryan's family. His son is the general manager.

In August 2000, I saw a Roundrock Express game there with Glen Wilburn, the Red Sox Public Information Director. Glenn was a student of mine at Northeastern, and our intern in 1991–1992. The Express is the Astros's affiliate in the Class AA Texas League.

On the way to Austin, we stopped in Waco to see Baylor University. Jerry Trupiano says that Waco is so exciting, when Baylor wins—they paint the town beige. (Baylor's colors are green and gold.) He also says that if Baylor wins, "you can't find a bottle of milk in town!"

We've also been to the campus of Texas Christian University in Fort Worth, where I saw *Out of Left Field*, Jeffrey and Douglas Lyons's book nicely displayed in the bookstore.

One of the perks of being a big league broadcaster is renewing acquaintances with broadcasters around the league. In Texas, I used to see my friend, the late Mark Holtz, who broadcast Rangers games from 1982 to mid-1997. Mark's wife Alice battled cancer for many years, then Mark developed anemia and then leukemia. I will never forget getting a phone call from his partner, Eric Nadel, a good friend of mine, in September 1998, to inform me that Mark had passed away. Mark had received a bone marrow transplant earlier that year and we thought he would recover. But the cancer was too strong and he passed away about a year and a half before Alice did.

Eric Nadel, a Brown graduate, has been with the Rangers since 1979. We speak with each other and compare notes a lot during the season and during the offseason via e-mail and phone. We discuss players, trades, players' salaries, broadcasters' salaries, working conditions, and other topics that help us all.

I also enjoy seeing Tom Grieve. He's one of the nicest people in the game of baseball—both when he was the team's general manager (1984–1994) and since 1995 as a Ranger broadcaster.

As a New Englander, it's always fun for me to see and speak with real Texans.

It's very difficult to walk anywhere in Arlington, because the team hotel and the ballpark are both at the confluence of a number of freeways. It's an interesting area. It's usually very warm (at least during the baseball season), but for some reason it does not feel as warm as Kansas City or Baltimore, for example. There is usually a breeze, which helps a little.

I remember a game on July 26, 1988, when the "Morgan Magic" was interrupted. The Red Sox had won 12 straight games, but that streak ended in Texas. The Sox had battled back, and had the tying run at second base with two outs in the ninth inning. Todd Benzinger, batting righty, hit a screeching line drive to leftfield. Cecil Espy, the Rangers' leftfielder came in and made a shoestring catch to save the game for the Rangers. The Red Sox win streak was ended. My son Tom, about 13, was on the trip with me, and we went over to Joe Morgan's suite after the game and ordered a pizza. I had a few beers and Joe had his usual Scotch. A little while later, there was just one slice left. Said Joe: "There it is—always that last piece." He said to Tommy, "Jump on it kid, with both hands!"

The next night, the Sox went on another win streak and won 19 out of their first 20 games under Joe Morgan. That was real Morgan Magic!

On the same trip, it was so hot that as Tom and I walked across the old ballpark's parking lot to a restaurant for lunch, Tom started to cry.

Kate took her first trip with me in 1989 when she was about ten. It was the first night she had been away from Jan. We took a commercial flight from Boston to Dallas, and as we drove to the hotel at about midnight, I got lost. Kate, who had fallen asleep, woke up and was in tears. But we called home the next morning, and she was fine. We had a great time at Six Flags over Texas, and then at Wet 'n Wild.

On another day at Arlington, Duke and I shagged balls in the outfield during early batting practice with Joe Morgan. It was very hot but also lots of fun.

The pressroom at the Ballpark in Arlington serves fat-free frozen yogurt throughout the game. I like to mix it with Diet Dr. Pepper, a very popular drink in Texas. The salad bar in the pressroom is also quite good.

I noticed that the Rangers were usually on page nine of the *Dallas-Fort Worth Star*, while the Dallas Cowboys were usually on page one, especially if training camp had started. But since the ballpark at Arlington opened in 1994, and the Rangers were in the postseason in 1994, 1996, and 1999, that has mostly changed, as there is a lot more emphasis on baseball than there used to be in Dallas. But if you have to battle Friday night high-school football, baseball—even major league baseball—has a tough time competing. Football is still number one in Texas.

It's a rather long ride—as everything is in Texas—to mass at Blessed Sacrament Church in an outlying area of Arlington. Trup and I went to mass and we saw Red Sox pitcher Jeff Suppan there. The van from the hotel had failed to pick him up. In the days before cell phones, there was no way to call a cab, so Trup and I gave Suppan, a very nice young man, a lift back to the hotel.

The day before Opening Day 1996, we had to get him back to the hotel for a meeting before the game. The mass was a very long one since it was Palm Sunday. Jeff was getting nervous, because he thought he would miss the meeting. We got him back on time. Trup and I always thought that we deserved a save for delivering Suppan on time.

21

Toronto

Toronto is one of the great cosmopolitan cities of the world. The crime rate is much lower than that of most U.S. cities. From the late 1960s on, the city has blossomed with an influx of many different ethnic groups—a true metropolis of more than 3 million people.

The first time I went to Toronto was in 1969 while I was still in graduate school at Syracuse. My first *baseball* trip to Toronto was in 1977 when I was with the Indians to do a story on the Indians's new manager, Jeff Torborg.

During my first six and a half years with the Red Sox, the Blue Jays played at Exhibition Stadium. They moved to Skydome (they don't use "the") in mid-1989. Exhibition Stadium is part of the Canadian National Exposition Fairgrounds, right on the shore of Lake Ontario. It was really a football stadium, converted to baseball. It was the home of the Toronto Argonauts of the Canadian Football League, which uses a 110-yard field.

The field had artificial turf, and although the sign said that it was 315 feet down the rightfield line, it was probably shorter than that. The centerfield bleachers were about 800 feet from home plate. They were pretty bad—about 400 feet from the centerfield fence, then another 400 feet to home plate.

It was hard to see at the stadium, too, particularly during the day, when there was glare off the turf.

The Blue Jays were always a first-class organization and they did everything they could to improve things at the old stadium. The press accommodations were first rate. The dining room was excellent, and the clubhouses were pretty good for a stadium built for football.

Ontario Place, an amusement park, was close to the stadium, and we took our kids there to enjoy the Ferris wheel and water slides.

The Canadian Baseball Hall of Fame is also at Ontario Place. There's an exhibit there about Babe Ruth's first home run in professional baseball, hit there.

The old Hockey Hall of Fame was in the exhibition fairgrounds, too, shaped like a puck.

The thing I remember most about Exhibition Stadium was long rain delays. As with other Great Lakes cities (Chicago and Cleveland, for example), there's a lot of cold wet air coming off the lakes. Some of the rain delays lasted as long as three hours. I remember one in particular, on a Sunday afternoon. Eddie Jurak had been the batting champion of the Eastern League, with a .340 average. He hit his first and only major league home run in the fourth inning. Then it rained in the bottom of the fourth, and there was a rain delay of about three hours before the game resumed. I spoke with Jurak after the game, and I asked him, "Eddie, were you sweating that your first home run was almost washed out?" He replied, "What do you mean? It would have counted." "No," I explained, "if the game had been postponed before the end of the fifth inning, it would not have been an official game, and the home run would have been washed out." Jurak did not know that. Jurak was a utility player who was one of the best I have ever seen at driving in the runner from third with less than two outs. He hit almost everything to the right of second base. But Eddie Jurak was probably best known for introducing Wade Boggs to Margo Adams on a West Coast trip, setting up an infamous part of Red Sox history.

During rain delays, Ken Coleman and I used to fill the time with talk, which could be very exhausting, especially when the delays ran to three hours. We did have some tapes to play, such as Ken interviewing

Jonathan Winters who did some of his baseball skits, or interviews with Ted Williams. I had some rain delay tapes of my own, including interviews with Bob Feller.

These delays were very tiring, and by the time the game resumed, I sometimes felt as though I had already broadcast a doubleheader.

Now, when the delay is more than five minutes, we send it back to the studio.

◆ ● ◆

Jim Rice had a three-home run game in Exhibition Stadium on August 29, 1983.

One game I remember quite clearly was a game pitched brilliantly by Luis Leal. He shut out the Red Sox in a two-hitter on June 16, 1984, at Exhibition Stadium, a bright Saturday afternoon. He was unhittable.

For some reason, I also remember one nemesis: Rance Mulliniks. He always seemed to have a big hit against the Red Sox.

Over the years, you could really see the Blue Jays develop into a contending team. They had an excellent outfield: Jessie Barfield (1986 home run champion with 46), George Bell (MVP in 1987), centerfielder Lloyd Moseby, and pitcher Dave Steib.

With that talent, the Blue Jays went from an American League expansion team in 1977 to a contender pretty quickly with astute drafts and homegrown talent. The Blue Jays were an outstanding organization.

When I went to Toronto, I liked to visit with two friends who were Blue Jays. One was pitching coach Al Widmar. Al was a native of Cleveland, and went to Cathedral Latin High School, which had been a great athletic power there. He pitched for the Red Sox, the St. Louis Browns, and the Chicago White Sox in the 1940s and 1950s. He also played in the NBA.

My other friend with the Blue Jays was James "Jimy" Williams. Our paths crossed again when Jimy managed the Red Sox from 1997 through most of 2001. Over the years, I did more pregame interviews with Jimy than with anybody else.

On June 5, 1989, the Blue Jays moved to their new park, Skydome. It was the first park with a working retractable roof. Everything was state of the art. When it opened, it looked like it would be a real pitcher's park. It turned out to be a hitter's park. Whether that's because the air currents changed, or they opened the roof, or moved the fences, it's a hitter's park now. In the Red Sox first series at Skydome, the Sox tied the game late. In the tenth inning, Tom Henke, an outstanding hard thrower for Toronto, faced pinch hitter Danny Heep. (Heep's middle name is William, but Chris Berman gave him the inevitable nickname Uriah.) Heep hit a three-run home run for a dramatic win.

Skydome is glitzy, without the panache or ambiance of the ballparks in Baltimore or Cleveland. The video boards are enormous. From the visiting broadcast booth, we can't see the bullpens, which are in left- and rightfields but we have monitors in the booth and can look at the closed-circuit picture to see who is warming up.

One of the longest home runs I ever saw was a walk-off homer hit off Kip Gross (in one of his two games for the Sox) by Carlos Delgado off the window of the restaurant in right centerfield, May 16, 1999.

Another was hit by Manny Ramirez on June 3, 2001, a 500-plus-foot job into the fifth deck.

The Sox have changed hotels in Toronto a number of times. They have stayed at the Westin Harbor Castle, a very nice place right on Lake Ontario, and close to Skydome, at the Toronto Marriott, near the Eaton Shopping Center, a two-block mall, at the Toronto Hilton, which used to be the Hotel Toronto. I stayed there when I was with the Indians, too. The hotel used to have bellhops and doormen dressed in kilts. When my daughter Kate came with me in 1983 when she was four, she referred to them as the "lady man." We have since moved up to a hotel in the Yorkville section, a high-rent district.

The expensive Barrister's Bar at the Hilton Hotel features a legendary bartender named Mr. Yu. He has been tending bar there for nearly 30 years, and often served Billy Martin. The Kon-Tiki Lounge in the basement made very potent Mai Tais. One was enough.

One of the great things about downtown Toronto is the ability to walk almost anywhere underground. Underground shopping is very popular, and is outstanding. You can go right from the hotel lobby to an underground mall and walk a few miles of shop after shop. It must be great in the winter.

You can walk to the Hockey Hall of Fame, which moved from the CNE Fairgrounds to a new facility at BCE Place and Yonge Street. The interactive exhibits are very modern, and the place is very well run. I am not a great hockey fan, but the Hall of Fame is worth a visit.

The harbor tour of Toronto is outstanding. From May through September, the weather is beautiful and perfect for the tour. The boat goes around Toronto Harbor, and some of the outlying islands. Center Island is a beautiful garden spot with a beach about a one-minute ferry ride from downtown Toronto. It is also the former site of the ballpark belonging to the Toronto Maple Leafs of the International League. In 1914, Babe Ruth was playing for Providence, and he hit his first professional and only minor league home run there. Legend has it that the ball went into Lake Ontario. Jan and I like to rent bikes and ride all around the island—about seven miles. There are swan boat rides and an amusement park.

Toronto is one of the few cities, certainly in the American League, which boasts a "clothing optional" beach. Jan and I were riding on Center Island in 2001. She stopped to look at some flowers while I pedaled on ahead. I saw the sign, "Clothing Optional Beach." That's about as far as I went. I mentioned the sign and the beach to Jerry Remy, former Red Sox second baseman, who is one of the Red Sox television broadcasters. Jerry embellished the story when he went on the air. He had Jan and me at the clothing optional beach and said that Jan made me bury my head in the sand. By the time I got home, a number of people asked me how Jan and I enjoyed the nude beach.

Joseph Aboud, the clothing designer, is an old friend and a devoted Red Sox fan. He was visiting Sean McDonough and Jerry in the TV booth, and at one point the camera was on me in the radio booth next door as I was doing play-by-play. Then, during a commercial break, Aboud presented me with a pair of designer swim trunks, probably worth about $200. They were "easy on, easy off" he said, for me to use the next time I went to the clothing optional beach.

You can also rent bikes near the lakefront by Skydome and ride by the old ballpark site. When Elston Howard played for the Toronto Maple Leafs in the International League, he hit 19 triples—amazing, considering that he was a very slow runner. Howard was the MVP in the League in 1954. The Maple Leafs were an independent team, not affiliated with any major league team. They were owned by Jack Kent Cooke, later the owner of the Washington Redskins. Elston Howard is the first major league player I ever interviewed, during the winter of 1966 in Binghamton, New York. I was a sophomore at Colgate and working part time at WCHN Radio in Norwich. The station sent me to interview Howard who was on the Yankees Winter Caravan Tour, designed to help sell the team and to sell tickets. What a great guy.

Pete Castiglione (pronounced CASTLE OWN—same spelling, not related) played for the Maple Leafs in the 1950s too. I used to hear a lot of stories about Pete from Neil MacCarl, a Toronto sportswriter, now retired, who is an official scorer for the Blue Jays.

Toronto is where Dick Williams managed a AAA team for the Red Sox. He was the manager of the Maple Leafs in 1965–1966, and many of the players who were on the "Impossible Dream" team of 1967 had come up with Toronto, including George Scott and Mike Andrews.

Over the years, the Red Sox have played well in Toronto, which is a little surprising, because the Red Sox have not really done well on artificial turf. The Sox have never been built for speed.

On August 25, 1990, Dwight Evans homered off David Wells for the only run of the game as Roger Clemens stranded a runner at third base *four times* and walked away with a 1-0 complete game victory. He ended the game by striking out Manuel Lee with the bases loaded. Catcher Tony Peña told him, "You throw that splitter. Don't worry about it being in the dirt or getting away from me. I will stop it." And he did.

Greg Harris won the last game of that series 1-0—three straight shutouts in Toronto.

◆ ● ◆

Howard Starkman was the media relations director for the Blue Jays from the team's 1977 debut in the American League through 2000. He was later promoted to vice president in charge of special projects. He always did an outstanding job.

I am also a friend of Tom Cheek, who has been the Blue Jays broadcaster since their first game. He's from Pensacola, Florida, but cut his broadcasting teeth in Burlington, Vermont. The effervescent Jerry Howarth, a very upbeat guy, also broadcasts for the Blue Jays, and he has been an excellent source for the kind of information we, as visiting broadcasters, need—who is injured, who missed a start, and other personal anecdotes about the players.

Buck Martinez was fun to be with when he was a broadcaster and also as the team's manager. When I was with the Brewers in 1981, Buck was one of four catchers on the team. Before Buck was the skipper, I thought Cito Gaston was an outstanding manager. He led the team to world championships in 1992 and 1993 and never got the credit he deserved.

The Blue Jays's current general manager is J. P. Ricciardi, an old friend from Worcester. J. P. played minor league ball, scouted for Oakland, became the Athletics's assistant general manager, and moved to Toronto in 2002 as general manager, where he is building a winner. He is a real down-to-earth guy and a great judge of talent. During his offseasons in Worcester, J. P. coached the Holy Name High School basketball team to the Massachusetts state finals. He also got my son Tom his first medical job, as an emergency medical technician at the Holy Name football games.

The Toronto fans, if not very passionate, are very polite. The crowds are very well behaved. Having won the Series in 1992 and 1993, Toronto was hurt badly by the strike of 1994. In each year from 1991 through 1993, the Blue Jays drew more than 4 million fans. They have not come close to that since then.

Toronto is a great city for public transportation and for walking. I rarely rent a car in Toronto. The city has a wonderful subway system— very clean, very safe, and very quick. The streetcars are great, too. In fact, they used to be Cleveland's streetcars. Toronto bought them from Cleveland when Cleveland stopped using streetcars in the 1950s.

The Ontario Science Center is full of interactive exhibits and is a fun place to visit. I went there with my kids.

Toronto has some terrific theater. The Toronto Truck Theater has been playing Agatha Christie's *The Mousetrap* for many years, as was *Phantom of the Opera*. We've seen *Mama Mia* in Toronto, too. The theater district also has some fine restaurants.

Three blocks from Skydome on Adelaide Street is the Loose Moose, one of many enjoyable clubs and restaurants in downtown Toronto.

Alice Fazooli's Crab Shack is one of our favorites in Toronto. It's sort of a loud and large Italian restaurant with good fish and good chicken. Considering the exchange rate with American dollars, the prices are not bad.

The Movenpick, a Swedish place, is good for breakfast and desserts. When Jack Rogers was the Red Sox traveling secretary, he'd take us to Hy's Steakhouse, an outstanding place. I liked it even though I don't eat much steak. The fish and chicken were very good.

There are more than half a million Italians in Toronto, and most of them have come there recently—much more so than in the states. Many of them came to Canada in the 1950s and 1960s. Toronto has two Italian neighborhoods. One is in the St. Claire area. Jan and I went to a romantic spot called San Remo, which had strolling musicians come by our table. Closer to downtown is the College Street Italian neighborhood, which includes good shopping as well as restaurants. We like a place there called Grappa, and the Sicilian Ice Cream Company for lemon ices.

When they were younger, my kids worked out on the field at Skydome, and so did I, catching fungoes off the bat of Johnny Pesky.

Casa Loma is a 98-room castle not far from downtown. It was built between 1911 and 1914 and contains lots of hidden passageways.

The CN Tower, the world's tallest building, is in downtown Toronto, right next to Skydome. There's an elevator to the restaurant on top.

Fort York is down by the C&E Fairgrounds. It is the site of one of the bloodiest battles of the War of 1812.

Lester B. Pearson Airport in Toronto has a curfew—no landings after a certain hour. So more often than not, the team plane has flown into Hamilton airport, which seems to be in the middle of a farm. Going through customs is much faster there than at Pearson, so even though it's an hour-and-ten-minute bus ride from Hamilton to the team hotel, it's just about as fast.

We've driven to Toronto from Detroit, which is a nice three and a half hours. Someday, I'd like to go by train.

22

National League Cities

Most of the cities I visit are in the American League. But since 1997, with the advent of interleague play, the Red Sox have traveled to most of the cities in the National League, too. I have enjoyed myself in those cities, but I don't know them as well as the American League sites that I visit every year.

I've written about San Francisco in the Oakland chapter, and my visits to San Diego and Los Angeles are covered in the Anaheim chapter.

Atlanta

I first went to Atlanta with the Red Sox for an exhibition game against the Braves at the end of Spring Training in 1996. Then, with the onset of interleague play, Boston played regular season games in Atlanta starting in 1997. The Red Sox were 0-3 against the Braves that year. The team ended Spring Training with another exhibition game there at the end of 1998, too.

Atlanta-Fulton County Stadium was rightly dubbed "The Launching Pad" because home runs really flew out of there. While the crowds were very small and the games weren't memorable, I am glad to have had the opportunity to see the old stadium. In 1997, the Braves moved into their new stadium, Turner Field, built for the 1996 Olympics.

Turner Field is very big and very glitzy. There's a big Coke bottle on the roof. (Atlanta is the corporate home of Coca Cola.) The centerfield concourse is filled with shops, interactive activities, and concession stands. The Braves's Hall of Fame is in left centerfield, and it is filled with some great memorabilia. Scouting boards are displayed there, too, showing the progress of such players as Henry Aaron and more recent players, like Mark Lemke. The boards show how the players were scouted and advanced through the Braves system up to the big club. I've never seen a display like it anywhere else.

Considering the Braves's great pitching staffs in recent years, the Red Sox have played fairly well in Atlanta.

John Kramer, our engineer in Atlanta, doubles as a college umpire who told us that he worked Georgia Tech baseball games when Nomar Garciaparra played there.

The broadcast booths in Atlanta are big and comfortable. We also like to see the Atlanta broadcasters. Don Sutton is an old friend. He was nice to my son when he was with the Brewers and Duke worked in the Milwaukee clubhouse. Skip Carey is a colorful guy. A lot of people like to do imitations of Skip. He tells it straight. Pete Van Wieren is a solid, professional baseball broadcaster. He came up from the International League, and has had a long tenure with Atlanta.

The Braves are a great organization for which I have tremendous respect. They have perhaps the best manager of his era in Bobby Cox, who has won every National League Eastern Division title since 1991. The architect of that team is the general manager, John Schuerholz. John and Bobby have guided the Braves through an ownership change and through turnover in players.

John was a teacher in Baltimore when Lou Gorman hired him to work for the Orioles in their farm department. John did very well first in Kansas City, where he built their World Champion club in 1985, then moved to Atlanta to begin his outstanding career with the Braves. Whenever I mention John to Lou, he says, "I hired him, hired him, hired him!" John loves Uncle Lou. We all do.

The clubhouses in Atlanta are very large. The food in the media cafeteria is good. It is sometimes hard to get a cab at the stadium after the game.

Atlanta has a lot to offer the visitor. I've been to Dr. Martin Luther King Jr.'s birthplace and the Martin Luther King Center for Nonviolence and Social Change on Auburn Avenue. At the nearby Ebenezer Baptist Church, I've seen where Dr. King's father, "Daddy" King, also preached. The center has a montage of photos of the civil rights movement, from the Montgomery Bus Boycott, the March on Washington, through Dr. King's life.

Nearby is the Jimmy Carter Museum and Library on Freedom Parkway. I think Mr. Carter is the best ex-president we've ever had, and the Nobel Peace Prize he was awarded in 2002 is evidence of that. He has been a real gentleman, a force for peace in the entire world, and a true Christian—an inspiration for many. He lives what he preaches. The grounds around the Carter Center are beautiful. I have wanted to visit his birthplace in Plains, Georgia, but it's a two-hour drive from Atlanta.

I did visit Kennesaw Mountain Park, about an hour from Atlanta. Kenesaw Mountain Landis, the first commissioner of baseball, was named for the battle site where his father, a Union officer, was severely wounded.

I've been to Stone Mountain Park about 30 minutes from Atlanta, where Robert E. Lee, Stonewall Jackson, and Jefferson Davis are etched into the mountain. There's an amusement park nearby, and the area includes fishing, hiking, and boating.

When I was in Atlanta in 2002, I had a chance to visit the Ty Cobb Museum in Royston, Georgia. The hospital Cobb funded is adjacent and the museum's portrayal of Cobb is interesting. He is referred to as "complex," rather than as a miserable, bigoted individual.

Chops is a very good restaurant in the Buckhead neighborhood of Atlanta. Jimy Williams sent us there. It's about a $25 cab ride from downtown, but it's a very good steakhouse that also serves good chicken and fish. Jimy says that every time you use your fork, they bring you a new one.

Jan likes Pitti Pat Porch, where the pork chops, Savannah crab cakes, and peach cobbler are the house specialties.

We've stayed at the Marriott, the Westin, and the Ritz Carlton in Atlanta.

There are not as many stores and shopping areas in downtown Atlanta as you might expect for a city this size. The underground shopping area is well known, and has a food court and specialty shops, but I did not find it memorable.

There's a fun tour of the Coca Cola plant near their world headquarters. You can taste different Coke brands and flavors from all over the world. Some of them are really dreadful—just too sweet.

CNN headquarters also has an interesting tour in downtown Atlanta. You can watch the 3:00 PM show, and ask questions of various newsmakers. Downtown Atlanta retains much evidence of the 1996 Olympics, including Olympic Park.

Yes, it can get hot in Atlanta, but not much more than, say, Baltimore in the summer.

Los Angeles

Over the years, we have visited many of the attractions in and around Los Angeles: Beverly Hills, Rodeo Drive, Hollywood, the Walk of Fame, Universal Studios, and some of the nightclubs, but it wasn't until 2002 that we saw a game at Dodger Stadium.

The Red Sox played a three-game interleague series there in June and while the games were disastrous for Boston—the Red Sox were swept—the trip to Chavez Ravine was memorable.

Dodger Stadium opened in 1962 but it still looks clean, sparkling, and new some 40 years later. Vin Scully, the Hall of Fame broadcaster, and his partner, Ross Porter, welcomed us graciously and the visiting team's broadcast facilities were outstanding. You know the jokes about everyone having a car in L.A. and L.A. being a great big freeway. Well, they are accurate. The traffic in and around the stadium and the downtown area can be horrific, so allow plenty of time. Once you get near the park, though, there is wonderful access from the freeways to the parking areas and you can park and then enter the stadium on the level in which your seat is located.

Miami

I first went to Joe Robbie Stadium in 1989, before the Marlins franchise existed. The Red Sox played an exhibition game during Spring Training against the Baltimore Orioles there. The stadium had not been reconfigured for baseball, so they built a plywood fence around the outfield. It was only about 260 feet to leftfield. I remember some of the little left-hand batters hitting them out there. Danny Heep, for example, lined a homer over the fence.

The first time the Red Sox went to Pro Player Stadium (which Joe Robbie had become), to play the Marlins was in 1998. Fort Lauderdale and Miami are much different in the summer than they are in Spring Training. Yes, it's hot and humid, but you can get around quickly and there is not much traffic.

The team stays at the Marriott Marina in Fort Lauderdale, on 17th Street, near the Intercoastal Bridge. You can see numerous large yachts. Fort Lauderdale is known as the Venice of America, and it lives up to that name with lots of canals. I've taken a water taxi there, and I've been on some private boats. We've also rented bikes on the beach and ridden around some of the side streets by the private canals and in the Hugh Taylor Birch State Park. That was fun!

Fort Lauderdale Beach is beautiful, and the water feels great, but you do have to watch out for jellyfish. The water is about 80 degrees and the beach is not crowded in the summer. It is also a great place to leave teenagers—they love it.

Jan and I have also stayed at the Sheraton Yankee Clipper, the Sheraton Yankee Trader, and the Bahia Mar (now a Radisson), all on Fort Lauderdale Beach in the winter. There's good outdoor dining all around the area.

Bravo is an excellent modern restaurant featuring both northern and southern Italian food. Chicken, pasta, beef—everything's terrific. In fact, it's one of the best restaurants I've ever eaten at in the entire country. It is on 17th Street in Fort Lauderdale near the Intercoastal Bridge.

Concha D'Oro (shell of gold) in nearby Hollywood, Florida, also has excellent food, great pizza, and great prices. It has red-checkered tablecloths. Senior citizens line up to get in.

Doria's Pier Five in Hallandale on U.S. Route 1, across from the Gulfstream racetrack, is also one of my favorites in Florida. Italian cuisine and a New York style.

Don Shula's restaurant is a steakhouse in the Sheraton Yankee Trader. For fish, try Sea Watch on AIA near Pompano Beach or Max's Grille in Boca Raton's Mizner Shopping Plaza.

Los Olas Boulevard has some of Fort Lauderdale's best shopping—and most expensive.

You can take a snorkeling boat to go about 500 yards from the beach off Bahia Mar for some excellent snorkeling.

Although there are many Red Sox fans in the Miami area—including many who moved from New England—the crowds at Pro Player Stadium are usually quite small. The facilities and the broadcast booth at the stadium are good. But what bothers me there is that the stadium is right off the Florida Turnpike. So when you leave the stadium, you have to pay a toll to get out of the park. Also, there is very little public transportation to the ballpark. It's just too far from downtown Miami.

Montreal

I've only been to Montreal three times, but one thing is clear: Olympic Stadium, home of the Expos, is the worst ballpark in the major leagues. It's ugly. The only good thing I can say about the stadium is that you can reach it easily by subway. In fact, the subway runs from downtown directly into the ballpark. You don't even have to go outside.

We stayed at the Sheraton in downtown Montreal when the Red Sox played there starting with three games in 1997, and it seemed as though we were in a European city. Montreal is that different. The old cathedrals, the architecture, all have a European flavor. Yes, Montreal is a modern city with great shopping, and I really like Old Montreal. The neighborhood around the cathedral of Notre Dame is a great place to walk, although it is quite far from downtown. There's a nice Italian neighborhood near Mont Real. The ride up the mountain is a beautiful drive, and there's a good view of the city at the top.

In the Red Sox first game in Montreal, on Labor Day 1997—not a holiday in Montreal, of course—Vladimir Guerrero hit a walk-off home run in the bottom of the tenth inning to beat Boston 4-2 before a crowd of 29,000.

I also remember Guillermo Mota, a pitcher, hitting a home run off Boston in his first major league at bat on June 9, 1999.

The Red Sox were swept in Montreal in 1997 and again in 1999—0-3 in both visits. Then, they won two out of three in 2001. What I found interesting is that the Expos had been drawing about 5,000 fans per game, until the Red Sox came to town. Then, they drew about 32,000. A lot of Red Sox fans from northern New England, especially Vermont, drove up to Montreal to see the team play. It sounded like a Red Sox home game.

Montreal is on an island surrounded by the St. Lawrence River. There's a big casino there. Visiting the casino is a good way for baseball people to unwind after a game.

Montreal was a good minor league city for the Montreal Royals, where Jackie Robinson broke into the Dodger organization, but it is not a very good major league baseball city.

Philadelphia

I've been to Philadelphia with the Red Sox four times for interleague play. Veterans Stadium was one of the worst facilities I've ever been to. It's very hot in the summer, and the broadcast booths were about as hot as any I've ever worked in because the air just doesn't move. The artificial turf at the Vet was also dreadful.

We stayed at the Sheraton Hotel near Bookbinder's, Philadelphia's famous old seafood restaurant. It was a fun, tourist place to go to, but it has since closed. I went to the Italian market in Philadelphia, which was featured in *Rocky*. I also had a chance to visit Franklin Field, where Jeffrey Lyons once kicked off for the Penn Quakers. That's also the field where the Eagles and the Packers played the famous NFL championship game in 1960. And I saw the Palestra, where there have been many Big Five basketball games over the years. I did the Independence Hall Walk, tracing the path from the building where the Declaration of Independence was signed. The fans in Philadelphia are rabid about their teams, but can also turn very negative when things are not going well. They can really boo.

I think the best thing about my visits to Philadelphia was seeing Harry Kalas, the Voice of the Phillies and NFL Films and his partner

Chris Wheeler. Several years ago, we had a seminar at New York's Museum of Radio and Television, which featured a number of major league broadcasters from the Mets, Yankees, Phillies, Bob Wolf (formerly of the Senators), author Curt Smith, and me. My son Duke asked Harry Kalas to record a message for his answering machine. Harry asked him, "Do you want the baseball or the football?" Duke chose the football voice, and Harry made this recording for him: "Duke is not home right now, he's at the frooooooozen tunnnnnnndra of Lambeauuuuuuuuu Field awaiting the Greeeeeeeeen Bay Packahs."

I enjoyed seeing Andy Musser, Chris Wheeler, and particularly the late Richie "Whitey" Ashburn. In one of my classes, a student wrote a glowing paper on Richie Ashburn, and what a wonderful gem he was for Philadelphia. Richie was probably the most popular Phillie of all time. Richie was beloved not only because of his talent as a player, but also because of his many years broadcasting Phillies games.

◆ ● ◆

A highlight of going to Philadelphia is a chance to visit with one of my favorite Red Sox players, catcher John Marzano. Marzie now does the postgame TV show on Comcast after the Phillies games. He is a natural and is never at a loss for words. John still has the tape of his first major league home run called by Ken Coleman, August 15, 1987, at Arlington Stadium in Texas, as well as my postgame interview with him. He keeps the cassette in his safe deposit box and brought it to Veterans Stadium to play for me in June 2003.

We always kid Marzano about being a friend to the stars. He used to pal around with Roger Clemens in Boston and once tackled the Tigers John Shelby from behind when he charged the mound after Clemens hit him with a pitch. When he played for Seattle, Marzano hung around with Alex Rodriguez.

Marzano, who went to Temple and grew up in South Philly, is South Philly personified.

He also knows his restaurants. He sent us to a great place called Michael's in 2003, located at 8th and Christian in South Philly, which features the best antipasto I have ever had—stuffed mussels, eggplant, stuffed peppers, mushrooms, shrimp, and more. Michael's is reasonably priced and a short ride from city center.

Phoenix

I have only been to Bank One Ballpark in Phoenix once. We arrived at midnight on a late March night in 2000, did an afternoon exhibition game and flew out after the game to Seattle to open the season. The BOB is state of the art. It looks like an airplane hangar—not the most beautiful of the new parks but spectacular. The swimming pool in right center is its most distinguishing feature. As for Phoenix, I hadn't been there in 20 years, since I was in Spring Training with the Indians. Of course, it is now a much bigger city but I didn't get a chance to see much.

When I was with Cleveland, we used to make the trip several times a week, about 110 miles up I-10 from Tucson to the Phoenix area. The highlight, besides the cacti, was Picacho Peak, site of an 1862 Civil War engagement.

Pittsburgh

I have seen major league baseball in three ballparks in Pittsburgh. When I first got to Youngstown in 1970, I saw the Pirates play at old Forbes Field and did pregame TV interviews there. Forbes Field, located in the Oakland section of the city, opened in 1909. It had ivy-covered walls and deep dimensions especially down the leftfield line and to the power alleys and centerfield.

I remember entering the tiny broadcast booth to visit Bob Prince, the Hall of Fame broadcaster, and having to duck to avoid the pipes and girders. Forbes Field was located in a very busy part of the city and part of the University of Pittsburgh now sits on its location, where a plaque marks the spot where Bill Mazeroski hit the walk-off home run to end Game Seven and beat the mighty Yankees in the 1960 World Series.

Prince was a college graduate who went to Harvard Law School. But his father came to visit him at Cambridge, and saw a newspaper photo of Bob dancing with a stripper. The elder Prince pulled Bob out of law school on the spot. Bob moved to western Pennsylvania and wound up with the Pirates. *If I Hadn't Danced with a Stripper* was the original title of Prince's book, which was to have been written with my good friend Bill Christine.

Bob went on to a Hall of Fame broadcasting career. Bob was one of the best storytellers ever. He'd spend the first two innings sending birthday wishes to senior citizens, then get down to the game.

His firing by the Pirates after the 1975 season was one of the worst public relations moves in history, rivaled only, perhaps, by the Tigers's firing of Ernie Harwell after the 1991 season. The Tigers rehired Harwell after one year and the sale of the team to Mike Illitch. In 1993, Harwell was back, much to the delight of his many Detroit fans.

Prince was so popular in Pittsburgh that there was a march on radio station KDKA to demand that he be rehired, but he wasn't—until a decade later when he did cable TV games. Prince went to Houston in 1976, then on to ABC television.

On a close play, Bob would say, "He got him by a gnat's eyelash." Prince's favorite expressions were, "We need a bloop and a blast," and "We had 'em all the way." That kind of phrase, while both memorable and popular in Pittsburgh, simply would not have worked in Boston or New York. Those cities wanted knowledgeable, personable broadcasters, but not Homers who referred to their teams as "we." That is a Midwest style, made famous by Prince and Harry Caray. To my knowledge, no one in Boston baseball has taken that approach. I have never worked with someone who openly rooted, though there is no question that I want the Red Sox to win. Fans tell me that if they tune in to one of our broadcasts and don't know the score, they can tell by the tone of my voice whether the Red Sox are winning or losing. I take that as a compliment.

◆ ● ◆

In the middle of the 1970 season, the Pirates moved to Three Rivers Stadium. I covered the first game won by the Cincinnati Reds. Tony Perez, a future Hall of Famer, hit the first home run. Three Rivers, which the Pirates shared with the Steelers of the NFL, was a cookie-cutter all-purpose stadium similar to those in Cincinnati, Atlanta, and other places. But at the time, it was state of the art with modern conveniences, a big press box, and extra broadcast booths so I could do my practice play-by-play tapes through the courtesy of Bill Guilfoile, the Pirates public relations director.

It was one such recording of Bob Gibson's no-hitter that I used as an audition tape for job applications. I got to cover the 1970 and 1971 National League Championship Series at Three Rivers and the 1971 World Series there. Three Rivers Stadium was in a good location at the confluence of the Allegheny and Monongahela Rivers where they meet to form the Ohio.

I also saw Game Five of the 1979 World Series at Three Rivers, a key win for the "We Are Family" Pirates in their come-from-behind win over the Orioles, and I covered several Cleveland Browns-Pittsburgh Steelers games there.

One of the good things about interleague play is the chance to visit new parks, and in June 2003 the Red Sox played the Pirates at the new PNC Park. What a gem. You can walk from downtown Pittsburgh across the Roberto Clemente Bridge, which is open to pedestrian traffic only before and after games. You see the Roberto Clemente, Willie Stargell, Honus Wagner, and Ralph Kiner statues outside the park. The ballpark complex includes restaurants and bars and behind the center-field stand is Manny Sanguillen's Barbeque. I walked out to see Manny, whom I knew when he caught for the Pirates in the 1970s, and he is still a delightful guy. As we visited, we called Manny's former minor league manager and Pirates coach, Joe Morgan, on a cell phone and they were thrilled to talk to one another.

The highlight of PNC Park, though, is the view. Our broadcast booth is about five stories up—very high—which gives us a panoramic view of the river. You can see the ferry cruises moving up and down the Allegheny during the game, as well as barge and pleasure boat traffic. Less than a mile downriver is Heinz Field, new home of the Steelers and the University of Pittsburgh football team.

An activity I enjoyed was taking the Duquesne Incline, a cable car that goes from the Ohio River bank up Mt. Washington to the Mt. Washington section of Pittsburgh. I went with the great Red Sox fan,

Stanford law professor Bill Gould, who timed one of his lectures to coincide with the Red Sox visit to Pittsburgh.

There are several restaurants on top of Mt. Washington and the Georgetown Inn, which we chose, has a great view of the city and the stadiums. Downtown Pittsburgh is fun to walk but traffic is very congested and that is usually the case after a Pirates game.

St. Louis

Jan and I were honored to be invited to the Brian Daubach-Chrissie Geppi wedding in St. Louis.

Brian has been with the White Sox for one season, but they still thought to invite us to their wedding. Both families are so warm and friendly and made us feel so welcome. We were introduced as the people who first got Brian and Chrissie together. Chrissie asked me to do the second scripture reading at the mass, held at St. Peter and Paul's Church, in a renovated section of St. Louis. The reception was very elegant and we had a marvelous time. Two days after Christmas 2003, Jan and I got a call from an excited Chrissie Daubach who told us that Brian had been offered a minor league contract to rejoin the Red Sox. Both Chrissie and Brian were thrilled to be coming back to what they feel is their second home.

We also had a chance to visit Busch Stadium for the first time on this our first visit to St. Louis. For a mid-1960s all-purpose cookie-cutter facility, Busch Stadium does have some charm. The many statues out front including those of Jack Buck and Stan Musial give the area a unique feel.

We also got a quick tour of The Hill section from Mark Starr, son of my late partner, the Burly Broadcaster, Bob Starr. Mark showed us the field where Yogi Berra and Joe Garagiola developed their skills as kids.

San Diego

The Red Sox have been to San Diego twice—in 1984 for an exhibition game at what then was called Jack Murphy Stadium and in June 2002 for an interleague series against the Padres at the renamed Qualcomm

Stadium. Qualcomm is one of those 1960s-type cookie-cutters a la Three Rivers Stadium and Riverfront Stadium, but the Padres, through the efforts of Larry Lucchino and his group who ran the club until 2001, have built a beautiful new downtown park, Petco Field, opening in 2004.

It should fit in well with the delightful San Diego landscape.

Yes, the weather is beautiful and so is the scenery. One of the highlights is the nearby village of La Jolla, featuring high-end retail shops, art galleries, and fine dining. Just be careful of the parking codes. There are no meters but the time limits are strictly enforced by chalking the tires. The fine for staying overtime is hefty, as we discovered. La Jolla's public beaches are breathtaking, too, and the Pacific water is warm and refreshing. Another outstanding beach city, though much different from La Jolla, is Coronado, just across the bridge from downtown. It, too, has marvelous ocean views and shopping but is known for its old Victorian mansions and its large U.S. naval base. We had lunch at the Hotel del Coronado, an old resort and landmark hotel.

As for entertainment in downtown San Diego, the Gaslamp Quarter features outstanding restaurants and nightspots. We found Croce's, run by the family of the late musician Jim Croce, to have a great menu and excellent live music. Of course, we also found the Little Italy section, located just a few blocks from the financial district, and sampled the cuisine, which is outstanding.

For shopping and dining, Seaport Village, located near the major downtown hotels and the convention center, has more than 50 special stores and bay front restaurants.

Two of the top tourist's attractions are Old Town, the original center of San Diego and Balboa Park, home of the San Diego Zoo, and much more. We took our kids to the zoo several years ago and it is as spectacular as advertised with its pandas, hippo beach, and petting area. But if you are going to Balboa Park, you should also see the Japanese Gardens, art and historical museums and, our favorite, the San Diego Hall of Champions Sports Museum. San Diego natives are honored including, of course, Ted Williams, Tony Gwynn, and Bill Walton and there is a great display on the history of professional baseball in San

Diego including the Pacific Coast League Padres for whom Bobby Doerr and Teddy Ballgame starred. One regret was not having the chance to visit the small bungalow at 4121 Utah Street, number nine's boyhood home, which still stands.

We did make the obligatory 30-minute drive to the Mexican border, where we parked and crossed into Tijuana. The border stores were very disappointing unless you are into "health" stores featuring human growth pills. It was a very short visit.

PART III

Along the Way

Among My Favorite Players

After 38 years in sports broadcasting, including 25 at the major league level, and 22 with the Boston Red Sox, I think I have worked with hundreds of baseball players and executives.

I see the players and their families in Spring Training. At some point during the season, I probably interview every player on the roster for a pre- or postgame show. And I've had the opportunity to get to know many of them quite well. When a rookie is called up, I like to ask him how he pronounces his name. When a veteran is obtained through a trade, I introduce myself and seek some personal anecdotes.

One afternoon in 1972, I found myself all alone in the Pirates clubhouse with Roberto Clemente. The rest of the team was taking infield practice. He spoke with me about the pressure put on him for interviews, for charity work, for his time in Pittsburgh. I wish I had been recording the interview, but perhaps he spoke more freely because I was *not* taping our conversation. He said that the pressure on him was 100 times greater when he went home to Puerto Rico, because he felt the need to help people so much there, where he was revered as a demigod.

◆ ● ◆

Al Oliver was probably my best friend on the Pirates. I saw him recently at a Baseball Assistance Team dinner in New York. We spoke quite often when I was working in Youngstown. Al is from Portsmouth, Ohio. He spoke very well. In fact, he had a second career as a motivational speaker. I brought him to Youngstown twice. First, he spoke to our group, the Curbstone Coaches, a group of businessmen and athletes who are sports fans. We got him $50. The second time, I got a permit to use Pemberton Park, where Youngstown State played its games, for a clinic for kids. The Pirates had played a game on Sunday afternoon. After the game, he and his family got in a car, and drove to Youngstown where they rented a hotel room, which they paid for, and on Monday morning, Al did the clinic for about 150 kids. That took about three hours. His fee for the clinic was a whopping $100. The clinic was very good, particularly because of the wonderful way Al had of speaking with the kids.

I was pitching batting practice at the clinic, and Oliver kept hitting pop-ups, probably because my pitches were so slow. Without showing me up, I was asked to bring in the lefthander—a college pitcher who was helping us at the clinic. He pitched much faster than I did, and Al was able to hit a few out of the park. The kids loved that.

Al wound up with 2,743 hits during an 18-year career (1968–1985) with the Pirates, Rangers, Expos, Phillies, Giants, Blue Jays, and Dodgers.

By the time I went to Cleveland in 1972, I already knew some of the Indians because I had interviewed them in Cleveland and when I was a TV anchor in Youngstown. I had interviewed Buddy Bell, for example, while I was a TV anchor before I went to Cleveland. He and I have remained friends.

◆ ● ◆

My best friend on the Indians was Andre Thornton, and he remains one of my closest friends.

I met Andre when he joined the Indians in 1977. The Indians got him in a trade with the Expos for Jackie Brown—a great trade for the

Indians. Andre had a fine career with Cleveland, and retired as an Indian. He wound up with a record that will never be broken—Most Home Runs in a Career at Cleveland's Municipal Stadium (119), which the Indians left after the 1993 season for Jacobs Field.

Even during our first interview, something clicked and we had an instant bond. He was bright, articulate, and considerate.

One day in October 1977, I was pulling into the parking lot at WKYC, Channel 3 in Cleveland, where I was writing news, when I heard on the radio the tragic news of a car crash on the Pennsylvania turnpike. Andre's car had flipped over in the snow. His wife Gertrude and their three-year-old daughter Theresa were killed. Andre and his son Andre Jr. (Andy) survived. The funerals were held in his hometown of Phoenixville, Pennsylvania, near Philadelphia.

During the season, Andre lived in Bainbridge, Ohio, about seven miles from our home in Solon, Ohio. Jan and I wanted to do something for Andre and his son, so a few weeks after the crash, Jan made a pan of lasagna, and I called to ask whether I could bring something over. Andre was home with Andy. I went to try, somehow, to console Andre after this unimaginable tragedy, but he was such a strong person, and a strong Christian that, as it turned out, he consoled me. I left his house uplifted by his faith and his spirituality. We were able to talk quite frankly about what had happened, and how he would cope with his future and Andy's. I did a lot of listening, and that conversation brought us even closer.

In 1978, Andre had a big season with the Indians, and I visited with him often in the clubhouse or on the field, even if it was not for a formal interview. It was during that season that Andre met Gail Jones, a wonderful young lady whom Andre would soon marry. Gail and her sisters are gospel singers. Their father is Howard Jones of Oberlin, Ohio. He was with the Billy Graham Crusade. Gail's sister married Pat Kelly of the Baltimore Orioles. Pat Kelly once told Orioles manager Earl Weaver that he ought to walk with the Lord. Weaver said he'd rather walk with the bases loaded.

Jan and I were invited to Andre and Gail's wedding in Oberlin.

I have probably socialized more, and had more conversations with Andre Thornton than with any other ballplayer I have been around. I always thought that we'd have been friends even if he was not a ballplayer and I was not a broadcaster. We still visit with each other quite often.

In Cleveland, during the offseason, we'd go to Cavaliers games. One Spring Training, Andre and Gail went to Tucson and left Andy with us. Andy was Duke's age, and we brought him to school every day. We had a great time with him, and he was a fine influence on Duke.

In 1979, I traveled with the Indians, and we spent more time together. Andre introduced me to Baseball Chapel, which has become an important part of my Sunday routine. Players get together in a room off the clubhouse, and hear a speaker—a clergyman, an athlete, a coach, or somebody else—and I've been going ever since. Baseball Chapel was not as highly thought of at the time as it is now, and occasionally somebody stood outside the door and said nasty things one might not expect to hear. A small group of anti-Chapel players later told Andre that they respected him for his strong leadership by example, which had turned them around, and that they now supported Baseball Chapel. There is nothing formal about it—just people who work together taking time each week to share their faith and their spirituality.

Whenever players had personal issues—marriages, divorces, children, whatever—they went to Andre. He was, without a doubt, the strongest player I ever met—emotionally and spiritually. And he was very strong physically, too. He was a fine first baseman and a smart baserunner, though not blessed with great speed.

Unfortunately, Andre never got to play in a postseason game, because the Cleveland teams he played for had no money and no pitching.

During the latter part of his career, when he was not playing much, he studied with the people at Key Bank, with an eye on his post–baseball life. After his playing career was over, Andre continued to live his faith, creating Christian Camps. He took inner-city kids to a rural part of eastern Ohio, about 30 miles east of Cleveland, for Bible studies and outdoor activities.

Andre is now a major entrepreneur. He owned several Applebee's restaurants and also owned factories in Ohio and Michigan that produced heavy machinery. He has since sold those. Andre's business interests include a diversity training program, which helps major companies comply with equal opportunity laws, and a company called Global Promotions, which does promotions for sports franchises and major corporations and businesses. Andre is a member of the President's Council, a group of Cleveland's most influential business leaders that promote economic growth in Northeast Ohio. He is a true leader and innovator.

Whether on or off the field, Andre has been successful at whatever he does. His integrity and spirituality are always there. When the Red Sox visit Cleveland, Andre drives in about 30 miles from his home to see me, even if he does not go to the game. Sometimes he takes me out to his house to see Gail and their two college-age sons, Dean and Jonathan. Andy now lives in Chicago. Whenever I'm with Andre, I feel refreshed—emotionally and spiritually. He reassures me of the basics of life, and he is a true friend, and one of the best friends I've ever had in baseball.

◆ ● ◆

Johnny Pesky is "Mr. Red Sox." An outstanding shortstop who hit .307 during his ten-year career (1942–1954, with time out for World War II) with the Tigers, Senators, and the Red Sox, Johnny has served the Red Sox as player, manager, coach, special assistant to the general manager, broadcaster, and advertising salesman. He also managed the Sox AAA team in Pawtucket, Rhode Island. He has been a goodwill ambassador for nearly 60 years. Johnny is in uniform at Spring Training and visits Pawtucket and Lowell—and also the parent club when it is home during the season. Johnny is among the best fungo hitters of all time. I have calculated the number of fungoes he has hit in his career—enough to stretch about one third of the way around the world.

He was instrumental in helping me establish myself in Boston. My first year in Boston, 1983, Johnny was on the coaching staff but was losing weight and was too weak to stay on the bench. He lost over 50 pounds and looked terminally ill but was finally diagnosed with Celiac Sprue, a disease of the digestive system. That was nearly 20 years ago and he returned to robust health once the diagnosis was made but, in the meantime, he would sit in with me for the fourth and fifth innings of our home broadcasts. Johnny did the color while I did play-by-play. His presence and his very strong support gave me more credibility and acceptance. No one ever had a better or more loyal booster than I had with Johnny.

Johnny also took special interest in my sons, Duke and Tom, and hit them thousands of fungoes during early batting practice at stadiums on the road when they would travel with me. He was especially fond of Duke's strong arm and would tell everyone, "That kid's got a great arm." However, neither Duke nor anyone else could throw it by Pesky when he had a fungo bat in hand. One regret I have: when Duke married his lovely bride Kiki in 1999, I failed to invite Johnny and Ruthie Pesky to the wedding. I was mortified. Johnny, the most honest and sincere guy you could meet, called me on the carpet for the oversight. A year later, Tommy married Rachael and this time Johnny and Ruthie were invited. But in my presence, he told some mutual friends, "Yeah, I did get invited to this wedding. I shamed the old man into it after he didn't invite me to Duke's wedding." Johnny did forgive and forget, though, and we love him dearly. Every year, I try to attend the annual Johnny Pesky Friendship Dinner during the winter, thrown by some 500 of his closest friends. The 50th Pesky Friendship Dinner was held in January 2002.

◆ ● ◆

Rick Waits and I have also been friends for many years. Waits was a pitcher and he beat the Yankees the last day of the 1978 season, which forced the dramatic one-game New York-Boston playoff—the infamous "Bucky Dent game."

When I was working at WKYC-TV in Cleveland, I did a story on Rick, a lefthander with a good curveball—who was also a tenor. He grew up singing in church in his native Atlanta. The *Today Show* saw the piece, and liked it. So I put him in touch with the producer, and he got to sing on the *Today Show*. He had pitched the night before, and gave up a three-run homer to Lou Piniella in the bottom of the ninth inning to lose the game—a crushing defeat. Rather than go to bed after the game, and try to get up and get his voice in shape to sing, he decided to stay up all night, and he did. When he went on the air the next morning, he sang "The Impossible Dream," from the Broadway hit *Man of*

La Mancha, a very difficult song. Unfortunately, at one point he forgot the lyrics and just sang "tra la la." But his voice sounded fine.

Rick later coached in the Mets system.

◆ ● ◆

When I came to the Red Sox in 1983, I was 36—younger than Carl Yastrzemski, but older than many of the other players. My first year with the Sox, we had a team of very nice players. Rick Miller, our Baseball Chapel leader, became a close friend. He was the top pinch-hitter in the league, and had won a Gold Glove as an outfielder in 1978. Rick's wife Janet is Carlton Fisk's sister. We still see each other at Fantasy Camp and have always had lots of conversations about baseball and life.

◆ ● ◆

Mike Easler is from Cleveland, and had spent a long time in the minor leagues. I did a "Why isn't this guy in the majors?" story about him while he was with the Columbus Clippers. His family liked the story, and we became fast friends. Mike joined the Sox in 1984, and became a really good friend. We talked a lot on buses and planes, and spent time together in Red Sox chapel. He had a really good year in 1984, hitting .313 with 27 home runs.

Mike later became the Red Sox hitting coach, where he became Mo Vaughn's "personal" hitting coach. Mike is a very solid, uplifting guy. If you spend five minutes with him, you'll feel better about the world.

◆ ● ◆

Marc Sullivan was a catcher for the Red Sox in 1982 and from 1984 to 1987. What a nice guy. You could spend hours with him and the fact that his father owned the team never came up. I still see Marc at Red Sox Fantasy Camp.

◆ ● ◆

Many of us used to go out to Snoqualmie Falls together, outside of Seattle, for a 13-course breakfast. Rick Miller, Glenn Hoffman, a quality guy, a steady shortstop, and later, albeit briefly, the manager of the Los Angeles Dodgers.

Dave Stapleton was also on the team. Yes, I agree that he should have been used to replace Bill Buckner for defense in Game Six of the 1986 World Series. They all made me feel welcome in 1983, my first year with the team—and my first year being the regular, 162-game broadcaster for a major league team.

◆ ● ◆

Dennis Eckersley was also a member of the 1983 Red Sox team. He remembered me from Cleveland, and was always fun to talk to, either in an interview or just to chat. He had a unique way of expressing himself—his own language. He used to say about a particular pitch, "That ball had hair on it," meaning that the ball was thrown hard. Dennis was considered very cocky when he played—he used to shoot guys out after he struck them out, but he was down to earth and humble. Cocky yes, arrogant, no. There's a difference. He was also direct and honest, and he was one of Jan's favorites. She loves his directness—the way he looks you in the eye.

After he retired, Eckersley broadcast a few games with me, and his unusual take on the English language continued. In 2000, the Angels had a short little second baseman from Australia named Trent Durrington, just up from AA. Dennis was on the air with me in Anaheim, when Durrington came to the plate, and Dennis said, "This guy is a sand blower." I said,"You have to explain what a sand blower is." He said, "that's a short guy, built so low to the ground that when he passes gas, he blows the sand or dust all around." After we broke for the next commercial, Eck said to me, "aren't you proud of me? I didn't say fart."

We are thrilled that Eck was elected to the Baseball Hall of Fame in 2004, his first year of eligibility.

◆ ● ◆

Tony Armas Sr. and I spent a lot of time together. Most of the time when we met at the hotel bar, he bought. I enjoyed being with him. For a guy with a lot of baseball talent, he was quite humble. He was also a very intelligent baserunner. I never saw him make a mistake on the base paths. I have found that most Venezuelan players, like Tony, have very good baseball instincts, and are well coached and knowledgeable about the game. Armas did strike out a lot, but he also won a home run crown with 43 in 1984. When somebody congratulated him on a good catch, he became very humble. "If you don't hit, you've got to do something," he used to say.

◆ ● ◆

Marty Barrett appeared briefly with the Red Sox in 1982 and again in 1983 and came to stay in 1984. From the mid-1980s, he lived in Pembroke, not too far from me, and we occasionally drove to Fenway together. In 1986, Marty had 24 hits in the postseason—which at the time was the League Championship Series and the World Series record. Even now, with the extra layer of playoffs added in the Division Series, his record of 24 hits has not been broken.

Marty was a very heady player and you could almost see him thinking on the field. I saw him involved in the hidden ball trick three times. The first was on July 7, 1985, in Anaheim. Barrett got Bobby Grich at second base. Two weeks later, on July 21, he flipped to shortstop Glenn Hoffman who tagged out Doug DeCinces. Barrett did it again on September 5, 1988, as he tossed to shortstop Jody Reed who tagged Jim Traber of the Orioles.

Also in 1988, I saw Barrett steal home in Baltimore—the first time a Red Sox player had done it in 15 years.

Marty was very unhappy during 1990, his last year with the Sox. Manager Joe Morgan replaced him at second base. Marty was angry when he left the club. Unfortunately, after his knee operation in 1989, he had lost a step, and after just 12 games with the Padres in 1991, his major league playing career was over.

◆ ● ◆

Don Baylor joined the Sox in 1986 after a trade for Mike Easler. I always liked being around Don. He was a strong guy, and you could sense his leadership qualities. When he came to the Boston clubhouse, he saw problems that needed to be fixed, and he fixed them. He established himself as a star in 1986, and hit a big home run for Boston in the ninth inning of Game Five of the ALCS that year, which cut the Angels's lead to one run.

◆ ● ◆

Tom Bolton (Red Sox 1987–1992) and Dana Kiecker (from Sleepy Eye, Minnesota, Red Sox 1990–1991) won some big games for the Red Sox in 1990. A UPS deliveryman in the offseason, Kiecker got hurt during the 1991 season and quickly faded. Bolton won a game against the Tigers in September 1990, which put the Red Sox in front to stay in the American League East.

◆ ● ◆

Wade Boggs and I did not spend a lot of time together, but we respected each other as professionals. Occasionally, I would give Boggs some numbers he found amusing. When I keep my score book during a game, instead of just putting down a number, such as 6, to indicate which fielder made a put-out, I write PO 6—indicating a pop-up rather than a line drive. In August 1985, I reviewed my scorebook and noticed that Wade Boggs had not popped up to an infielder all season. (Later in the season, I think he did so once or twice.) When I mentioned this unusual statistic to Boggs, he liked it.

He also liked to hear the wall-ball statistics that I also kept before most other people did. Wall-balls are balls hit off the Green Monster in Fenway's leftfield, for example.

Boggs was without question the best two-strike hitter I have ever seen. His ability to wait on a pitch, even with two strikes, was amazing. He could hit the leftfield wall better than anybody, about 24 times a year, until 1992, when he struggled and didn't hit the wall after May. (That was Boggs's worst year. He hit only .259.) But he won the American League batting title five times, including 1983, his second season in Boston and my first.

Thereafter, he won it every year through 1989, except for 1984, when Don Mattingly of the Yankees won it. But Boggs was the best contact hitter I've ever seen. He could hit the ball right out of the catcher's mitt. He also had an uncanny ability to foul off difficult pitches until he got a pitch he wanted.

Why didn't Boggs hit more homers? He probably could have hit 30 homers a season, and still batted .310. But with his five batting titles and .328 career average, he's going right to the Hall of Fame.

During his years with the Red Sox, I watched Boggs improve his fielding at third base, going from below average to a Gold Glove. He really worked at it.

Some people have denigrated Boggs's athletic ability. He was very fast leaving the batter's box, though not very fleet afoot. To be sure, speed is a valuable asset in baseball. But, to me, eye-hand coordination is just as important in athletic competition as the ability to run fast or to jump high. Boggs certainly had that.

A final word or two about Wade Boggs. In the ten years (1982–1992) he was with the Sox, I never met and I never saw Margo Adams. I don't think I led or lead a sheltered life. Her presence only came to my attention when the affair became public. Right after that, the issue blew up in a flurry of dreadful publicity for Boggs and the team.

I never discussed the issue with Boggs, either in person or on the air, because it did not affect what he did on the baseball field. He was paid to play every day, and he did. And he played very well.

Over the years, we got to know and like Wade's wife Debbie, his daughter Meghan, and his son Brett, named for George Brett.

Boggs did have some unusual idiosyncrasies, besides being very superstitious. (His habit of eating chicken before every game is quite well known.) Less well known is the incident when he fell out of his pickup truck on Route 17 in Winter Haven, and once claiming that when he was threatened at knife-point, he had willed himself invisible.

◆ ● ◆

One of my all-time favorite ballplayers was Dennis Oil Can Boyd (OCB), all 155 pounds of him (maybe less). He was called Oil Can because, as a kid in Meridian, Mississippi, he drank beer and called it oil. His father had played in the Negro Leagues. Even though Dennis was considered a "character," and off the wall, he was a very astute

pitcher. He knew what he was doing on the mound—how to set up hitters, how to work hitters. He had a wide assortment of pitches, and
good control. He threw a "slide ball," as he called it, a fastball, and several other pitches. He loved Satchel Paige.

John Lincoln Wright and the Designated Hitters recorded a song
called "The Ballad of Oil Can Boyd." How many players have songs
written about them? We played the song once on the air and our station
owner, Jack Campbell, complained. He liked only Big Band music.

Although Boyd was said to have had a number of clubhouse
tantrums—including a legendary one in 1986 when he was not named
to the American League All-Star team—I never saw any myself. I just
loved to talk pitching with him. He was a very intellectual pitcher, and
always friendly to me. I always found him charming and engaging, but
I understand that he can be emotional. I still see him at Red Sox Fantasy
Camps. In 1986, he won 16 games, helping the Sox to the American
League pennant. A circulatory problem shortened his career.

◆ ● ◆

I liked Bill Buckner. He played hard and was well spoken. He had more
than 100 RBI in 1985 and 1986, his two full seasons with the Red Sox.
Bill swung at everything.

He was always straight up with me. During the years he was with
the Red Sox, I was the number two radio announcer (number one was
Ken Coleman), but Bill always treated me with respect.

Bill Buckner had an outstanding 22-year career with the Dodgers,
Cubs, Red Sox, Angels, and Royals. He had 1,208 RBI and 2,715 hits.
He must have been doing something right.

But he will always be remembered for the error he made in
Game Six of the 1986 World Series in which the Red Sox played the
New York Mets. When the game started, the Red Sox led the series three
games to two. So the Sox only needed one more win to be World
Champions, something they had not been since 1918.

I always thought that Buckner, who was 36 and had bad ankles,
should have been removed for defensive purposes in the last of the tenth

inning. But John McNamara kept him in the game, and Buckner made a terrible error. But that error did not cost the Sox the Series. Even if he had not made the error, the game would have been tied, and gone into extra innings. And that was only Game Six. The Sox had a 3-0 lead in Game Seven and could have won it. But they did not. The Mets were World Champions.

In 1987, Buckner had a bad year with the Red Sox, and was traded late in the season to the California Angels. He came back to the Sox for 22 games in 1990. The fans at Fenway gave him a standing ovation when the entire team was introduced on Opening Day that year. Later, he was hounded out of New England and retired to Idaho.

◆ ● ◆

One of my oldest friends in baseball is Lynn Jones, the former backup outfielder with Detroit and Kansas City who served as Lonnie Smith's caddy in leftfield during the Royals's World Championship season in 1985.

Lynn would replace Smith in leftfield when the Royals held the lead late in games and hit a triple in the 1985 World Series. Lynn, a Thiel College graduate is one of the very few graduates of the President's Athletic Conference to make the major leagues. (Don Shula and Carl Taseff of NFL fame went to conference rival, John Carroll.) Lynn's brother Darryl played for the Yankees briefly after graduating from Westminster College. The Jones brothers grew up and still live in Conneautville, Pennsylvania, where my in-laws vacationed, so we'd get together during the All-Star break. Lynn, as it turns out, used to watch me on television in Youngstown when he was in high school and I later worked with his brother Paul at NBC-TV in Cleveland. Lynn managed at the A, AA, and AAA levels in the Florida Marlins's system and also the Braves Class A Club in Macon. He also coached third base for the Marlins and has worked as a financial analyst, stockbroker, and investment specialist. In 2003, Lynn joined the Red Sox as a roving minor league outfield instructor. I think he will make an excellent major league manager in the near future. He is the Red Sox first base coach in 2004.

◆ ● ◆

Ellis Burks was a special favorite of mine. He came up to the Red Sox in 1987, when they were having a bad year. He gave the Sox a dimension they had not had in a long time, at least since I had been with the club— speed. He stole 27 bases and hit 20 home runs in his rookie season. He had a very quick bat. I always found him well spoken and a gentlemen. He was 23 when he came up, and we talked a lot. He was also my daughter Katie's favorite player. He spoke to Katie, who was eight that year, as he would speak to an adult. She kept his picture (which he signed for her) on her bedroom wall. It's still there, along with a bat and a glove he gave her.

Ellis had some very good years with the Red Sox, but he suffered some serious injuries. Mike Greenwell ran into Burks in the outfield a few times, and he hurt his shoulder sliding on a triple in Detroit in 1990.

I think the Sox made a mistake letting Burks go after the 1992 season. They did not offer him a contract for 1993, because they were afraid that his bad back would hamper his play. Burks has hit over 300 home runs and has had a very solid career. He re-signed with the Red Sox for 2004.

◆ ● ◆

José Canseco—one of the more disappointing players I have ever been around. The players called him "Elvis." The Sox acquired him from the Texas Rangers in 1995, and he was with the Sox for just two years. But he only played 198 games over those two years, because he spent a considerable amount of time hurt. Tremendous power, of course, but he was an excellent and underrated situational hitter when he was not trying to hit 500 home runs. He could drive in a runner from third, or simply advance a runner. Canseco retired early in the 2002 season, just 38 home runs short of 500.

Canseco was a natural and a disciplined hitter at times, again, when he was not trying to crank one out.

He did not really work at his trade. When the team was stretching, he was talking to players in the batting cage. I don't think Canseco really enjoyed playing baseball. He seemed to enjoy the show business aspect of the game. He was the best player in the game in 1988 (42 homes, 124 RBI, 40 stolen bases, .307 average), and had he worked at it, he could have stayed there for several years.

◆ ● ◆

Roger Clemens is one of the most interesting people I have been around during my years with the Red Sox. I will never forget the first time I saw him. Spring Training 1984. He had been the Red Sox first round draft pick in 1983, and he pitched briefly in New Britain (AA) and Pawtucket (AAA). He faced three Detroit Tigers batters in Chain O'Lakes Park in Winter Haven. The Tigers were a wire-to-wire winner in 1984, and they won the World Series. Nevertheless, Clemens struck out three outstanding righthand batters—Chet Lemon, Tom Brookens, and Larry Herndon on ten pitches. I knew I had seen the real thing when I saw Clemens. I broadcast all 192 of his Red Sox wins. I got to know him quite well, because he was young, and at 37, I was the youngest Red Sox broadcaster.

Clemens was warming up in the Anaheim bullpen in 1985. John MacNamara, the Sox manager, walked out to talk with Clemens. Clemens must have told Mac that something was wrong, because he went right from the bullpen to the airport for a flight back to Boston to be examined by the team physician. Al Nipper, one of Clemens's good friends on the team (and a good friend of mine) went with him. Clemens wound up having arm surgery and it was unclear whether he'd recover enough to be a dominant pitcher. He came back better than ever.

Clemens had a great year in 1986. He did everything he wanted to do. When we were in Milwaukee for a series, he went to a Monday Night Football game to see the Packers play in Green Bay. We went to the White House on September 10 that year.

Clemens pitched Game Six of the World Series, and left with a lead (to this day, probably only three people know whether he asked out of the game, or whether he was removed by manager John McNamara) and won Game Seven of the ALCS. The only person besides Clemens and McNamara who might know is Bill Fischer, the Red Sox pitching coach. He's not saying. But I think Clemens noticed a blister on his finger, and said

"I have a blister, and I don't know if I can throw my slider." So McNamara took him out. I cannot believe that Roger asked out of the game.

I was always fond of Roger, and we continue to have a good relationship. One of his problems with the media was that his wording was often misinterpreted.

Roger once made the statement, "If they don't protect the families of the players in the stands, someone is going to get hurt." Some took this as a threat on his part. But I think Roger meant innocent family members might get hurt. He was seeking a section for Red Sox families in the stands. Another time he made the statement, "You have to carry your own bags around here." He meant it figuratively, but some took it literally.

Red Sox Manager Joe Morgan told me that Clemens always cheered for his teammates while he was on the bench. It bothered me when Clemens left the Red Sox, especially later when he went to the Yankees. There was nothing really wrong with Clemens, except that he had been with bad ballclubs with bad bullpens. The Sox couldn't score, and the relievers could not close games for him.

Six of us saw both games in which Roger Clemens struck out 20 batters. The first game was on April 29, 1986, against the Seattle Mariners, and the second was on September 18, 1996, against the Detroit Tigers.

The lucky six were Rich Zawacki, Red Sox physical therapist; Jim Rice—player in 1986, coach in 1996; Bill Moloney, the Sox batting practice pitcher; Jack McCormick the Red Sox traveling secretary since 1996 (during Roger Clemens's first 20 strikeout game, he was a Boston police officer, assigned to keep intruders out of the Red Sox dugout), grounds crew member (and later clubhouse manager) Joe Cochran, and me.

I was the first to interview Roger after his first major league win on May 20, 1984, in Minnesota. My son Duke, now a sportscaster with WCBS-TV in New York City, was the first to interview Clemens after his 300th win on June 13, 2003.

◆ ● ◆

Brian Daubach is also one of my favorites. He's a self-made player who worked hard for almost a decade in the minor leagues. He was one of Jan's favorites. Daubach, from Bellevue, Illinois, is the son of a letter carrier, and he retains his blue-collar values, including dedication to hard work.

◆ • ◆

The worst injury I ever saw was the line drive off the bat of Ryan Thompson of the Yankees on September 8, 2000. The ball hit Bryce Florie, the Red Sox pitcher, square in the face by his right eye, and he went down, his legs kicking spasmodically on the pitcher's mound at Fenway. He was taken off the field in a golfcart and taken to the Red Sox medical room at Fenway, where he was treated briefly until the ambulance arrived to take him to the hospital. Florie made an amazing comeback and returned to pitch again for the Red Sox the following June 28, but his stay in the big leagues was brief.

◆ • ◆

The fastest Red Sox runner I ever saw was Donnie Sadler. He broke in with the Red Sox in 1998, and was used sporadically through 2000. Sadler went on to play for the Reds, the Royals, and the Rangers.

◆ • ◆

Johnny Damon and Tony Armas Sr. were the best (not necessarily the fastest) baserunners I ever saw. Damon was the best base stealer during my years with the Red Sox.

◆ • ◆

The most unusual pitching motion is easy to select: Tom Brennan, known as the Gray Flamingo. I first saw him with the Indians in 1981. He perched on one leg and hesitated in the midst of his delivery—sort of like a flamingo. And he had gray hair.

◆ • ◆

Dwight Evans hit the first home run I ever called. I was doing Indians TV in 1979, a fly ball off Rick Wise into the screen at Fenway. I traveled with him from 1983 through the end of his stay with the Red Sox in 1990.

Dwight was a great rightfielder with a great arm. He was a disciplined hitter, and drew a lot of walks. Had a big homer in Game Seven of the 1986 World Series, and he had a penchant for hitting walk-off home runs on Saturday afternoons at Fenway. He did it four times.

We had many conversations about baseball and about families. Dwight was very pensive and was an enjoyable guy to listen to. But he did not want to know his stats. He always told me "Don't tell me my stats. I don't want to know." But I think he knew them anyway. He worked hard at staying in shape. The Sox got a Versaclimber, which exercises the legs by simulating mountain climbing. He used it and he was able to stay an excellent outfielder for many years. Dwight was the Red Sox hitting coach in 2002.

◆ ● ◆

Tony Fossas. A left-handed reliever. Red Sox manager Joe Morgan helped Fossas make a lot of money. He could throw a hook to left-handed batters to get them out. Ken Griffey Jr. bunted off him because he was so frustrated—but later hit a three-run home run off Tony.

Morgan saw Fossas at a tryout in Pawtucket when Fossas was quite young and years later gave him a chance with the big club. Fossas is a native of Cuba, who grew up in Jamaica Plain section of Boston. He lives in Ft. Lauderdale now. A very religious guy, he was also very loyal to Joe and to the Red Sox.

◆ ● ◆

Nomar Garciaparra—the best all-around player I have ever seen with the Red Sox. He's very bright and knows what he's doing in the game. Nomar does not brag, but he once told me that his grade point average at St. John Bosco high school was 4.02—because he took honors courses in math. He went to Georgia Tech.

Nomar is a tremendous worker, and knows his body well. Like Wade Boggs, he takes 100 ground balls before every game. He regularly makes the most spectacular plays I have ever seen at shortstop, especially the one where he moves toward third base, grabs the ball while moving, makes a pivot, and makes a turnaround jumpshot to get the runner at first base. I've had the chance to meet his family, including his father, Ramon, and mother, Sylvia. He understands the fans in Boston. A real five-tool player who, if he stays healthy, will wind up in Cooperstown.

◆ ● ◆

Mike Gardiner was a journeyman pitcher obtained by the Red Sox in a trade with Seattle. A Canadian, he was one of the brightest players I have ever known. He persuaded some minor league teammates to invest with him, and after he retired from baseball, he became a stock analyst. He knew what he was doing on the mound, and could always explain what he was doing. He did not have a great fastball. He worked out with my son Duke at Stonehill College in the offseason. I thought Mike would have been a fine broadcaster. He enjoyed his stay in the majors as much as anybody I have known in the majors.

◆ ● ◆

Tom "Flash" Gordon came to the Sox as a free agent pitcher from Kansas City. He set the Red Sox record for most saves in a season in 1998. He got Trup and me into a Stephen King book called *The Girl Who Loved Tom Gordon*. In the book, the girl listens to Trup and me broadcast Red Sox games while she is lost in the Maine woods, and she hopes that Gordon will get into the games. That season, King was hit by a van in Maine while he was jogging and he required painful hip surgery. Gordon also had a severe injury and had to undergo "Tommy John" surgery. Jimy Williams and I always called him "Thomas." Whenever I stopped by his locker in the clubhouse, he was always easy to talk to.

◆ ● ◆

Another of my favorites was Jeff Gray, a journeyman middle-reliever. He could throw his fastball and splitter for strikes. A Florida State product, he was Jody Reed's roommate. He thought very hard about the game, and worked hard at it. He was always quite serious. No fooling around at all. He had a stroke while he was in college, and had another one in the Red Sox clubhouse, which really finished his career as a pitcher. A

sad case. But a guy who had a lot of success by hard work who appreciated what he had.

◆ ● ◆

Jason Varitek is a catcher I respect very much. He is a rock—and has
never missed a game because of injury except when he broke his elbow
diving for a pop-up in June 2001. He knows how to work pitchers and
how to call a game—a very cerebral catcher and a solid pro.

◆ ● ◆

Mike Greenwell. As Jerry Trupiano said first, "I don't know where he is
right now, but I do know that wherever he is, he's talking." Mike was
the most talkative player I have ever met.

24

Managers

The first big league manager I had was Jeff Torborg. He was managing the Indians when I started with Cleveland in 1979. When Indians manager Frank Robinson was fired in June 1977, Jeff took over the reigns in Cleveland. Since then, he has managed the White Sox, the Mets, the Expos, and the Marlins. He remains one of my best friends in baseball.

Jeff is a great manager and a strong family man. If you meet Jeff, you meet his family—his wife Suzie (a former Miss New Jersey), and their three sons, Doug, Greg, and Dale. Jeff is very proud of his family and is devoted to them. He was a backup catcher, hitting .214 for his career, but he caught three no-hitters, including Sandy Koufax's perfect game. As a collegiate player at Rutgers, he set the NCAA batting record with a .537 mark in 1963.

Jeff was very sensitive as a manager, particularly to the guys who did not play every day. He was one of those guys when he played for the Dodgers under Walter Alston. Jeff never caught 100 games in a season until his last year, 1973, when he caught 102 games for the Angels.

We used to see the Torborg boys escort Suzie to her seat at the ballpark, and Jan and I were impressed by their gentlemanly manners. I knew Greg and Dale the best. Greg is a lawyer and an agent in New York. He worked the computers in the front office for the Expos when his father was the manager. Dale became a professional wrestler after a good baseball career at Northwestern University and in the minors. He's known as "The Kiss Demon." His wife, Christie Wolf, is also a professional wrestler, who goes by "Asya."

Unfortunately, when Jeff managed in Cleveland, he did not have a good ballclub. (His Cleveland teams, 1977 to 1979, finished fifth, sixth, and sixth in the American League East.) Gabe Paul, the Indians's president, was very tough on managers. For example, in early July 1979, the Indians had just broken a ten-game losing streak. Rumors started to circulate that Gabe Paul had offered the Indians's managing job to Hall of Fame pitcher and Indians legend Bob Lemon. At the time, Lemon was between managing stints with the New York Yankees, because Billy Martin was running the club. Yankees's owner George Steinbrenner had leaked the story about Lemon to the Cleveland press because he was upset with Gabe Paul, who had recently left the Yankees.

Lemon turned the job down. I was in Detroit with the Indians, and Gabe Paul held a press conference in a hotel room to tell us that Jeff Torborg was still the Indians manager—"But don't ask me for how long." I thought it was an awkward and embarrassing situation for Jeff, who deserved better.

About three weeks later, Jeff was fired and replaced by Dave Garcia. I'll never forget it. I walked into the clubhouse that day. The Torborg youngsters had written on the chalkboard, "Good luck, Uncle Dave." The Torborg family was very close to Dave Garcia and his family.

Torborg then coached for the Yankees for ten years, and got back to managing as the skipper of the Chicago White Sox, where he had his best days. After finishing in seventh place in 1989, the White Sox, under Torborg, finished in second place in the American League West in both 1990 (when he was named American League Manager of the Year) and 1991.

In 1992, Torborg went to the Mets. A good move financially, but he took over an old team with high salaries and big egos. The Mets finished fifth in 1992 and seventh—dead last—in 1993. He was fired during the

1993 season, but went on to become an excellent broadcaster. He and I had talked about broadcasting before he became a broadcaster. We always wanted to work together because we liked each other, had (and still have) an excellent rapport, and thought that our styles and approaches would complement each other.

Jeff was a frequent guest on our Red Sox broadcasts—and not just because we were friends. He was intelligent and was articulate enough to share his insights with the listeners. He did the ESPN radio broadcasts on their Sunday night games, before moving to the Fox TV network.

Jeff returned to managing with the Montreal Expos in 2001, and the Florida Marlins from 2002 to early 2003.

I see Jeff and Suzie Torborg at the B.A.T. dinner in New York in January, and at Spring Training or interleague play.

◆ ● ◆

Dave Garcia is a great storyteller and a great lobby sitter. He never played in the majors, so most of his stories are about the minors. I learned a lot about baseball and people from Dave. He grew up in East St. Louis. His wife Carmen, a wonderful lady who passed away a few years ago, was a very dedicated baseball wife. She went to all the games. Carmen had an uncanny ability to predict the sex of a newborn by feeling the mother's belly. I don't know how she did it, but she was right about 98 percent of the time, especially in 1979—the year Dave became the manager—because the Indians had a very fertile ballclub. Jan was pregnant that year. After Carmen put her hand on Jan, she pronounced, "It will be a girl." Kate was born May 31, 1979. I still don't know how Carmen did it.

Dave had some conflicts with Gabe Paul, but did things the way he thought was the right way. Before taking over the Indians, he had managed the Angels for parts of 1977 and 1978. After his dismissal in Cleveland following the 1982 season, he stayed in the game as a scout and then as a coach for the Colorado Rockies.

Dave was a solid baseball man and manager who was loyal to his players, and never showed them up.

◆ ● ◆

When I got to Milwaukee in 1981, the Brewers's manager was Bob "Buck" Rodgers. He had been a switch-hitting catcher for the Angels. In 1962, the expansion team's second year in the league, they challenged the New York Yankees for the American League pennant. Buck was a big, strong, good-looking guy, and there was no question who was in charge when you were around Buck Rodgers. He ran a game tightly and ran a ballclub well.

I always appreciated the way he treated me. Buck knew that I didn't live in Milwaukee, and that my time there was rather limited. When I would come into Milwaukee from Cleveland, he'd ask me, "What do you want, what do you need?"

◆ ● ◆

When I came to the Red Sox in 1983, the manager was Ralph Houk. It was great to be around him because he had managed the great Yankee teams of the early 1960s, which I had followed as a kid. He was very nice to me, and we talked a lot of baseball. He talked and I listened.

I never saw Ralph except at the ballpark—never at the hotel, at a restaurant, or at a bar. But one day in Baltimore, late in the 1983 season, I saw Ralph at the hotel pool. I was wondering whether I'd be back for a second year. I said, "Ralph, I hope I'm coming back next year." Ralph had a great way of reassuring people and he told me, "Everything I've heard has been good. The baseball people like you. You'll be fine." I felt ten feet tall. I was relieved to hear it, because Jan and I were buying a house near Boston at the time.

Houk was a good guy. Whenever I needed an interview, a quote, or an explanation of why he made some move, he always gave me what I needed.

Ralph decided to retire after the 1984 season. The team gave him a golf cart. He and his wife Betty went back to Florida to live. He returned to the game as a Spring Training instructor with the Twins. With the possible exception of Earl Weaver, nobody put on a better show when he was ejected by an umpire—tossing his cap, waving his arms, and stomping his feet.

The media might have been a little intimidated by him, because he was never really ripped in the papers, at least not during his years in Boston. Some of that may have been because of his reputation as a soldier—"the Major," who earned a battlefield commission.

Ralph was generally friendly and soft-spoken.

You never talked to Ralph about a tough loss, especially the next day.

I remember watching a college World Series game in Ralph's office in 1984. Cal-Fullerton was in the game, and they were way behind. In the late innings, I told him I thought that they were going to lose. But Ralph knew that the game was "live on tape," so he bet me that they would come back and win. He already knew the final score! The next day, he told me that he knew they were going to win—"I knew it all along!" Ralph got a big kick out of that.

◆ ● ◆

John McNamara succeeded Ralph Houk when he retired after the 1984 season. I think John's greatest contribution to the team was that he emphasized pitching and he was very good with the pitching staff. John also had an excellent pitching coach in Bill Fischer. Mac always acted like he had the weight of the world on his shoulders. He was very serious, and he suffered every defeat as a personal insult. He lived and died with every game. In 1985, Mac's first season with the Red Sox, the team finished in fifth place in the American League East with a dismal 81-81 record.

But I also remember that when the Sox won the Division the very next year, Ken Coleman and I were in the clubhouse for the team celebration, and we interviewed Mac. He said, "You and Kenny are part of this. You're with the team every day." A very gracious thing to say.

The thing I remember most about John McNamara was how hard he took the team's World Series loss in 1986. Everybody in Boston and in New England took it hard. Everybody associated with the team took the loss very hard, but John took it the hardest of all. I remember the trip back to Boston after the team's loss in Game Seven. There was a very short bus ride from Shea Stadium to LaGuardia Airport, where we boarded the team plane for the flight to Boston. He tried to put on a smile, but we could all see how forced it was. I sat next to Dave Sax, who was not eligible to play in the series.

A few days later, Boston had a parade for the team which had, after all, won the American League pennant. The players rode in trucks, but I was covering the parade for WPLM, the team's flagship station, so I watched from Boston's City Hall Plaza. About a half a million people came out to see the team that had suffered a crushing defeat in the World Series. Mac spoke, but he wasn't very happy. He said that he really didn't want to be there, but the fans lifted him up.

After the parade, the team went back to the ballpark to clean out their lockers. I went into Mac's office and told him that I thought he had a great season despite the World Series loss. What he said was, "Why me? WHY ME? I go to church every Sunday. I live right. Why did this have to happen to me?" I knew that he went to church, because I went with him a number of times, and saw him in church on other occasions. "Why me?" He sounded a little like Ralph Branca, after he gave up the pennant-winning home run to Bobby Thomson in 1951. "Why me?"

I don't think Mac ever got over that 1986 loss. To this day, baseball people who spend time with Mac say that he can't go more than a few minutes without somehow bringing up 1986. The loss in 1986 is constantly with him. I don't think he'll ever get over it.

McNamara was back with the Red Sox, but he and the team had a very tough season in 1987, finishing fifth in the division with a 78-84 record. The next year, 1988, was the year of Margo Adams, the woman who announced that she was Wade Boggs's on-the-road mistress. It was also the year of the fight in Cleveland. Mac was replaced at the All-Star break by Joe Morgan, who had been the third base coach.

McNamara went to see Haywood Sullivan, who was running the team for Mrs. Yawkey. Mac and Sullivan were good friends, so it must have been hard for Sullivan to tell Mac that Mrs. Yawkey ordered him to be fired. I remember seeing Mac on the news that evening. He said, "The golden rule applies—she who has the gold makes the rules." So John McNamara was out and Joe Morgan was in.

◆ ● ◆

Joe Morgan and Jimy Williams are probably the best managers the Red Sox have ever had, certainly during my years with the team. Joe is probably my closest friend in baseball. Jan and I have socialized with Joe and his wife Dot more than with anybody else in the game.

Joseph Michael Morgan—a unique character, one of the most interesting people I've ever met. Joe has a unique, very colorful way of speaking. Jan jokes that Joe taught my children all the bad words in both English and Spanish that he learned playing winter ball in Venezuela and Puerto Rico. Joe always smiles when Jan chides him about that. "Not the bad words—not the really bad ones." But Joe had a way of saying those words in a way that did not conjure up a lot of anger and nastiness.

I recited a list of the things Joe used to say when Mrs. Yawkey had a dinner to honor him after the 1988 season. The "greenflies" were the fans who hung around out at the team hotel, or where the bus emptied at the ballpark, pleading for autographs. When it was time to leave, he'd say, "Let's emulate the Arab." That meant, fold up your tent and get out. "Six, two, and even" was his favorite sayings. Nobody quite knows what it means or where it came from. Some think it came from Dick Tracy. Others think it's a racetrack expression. He called each game a *juego*—Spanish for game. "Throw the number one," he'd say to pitchers who become slider-happy.

I think the most fun time of my entire career were the years Joe Morgan was the Red Sox manager, 1988 to 1991. Joe had managed the Sox's AAA team in Pawtucket for nine years, then became a Red Sox scout for two years. He scouted Roger Clemens at the University of Texas and Greg Maddux in Las Vegas.

I never met Joe before he came to the Red Sox as a coach—first in the bullpen then as their third base coach in 1985–1986. We'd spend time together talking baseball, players, trivia, or whatever in the coffee shop at the hotel or for a postgame nightcap. He made the players come to life—the players whose baseball cards I had from the 1950s and 1960s.

Joe's major league playing career was limited to just 88 games over parts of four seasons with the Milwaukee Braves, Kansas City Athletics, Cleveland Indians, Philadelphia Phillies, and St. Louis Cardinals. In fact, Joe likes to say that he played for more teams in fewer games than any other player since 1926. His teammates included Hall of Famers Hank Aaron, Warren Spahn, Eddie Mathews, Enos Slaughter, Red Schoendienst, Robin Roberts, Lou Brock, and Bob Gibson. A number of his teammates, such as Chuck Cottier, Whitey Herzog, Dick Williams, Harvey Kuenn, Russ Nixon, Ken Aspromonte, Alvin Dark, Bobby Wine, Dallas Green, and Roger Craig, also went on to become big league managers.

Joe is a very honest, down to earth, upbeat guy who can talk with anybody about anything. He can always find a topic of conversation.

I learned (and continue to learn) more about the game of baseball from Joe Morgan than from anybody else. Whether it's strategy, knowledge of big things, little things, people, or plays, he knew it. Joe also has a tremendous capacity to remember names, people, and plays. Joe is an excellent judge of talent, and as far as I know, was always fair with his players. He said what was on his mind. If he thought a player had lost a step, he'd say so. Of course, most players don't like to hear that sort of thing, but Joe continued to be blunt and direct—always honest.

Once Joe took over the team following the 1988 All-Star break, the "Morgan Magic" began. The Red Sox won 12 in a row, 19 out of 20, and 24 straight at home. (McNamara managed the first five in that streak.) I don't think those streaks will ever be repeated. When he was given the job, he was told that he was the "interim manager." He didn't know whether he'd be there for a day, two days, or whether the front office was trying to talk Whitey Herzog into taking the job.

But the team won. When a reporter asked Joe, "What does 'interim' mean?" Joe replied, "Interim, sir, is not in my vocabulary."

As I mentioned, Mrs. Yawkey had a dinner to show her support for Joe after the 1988 Morgan Magic season, when he brought the team the American League East title. (Oakland, with a far better team, swept Boston 4-0 in the League Championship Series.) The dinner was at Dmitri's in Joe's native Walpole, where he still lives. Mrs. Yawkey came in and gave Joe a manila envelope. He put it in his pocket unopened. Mrs. Yawkey said, "Joe, I think you should open that now." So he did: inside was his bonus for having such a great half season: $50,000. He couldn't believe it.

Mrs. Yawkey went to every Red Sox home game, where she sat in her private box with other team executives. She never was interviewed on the air or even on tape and never went to Spring Training, but she occasionally went to team functions during the baseball season.

I started doing a daily manager's show in 1988 when Joe Morgan was the Red Sox manager. Most shows are standard—an analysis of the previous day's game, an injury update, lineup changes, and pitching matchups. But if there is something controversial or newsworthy, such as Carl Everett being suspended, I will alert the manager before we go on the air of what I need to ask. I don't see my job as trying to surprise or shock the manager, or to catch him in any trap. I'm going to be back the next day and the day after—for all 162 games. My rapport with the manager is critical. So is trust.

The Sox didn't do quite as well in 1989, Joe Morgan's first full season as manager, as they had in 1988. They finished in third place, six games behind the Blue Jays.

But in 1990, the team battled to win with less talent than Toronto had, with players such as Tom Bolton and Dana Kiecker. Once again, just as in 1988, the Red Sox finished first in the American League East, but lost in a 4-0 sweep by the much superior Oakland Athletics.

In 1991, the Red Sox finished seven games behind Toronto. The Sox nearly fired Joe after they were swept in Kansas City in late July. Once again, Whitey Herzog was considered but didn't take the job. We then went to Toronto and swept four games there. By September 22, Boston was only half a game out of first place. Then, at home against the Yankees, with the Red Sox up 5-4, with two out and an 1-2 count, Jeff Reardon hung a pitch and Roberto Kelly hit a home run into the screen to tie the game. Rookie Bernie Williams's two-run double in the tenth gave the Yankees a crushing 7-5 victory. That was pretty much the end of the Red Sox season as they lost 11 of their last 14 games.

◆ ● ◆

On October 8, two days after the season ended, Joe was called into a meeting at Fenway Park. He thought the purpose of the meeting was to discuss his coaches. But when he entered the meeting room, he saw Haywood Sullivan, John Harrington, and other team executives. He looked around and immediately knew the purpose of the meeting— to fire him. He asked, "Am I out of there?" "Yes," he was told. Before he turned around and walked out, Joe said, "I just want to say one thing: your team is not as good as you think it is." He was right. He left the room and came to our house—to stay away from the media.

He knocked on the door but we were out. Jan was at the dentist where she heard the news of Joe's dismissal. I was taking our son Tommy for his driver's test. Kate was home alone. She was 12. But she knew Joe well enough to open the door for him. He said, "Did you hear?" She had heard, but was too polite to say so. Joe said, "I got axed." He left, but by the time he and Dot returned in about half an hour, Jan and I were both home. Jeffrey Lyons called to commiserate and said a few words to Joe. That made Jeff feel better. Bill Ballou of the *Worcester Telegram* was the only reporter who found Joe at our house. (I think Joe's son Billy tipped him off.) He went to the center of town and asked people where I lived.

◆ ● ◆

Clell "Butch" Hobson was named as Joe's successor as Red Sox manager for the 1992 season. Butch was a good guy who had played quarterback at Alabama, and became a hard-nosed baseball player. He made some errors but had some power. Batting ninth in the batting order in

1977, Hobson had hit 30 home runs with 112 RBI for the Red Sox. After his playing career (1975–1982), almost all of it with the Red Sox and another playing stint in Columbus of the International League, Butch had managed in the minor leagues.

Butch meant well, but as Joe had said, the team really wasn't very good.

The 1992 Red Sox, in Hobson's first year as manager, did something that no Red Sox team had done in 60 years—they finished dead last: 73-89, 23 games behind American League East Division–leading Toronto.

Hobson never really had a chance that year. Mrs. Yawkey died in late February; first baseman Carlos Quintana was in an auto accident and never fully recovered. Roger Clemens reported late to Spring Training. When he did show up, he ran around the outfield with Butch, but Clemens was wearing headphones and it looked like he wasn't listening to Butch. I don't think he meant to be disrespectful, but the scene was shown on television, where perception is everything.

In 1992, the Red Sox had no power (Tom Brunansky led the team with 15 home runs!), no speed (Jody Reed led with eight stolen bases), and just a little hitting. They really struggled. Even the rookies had a hard time. Phil Plantier had some troubles with Hobson, as did Mo Vaughn, who wound up being sent down to the minors for a while.

Hobson lasted three years as Red Sox manager, from 1992 to 1994 and was let go after the strike in 1994.

◆ ● ◆

Kevin Kennedy replaced Butch, and he had the good fortune of winning in his first year with the club. The team finished 86-58, seven games ahead of the Yankees in the American League Eastern Division. Kevin was a very good game manager. A minor league catcher, he never played in the big leagues. He was impressed by big strong guys and by power hitters like José Canseco, Kevin Mitchell, and Mo Vaughn. He focused a lot on the team's stars. That might have caused some resentment among the other players. He also did not pay as much attention to the front office as they would have liked, and that probably led to his eventual dismissal after the team's third-place finish in 1996.

Kevin has very strong opinions and is not afraid to step on people's toes. After one of our pregame manager's shows, I told Kevin that I thought he had a real future as a broadcaster. He wound up with a very good job on FOX-TV. His ability to speak his mind articulately has helped him there a great deal.

◆ ● ◆

Kevin Kennedy was replaced by Jimy Williams, one of the best managers I've ever been around. He knows people and he knows players. He's the best instructor I've ever seen in a manager, particularly when instructing infielders in the art of throwing a baseball. He worked countless hours with Nomar Garciaparra, hitting fungo after fungo. Jimy has very little ego, and always tried to give credit to the players, not to himself. He believed in doing things the right way. And he could be stubborn. Toward the end of the 1997 season, he gave a starting assignment to Steve Avery because, he said, "I thought it was the right thing to do." But the front office was upset. If he hadn't started that day, the Sox would not have been obligated to pay Avery a big bonus. Jimy said that he wasn't aware until the day before that Avery's contract clause would kick in.

Mo had liked Kevin Kennedy a lot, but Mo was very loyal to Jimy and had a lot of respect for him even though he was having a lot of troubles with the front office.

One of the things that Jimy emphasized was team defense. Also, he wanted batting practice conducted the right way. Batting practice had fallen into what he considered disarray, with the stars running the show. But Jimy added some discipline to batting practice. He assigned times for each hitting group. Everyone stayed on the field throughout batting practice instead of heading for the clubhouse. He did a very good job and most of the players responded to Jimy's way of doing things.

But Jimy continued to have his problems with the front office. Things really came to a head over Carl Everett. Everett was often late getting to the ballpark and Jimy cracked down by benching him and fining him.

Jimy did not get the support he thought he deserved from management, especially in the Carl Everett controversy. In the pregame show with us, he said that if the manager doesn't get backing from the front office, perhaps the manager should be fired.

Nothing happened. Jimy had a contract for the next season too, and he was not going to quit. But during that next season, 2001, things fell apart. Despite long stints on the disabled list by Nomar Garciaparra, Jason Varitek, and Pedro Martinez, the team was in the pennant chase. But when the team lost six out of seven games, Jimy was fired on August 16 (also the date the Babe and Elvis died) and pitching coach Joe Kerrigan was named as the manager. After that, the team collapsed.

I have a lot of respect for Jimy. He was always very considerate with me. If I screwed up the taping of the pregame show, either by having my tape recorder's batteries die, or by hitting the wrong button, he'd come back and was gracious enough to do the interview again. Sure, doing the interview was part of his job, but he never gave me a hard time about things like that, which might have rankled other managers. He was always considerate of my time. If he was late or had to keep me waiting because he had to deal with a player, he always apologized.

Jimy and I often spoke about being from big families. Jimy came from a family of seven children. I am the oldest of eight. Jan is the second of ten kids.

Jimy Williams did a great job managing the Red Sox in 2001—he had the club in contention virtually all season. The team was in second place on August 16, the day he was fired, with a record of 65-53, just five games behind the Yankees and they were only a few games out of the wild card race. They finished the season 82-79.

But the front office feeling, probably a desperation move, was that a sudden change in the team's on-field leadership might help them catch

"Morgan Magic" again. So Jimy Williams was out and Joe Kerrigan was in.

◆ ● ◆

Kerrigan never really had a chance. No Pedro, no Nomar, no Varitek, and a very difficult situation. The Yankees were on a roll and the Red Sox were going backwards. Kerrigan complicated his problems by losing Manny Ramirez. Ramirez was hurt and he actually went home for a while. On September 7, Pedro Martinez, though still ailing, was forced to pitch a game against the Yankees. He lost it 7-3. The game didn't mean much, as the Red Sox were out of the race by then. No one questioned Pedro's heart and dedication, but the situation on the team was almost anarchy. The players were very unhappy. We were in New York for a wraparound series (Friday through Monday) starting on September 10. Then came the events of September 11.

Joe Kerrigan had been a very good pitching coach for two years, and he loved being manager, but the finish was a disaster.

The Red Sox had announced before the 2001 season began that the club was for sale, and there was speculation all during the season in the Boston papers as to what would happen to the team. Just before Christmas, it was announced that a group headed by John Henry, Tom Werner, and Larry Lucchino had been awarded the franchise for a price of about $660 million. It was interesting to sit and watch the sale develop. Would the new owners be a local group or from out of town? I didn't know any of the prospective owners, but I was as interested as any fan. Not much happened until the second week in January. That was when John Henry and Larry Lucchino were given a tour of the Jimmy Fund clinic. They announced that the long relationship between the Red Sox and the Jimmy Fund would continue.

Spring Training started, but the sale of the team had not become final. Trup and I arrived in Fort Myers on February 26 and went to the workout at the minor league complex. Rumors were circulating that general manager, Dan Duquette, would be fired. We saw Dan, but he gave no indication of the turmoil swirling around him. In fact, Dan asked whether he could appear on our first broadcast the following night to talk about a new ticket package. The next day, on the 28th, the team announced that Dan had been released. I went to the news conference at the Sanibel Harbor Hotel and Dan was emotional.

Mike Port, who had been Dan's assistant, was named interim general manager. Mike is one of the most solid, respected people in the game of baseball. I first met Mike when he was the general manager of the California Angels. I'll never forget sitting in the broadcast booth, in Game Five of the 1986 ALCS, and looking over to see Mike's face in the next booth when Dave Henderson hit his home run. It looked as though Mike's Angels were going to beat the Red Sox for the American League pennant. In my elation for the Red Sox, I felt sorry for Mike at the time.

He joined the Red Sox before the 1993 season as an assistant to Lou Gorman. When Lou moved upstairs, it looked as though either Dan Duquette or Mike Port would be the new general manager. Dan got the job, but Mike stayed on and continued to work efficiently and quietly behind the scenes. He took care of player contracts, waivers, and baseball procedural rules. Mike Port earned the respect of agents, other general managers, and front office staffs throughout baseball—and of everybody associated with the Red Sox.

Now Mike was the interim general manager. He brought a sense of integrity, stability, professionalism, and continuity to the team. He also has a sense of humility and is usually the last to toot his own horn.

In my view, the fact that Mike went to the December 2002 news conference in which the team announced that 28-year-old Brookline, Massachusetts, native Theo Epstein would be the team's new general manager speaks volumes about Mike. I am very happy that Mike is staying with the team as vice president of baseball operations. Theo is a Yale graduate, and we've spoken about New Haven and Yale, since many of my relatives went there and I grew up in New Haven. Theo's dad, Leslie Epstein, is the head of the creative writing department at Boston University and a novelist. My nephew, Tyler Petersen, was one of Professor Epstein's students. Professor Epstein has encouraged Tyler to pursue a career in creative writing.

While he was still a Yale undergraduate in 1992, Theo had an internship with the Baltimore Orioles. He was interviewed by former Yale football star Calvin Hill, who was an Oriole executive at the time. Theo moved to San Diego with Larry Lucchino and became director of baseball operations for the Padres, coming to the Red Sox in 2002.

After Dan Duquette was fired, Joe Kerrigan was still the manager. It was an even tougher situation for Joe Kerrigan now that "his guy" was out. The feeling around the team was that there had to be a change to put an end to all the rumors, turmoil, and dissatisfaction in the clubhouse, so Joe Kerrigan was let go. Mike Cubbage was named the interim manager.

The owners interviewed a number of people for the manager's job, and I remember calling my friend Grady Little around March 5. He was coaching for the Cleveland Indians in Winter Haven. I asked him if he thought he was going to get the job, and he told me that he hoped so. Grady and I had known each other for years. He had been the Red Sox bench coach from 1997 to 1999.

So I was thrilled when, on March 11, Grady was named as the new Red Sox manager. He drove down from Winter Haven the night before, and the owners put Grady in a back room. The players were in the clubhouse at Fort Myers, and the reporters were waiting outside in the dugout and on the field. All of a sudden, the media heard a big cheer from the clubhouse as Grady was introduced to the team. The players had given him a standing ovation. The choice of Grady Little as the new manager of the Red Sox was very happy news for everybody associated with the team.

Grady has been in baseball a long time, although he never had a chance to play in the majors. Grady had left baseball for some years in the 1980s to become a cotton farmer in Texas. After managing in the minors for many years, mostly with the Braves system, he went to the majors as a Padres coach in 1996.

Grady and his wife Debbie have remained good friends of ours for years. They live in Pinehurst, North Carolina.

Not only was he received well, he got the team off to a 40-17 start. They played well and won a number of close games early in the season.

But as the season wore on, the lack of depth on the team caught up with them. They looked great on paper, and were filled with stars.

There was a lot to be said for the 2002 season in terms of individual performances and for the fact that Grady Little did an excellent job after taking over the team. He brought a calming atmosphere and better chemistry to the clubhouse. Grady was also tested during the season. I remember a game in September in which Manny Ramirez hit a grounder to the pitcher. Instead of running to first, he took a left turn to return directly to the dugout. That caused a big brouhaha. Knowing he had made a mistake, Manny instantly apologized to his teammates, and Grady did not take him out of the game. The next day, Grady said that he should have taken Ramirez out of the game after the incident.

25

Quick Pitches

Rich Gedman was a good friend of mine when he was with the Red Sox from 1980 to 1990. In 1983, my first year with the Red Sox, he wasn't playing much. One day I sat next to him on the team bus. He told me he was thinking of asking to be sent down to the Sox's AAA team in Pawtucket, Rhode Island. There, he thought, he could hone his skills playing every day, rather than just sitting on the bench most of the time *not* playing in Boston. In his first three years in the majors, Gedman shared catching duties with Carlton Fisk and Gary Allenson. But I asked what would happen if he suffered a freak injury and never came back to the big leagues?

In the end, he never asked to be sent down and he blossomed in 1984 as a full-time starter. In 1984 and 1985, nobody hit the ball harder or more often than Rich Gedman. He had a big season in 1986, the year the Sox won the American League pennant. I remember one game in which manager John MacNamara sent Gedman up as a pinch hitter against left-hander Willie Hernandez on a rainy Sunday afternoon at Tiger Stadium. Hernandez threw a screwball. A lefty screwball breaks down and away to a righty—just the opposite of a curveball—and down and in to a lefty. That's why left-handed batters can sometimes be more effective against the screwball than righties. Gedman lined a pinch-hit grand slam into the lower deck.

◆ ● ◆

Bart Giamatti was president of Yale when I first met him, but our families had been friends for years. My uncle Salvatore and Bart's father, Valentine, grew up in the Italian section of New Haven, Connecticut. They went to the same elementary school and the same high school, and then both went to Yale together on full scholarships. They walked to classes from home. Both became professors of Italian. In addition to teaching at Yale, my uncle Sal was at the Georgetown University Foreign Service School and started the Italian Department at Middlebury College.

Bart's father taught at Mt. Holyoke College so Bart grew up in South Hadley, Massachusetts.

My father also went to Yale (class of 1936), and Giamatti graduated from Yale in 1960. They knew each other as members of the Amity Club, an association of Italian professionals in New Haven.

In 1987, I went to Yale for a symposium on baseball featuring Bart and Peter Gammons of the *Boston Globe*. While there, I did a pregame interview with Bart. A lifelong Red Sox fan, he told me that he wore his Red Sox cap to classes at Yale. Bobby Doerr was his favorite player. Ted Williams was a great player, but seemed almost superhuman to the young Giamatti, beyond mortal comparison. Doerr, on the other hand, was a little more realistic.

My father and his brother, my uncle Charlie, would sit with Giamatti to watch Yale games when my brothers Frank and Charlie pitched for the Elis.

It was a real shock to all of us when Giamatti died suddenly on September 1, 1989, right after banning Pete Rose from baseball for life.

Had Giamatti survived, perhaps the nuclear war that befell baseball in 1994 could have been avoided. He had an ability to compromise, which is now sorely missed.

My father frequently said that Bart could have been president of the United States because of his intelligence, his demeanor, and the aura around him. But Giamatti was not arrogant. He had the most incredible vocabulary I ever heard; yet he never flaunted it. He was a modest man, even as president of Yale.

In May 1989, while he was president of the National League, Giamatti came to a Red Sox-Royals game, and we had him on the air before the game. He was going to sit with us for one inning. My broadcast partner Ken Coleman was out with the flu, so Johnny Pesky was sitting in for him in the broadcast booth. Giamatti was thrilled to meet one of the heroes of his youth—he'd never met Pesky before. Giamatti was supposed to "work" just one inning with me, but he was so thrilled to be there, he stayed for four innings, and wished he could have stayed for the whole game. Pesky's reaction? "He's the president of Yale, and he wants to meet *me?*"

Fay Vincent, who succeeded Giamatti as commissioner was also an old family friend. He's from New Haven. My Aunt Anne Schwab and his mother taught together in New Haven schools. His father was a football referee. Vincent was doing a very good job as Giamatti's deputy and later as his successor, but the owners wanted somebody they could control. They did not find that person in Fay Vincent.

◆ ● ◆

Jackie Gutierrez was a favorite of mine. He was the Red Sox regular shortstop in 1984.

He had come up to the Sox late in 1983, and played in Carl Yastrzemski's last game, October 2 of that year. In 1984, he took over at shortstop, and made an error in the opening game of the season. Despite that bad start, Jackie had a very good year. He hit .263 and made some of the most spectacular plays I've ever seen a shortstop make. He used to whistle all the time. In fact, his shrill whistle earned him the nickname, "the Whistler." You could hear it all over the ballpark, even when the crowd was rumbling. He played the game with verve. I spent a lot of time with him and his roommate, Al Nipper. After a Sunday afternoon game that season when Jackie's mother was visiting from his native Cartagena, Colombia (he was just the third Colombian to play in the majors), we had Jackie, his mother, Al Nipper, Jim Healey, the Red Sox director of broadcasting and his wife Janis, and Ken Coleman and his wife Ellen over for dinner. One of the funniest things I have ever seen was watching Ken, who spoke no Spanish, trying to speak with Señora Gutierrez, who didn't speak a word of English. Ken was speaking slowly and emphatically, and was using hand signals, all of which just served to confuse Mrs. Gutierrez.

Jackie was another favorite of my daughter Kate. In 1985, Gutierrez was replaced at shortstop by Glenn Hoffman, and Jackie moved on to Baltimore. He was probably a lot older than he said, and he was a very emotional guy. He really played some spectacular shortstop. He finished his career with the Phillies in 1988.

◆ ● ◆

Dave Henderson—Hendu. He played the game with a smile, and was one of the best big-game players I have ever been around. Hendu hit the two biggest home runs of the 1986 postseason. His home run in the ninth inning of Game Five of the ALCS kept the Sox alive. He homered again in the tenth inning of Game Six of the World Series to give the Red Sox a 4-3 lead over the Mets.

Of course, the Mets won the game in the bottom of the tenth, but overall, Henderson had a very good series.

Dave was always smiling and laughing. Some managers didn't take him as seriously as they should have, perhaps mistaking his jovial demeanor for a lack of seriousness. But he was a superb, well-conditioned athlete, and when the game was on the line, he delivered. During the 1986 Series, I worked with Sparky Anderson during the "home team inning," and I mentioned that Dave Henderson was the fastest runner on the team. Sparky commented that if Henderson was the fastest on the team, the Red Sox had a slow team. He was right.

After leaving the Red Sox, Henderson had some big years with Oakland, and I remember in 1988, Ken Coleman and I were working directly behind the screen, near the on-deck circle at the ALCS at the Oakland Coliseum. In Game Three, Ken and I made eye contact with Henderson, and while standing in the on-deck circle, he waved to us. Typical Dave Henderson. These days, Dave is a broadcaster for the Seattle Mariners.

Dave Henderson's home run in Game Five of the ALCS is one of the greatest moments in Red Sox history, and was honored at the Sox Hall of Fame. (Dave was only with the Red Sox for 111 regular season games over two years, not long enough to make the team's Hall of Fame.)

◆ ● ◆

Bruce Hurst is a guy who had a lot of fun playing the game of baseball. When he first came up to the majors in 1980, I think he was a little shocked by the lifestyle of professional baseball at the major league level. His hometown of St. George, Utah, was a long way from the East Coast both geographically and in lifestyle.

He became a big-game pitcher. He would have been the MVP of the 1986 World Series if the Sox had not lost Game Six. In fact, because the guy running the Shea Stadium message board was a little premature, the sign flashed: "Congratulations Red Sox MVP Bruce Hurst" with two outs in the bottom of the tenth inning, when the game (and the series) turned completely around. Hurst had pitched eight innings and won Game One. He had won Game Five with a brilliant complete-game performance, and he pitched well in Game Seven, leaving the game tied 3–3.

In 1988, Hurst was a big factor in the Red Sox first-place finish in the American League East. He won 18 games for Boston that year. The myth that left-handers can't pitch at Fenway is just that—total myth. Hurst was especially effective at Fenway in 1988, where he was 13-2. He came right over the top with a big curveball and right-hand batters had a tough time picking up his release right out of the centerfield bleachers in day games. Hurst enjoyed it, and always had a smile. He and Roger Clemens hung out together—both great competitors. When my wife Jan first met him around 1984, she said, "This is the nicest player I have ever met." Bruce was very devoted to his wife Holly. He left Boston after the 1988 season because he might have thought that baseball was too important and that he was under the media microscope too much playing in Boston. The Boston press can be very tough because of intense media competition. Many of the Boston sportswriters who cover and write about the Red Sox also appear on television and radio programs to talk about the team. The many talk radio programs in Boston also add to the toughness of the Boston media.

Bruce Hurst went to San Diego, where he was dismayed, I think, to find that people there did not care nearly as much about the fortunes of the Padres. It's not that he regretted leaving, but he tried to come back to Boston later. Unfortunately, he had hurt his arm and retired after a brief stint with the Texas Rangers.

I always enjoyed being around Bruce Hurst.

◆ ● ◆

I had known Dennis Lamp when he was with the Blue Jays. He did impressions of announcers. He did a terrific Jerry Howarth, the Blue Jays announcer. Lamp threw a sinker/slider over the back part of the plate very effectively. Although he had been a starter with the Cubs, he was a middle reliever in Boston. He helped the Sox to division titles in 1988 and 1990. When he was with the Red Sox, Dennis lived in Cohasset, not far from my home. His wife Janet was from Brockton, Massachusetts. We went out to dinner on occasion in the offseason. He wanted to be a broadcaster after his playing days, and he studied for it, but it didn't work out for him as far as a second career was concerned. He was funnier without a microphone than with one. A good pitcher and a funny guy.

◆ ● ◆

Darren Lewis is the only player with whom I have exchanged books. (During the 2002 season, I lent Tony Clark a few books, but with Darren it was a regular exchange.)

I had a lot of respect for Darren Lewis as a person and as a player. When he went to the University of California, Berkeley, he never expected to be a big league baseball player. He studied with Harry Edwards, the noted sports sociologist, and majored in sociology. Darren continues to work toward his degree. He still needs a few credits. He was an excellent defensive outfielder. We used to exchange books, mostly about baseball. He gave me books about arbitration, and *The Orlando Cepeda Story*. Over his four years with the Red Sox from 1998 to 2001, I gave him many books including Josh Gibson's biography. He trusted me with his opinions about other players, acquisitions, and relations, and I respected his opinions. He also had strong opinions about how different players were being used by their managers. If Darren decides to stay in baseball, he will make an excellent manager or general manager one day. He was a very pensive guy who really appreciated what he had as a major league baseball player.

One of the things that impressed me about Darren was that I never saw him waste a minute in the clubhouse. He did not play cards or video games in the clubhouse. He would watch videos of his at bats or of upcoming opposing pitchers, work in the batting cage, work out, or do something else to prepare for the upcoming game. Darren was not a great hitter but he was a self-made player. He worked at it. He was the best-prepared player I have ever been around. It was not a surprise to me that he held the record for the most consecutive errorless games in centerfield (392), and most chances in a season without an error by a non-pitcher (938). Through 2000, he also had the highest fielding percentage by an outfielder, .995

◆ ● ◆

Pedro Martinez is the most spectacular pitcher I have ever been around. Great stuff. Like many pitchers, Pedro throws three pitches—fastball, change-up, breaking ball. But I've never seen anyone else who has such command of all three pitches. What I like about him is his charm. He is also extremely bright. He is one of the most articulate, if not the most articulate, baseball players I have ever been around—and English is his second language. He is in fact more articulate in English than most English-speaking ballplayers and announcers. Indeed, he is articulate in both English and Spanish. His English vocabulary is outstanding and his grammar is excellent. He told me that his brother Ramon, also a big league pitcher, told him when he signed that if he could not communicate, he didn't have much going for him. So he learned how to communicate very well. He is a great pitcher in the biggest games, as well as a great overall pitcher. He seems to relish the big moments, such as the most heroic moment I've ever seen in baseball—when he came out of the bullpen to no-hit the Cleveland Indians over six innings in Game Five of the 1999 ALDS without his good fastball to put the Red Sox in the 1999 ALCS with the Yankees. His 2-0 win over Roger Clemens of the New York Yankees on May 28, 2000, was a classic—two future Hall of Famers, two complete games, and a shutout. I also remember the 17-strike-out, one-hit game he had against the Yankees in 1999—one of the best single-game performances I ever saw.

Pedro is a star and he knows it, and he has a lot of fun playing. We spoke once about Mother's Day, and he told me what an important holiday that is, because, he said, a mother is like a saint, like the Virgin Mary in the Dominican Republic. Part of the custom in the Dominican Republic is that mothers are truly honored. I enjoy speaking with Pedro about his culture, and the differences between American and Dominican culture. Pedro also understands the responsibilities that come with being a national hero. In fact, in 1997, he helped to end a general strike in the Dominican Republic by asking both sides to compromise.

Pedro has invited me to his home in Santo Domingo, Dominican Republic, and I hope to take him up on his offer.

◆ ● ◆

Lou Merloni provided one of the most thrilling moments I've ever had at Fenway Park. In his very first at bat at Fenway Park, the Framingham, Massachusetts, native homered into the screen off José Rosado of the Kansas City Royals on May 15, 1998. Lou grew up a Red Sox fan, and went to Providence College. Because he was a self-made player—a low draft pick and a so-called "blue collar" player—and because his name ends in a vowel, frankly, his debut home run was especially meaningful. I always liked talking with Lou and his family. He's a good friend of Nomar Garciaparra. Lou gets everything he can out of his tools.

◆ ● ◆

Tim Naehring is one of the nicest guys I've ever met on the Red Sox, and he was a fabulous third baseman. In fact, he may have been the best defensive third baseman I've ever seen with the Red Sox. He really came to play. Tim would have done better had he remained injury free. He had a succession of major injuries. A back injury, a wrist injury—then finally he threw out his elbow on a throw in Toronto in 1997, which effectively ended his career. But I remember when he came up to the Red Sox in 1990. Joe Morgan was the manager. Naehring made an error in his first game. But Joe stayed with him, and Tim won the second game with a timely hit. I remember a big home run he hit in Cleveland on April 11, 1992, only a few days after the season started. It was the Indians's home opener. The game was also memorable because the temperature was in the 60s when the game started, then plummeted to the 30s. Nahering's home run came in the 19th inning and gave the Sox a 7–5 victory.

Tim homered in the first game of the ALDS on October 3, 1995, in the 11th inning, but the Sox lost that game on Tony Peña's home run in the 13th off Zane Smith. In 1995, when the Red Sox clinched the AL East title, they were all whooping it up on the field. Tim waved up to Jerry Trupiano and me in the broadcast booth, as if to say, "You guys are part of this celebration too." He was a thoughtful and considerate guy. He was also a very handsome man. We had him on the air once during a game when he was on the disabled list. Bob Starr called him "Boston's most eligible bachelor" on the air, and Tim turned red. After his playing days ended, Tim stayed in baseball, and is now an executive with the Cincinnati Reds.

◆ ● ◆

Steve "Psycho" Lyons was one of a kind. When he came up in 1985, he gave the Red Sox a little bit of speed, something they have rarely had. Steve also managed to pitch an inning for the Red Sox against the Twins on July 21, 1991, allowing just two hits, no runs, no walks, and one strikeout. In a game against the Brewers in June 1986 with the Sox down two runs, Wade Boggs at the plate, and Marty Barrett on first, Lyons, on second base, tried to steal third and was thrown out. That ended the game. It also ended Lyons's Red Sox career. Or at least that stint with the Red Sox. He was traded to the White Sox for Tom Seaver later in June. Steve had four separate tours of duty with Boston— 1985–1986, 1991, then 1992–1993. Steve knew his limitations and liked to play to the TV camera. Since retiring as a player, he has become a baseball analyst for Fox. He is the best ex-athlete I have ever seen at reading a script in the studio. He is extremely disciplined in the studio, although he is certainly an extrovert and a showman.

I always liked Steve and his wife Christa. I also liked him because he was nice to my son Duke. When Steve's playing days ended after an abbreviated 1993 season, he lived briefly near us, while trying to break into broadcasting. He knew that Duke was also looking for a sports-casting job. Shortly after Steve was hired by Fox, he walked into the news director's office in Los Angeles and told him that they should hire Duke right away. So Steve will always be a favorite of mine. He's not afraid to voice an opinion, that's for sure.

◆ ● ◆

In 1983 and 1984, we spent some time hanging around with Reid Nichols. He was traded in 1985 to the White Sox. Reid is a strong Christian guy. He went on to be the farm director for the Rangers and the Orioles, then a Rangers coach. More recently, he's joined the Milwaukee Brewers's front office and development staff and directs minor league operations.

◆ ● ◆

Al Nipper won the last game of Carl Yastrzemski's career, in 1983. In 1987, even though Phil Rizzuto said, "This guy can't break a pane of glass," Nipper beat the Yankees four times. Nipper was a good friend of Roger Clemens. I was pretty close with Al when he was with the Red Sox. Nipper got everything he could out of his pitching talent, and he became the pitching coach for the Red Sox and the Kansas City Royals. As a rookie, he had already read 26 books on pitching.

◆ ● ◆

Al Nipper suffered another of the worst injuries I ever saw when, in 1986, he was covering home on a play at the plate when Larry Parrish slid home with his spikes up, because he had recently had a knee operation and could not tuck his leg under his body. Parrish's spikes caught Nipper the wrong way, and he had an ugly, bloody gash on his knee. Nipper was hospitalized, but was able to bounce back.

One Spring Training, when Kate was 5, Al Nipper, who was staying at the Holiday Inn in Winter Haven where we were also staying, taught Kate how to roller skate. Al kept a big bin of rice in his room. He strengthened his forearm and hand by shoving his fist into the rice over and over again, a technique also used by Steve Carlton.

◆ ● ◆

Trot Nixon is a very hard-nosed player. He's all business on the field and plays the game as intensely as anybody I've ever seen. I think his injuries during his minor league career slowed his progress to the majors. But he is a winner and is not afraid to speak his mind. His father, Dr. Bill Nixon, is a nephrologist. In fact, he was Willie Stargell's nephrologist. Trot's brother-in-law is a dermatologist, and his brother, Bud, is in software. Trot's wife Kathryn is a lovely person who has done a lot for the Jimmy Fund. Trot is a no-nonsense guy—a humble guy who really appreciates where he is, and never stops working. He does an outstanding job as the Red Sox Chapel leader.

◆ ● ◆

If I had to pick a favorite catcher of all time, it would have to be Tony Peña. Tony came to the Red Sox in 1990, after stints in Pittsburgh and St. Louis, and brought tremendous enthusiasm to the ballclub. He was always very excited to play and he worked hard at it. He wanted to play every single day and wanted to catch every single day. He played with a lot of flair and he could really block pitches. When he was younger, he could really throw, too. Tony's first year with the Red Sox, 1990, started out well for him at the plate, but he tailed off after that. He didn't hit much, but his catching was very solid.

Tony took a special interest in my son Duke. He had Duke on the field at Fenway, instructing him on his catching and he was popping up and down, excited about the way Duke threw. We spent a lot of time together. We also loved to be with Tony's son T. J. I first saw T. J. play when he was just eight or nine, and I thought, "Here's a kid who's going to be a great ballplayer. What an arm!" T. J. had long arms and a whip-like motion. Tony had a very nice family, and still does. T. J. now plays in the Atlanta Braves's system.

The Worcester, Massachusetts, police force always invited one Red Sox player to attend their Saturday night softball game to benefit the Jimmy Fund. I asked Tony to go one year, told him that the drive was about 45 minutes each way, and that he'd be expected to be at the event for about 45 minutes. He agreed. The day of the game was very hot, and Tony had caught all nine innings for the Red Sox. He went 0-4 with a few strikeouts, and he sweated so much that he lost about ten pounds. Not a good day. After he showered and dressed at Fenway, the Worcester police picked him up and took him to their game, where they kept him for four hours. He didn't get home until about 11 o'clock at night. And he had to catch the next day. When I saw him the next day at the park, he told me, "You lied to me. You lied to me. You said they'd keep me 45 minutes. Instead, they kept me four hours!" I said, "Tony, why didn't you tell them you had to leave?" His answer was most revealing. He said, "Because they honored me. How could I leave?" He got over it.

Shortly thereafter, I tried to make it up to him. We gave gift certificates for Eastern Clothing to the guests on our postgame show. John and Paul Airasian own Eastern Clothing, and they are the best I have ever found at matching the perfect outfit for different individuals. Tony was not very familiar with the Boston suburbs, so, begging his forgiveness for the Worcester fiasco, I offered to take him to the Eastern Clothing store in Watertown. He had been our guest on about six postgame shows and he had about $600 in gift certificates, but wound up spending about $6,000. Tony told me that he loved shoes. He must have really loved shoes because he told me that he had more than 100 pairs at his home in the Dominican Republic. Tony was a very generous guy.

Tony was only six feet tall. He told me that he used to help build up his strength by helping his father lift bananas. Tony is a great student of the game, and he was interviewed for the manager's job in Houston a year or so ago. While he didn't get that job, he was named manager of the Kansas City Royals in 2002 and was manager of the year in 2003. He's one of my all-time favorite Red Sox players.

◆ ● ◆

Paul Quantrill, from London, Ontario, was a great competitor. He came up to the Red Sox in 1992 from the University of Wisconsin, which later dropped baseball. We first saw him pitch in the Hall of Fame game at Doubleday Field in Cooperstown in 1989 when he was a rookie league player. Like a number of other players, Paul was very nice to my son Duke when Duke was an impressionable 19-year-old. Paul took Duke under his wing a little, and helped him with his pitching. Paul has always been ready to take the ball. It's all about winning for him. He's one of the most solid individuals I have ever been around. Also one of the brightest and most realistic. He appreciates being a major leaguer.

◆ ● ◆

Jeff Reardon, a native New Englander (born in Dalton, Massachusetts), was signed by the Mets out of a tryout camp after playing college ball at the University of Massachusetts. He blossomed with the Montreal Expos, where he put up big numbers, and also with the Twins. In 1987, he saved the ALCS clincher against the Tigers in Game Five, and closed the World Series for the Twins that year saving a 4-2 win over the Cardinals in Game Seven.

Reardon came to the Red Sox in 1990, and started out well. Then he had a midseason back operation, but miraculously came back in a little over a month. He helped the Red Sox win the American League East title that year. He saved the last game of the season when, in the bottom of the ninth inning against the White Sox at Fenway, Tom Brunanski made an outstanding catch of an Ozzie Guillen line drive in rightfield. Red Sox 3, White Sox 1.

Jeff didn't have a big ego. He always remembered where he came from and his roots.

I had the pleasure of hosting the Rolaids luncheon at Fenway Park in 1991 when Jeff broke the major league career record for saves—a record that has since been surpassed by Lee Smith and Dennis Eckersley.

◆ ● ◆

Jim Rice. During my career, I think I have traveled more with Jim Rice than with any other uniformed person. As a player, I traveled with him from 1983 through the end of his playing career in 1989. (He had come up in 1974.) He was later the batting coach for the Sox from 1995 to 2001. I always had a good relationship with him. Occasionally, we'd discuss hitting or other players. Jim is stoic—not a man of many words. On some days, he's glad to talk. On other days, he's very quiet. Jim once said that he had a lot of acquaintances in the game of baseball, but not a lot of friends.

Jim had some excellent years for the Red Sox. In 1977, 1978, and 1979 he put up some very big numbers (39, 46, 39 homers). And in 1983, he had a monster year: 39 homers, 126 RBI, 344 total bases. In 1986, he knocked in 110 runs. But a bad elbow, cranky knees, and some questions about his eyesight ended his playing career at 36. If he had had one more big year, I think he'd have been in the Hall of Fame by now. He's still very close.

In addition to his prowess on the field, Jim was also the best-dressed player I have ever been around. He and I used to talk about sweaters. He had the Coogis, I had the St. Croixs. He liked my choice of sweaters, but his were a little bit more expensive. Jim Rice is a big part of Red Sox history.

◆ ● ◆

Little Luis Rivera, from Cidra, Puerto Rico, was the main Red Sox shortstop on the 1990 team that won the American League East pennant. He was with the Sox from 1990 to 1993. I liked him because he was a fun guy with a deep voice and a great sense of humor. His daughter Carla, then about five years old, was a beautiful girl. Joe Morgan said that Rivera was a little guy with a big man's swing. He had some power, but never hit for a high average. In one game, the Red Sox were trailing in the seventh inning and Joe went up to him and said, "Luis, I think we're going to use a pinch hitter." Luis looked at Joe and said, "What, for Boggs?" Boggs was only hitting about .360, and Rivera was hitting a solid .240. He knew what Joe meant. The writers liked Rivera, too. He seemed to play his best when he played two or three games in a row. A good guy who made some outstanding plays. He's coaching in the minors now, but I think he could make a good major league manager someday.

◆ ● ◆

Aaron Sele won his first six decisions after he came up to the Red Sox in 1993. The Golden Valley, Minnesota, native had a great curveball. He got an unfair rap in Boston, but some questioned his competitiveness after the 1995 season because he spent time on the disabled list. With the departure of Roger Clemens after the 1996 season, Sele became Boston's number one pitcher in 1997. After the Red Sox, he played for the Texas Rangers, the Seattle Mariners, and the Anaheim Angels. My wife Jan had a special fondness for Sele because she thought he was a real gentleman.

◆ ● ◆

Bob Stanley, the Steamer. In a fair and perfect world, Bob Stanley gets the last out of the 1986 World Series. He is Mr. Red Sox pitcher. Number one in Red Sox career appearances (637), saves (132), and relief wins (85).

Bob Stanley is a real down-to-earth guy. Our rooms were just a few doors apart at the Holiday Inn in Winter Haven, Florida, during Spring Training for seven years.

Bob mixed with the fans better than any player I have ever seen. He'd be at the hotel or around the pool with his wife Joan, his son Kyle, and his daughters, Kristin and Kerri, and he'd talk with the fans. Everybody knew him and his family. He was a very emotional guy and was very hurt when the crowd booed him. He was 15-2 with 10 saves in 1978 as a starter and reliever.

I remember a game where he came in in the third inning on a Sunday afternoon against Minnesota in 1983. He pitched scoreless ball through the 12th inning, and wound up with a no-decision. (The Red Sox eventually lost that game.) Bob had a rubber arm—he could pitch every day. Sometimes he said things to reporters that caused some waves, usually in the heat of the battle. He always wanted the ball, and knew what to do with it.

Bob Stanley was one of the most generous guys I have ever been around, particularly in the work he did for the Jimmy Fund. During his stay with the Red Sox, nobody did more than Bob to help. He did much of it privately, visiting kids being treated for cancer. One boy had retreated into a shell—he didn't talk with his parents or with anybody else. Bob went to see him and got him going, telling him how much his parents cared. The kid responded and started speaking with his parents again. Unfortunately, the youngster died, but Bob didn't know this, and when Bob saw the kid's father about a year later, he asked about his son. The father told Bob that he and his wife really appreciated what he had done for the boy, and that he had been buried in the Bob Stanley Red Sox jersey that Bob had given him.

Bob retired after the 1989 season. On January 19, 1990, his son Kyle was diagnosed with cancer—a sinus tumor. He had facial surgery and made a full recovery. Kyle went to Providence College and has been pronounced cured.

Bob was a pitching coach in the Mets's farm system for several years. He's now the pitching coach with the San Francisco Giants Class AA team in Norwich, Connecticut.

Nobody would have been more perfect to close the 1986 World Series than Bob Stanley. Nobody did more for the club, and he deserved it. But a wild pitch (I thought it was a passed ball) in Game Six, and that was that. It didn't happen.

◆ ● ◆

Mike Stanley had two tours with the Red Sox as a player—1996–1997 and 1998–2000. A real gentleman, he was our Baseball Chapel leader, and he had a great perspective about the game and about life. Mike was one of the more mature players I've known—a quiet leader. He was back with the Sox as a bench coach in 2002.

◆ ● ◆

Dave Stapleton, a Red Sox from 1983 to 1986, was a very nice guy from Alabama. He played for coach Eddie Stanky at the University of South Alabama. He knew all the little things a major leaguer has to know—where to play and how to play. He played first, second, third, and shortstop. Although he did not have a lot of power, he was a very good defensive player—an intelligent, instinctive player.

◆ ● ◆

John Valentin, like Bob Stanley, did a great deal for the Jimmy Fund, much of it with no publicity. He once drove through a snowstorm to visit a kid at Hanscom Field, north of Boston. The young man was dying of cancer and this kind of visit was something he did quite regularly. When he signed his big contract ($2.6 million for the 1996 season), he made special mention of the Jimmy Fund, and gave a lot back, both in time and in dollars. He was a big-game player. He had seven RBI in Game Four of the 1999 ALDS against the Indians.

Then, in Game Three of the 1999 ALCS, in the Pedro Martinez-Roger Clemens game, he helped knock Clemens out of the game early, as the Sox humiliated the Yankees 13-1.

John did not always wear a smile. Sometimes, he had a rather stern countenance. But I enjoyed speaking with him and being around him. We had a mutual trust. After Jan and I were held up at gunpoint in Kansas City, he came up to me after reading about it in the paper and said, "I'm sorry about what happened to you and your wife." That's not something I would expect from a player. But he was a considerate guy. He got upset when he was asked to switch positions to let rookie Nomar Garciaparra play shortstop. Valentin walked out for one day, but he came back and moved to second base. Later, he moved to third, where he became an outstanding defensive third baseman before his career was cut short by a series of leg injuries.

John once told me that as a young player he thought that he had a choice between being a defensive shortstop and building himself up to become a power hitter. He chose the latter. It really helped him, because he was made for Fenway Park—a dead pull righty hitter. He hit that wall up to 20 times a year. He also had 20 home run seasons for the Red Sox in 1995 and 1998. He played only ten games in 2000, then suffered one of the worst injuries I've ever seen. The ball was hit to him at third, and as he tried to field it, the ligament snapped off the bone by his knee. I could tell that the pain was excruciating. That was one of the most frightful moments I ever saw in baseball.

John tried to make a comeback in 2001. He played only 20 games that year, but was back with the Mets in 2002. He went to Spring Training with Houston in 2004.

◆ ● ◆

Maurice "Mo" Vaughn is one of my all-time favorite Red Sox players.

Mo did so much for the team—including a grand slam in the Red Sox home opener against Seattle on April 10, 1998. His first home run nearly went out of the stadium in Baltimore on June 30, 1991. All the walk-off home runs he hit. I remember his tremendous power and his big smile. Mo had big shoulders, never looking for an excuse. He always took the blame when he thought he hadn't done as well as he should have. It's unfortunate that Mo got into disputes with the front office. It was like a divorce, pure and simple. He should have been a Red Sox player for his entire career, but in 1999 he went to the Angels. He was out for the entire 2001 season with an injury. In 2002 he went to the Mets and was injured in 2003.

We've stayed quite friendly with Mo's parents, Leroy and Shirley. We see them for dinner and speak with them periodically. When Mo was traded to the Mets, my son Duke was able to break the story in New York first about Mo agreeing to the trade thanks to our contacts. Mo remains a special guy to me, and I wish him well.

◆ ● ◆

Greg Pirkl had two at bats for the Red Sox at the end of the 1996 season. He's best known for leading major league baseball in tattoos (well before the prevalence of tattoos in the NBA.)

◆ ● ◆

Toby Borland had 19 hunting dogs and he knew them all by name. In his final game for the Red Sox, he could not throw a strike. After walking four straight batters, he was pulled from the game and never pitched again for the Red Sox.

◆ ● ◆

We got back from a road trip one night at 4 AM. While we were away, we parked our cars right under Fenway. I looked at my car and found that I had a flat tire. I'm not very handy. Wes Gardner, a good ol' boy from Benton, Arkansas, changed the tire for me. That's something I'll never forget.

◆ ● ◆

Jeff Plympton pitched just 5.3 innings in four games for the Red Sox, all in 1991. He was a Framingham, Massachusetts, native who went to the University of Maine. He did the best impression I have ever seen of former Red Sox manager Joe Morgan: "Slider, slider, slider. Throw the number one, kid, throw the number one."

◆ ● ◆

David Cone was with the Red Sox for just one year, 2001, but he was the best player I ever saw at talking with the media. He is so in command, and so at ease with the press, it's almost presidential. I always had a special feeling for David because his mother-in-law, Angela Corso DeGioia (Miss Corso to me), was my ninth grade biology teacher. She was a very pretty woman. The guys really liked her, but they respected her and feared her, too. She was the first teacher I had who really made me think, not just repeat what was in the textbook. She also gave me a C.

Ms. Corso came up to see me in the broadcast booth at Fenway in 2001. We hadn't seen each other in years, and we had a lovely visit.

◆ ● ◆

Rich Rowland. As Trup said, Credence Clearwater Revival sang a song about him—"Proud Mary: Rowland, Rowland, Rowland down the river." Rich was a backup catcher and worked as a lumberjack in the offseason in Northern California. After he was acquired by the Red Sox in 1994, Nick Cafardo of the *Boston Globe* found that he was three years older than he said he was.

◆ ● ◆

John Trautwein. He was acquired as a Rule 5 draft pick with a chemistry degree from Northwestern. He was a marginal pitcher (0-1 in nine games), but John was a bright, well-spoken young man. When his baseball career was over after the 1988 season, he was very successful as a chemical engineer and chemical salesman in Europe.

◆ ● ◆

Matt Young signed as a free agent for the 1991 season. The year before, in Seattle, he earned a reported $587,000, but the Red Sox signed him to a big contract—$2,226,667. His was the kind of contract that typified free agent signings that didn't work out. He had a lot of trouble throwing to bases. I remember the no-hitter he threw and lost on a frigid day in Cleveland on April 12, 1992, during the first week of the season, the first game of a doubleheader. Young pitched an eight-inning no-hitter but lost 2-1. His accomplishment was stricken from the books by Commissioner Fay Vincent, who didn't recognize it as a no-hitter because he didn't pitch nine innings.

◆ ● ◆

Tim Wakefield—2003 was his ninth year throwing the knuckleball for the Red Sox. Tim is a great competitor and the most versatile pitcher the Red Sox have had since Bob Stanley—starting or relieving.

Like Stanley, he is also among the most generous players I know—contributing his time and funds to the Jimmy Fund, the Franciscan

Hospital for Children, and his own charity for Special Needs kids in his native Melbourne, Florida.

◆ ● ◆

Now, some short takes.

Rick Waits is the best singing ballplayer I know. As mentioned earlier, he was good enough to sing on the *Today Show*. Waits is now the minor league pitching coordinator for the Mets.

Jim Rice was the best-dressed player I ever knew. Whether it was his Coogi sweaters, his suits, or his golf attire, his clothes were always stylish and they fit him well.

Darren Lewis was the most knowledgeable about the history of the game.

The best sign-stealer was Joe Nossek when he coached for the Indians. He now coaches for the White Sox.

I didn't know Jackie Jensen, who retired from baseball because he couldn't stand flying, but I do know Dick Pole, who was the Red Sox bullpen coach for two years. Dick was a big, burly pitcher who always did a good job as a coach regardless of which team he was with. He is scared to death every time he gets on a plane. I usually sat behind him on the team plane. On one flight, Dick asked me to change my seat. He said it would affect the karma, and you don't mess with karma on a plane. He also got us what he called "diet beers" to make the flights more palatable. Dick is now with the Cubs.

The pitcher with the best pickoff move I ever saw was Bruce Hurst. He was very deceptive . . . looked like he was throwing home when he threw to first.

The outfielder with the best arm I ever saw was Dwight Evans. He could throw lasers; runners seldom challenged him.

◆ ● ◆

About the only time I play golf is in the fall, occasionally with my good friend Monsignor William Glynn. He's very kind, and does not ridicule my "technique." Monsignor Glynn is the pastor of Holy Family Parish in Duxbury, Massachusetts. He is such a Red Sox fan that he flies the Red Sox flag from the church steeple—full staff if they are in first place, half-staff if the Yankees lead.

Monsignor Glynn celebrated his 80th birthday in 2002 and 400 of his parishioners hosted a party for him at the Holy Family Church. I recorded and played a fantasy audiotape where Monsignor Glynn hits a home run off Mariano Rivera to win the ALCS for the Red Sox. He loved it.

26

The Extended Family— From Coaches to Owners to Umps

One of the coaches I know best is Bill Fischer, the Red Sox pitching coach from 1985 to 1991. His nickname was "Uncle Fish." He pitched for Washington, Detroit, Kansas City, and the Chicago White Sox. When Bill was with the Kansas City Athletics, he served up a home run to Mickey Mantle on May 22, 1963. In fact, during one of our visits to Yankee Stadium, we asked him for his strongest memory of the stadium. He pointed, and said, "Look up there. See that façade? Mickey Mantle hit one up there off me. Almost went out of the stadium."

Fish is a big, burly, gruff guy, but was one of the best pitching technicians ever. Tom Seaver loved him, and Roger Clemens really looked up to him. Fish coached into his 70s and is still a minor league instructor in the Atlanta Braves system. I've always liked Fish and his wife Val.

Fish was always a funny speaker and was most entertaining at the BoSox Club dinners. As he got older, he became easier to interview. To this day, he insists that there are only three people who know what happened when John McNamara took Roger Clemens out of the sixth game of the 1986 World Series in the eighth inning—Clemens, McNamara, and Fish.

Fish likes to tell the story of how other teams used to steal the Red Sox signs.

Second baseman Marty Barrett would give the pitcher's signs to Dwight Evans in rightfield. The Texas Rangers would steal the signs from the bullpen and relay them to the batter.

After leaving the majors, Bill went down to the minors. When Fischer got to the Richmond Braves in 1994, his new teammates who had been in the American League told him, "We knew all your signs!"

Bill told me that when he was in high school in northern Wisconsin, it was so cold one day that he pitched a game in a ski parka. Bill was nice enough to work with my son Duke on his pitching when Duke was at Stonehill College.

Some time around 1986, the Sox gave their players certificates for Eastern clothing. They told Bill that if he lost weight and stopped smoking, they'd buy him an entire new wardrobe. He lost the weight and quit smoking, and the other pitchers, including Roger Clemens, Bruce Hurst, and Al Nipper, did indeed buy him a new set of clothes.

When he was with Tampa Bay some years later, the players again bought him an entire new wardrobe after he lost weight.

◆ ● ◆

Al Bumbry has been a good friend for many years. He was an excellent outfielder for the Orioles, where he played for some good teams, and from 1988 to 1993 he was the first base coach for the Red Sox when Joe Morgan and Butch Hobson were the managers. Al's significant other is Annette Bradley, sister of Phil Bradley. We'd spend time with Al and Annette when we were on the road. In New York, Al made a true friend when he went to a game in Central Park to watch Jeffrey Lyons play rightfield in the Broadway Show League.

◆ ● ◆

Dick Berardino is another good friend and coach. Dick was a high-school teacher and coach in Waltham, Massachusetts. He also managed the Red Sox short season Class A team in Elmira, New York, where one of his players was Wade Boggs. Dick likes to say that this was the only team for which Boggs did *not* hit .300. Dick was a defensive back and a receiver on the Holy Cross football team, and one his proudest moments was when he tackled Jim Brown of Syracuse. (Of course, he got dragged a few extra feet.)

◆ ● ◆

Wendell Kim was the Red Sox third base coach from 1997 to 1999 and got a lot of heat when runners were out at home, but I thought he did a good job. It wasn't his fault that the Sox had bad and slow baserunners during his tenure. Fenway was also a tough park to coach third because the leftfield wall is so close to the diamond, meaning that the leftfielder is closer to the plate, making it difficult to score on a single to left. Another reason it was tough to be the Red Sox third base coach was that until 2002, the Red Sox had slow runners.

Wendell did magic tricks in the clubhouse, and he came to Jan's second grade class a few times to do magic tricks for the students.

◆ ● ◆

Mike Roarke, a Boston College graduate, was a longtime National League pitching coach from Rhode Island. Mike had been with Joe Morgan at Pawtucket. He was with the Red Sox in 1994. Pitchers liked him and respected him. Mike had the misfortune to be with the Sox during the strike year.

◆ ● ◆

Rac (short for Rachel) Slider was an infield coach with the Red Sox from 1987 to 1990 and a longtime minor league manager. He was a Texan who was probably the only man with whom I ever discussed cattle branding techniques.

◆ ● ◆

Eddie Yost, "the Walking Man" (he had led the American League in walks in 1950, 1952, 1953, 1956, 1959, and 1960) and coach with the Red Sox from 1977 to 1984, was one of the best third base coaches the Red Sox ever had. Even as a coach, he was in top condition. I used to have his baseball card when I was a kid. When he was with the Sox, his hobby was repairing clocks.

◆ ● ◆

Gabe Paul was the president of the Indians when I got my job with Cleveland. Players had strong opinions about him because he was from an era when management told players what their salaries would be, and that was it. No room to negotiate, no free agency. Take it or leave it. Dick Radatz told me that Paul once cut his salary by $11,000. Management could cut any player's salary by up to 25 percent in those days.

But Gabe had a very different personality with the media. He had what was called a "Mona Lisa" smile. He could be quite charming—in fact, he charmed my parents. Gabe worked well into his 70s, and I got along well with him.

◆ ● ◆

Phil Seghi was the Indians's general manager when I was with Cleveland. A good guy, Phil was very guarded around the media. Phil was a very good judge of talent but he had very little money to work with in Cleveland. He talked to me a lot about baseball and about players, and I learned a great deal from him. Phil passed away in 1985 shortly after he retired from the Indians.

◆ ● ◆

I was with Commissioner Bud Selig in Milwaukee when he was the president and owner of the Brewers. He was always nice to me. What I liked about him was his passion for the game. He knew everybody's name—all the media, all the reporters. He was a very friendly guy—not arrogant at all. I liked the way he smoked his Tiparillos—which I think he has since given up—pacing up and down behind the press box. Sometimes he couldn't bear to watch the games—the tension as so great.

◆ ● ◆

When I came to the Red Sox in 1983, Haywood Sullivan was the general manager, and later the club president when Lou Gorman came in. Tom Yawkey, the team's owner, took a liking to Haywood when he was a bonus baby in the 1950s. He had been a catcher. He was always gracious to me. With the help of Mrs. Yawkey, Sullivan borrowed enough money to take over the club in 1978, with Buddy Leroux. I didn't really deal with Sullivan on a day-to-day basis, but he was always loyal to me. He really knew how to throw a party. Whenever the Red Sox had a team Christmas party, or a Spring Training party, he was always a gracious host. I enjoyed being around him.

◆ ● ◆

James "Lou" Gorman is a great guy. When he was general manager of the Red Sox from 1984 to 1993, I did a radio show with him every day. Although the on-the-air portion of the show was only four minutes, we normally spent an hour together each day because Lou was a great storyteller. He loves to talk, and he's one of the most charming men I know.

Lou has a special love for the U.S. Navy. He was on active duty for eight years, including time on the USS *Hornet*, and spent some 34 years as an active navy reservist.

Lou and his wife Mary Lou didn't have any children, but he loves children, and is wonderful with them. He knows the names of all the wives and children. He took a special interest in my children whenever they came to his office when I was interviewing him. "What to give you, what to give you," he'd say, always looking for a souvenir of some kind which he knew they'd like. If he didn't have any candy in his desk, Lou would look in other people's desks for candy.

I loved traveling with Lou because he knew every restaurant in every city we visited. When we were on the team bus together, he'd point to restaurant after restaurant, saying, "That's a good place, that's a good place." My mother-in-law loved him, my father loved him, and my kids love him, too. Lou Gorman is the reason my son Duke went to Stonehill

College. He is the best spokesman any college ever had. He went to Stonehill when the school opened in the late 1940s. And he preached its charms to my kids for years, after he first came to Boston in 1984, a year after I did. He's a native of Providence.

When Duke was unhappy at Ithaca College, stuck on the junior varsity too far from home, he remembered Uncle Lou preaching about Stonehill. So, after one semester, he transferred to Stonehill, where he was very happy.

Lou helped build the Mets in the early 1980s and then came to the Red Sox in 1984. So he had a key role in building both clubs that played in the 1986 World Series. As Red Sox general manager, he did a good job of keeping the Red Sox competitive.

◆ ● ◆

John Harrington, who ran the team for the Yawkey Trust from 1994 to 2002, was a gracious, soft-spoken gentleman. He did not really like the media limelight. John, who was associated with the Red Sox for almost 30 years, was always very loyal to me, and took a great interest in my family. He encouraged my daughter Kate to attend Boston College, from which she graduated in 2001. John was also very good to the Jimmy Fund, a subject that frequently made him quite emotional. He was also very loyal to the Yawkeys. When he owned the team, he stayed in the background a great deal and let the "baseball people"—the general manager, the scouting director, the farm director—run the show. When the team was sold, he took a lot of heat—much more than he deserved. He was an excellent caretaker for the Yawkey Trust.

◆ ● ◆

I've known Dan Duquette since 1981 when he was in his second year as an assistant in the Milwaukee Brewers's farm system office. He was always dedicated and professional. He can be very friendly and very funny but did not reveal his personality often in public. The media was very critical of his methods and style and portrayed his style as being harsh.

When Dan came to the Red Sox from Montreal in 1994, he had a tremendous buildup as being a boy-genius general manager. He was just 36. He brought Pedro Martinez to the Sox in 1998 from Montreal and drafted Nomar Garciaparra. It's too bad that Dan could not work things out with Mo Vaughn and Roger Clemens, who Dan said was "in the twilight of his career." Clemens went on to win the Cy Young Award with the Toronto Blue Jays in 1997 and 1998 and again with the Yankees in 2001. In 1997 and 1998, he also won the Triple Crown of pitching—quite a feat—leading the American League in strikeouts, wins, and ERA.

Another problem with the loss of Clemens to the Blue Jays after 1996 and the Mo Vaughn free agent signing by the Angels after the 1998 season was that the Red Sox obtained only draft picks in exchange. Both were given lowball offers and it was obvious that neither player was really wanted.

Dan's public image took a pounding because of several things, such as the Jimy Williams situation and the Carl Everett situation. If Dan had better public relations from the inside, he might have weathered these problems a little better. Dan should get credit for giving the Red Sox a much greater presence in the Far East and Latin America, especially in the Dominican Republic. For years, the Red Sox did not get the best players there, but Dan opened a camp in the Dominican Republic and beefed up the scouting and development staff there.

◆ ● ◆

Bill O'Donnell, one of my mentors, was the voice of Syracuse sports—basketball and football, mostly. I first met him in January 1965, when I accidentally picked up his gloves after a triple overtime game between Colgate and Syracuse, probably the greatest basketball game I have ever done. Colgate was a huge underdog. Syracuse had Dave Bing, Jim Boeheim, and other great athletes. Colgate's star was George Dalzell and our coach was Bob Duffy, who had played for the St. Louis Hawks and the Detroit Pistons in the NBA. A Colgate graduate, he was just 24. The game was played at Huntington Gym, a little bandbox, with bleachers going ten rows up. The Syracuse coach was Freddie Lewis, who waved an orange towel throughout the game. At the end of the game, Syracuse made one of two shots from the free throw line. The scoreboard had a manual clock. The scoreboard failed to register one of the foul shots. Dalzell made a shot from midcourt, and the Colgate players and fans went crazy, believing that they had won the game. But his shot had merely *tied* the game. No three-point shots then. The referee was Johnny Gee, who had pitched for the Pirates and the Giants and at 6 foot 9 inches had been the tallest player in baseball. The Colgate players were already carrying their coach off the court on their shoulders, but I knew that the score was still tied. So did Gee, and he waved the players back onto the court. The game continued into overtime, then triple overtime before the Orangemen ultimately prevailed. Colgate has played Syracuse in basketball every year but the Orangemen have won every game in the series since 1962.

Bill took a real interest in my career. He went on to broadcast for the Baltimore Orioles, and whenever they were in Cleveland, I would keep the scoreboard for Bill and Chuck Thompson, another great guy. Chuck is a Hall of Famer. Every time there was an opening with a major league club, Bill would call me to let me know, so I could get a jump on applying for the job. When I got my first major league job with the Indians in 1979, Bill was one of the first people I called. Unfortunately, he died of cancer in October 1982.

◆ ● ◆

Fred McLeod was 26 when we started working together in Cleveland. A very dedicated broadcaster, Fred could outwork anybody. He loves television and is an excellent anchor and reporter. He is now the voice of the Detroit Pistons in the NBA. After Cleveland, he made a stop in San Francisco, but he's been in Detroit for sometime.

◆ ● ◆

Bob Feller was fun to work with, and was always great to my kids. He can be a little gruff on the exterior, but when I worked with him, he was always self-effacing—he joked about his record for surrendering walks. Bob's wife Anne is a native of Connecticut. One weekend in 1983, Bob stayed at our home in Massachusetts, and we drove down to the University of Connecticut-Colgate football game. Anne is a graduate of the University of Connecticut.

Bob and I had a lot of fun together during the years I worked in Cleveland. Now, whenever I'm in Cleveland I call him and we usually get together at the ballpark. We also see each other during the winter.

◆ ● ◆

Bob Starr had one of the best voices I ever heard. He taught me how to relax in the booth—not to take everything so seriously. He used to say, "It's not my wife, and it's not my life." He got a big kick out of me when the Red Sox lost. Bob's father Harry worked in the Oklahoma oil fields, and when Bob told him that he wanted a career in broadcasting, his father said, "You can talk, can't you? There can't be much more to it than that."

Jan and I were with Bob two days before he passed away. He had left the Red Sox after the 1992 season to return to Anaheim. He developed fibrosis of the lungs and perhaps Legionnaire's disease. His lung problems set him back and he started getting worse. On our first trip to Anaheim in 1998, I wanted to see him, but his wife Brenda said that he didn't want any visitors. When we were back in Anaheim in August, I offered to stay with Bob while Brenda went out with Jan for a break. But she wouldn't leave him. So Jan and I went and had a wonderful visit. Two days later, when we were in Seattle, I got the sad news that Bob had passed away.

◆ ● ◆

I first worked with Jerry Trupiano in 1993. Bob Starr had left the Red Sox to return to the Angels. I had never met Jerry before, but I liked his audition tape.

Trup was recommended by our executive producer Luke Griffin. Luke had worked with Jerry at Mutual Radio where Jerry had done college and NFL football games. Trup had been the voice of the Houston Oilers.

Luke did a great job for us but American Radio, which broadcast the games then, let him go after the strike in late 1995.

Trup and I met during the offseason, and we did 20 games together in Spring Training in Fort Myers before the season started. The chemistry was good from the start.

Although Jerry was new to the Red Sox, he had plenty of experience as a major league broadcaster: He did Astros games in 1985–1986 and broadcast for the Expos 1989–1990. He had been to some of the American League ballparks and knew many of the people around the league.

◆ ● ◆

Hank Greenwald was a San Francisco Giants broadcaster and also worked for the Yankees in 1987–1988. From 1979 until his retirement in 1996, Hank never missed a game. His baseball book, *This Copyrighted Broadcast*, is very funny, just like Hank. He's not afraid to speak his mind. I met Hank in 1993 when the Red Sox had a day game in Oakland. Trup and I went to see the Giants night game at Candlestick Park in San Francisco; the only time I ever saw a game there. (I met Hank briefly when he was with the Yankees, but didn't get to know him until later.) At Candlestick, we met again in the press box, where he told me that his son Douglas was a student at Boston University. I told Hank to have his son call me. We got together, and our families became very close. We see Hank and his wife Carla regularly in Spring Training and throughout the year. After a seven-year retirement, Hank came back to broadcast Oakland A's games in 2004.

◆ ● ◆

Ken Coleman was my first partner in the radio booth when I came to the Red Sox in 1983, and I have written about him elsewhere.

◆ ● ◆

Ned Martin came to the Red Sox in 1961, and stayed for 32 years— a record that will never be touched. I think Ned should be in the Hall

of Fame. Ned was a very cultured gentleman, an English major at
Duke. He was a marine in World War II and landed on Iwo Jima.
One of the greatest moments I ever had was in the pressroom in
Cleveland during my first year as a baseball broadcaster. I met Ned,
and he said, "Welcome to the big leagues, young man." I'll never for-
get that.

Ned was a conservative Republican, and I loved to get him excited
about politics and about baseball. I loved to talk baseball with Ned, and
I learned a lot from him. After retiring from broadcasting, Ned lived on
a farm in southern Virginia. He and his wife Barbara were regulars at
our annual Christmas party.

Ned passed away while returning home from the Fenway Park tribute to Ted Williams in 2002.

◆ ● ◆

They're mostly all gone now, but there used to be a group of larger-
than-life broadcasters, such as Vin Scully of the Dodgers, Bob Prince,
Harry Caray (particularly when he was with the Cardinals and Cubs),
Jack Buck with the Cardinals, Ernie Harwell with the Tigers, and Mel
Allen with the Yankees. Marty Brennaman, another Hall of Famer, has
been with the Reds a long time and is well respected around the game
of baseball.

Some were resented by the owners because they were so popular—
frequently more popular than the players. Some also made more money
than the players. In 1967, Ken Coleman was the highest paid person on
the Red Sox plane. In 1989, Ken was among the lowest paid, followed
by the trainers, a few coaches, and me.

◆ ● ◆

Speaking of trainers, Jimmy Warfield was one of the nicest people I
ever knew in baseball. He was the Cleveland Indians trainer from
1971 until his death after a brain hemorrhage in July 2002. He was a
confidant of many players and a friend to all. Jimmy never said a negative word about anyone . . . even the robbers who mugged and

robbed him in his hotel room in Oakland. He said, "They probably needed the money."

Jimmy took quite an interest in my sons, Duke and Tom. They knew him almost all their lives. I would always visit him whenever we were in Cleveland, in the clubhouse or the dugout. Jimmy was also the greatest Penn State fan ever. Many players and managers from today and yester-year attended his memorial service at Jacobs Field. Andre Thornton was the moderator; one of the many players who were close to him and Andre's wife Gail sang hymns. Jimmy truly was one of the most beloved people in baseball. When the Indians made the World Series in 1995, I sent him a congratulatory message because he had seen so many Tribe losses over the years.

◆ ● ◆

Jack Rogers was the traveling secretary for the Red Sox for many years. He had been with the Braves in 1948, then left to work for Pan American World Airways in 1953. He started with the Red Sox in 1969 and traveled with the club through 1991. After that, he stayed with the club as a consultant. He gave the team a lot of class. Players had a great deal of respect for him. Nobody ever got out of line with Jack. Jack was great with the media. Jack always took us out to dinner when we were on the road. His wife Ellie was also very passionate about baseball and about the Red Sox. They became very good friends of ours over the years and were regulars at any parties we had. Jack passed away in January 2003.

◆ ● ◆

Dick Bresciani, the Red Sox vice president—of publications and archives—is very dedicated to and passionate about the Red Sox. He and I share our pain whenever the Sox don't do well, and the exultation when they do. He takes every loss personally. He and his wife Joanne have always been great to my kids. When my daughter Kate graduated from college, through the good graces of John Harrington, Dick gave Kate a job, and he's always been there for us.

◆ ● ◆

Tom Werner, Red Sox chairman, is a Hollywood TV producer, a brilliant programmer, and brings an important presence to the ownership group, especially with the continued growth of the New England Sports Network (NESN).

◆ ● ◆

John Henry, a self-made success in the commodities market, is a very gracious, soft-spoken man. He's brilliant at statistics and loves the game of baseball. He lets his "baseball people" do their jobs. He's also a very considerate man. We were flying from Atlanta to San Diego on a family trip. He greeted everybody on the plane, from the players to their wives to the equipment manager to the graphics operator for NESN—he welcomed everybody on board. When he got to me, he asked whether broadcasters' families were included on Red Sox family trips. I told him that they had been in previous years, but that the practice had fallen through the cracks recently. He told me, "We'll take care of that." I don't think most people in his position would have given the issue much thought. But he did.

I saw Larry Lucchino, the president and CEO of the Red Sox, play college basketball when Princeton played Colgate in the 1960s. He was a teammate of Bill Bradley—an outstanding guard who helped the Princeton Tigers to the Final Four in 1965. He has a Final Four ring. The Tigers finished fourth behind UCLA, which won the NCAA tournament.

He also has a 1983 Super Bowl ring because of his association with Edward Bennett Williams, the owner of the Washington Redskins.

Larry Lucchino also owns a World Championship ring he won with the 1983 Baltimore Orioles, where he was the chief executive.

He's a very personable, outgoing, hands-on executive. He has his finger on the pulse of the Boston community, as he did in Baltimore where he was instrumental in building the new ballpark at Camden Yards. He also played a key role in San Diego, where he was a prime mover in the building of the new Petco Park in San Diego. He helped lead the Padres to the World Series in 1998—a difficult thing to do with a small-to-medium-market, small-payroll team.

◆ ● ◆

Dr. Charles Steinberg is a dentist and was the Orioles team dentist. He got his start in baseball as an intern with the Orioles while he was in high school. He was a moving force in the game entertainment aspect of baseball. I was always impressed with the music and the big screen videos played at Memorial Stadium in Baltimore. He really knew how to keep the fans entertained and is very creative and innovative. He's bringing his expertise in this field to the Red Sox, as part of the new ownership group.

The new owners know how much the fans love the team. They want to show the reverse—how much the team loves the fans. The Red Sox have sponsored a Halloween party for inner-city kids, a Thanksgiving dinner for the homeless, a Veterans' Day celebration in the .406 Club, and the opening of the street fair on Yawkey Way adjoining the stadium in September 2002—all demonstrations of the team's concern for the community.

◆ ● ◆

Radio play-by-play broadcasters work hand and glove with umpires. Basically, we call balls and strikes on radio after the umpire decides what the pitch is. The umpires set the pace for our calls and it is good to be in sync with them. A slow umpire's call can be difficult to time. I have great respect for most umpires. They are proven right most of the time by the video replays.

There is no doubt who was number one during my tenure on radio—the pride of Oxford, Massachusetts, and a true American hero: Steve Palmermo. Steve had a great flair for umpiring and loved it. He hustled, had fun, and made good judgments. He was in charge of a game. Unfortunately, his career ended when he was shot and suffered spinal cord injuries while coming to the aid of some females victims who were being accosted by assailants. The attack happened in the parking lot of a Dallas restaurant after Steve had worked a game that night at

Arlington Stadium on July 6, 1991. Steve has had several operations since then and has vowed to work again. His courageous battle to make that happen continues and he has made great strides and can walk without the aid of crutches. Steve has been a mover in research for spinal cord injuries and has helped baseball as a supervisor. He is also a frequent guest on our games in his hometown of Kansas City and is one of the best analysts I have ever heard. He could easily be a national broadcast analyst. Steve and his dedicated wife Debbie persevere, even though he told me that he still has tremendous pain every day from the injuries. Steve deserves a high-ranking position in baseball.

Other top umpires include Rick Reed, a veteran from the American League. One time, former Red Sox manager Joe Morgan was watching a game on television and was so impressed with Reed's work behind the plate that he sent the ump a letter saying, "Hey Rick, I watched the whole game from Seattle and you didn't miss a single pitch." Of course, that was after Joe finished managing.

Rich Garcia, now a supervisor, was also a good umpire. Rich had a short fuse but great ability and was always in command. In my opinion, the best umpire working today is John Hirschbeck, a good friend who has endured the personal tragedy of the death of his son, John Jr., from a rare brain disease. John's surviving son, Michael, has the same condition but is doing better and often travels to games with his dad. John, a native of Stratford Connecticut and brother of major league umpire Mark Hirschbeck, lives in the Youngstown, Ohio, suburb of Poland, Ohio. Trup likes to tease me when I emphasize the umpires from Youngstown now working in the majors: Hirschbeck, Brian O'Nora, and Wally Bell.

Tim McCelland is another very good umpire working today and Tim Tschida is a personal friend—and a very good umpire, too.

The attitudes of the umpires have improved greatly since many of the veterans decided to resign en masse at the misguided and inexplicable direction of their union's leader, Richie Phillips, in 1999.

Some of those umpires were very arrogant and out of control and acted as if they were the most important people in the game. Some didn't hustle and acted as if they owned the game.

One of those umpires in question was working home plate one hot Sunday afternoon in Boston but refused to come out for the exchange of lineup cards saying it was too hot and he had to save himself for the game. With one or two exceptions, most of those arrogant umpires who made you wonder how hard they were trying are gone. Today's younger umpires may not be perfect but they try to be and bear down and hustle. That is not to say we don't criticize them, though. We try to be fair but will point out when they missed a call although I can't say we are neutral observers.

27

Scouts

When I travel with the team, I socialize a great amount with scouts. I see them in the press dining rooms at the stadiums, either at home or on the road. We go out to dinner with them whenever possible. Some of my best friends in baseball are scouts. They are the lifeblood of the game. Scouts are the most underappreciated, underpaid, and underpublicized people in baseball. They do the legwork. They do all the running. They find the players, and they see things that others do not. They see physical skills and raw talent, and try to project growth, maturity, character, and development. It's a very difficult job, and batting averages for scouts are not very high as far as signees making the majors.

Of course, some players are easy to scout—when you see top talent, anybody can recognize it. But it takes an experienced, incisive, bold, and courageous mind to project three, five, or eight years down the road—will this kid's arm improve? Will he grow enough to develop more power? How are his baseball instincts? Will he gain speed—foot speed and bat speed—as he gets older, bigger, and stronger? Baseball scouts answer these and a hundred other questions every day—and those are just the scouts who see high-school and college players.

The advance scouts usually stay one series ahead of the team. They e-mail or fax their reports to the manager and the pitching coach with their insights on who swings at the first pitch, hitters' and pitchers' tendencies, which outfielder's arm is showing his age, which pitcher to steal on, which base stealer is limping a little, and other tips that just might make the difference for a hit, stolen base, strikeout, run, or game.

Some of the best scouting jobs are done on players who initially seem small or have some other drawbacks. A good scout can see what this player will blossom into.

Deacon Jones is an advance scout for the Baltimore Orioles. He usually stays one series ahead of the team. He will file a report on each hitter and on each pitcher. What do they throw? What do they do in a particular situation? (i.e., what's his "out pitch"?) The pitches hitters like to hit in a particular count. Hitter's tendencies, pickoffs, first pitch swinging. This, and the large charts they compile, is the grunt work aspect of their jobs. The more interesting part, to me, is their life experience in baseball.

Grover "Deacon" Jones is a native of White Plains, New York. He is a member of the White Plains High School Hall of Fame.

Woody Hayes of Ohio State recruited him as a running back. When Hayes stood in Jones's living room, Deacon told Hayes that he wanted to attend college to play baseball, so he went to Ithaca College in New York.

Deacon became the American Legion player of the year in 1951. Later, he became the first African American inducted into the American Legion Baseball Hall of Fame.

Deacon had a tryout with the Brooklyn Dodgers at Ebbets Field and with the Pittsburgh Pirates. After he hit some balls at Ebbets Field, he met Jackie Robinson, who advised him to go to college. "You can always play baseball later," said Robinson.

Some years later, in the 1950s when Deacon was in the minors, he ran into the Dodgers in an airport and he spoke to Robinson. Although Robinson didn't remember Deacon's name, he asked him, "Hey, kid, you go to college, right?" Sandy Koufax had a tryout that day, too. The tryouts were in Pittsburgh under the watchful eye of Branch Rickey. He made offers to both of them. But Deacon turned down Rickey and went to college. After his junior year in Ithaca, he worked out for the White Sox and they asked him what he wanted to sign. He asked for about $9,000. The maximum bonus in those days was $4,000. If a player received a higher bonus, the team was required to keep him on the major league roster, whether they played him or not. (In the years before the major league draft, this rule was designed to keep the Yankees from stocking their minor leagues with all the talented players, and to keep the salaries down.)

The "Bonus Baby" rule hurt a number of players such as Frank Leja and Tom Carroll, who had to sit on the Yankees bench instead of playing and honing their skills for a few years in the minors.

The White Sox asked Deacon Jones what else he wanted to sign. (Of course at the time, anything else had to be under the table.) Deacon said he wanted a car like Marty Marion's, the manager of the Chisox. The general manager said, "Marty, give Deacon your car." He did.

He was also promised a $5,000 bonus after his first year in the minors. After that season, he drove to Chicago in his car, and picked up his $5,000 in cash. He had to stop at a motel to sleep. He was so nervous, he put the cash under his pillow. He later said that the happiest day of his life was when he put that $5,000 on his parents' kitchen table. They were thrilled.

In his early years, he had to battle to be permitted to play baseball. His father, whom he called the "real" deacon—was a deacon of the Baptist church—forbade his son from playing baseball on Sunday. When his father once caught his son playing on a Sunday, the son got a whipping.

But after young Deacon plunked $5,000 on the table, his father saw the light and realized that his son could make a living just by playing baseball and Deacon played on Sundays for many years thereafter.

Deacon had a fine minor league career. He hit .319 with 26 home runs and 110 RBI for the Savannah White Sox in 1962 before being called up to the big club on September 18. He hit a home run for the Sox in 1963, but seriously injured his right shoulder diving for a ball. He tried to work his way back into shape by playing winter ball, where he was a teammate of Roberto Clemente. He went to Clemente's chiropractor and tried all kinds of rubs and ointments, all to no avail. A lefty batter who threw right, he learned to throw left-handed, and became a very good first baseman when he returned to the International League. He was back with the White Sox for five games in 1966, and then retired.

From 1976 to 1982, he was the hitting coach for the Astros and the Padres under Dick Williams, where he was Tony Gwynn's hitting coach. The 1984 Padres won the National League pennant.

Deacon played with Don Buford in Savannah, Georgia, for the White Sox franchise in the Sally League. Deacon's wife Tiki and Don's wife Alicea integrated the stands at the stadium. They simply refused to sit in the "colored only" seating section. Deacon and Don looked up from the field one day and were surprised to see their wives sitting with the other players' wives in the box seats behind home plate. It caused quite a stir. The club's general manager sympathized, but thought that this would hurt his business. It did. Some sponsors terminated their support of the team, and attendance dropped. Eventually, the club moved to Lynchburg, Virginia.

Deacon was once chased through the woods near Columbus, Georgia, by the Klan.

He also was threatened with a gun in a bus station while he was in the minors.

Deacon is a great storyteller. I hope one day he will write his own book. He really understands people and has a knack for remembering everybody's name.

Duke, Tom, and Kate have spent lots of time with Deacon, and have learned a great deal from him—about race relations and about life in general.

Deacon and his family live in Sugarland, Texas.

◆ ● ◆

Tom Giordano, "T-Bone," has had many jobs in baseball. As of this writing, he's a special assistant to John Hart of the Texas Rangers.

Originally signed by the Red Sox, he played in the Philadelphia Athletics's minor league system for years before playing just 11 games for the 1953 A's. In 1953, he beat Henry Aaron for the Sally League home run title. He hit 24 at Savannah and Aaron hit 22 for Jacksonville. After his playing career, he worked in the farm system for the A's and the Expos and eventually became the farm director for the Orioles under Hank Peters. He then went to the Indians as a special assignment scout, again under Hank Peters. When Hank's protégé, John Hart, took over, T-Bone kept the same job. A special assignment scout is usually the top confidant of the general manager, sent on special missions to scout either specific players or players who would fill a certain need for the team—a player they might want to acquire.

T-Bone is the only scout I know who travels with garlic salt and garlic because he loves to cook. He's an excellent Italian cook. Whenever he stays at a hotel or a home with a kitchen, he cooks—sauces, complete dishes, whatever. He cooks for a few or for a group of other scouts. In certain cities, when he goes out to eat in a restaurant, he asks to work in the kitchen.

He is also a very funny guy and a practical joker. But primarily, he is an excellent judge of baseball talent. T-Bone is now in his late 70s and a great friend. He's from Long Island and has homes near Portland, Maine, and Tampa, Florida. T-Bone has a particular affinity for other Italians in and around professional baseball. He speaks Italian beautifully and has been especially nice to my son Duke.

◆ ● ◆

Tom Mooney was a special assignment and free agent scout for several clubs before joining the Red Sox. We saw him when he was a scout with the Seattle Mariners. He signed Ken Griffey Jr. and Mike Gardiner, among others. Tom is a native of Pittsfield, Massachusetts. When he was with the Houston Astros, he discovered Jeff Bagwell while scouting New Britain. When the Red Sox wanted to make the Larry Anderson trade, Tom told the Astros they should get Jeff Bagwell and nobody else. That confidence truly showed what a good judge of major league potential Tom was, because that season, Jeff Bagwell hit a total of four home runs for New Britain. Of course, New Britain, of the Eastern League, played in a terrible hitters' park.

Once Moons moved to the Red Sox before the 2000 season, we didn't get to see him as often as before. I don't see the Red Sox advance or special assignment scouts very often during the season, because they are scouting the teams that the Red Sox will play the following week. But in Spring Training or when I'm at Fenway Park occasionally during the offseason we renew our friendship. During the season, either at home or on the road, I see the advance scouts for the other teams. Mooney joined the Cincinnati Reds scouting staff in 2004.

◆ ● ◆

Buddy Kerr is one of my favorites. A native New Yorker, he grew up in upper Manhattan near the Polo Grounds and played for the New York Giants in the 1940s and for the Boston Braves in the early 1950s. He was with the Mets for many years before retiring. He loves to tell the story about how he used to get in shape for Spring Training during the winter. There were no indoor hitting facilities at the time, so he and some of his friends would have a catch in the subway station near the Polo Grounds at 8th Avenue and 155th Street.

◆ ● ◆

Bill Lajoie, a longtime baseball guy, taught and coached in high school when his playing days ended, then became a professional scout. He moved up to become the general manager of the 1984 World Champion Detroit Tigers. He then took semiretirement and became a special scout for John Schuerholtz of the Braves. He did an outstanding job there and became one of the most respected scouts in the game. Then it was on to the Milwaukee Brewers for two years before joining the Red Sox before the 2003 season.

◆ ● ◆

Bob Johnson scouted for the Expos and now the Oakland A's. Bob is a sharp guy who does a good job scouting against the Red Sox. I spent a lot of time talking with Bob about virtually every team in the league *except* the A's. He rarely saw them play.

◆ ● ◆

Ed Di Ramio is from Quincy, Massachusetts. He's one of my closest friends. For many years, he was a part-time scout for the Cardinals and the Phillies, and a full-time scout for the Cubs. Ed took a special interest in my son Duke when Duke was in high school—he loved Duke's arm. Unfortunately, Duke didn't have the bat or the speed to go along with his arm, but Ed used to take Duke along with him to a warehouse near Logan Airport in East Boston where the minor leaguers worked out in the greater Boston area atop a roofer's shack. Eddie took a professional and a personal interest in Duke.

After the 1991 season, the club decided that they no longer needed a full-time New England scout, and he was out of baseball for the first time in many years. I think that was a mistake.

◆ ● ◆

John Doherty, from North Reading, Massachusetts, was a longtime local hitting instructor who had a brief fling with the Angels in the mid-1970s. He worked with Duke and Tom and all the minor leaguers for no fee, just because he loved baseball. He coached in the Red Sox farm system in 1991.

◆ ● ◆

Arthur Hartung, another hitting instructor and minor leaguer, also worked with Duke. His son Andy was an All-American at the University of Maine, and led the Carolina League in RBI one year.

◆ ● ◆

John Koziak, a scout from Milford, Massachusetts, is another good friend of ours. He was with the Padres and now the Dodgers organization. John signed a number of New England prospects to professional contracts. One of his finds was Greenfield, Massachusetts, native Peter Bergeron, now of the Expos. He also signed Bryce Florie and Warren Newsome while scouting the Carolinas for the Padres. John is responsible for me getting an award from the New York Scouting Association in January 2003.

◆ ● ◆

Leo Labossiere was a scout for the Orioles and later a special assignment scout for Roland A. Hemond. He moved on to free agent scouting in New England. I used to see him at Fenway Park and in Lincoln, Rhode Island, just outside of Providence. We'd meet for lunch during the off-season, too. The first player he signed, Johnny Goryl, made it to the majors and went on to manage the Minnesota Twins.

The last player he signed, Chad Paronto, out of the University of Massachusetts, made it to the majors with the Baltimore Orioles.

Leo's son David is the longtime trainer for the Houston Astros.

Unfortunately, Leo passed away in September 2001. He had survived a bout with cancer in the late 1940s when he was still in high school. Even though he was only about 5-foot 4-inches tall, he was the captain of the Providence College basketball team.

◆ ● ◆

Tom Borque is another great scout. He happened to be Dan Duquette's college roommate at Amherst. Tom played baseball at Amherst and became a scout for the Milwaukee Brewers, where he signed Billy Jo Robidoux who later beat Nolan Ryan in a game against the Red Sox at Fenway Park with a double.

Tom went on to scout for the Montreal Expos and the Cubs. He's still a part-time scout for the Cubs. He currently is the business manager for the city of Lynn, Massachusetts, School District.

◆ ◆ ◆

Howie Haak was a great friend. He had been a backup catcher—a bullpen catcher—for the St. Louis Cardinals in the 1930s, but he never got into a big league game. Branch Rickey, who ran the Cardinals at the time, respected Howie's judgment. When Rickey took over the Dodgers, he took Howie with him as his special scout. At the time, the Dodgers had more than 20 farm clubs, and Rickey would visit them all. Rickey knew pitching. He had been a catcher himself during a brief major league career. He took Howie with him, and as Rickey stood behind him, like an umpire, Howie would catch all the pitchers on each club. After watching a number of pitches, Rickey would dictate to a secretary standing off to the side how far he thought each pitcher would go. He was probably right about 98 percent of the time.

When Branch Rickey left Brooklyn to join the Pittsburgh Pirates, Howie went with him again and stayed in Pittsburgh after Rickey retired. Howie spent his final years with the Houston Astros. He died in 1999.

Rickey, who did not drink, once offered Howie an extra $1,000 if he went all year without taking a drink. One thousand dollars was a handsome sum at the time, and Howie earned it. He said that the first thing he did after he got the money from Rickey was to go out and get drunk.

I used to give Howie rides to the hotel in Boston. He knew how to fill out his expense account documents, and he knew how to drink Wild Turkey. Virtually single-handedly, Howie opened up the American major leagues to players from Latin America. He signed many players, such as Tony Peña from the Dominican Republic, as well as Manny Sanguillen and Rennie Stennet from Panama, for the Pirates. He was treated like a king in Cuba before Castro took over. Howie had carte blanche to travel wherever he wanted. He was honored by the president of the Dominican Republic because of all the Dominican players he signed, although Howie didn't speak a word of Spanish. Howie also signed many players from Puerto Rico. He was loved and respected throughout Latin America because of the opportunities he provided to Latin players to play in the big leagues and earn big-league salaries. Many of the players he signed called him "My Daddy."

Gene Michael, "Stick," the head scout and former shortstop, manager, and general manager with the Yankees, is a very knowledgeable scout and a great guy. His instincts and judgment are usually right on the money. When Yankees owner George Steinbrenner was on a sabbatical of sorts and away from the day-to-day running of the club, Gene built the great Yankee clubs in the early 1990s. Gene was the general manager who signed Derek Jeter and Bernie Williams, for example.

◆ ● ◆

Al LaMacchia, longtime scout for Toronto, Tampa, and the Dodgers, recently turned 81. A former pitcher for the Browns and the Senators, Al speaks the best Italian of any scout I know.

◆ ● ◆

The Yankees are the only club I know of which double teams in advance scouting with former major league player and manager Chuck Cottier and Wade Taylor, a former Yankee pitcher.

Some teams try to save money by doing their advance scouting via satellite TV. It's unfortunate that when major league teams decide that they have to cut expenses, scouts are usually among the first employees to go. Without scouting, baseball would not be what it is today. Baseball is not like football and basketball, which rely on high schools and colleges to turn out ready-made professionals. A good baseball scout will look at a youngster of 16 or 17 and predict, with some accuracy, what he'll be like at 20 or 23. Baseball is so much more difficult to predict and to judge than other sports because there are so many variables.

Lenny Merullo, the former Cubs shortstop who recently retired at the age of 85, scouted from the late 1940s through 2002. Lenny played for the Cubs in the 1945 World Series. On September 13, 1942, he tied a major league record by making four errors in one inning. Lenny's son was born that day and of course was nicknamed "Boots." Boots played baseball at Holy Cross and was in the minor leagues, headed for the majors, when a leg injury ended his career. Boots's son Matt Merullo, Lenny's grandson, made the majors as a catcher with the White Sox and Twins and once tied the Red Sox at Fenway Park with a two-out, pinch-hit home run in the ninth inning off Jeff Reardon. Fittingly, Matt has followed in his grandfather's footsteps and is now scouting the Northeast for the Arizona Diamondbacks.

The Red Sox New England scouts have been special favorites of mine. No one works harder than Ray Fagnant, a Holyoke native and former minor league catcher. Ray, who has an MBA, scouts New England for the Red Sox and is considered one of the best in the game. His mother and sister listen to our games and bring us homemade brownies when they visit us in the broadcast booth.

Ray follows in the footsteps of Buzz Bowers, longtime New England scout who still works part time and the great Bill Enos. Bill has been in baseball since 1937 when he signed with the St. Louis Browns as a 17-year-old. He never played in the majors but has scouted for about 60 years. Bill lived in a 300-year-old house in Cohasset, Massachusetts, his entire life before moving to Arizona recently to be with his daughters. His late, lovely wife Grace was a wonderful cook and it was a badge of honor to be invited to their annual Christmas dinner for the area scouts.

Every year, Bill and Grace had mystery guests at the dinner, and Jan and I were honored with that distinction one year. The motif was baseball and Christmas. Bill signed a number of big leaguers including Rich Gedman.

◆ ● ◆

Another New England scout was the late Chick Whelan, best known for signing Richie Hebner for the Pirates. Chick, who had been a prisoner of war in World War II, loved to tell the story of beating the Pirates on an expense account report. One bright, sunny day while scouting a game, Chick was having trouble seeing the field so he bought a sun hat at the concession stand. He put the hat on his expense account, but some bean counter in the Pirates office rejected it. The next time Chick filled out an expense report, he made it several pages long and very complex. He said to the bean counter, "That hat is in that report somewhere. YOU find it!" Chick's son Bob is now the head baseball coach at Dartmouth.

◆ ● ◆

Another scout I love to visit with is the great George Digby, now semi-retired. George has scouted the south for the Red Sox since the 1940s and has signed players such as Haywood Sullivan, who became co-owner of the team, Wade Boggs, Bob Montgomery, Mike Greenwell, Jody Reed, and others. George told me how important it was for a scout to stay alert on the road because of the hundreds of thousands of miles they have to drive to find players. He said that his St. Christopher statue in his car has done well by him.

When we broadcast late at night, I always think of those scouts who are on the road, driving to the next stop and listening to baseball. We hope we keep them awake and alert.

I remember something Monsignor John Dillon Day, a retired Boston priest and renowned baseball and Boston College sports historian, told me at a banquet. He said, "Remember: what you have is an apostolate. You bring joy and entertainment to thousands of shut-ins, blind people, and the elderly. In some cases, your broadcasts are their only connection with the outside world and their only form of entertainment." I had never thought about my job this way until then. These shut-ins and elderly are not considered important in ratings or advertising circles, but Monisignor Day's comments put a new perspective on the importance of my job and on the responsibility involved. I thank him for that. By the way, Monsignor Day can name the starting lineups for the Boston Red Sox and the Boston Braves teams of the 1920s and the 1930s, who were usually keeping each other company in the basements of their respective leagues. Monsignor Day just celebrated his 90th birthday.

◆ ● ◆

Another of my favorite scouts is Dave Yocum who, along with Gordon Lakey, helped Pat Gillick build championship clubs in Toronto in 1992 and 1993. Now the assistant general manager of the Chicago White Sox, Yocum, a former minor league player, is one of the most respected judges of talent in the game.

◆ ● ◆

You know how Notre Dame has its subway alumni? Loyal and rabid fans who did not go to the school but act as though they did? Well, Dave Yocum is the sole member of the Colgate University Subway Alumni Club. He loves to listen in the stands at games he scouts at Fenway as my partner Jerry Trupiano teases me about the trials and tribulations of Colgate football. I once had Dave put on the Colgate football news mailing list.

◆ ● ◆

Gordon Lakey is one of the most respected professional scouts I know. Gordon is now the director of scouting for the Philadelphia Phillies. He spent many years with the Toronto Blue Jays. Gordon, a graduate of the University of Texas, manages to watch almost every pitcher in the major leagues, and often manages to see two major league games in different cities on the same day. He is a real gentleman, but don't ever mention Texas A&M in his presence—they are the Texas Longhorns's archrivals.

◆ ● ◆

I owe so much of my knowledge of the game of baseball to scouts and the scouting profession. To them, I tip my cap.

28

Spring Training

Spring Training is a great time of the year in baseball. Everybody is loose, except a few rookies trying to make the team. Wins and losses do not matter and many of the teams' front office workers are there.

My first Spring Training was with the Pirates in 1971 when I was with Channel 21 in Youngstown.

My roommate, disc jockey Mickey Krumpak, and I flew to Sarasota-Bradenton Airport from Youngstown and took a taxi right to McKechnie Field. The Pirates were to get us a rental car during our stay. Bill Guilfoile was the public relations director of the Pittsburgh Pirates, and he proved to be my introduction to major league baseball. Bill was later vice president of the Hall of Fame. His son Tommy holds the record at Cooperstown High School for home runs, set at Doubleday Field. Tommy later starred at Notre Dame and became chief financial officer of Lycos. Tommy now lives one town over from me in Massachusetts, and my daughter Kate has babysat for Tommy and Patty's five wonderful children.

After our first Spring Training game, Bill Guilfoile introduced us to some of the Pirates, including Willie Stargell, and told them that we were from Channel 21 in Youngstown. Guilfoile asked Stargell to give us a lift to the car rental agency. Willie said sure. So Mickey Krumpak and I got in the back of Stargell's big Cadillac with Gene Clines, Al Oliver, John Jeter, and Dave Cash.

Stargell could just have dropped us off at the car rental agency and we would have been grateful for the lift. But he got out of his car, entered the agency with us, and told the agent, "These guys are with the Pirates. Give them the special rate, will you?"

It is hard to imagine a star today of comparable stature going out of his way as Willie Stargell did to help two unknown broadcasters from a small city, not even his team's town.

The following season, Jan and I (we had been married in November 1971) went back to Bradenton and Bill Guilfoile made us part of the Pirates's family. He invited us to all team parties and affairs, and introduced us to everybody.

I asked the legendary Pirates broadcaster Bob Prince, "Bob, how do I get to be a major league broadcaster like you are?" He told me, "Either hit .300 or win 20 games!—there's no other formula." As it happens, Prince had done neither, but had been with the Pirates since 1948.

◆ ● ◆

By 1976, the next time I went to Spring Training, I was a freelancer with NBC. I was paid by the piece—a short, under-a-minute preview of the upcoming season. I'd go to the games all day, edit tapes all night, and send them in over the phone using alligator clips. It was a lot of work, but I got $33 for each tape that was used. I always tried to make enough money to cover the trips, which I did, and I also did enough stories to make a slight profit. Of course, I had to take vacation time from my television duties in Cleveland to go to Spring Training in Florida.

The next year, 1979, was my first at Spring Training in Arizona. We went to Tucson for two weeks. The Indians didn't broadcast Spring Training games from Tucson until 1982, so we practiced doing dry runs—we'd call the entire game. It was just not broadcast anywhere. I was hired the same day as Fred Macleod, who worked at Channel 8.

In 1982, we were back in Tucson and I broadcast some Spring Training games with Bob Feller. Satchel Paige always called him Bob Rapid, a play on his well-known nickname, Rapid Robert.

Feller was right down the hall from us at the Sheraton Pueblo in Tucson when we celebrated my son Tommy's seventh birthday. Feller kept most of the cake because he had the only room with a refrigerator. My son Duke had a catch with Bob Feller at Hi Corbett Field—an unforgettable experience.

We worked for Ted Stepien, who owned the Cleveland Cavaliers of the NBA and the cable rights to the Indians broadcasts for 1982. He was a widower with five daughters. Ted was in his mid-50s, and he would sit in his office in Cleveland watching the games. Ted called the broadcast truck and told the director, "Get that guy off! I want to see more cheese-cake!"—shots of pretty young girls.

In 1983, I went to Spring Training in Winter Haven, Florida, with the Red Sox. It's a different kind of town, not big city-influenced. Winter Haven is in central Florida and was "old South." Winter Haven is in a small area. When they had a team in the Florida State League, the Winter Haven Red Sox, they had the lowest attendance in professional baseball because there just were not very many people there. In Polk County, the Red Sox used to play the Tigers, who trained in Lakeland, for the Polk County championship. The winner got a cheap plastic tro-phy with an orange ball on it.

We stayed at the Holiday Inn, where many of the players stayed, too. Twice a week we had cookouts at the Howard Johnson's next door, and we hung out together. Bob Stanley and his wife Joan were two doors down from us. Jerry Remy was right nearby, too. Now he's one of the Red Sox television broadcasters, and he's still next door to me in the Red Sox TV broadcast booth.

The married families stayed in suites in the back of the hotel—Ken Coleman, traveling secretary Jack Rogers and his wife Ellie, Johnny Pesky and his wife Ruthie. There was not much to do in Winter Haven so we all got together. At the time, Winter Haven had only a few good restaurants. We liked Romeo's in nearby Lake Wales—great Italian food, owned by a guy named Romeo from Rome. His assistant Guido was a great guy. We liked to mimic him.

We also enjoyed a restaurant called Christy's—owned by Nick Christy, the first and oldest restaurant in town. It proclaimed itself the home of the Athenian Grouper. (Nick is of Greek descent.)

◆ ● ◆

I had one of the great screw-ups of all time in 1984. Jan was flying down to Spring Training, her first time there without the kids, and I drove to the airport to pick her up. Winter Haven was about halfway between Tampa and Orlando, an hour from each. When I got to Tampa Airport, I parked the car, went in to the terminal, and looked on the board for her flight. Not there. I was at the wrong airport! So I drove 71 miles to the Orlando Airport, and, an hour late, met Jan. It took me years to live that down.

◆ ● ◆

I spent ten springs in Winter Haven. Over the last few years, more rental condos opened up so we moved to the Lake Shore Club, a very nice apartment building on one of the many lakes that formed the Chain O'Lakes. Several players and their families were there as well and there was a real sense of community as was the case during our years in Winter Haven.

Then, in 1993, the Red Sox moved their training camp to Fort Myers on Florida's Southwest Coast. City of Palms Park, a beautiful new stadium, and still the best facility in all of Florida for spring baseball, opened in what had been a rundown section of downtown Fort Myers. The stadium, ringed by palm trees, seats close to 8,000 and has a practice field behind it. The Red Sox minor league complex, which has five fields and top-flight facilities, is just three miles east.

We use the minor league complex for Fantasy Camp, which I attend every February. At first, I went as a player but retired after 1999 to protect my lifetime .400 batting average. Now I go to do the public address announcing for the campers' games against the pros and to be master of ceremonies at the camp's awards banquet. Fantasy Camp is an adult's version of Disneyland. Guys and women from the ages of 30 to 75 play baseball games in Red Sox uniforms and get instruction from former Red Sox players and then eat and drink with the old pros during the evenings.

Outrageous kangaroo courts are part of the evening program where campers are fined for all sorts of indiscretions. Some are legitimate baseball omissions, others made up or silly transgressions. Lasting friendships are formed at Fantasy Camp between campers and the old pros. It is a true bonding experience and many campers come back year after year. Of course, the busiest guys at Fantasy Camp are the Red Sox trainers, who are hired to tend to the many aches and pains of these wannabe players. Being treated by the professional trainers seems to be a badge of courage for the campers.

I will never forget coming to bat in the ninth inning of a Fantasy Camp game, down by one run with a man on first. Steve "Psycho" Lyons, managing the opposing team, brought the outfielders in—right behind the infielders but I foiled his strategy by smoking an 0-2 hanging curveball from pitcher Dale Clarke over the head of the leftfielder for a game-tying double. Shortly thereafter, I scored the winning run on a hit by Don Lopes of Providence.

◆ ● ◆

The Red Sox share Southwest Florida with the Twins, who moved to South Fort Myers in 1991 to Lee County Stadium near the airport. Fort Myers is 110 miles and 180 degrees from Winter Haven. While Winter Haven is a small town, Fort Myers and Lee County are among the fastest growing areas in the nation. While Winter Haven has alligator-infested lakes, Fort Myers has the Gulf Beaches and vacation resorts and college kids on spring break.

There are many more people and much more traffic in Fort Myers but much more to do as well. The sense of community, though, is not the same because the baseball people are spread out over a large area.

Fort Myers Beach is the hot spot for the younger generation— beaches during the daytime and night life after dark. Sanibel Island, just across the Causeway from Fort Myers, is noted for its shell beaches— hundreds of thousands of beautiful shells that wash up upon the beaches each day. The island has many beautiful and pricey homes and condos and a wonderful wildlife preserve, but with only one way on and off the island, traffic can be brutal.

Fort Myers has thousands of new homes and condos and we have been fortunate to stay in two great developments, first Cross Creek and now Legends, which are near the airport. The location is most convenient for all the visitors who come south. It is amazing how much more popular you are with family members when you have a condo in Florida for the month of March.

◆ ● ◆

When we first went to Winter Haven, we all stayed at one hotel there—the Holiday Inn—because there were few other places to stay. Winter Haven is a collection of strip malls and fast food joints but there was a very limited restaurant selection for fine dining.

While many aspects of Spring Training, at least for the Red Sox, have changed since the days in Winter Haven, one thing has certainly improved.

Christy's and the Elks Club were about the only two decent places to eat. The manager of the Elks Club gave passes (it was a private club) to the Red Sox for the players and other personnel.

But they were only for white players, as the Elks Club did not admit blacks.

Many of us had no idea about this practice in the spring of 1985 when Mike Madden of the *Boston Globe* asked Tommy Harper about it. Harper, an African American who had played, coached, and worked in public relations for the Red Sox, was working as a special assistant to Lou Gorman and minor league instructor for the club at the time.

Harper spoke out against the segregationist policy of the Elks Club and the Red Sox's failure to do anything about it. Madden's column caused quite a furor . . . a furor made more intense because of the Red Sox's terrible racial history. The Red Sox had been the last team to integrate, some 12 years after Jackie Robinson broke the color line. In 1945, Robinson had a tryout at Fenway Park but was never called back.

Harper eventually was fired from his minor league instructor's job, sued the club, and won a large settlement. A condition of the settlement was that there would be no further public discussion of the issue or of the amount of the settlement.

Harper went on to coach for the Montreal Expos and in 2000 was rehired by general manager Dan Duquette to coach first base for the Red

Sox. The Red Sox got a lot of dreadful publicity as a result of the fallout from Madden's article.

In retrospect, I regret that I did not speak out on the matter publicly. My reaction to the Elks Club matter was simply to tear up my pass, which I did not use. It is not the type of place I would frequent anyway.

The Red Sox have made great strides in the area of race relations since then. John Harrington deserves much of the credit for increasing minority hiring and diversity and for supporting programs like RBI (Reviving Baseball in Inner Cities) and instituting special events. I had the honor of being master of ceremonies for a reunion of Negro League Players, hosted by the Red Sox in the mid-1990s and to introduce the Opening Day event in 1997, commemorating the 50th anniversary of Jackie Robinson's debut in the big leagues. The festivities featured his daughter Sharon, who threw out the first pitch that day.

The current management team seems very committed to inner-city programs and clinics and to diversity in hiring.

Fort Myers has all kinds of shopping, strip malls, and all the restaurant chains including the Outback Steakhouse, a popular dining spot for players and staff from both the Twins and the Red Sox. Fort Myers also has one of the best Italian restaurants we have found anywhere in baseball—the Mona Lisa, owned and operated by Joe Pirrone and his family. Joe, a native of Palermo, makes authentic Sicilian dishes and is well known for his eggplant lasagna, pasta, fish, and chicken specialties. He also has nightly karaoke in the adjoining bar. Joe, who has become a good friend, caters the annual St. Patrick's Day party Jan and I host at our rental condo. No corn beef and cabbage, just Italian cuisine, prepared Sicilian style by Joe Pirrone for our baseball friends. Joe, his wife Lea and their sons run the Mona Lisa in Fort Myers and Joe's sister, Anna, and her family, have another outstanding restaurant in Naples on Route 41, about 30 miles south, called Peppino's, featuring a similar menu. Another fine Italian dining spot is Nino's, also owned by a Sicilian. Nino's is located in a strip mall near the Twins's park and also has a location near downtown Fort Myers. Other excellent dining spots are the Prawnbroker, featuring fresh fish, the Stonewood Grill, and the University Grill.

As for sporting activities, Fort Myers is home to the Florida Everblades of the East Coast Hockey League, the lowest rung on the professional ladder. The games at the nearly new Teco Arena are very entertaining. Also a few exits south of I-75 is the Fort Myers-Naples Greyhound Race track. There are scores of beautiful golf courses in Southwest Florida and plenty of boating and fishing. We enjoy kayaking in the canals off the Sanibel Causeway and in one of the smaller lakes and there are plenty of level and flat bike riding areas in and around the condo units.

As for the baseball, the games are fun . . . sunshine, palm trees . . . players jogging on the warning track while the game continues . . . and a relaxed atmosphere for just about everyone except for those youngsters trying to make the club or those veterans trying to hang on.

Since winning is not essential, the games don't have the same edge or drama as regular season games and the complexion and flow of the games often change when the subs replace the regular players. It is amusing to see the fans leaving in the seventh or eighth innings. Trup says they are headed for the 4 o'clock buffet.

Home games or games with the Twins are very convenient and almost always played in the daytime. The other road games mean driving some two hours north on I-75 to the Tampa Area . . . or across Alligator Alley to Fort Lauderdale. While it is a treat to spend a month in Florida and escape the end of winter up north, most baseball people are anxious and ready to get on with the regular season come the beginning of April.

29

Teaching

I've been teaching sports broadcasting during the fall quarter at Northeastern University in Boston every year since 1985. Twice I also taught during the winter quarter.

Since 1997, I have also taught at Franklin Pierce College in Rindge, New Hampshire, also in the fall semester. It's a rather pleasant drive of about 100 miles door to door, especially in the fall as the leaves change color in northwestern Massachusetts and southwestern New Hampshire.

In the 1997–1998 academic year, I taught at Emerson College in downtown Boston during the fall semester and the first part of the spring semester before I had to go to Spring Training.

My course is a self-designed sports broadcasting course. I got the idea from Tom Hedrick, the author of *The Art of Sports Broadcasting*, a book for which I contributed a chapter on baseball broadcasting. After 25 years, Tom recently retired from teaching full time at the University of Kansas. Tom's nickname is "the Parrott," because he talks a lot. He's had some outstanding future broadcasters in his classes, including Kevin Harlan, who does NFL Football on Fox, Gary Bender, longtime network broadcaster, and Brian McRae, the ex-outfielder who has been on ESPN. Tom also had NFL Hall of Famer Gale Sayers in the early 1960s and worked with him individually on his reading and diction.

I modeled my course after Tom's syllabus, but I have added lots of my own idiosyncrasies. The course is a performance course. You have to know sports to do well in the course—I am not there to teach the rules of the game. Using both audio and videotapes, I try to help students overcome their inhibitions, stage fright, and any diction problems they may have, including those heavy Boston and New York accents. If they're too shy or don't know sports, I tell the prospective students not to take my course. Do something else. Students take the course for different reasons. Some just think it's fun. Others see it as a first step to a career as a professional broadcaster. Of course, some students take it because there is not a lot of reading involved in the course and they think they can get a good grade without much work. I am probably responsible for some of the grade inflation at Northeastern in recent years. As the chairman of the communications studies department told me when I started at Northeastern, "Nobody should flunk out of school because of sports broadcasting—it's not that important." He was right.

In 1984, our intern was Paul Kaplan, a Northeastern student. I was looking for a way to earn some extra money and I asked Paul whether he thought Northeastern might be interested in having me teach a sports broadcasting course during the offseason. I knew the money wouldn't be great but it would be something.

Paul spoke with the head of the speech communications (now called Communications Studies) department, Professor Carl "Pete" W. Eastman. He was a great promoter, and he jumped at the idea.

With a very few exceptions, a prerequisite for working as an intern with us in the Red Sox broadcast booth is that the individual has taken my class either at Franklin Pierce or at Northeastern. As it happens, Northeastern is walking distance to Fenway Park, where parking is always a problem. This lets me get to know the students, and I can determine whether they are interested, and whether they have baseball aptitude, intelligence, and knowledge of the history of the game. I also try to determine whether they will have the requisite chemistry to fit in in our booth. As Curt Gowdy once said, it's a small booth and a long, hot summer.

Leslie Sterling was a Harvard graduate who took my course in the late 1980s because she wanted to be a sports broadcaster. She also gave voice lessons and sang. She had a day job as a secretary, but her real love was baseball. She wanted to get a job covering the sport. Her favorite player was Frank Viola, then with the Minnesota Twins. She used to go to Red Sox-Twins games when Viola was pitching. After taking the course, Leslie worked as a radio stringer covering the Red Sox, the Celtics, and the Bruins. She was working for the Red Sox when Viola came to the Sox in 1992. She was great to have with us. She was a little older than the other students, probably in her early 30s, and she upgraded the entire class. Other students did their work properly and took it more seriously because of Leslie's presence. She had a delightful personality and delivery. Leslie was a voice coach, too. She helped me with my delivery. Later, I sent my son Duke to Leslie for help with his diction.

When Sherm Feller, the longtime Red Sox public address announcer died suddenly in the winter of 1993, the Sox came to me and said, "You've had many students. Is there one who would be right to replace Sherm? We're looking for somebody completely different—not somebody to imitate Feller."

I recommended Leslie. The team had never considered a woman. They brought her in just before the season started, and put her on the Fenway public address microphone, which can be very intimidating. It's not like talking into a radio or a TV mike, or like a mike connected to a tape recorder. There is a natural delay system, and an echo because of the vastness of Fenway Park. Leslie blew everybody away. She was so good, they hired her on the spot: she became the Red Sox public address announcer for the 1994 season. There was some backlash from some quarters about having a woman as PA announcer, but almost everybody thought she did a fine job. I thought she did an outstanding job. After her first year, she contemplated quitting, because she was thinking of entering the seminary, but she stayed for another two years.

Then in 1996, after three years as the Red Sox PA announcer, she left to enter the Episcopal Divinity School seminary near Harvard in Cambridge. In the spring of 2001, Jan and I got an invitation to attend her ordination. My experiences with Leslie Sterling were among the greatest I have ever had teaching. She is now preaching at All Saints Episcopal Church in Brookline, Massachusetts.

Don Orsillo was in Leslie Sterling's class in 1989. He was born in the Boston area and grew up in New Hampshire. He went to high school in

Palos Verdes, California. When he took my course, I could see his love for baseball. He had an outgoing personality and a good voice, and was serious about being a professional sports broadcaster. We liked Don so much we invited him to be our intern at the booth in Fenway. Don was very serious about it, and got a job as a professional broadcaster right out of college, doing the games for Pittsfield, the New York Mets affiliate in the New York-Penn League, a rookie league. He did the road games on the air, and was the public address announcer at home. The team did not broadcast its home games because the owners thought that broadcasting home games would cut down on attendance. I thought this was absurd, but that's what they thought. He earned less than $1,600 that year for 87 games, but stayed with the Pittsfield Mets for two years. Don also did Springfield Indians hockey in the American Hockey League for five seasons. After Pittsfield, he worked his way up to the Binghamton Mets at the AA level. He was there four years before going to the Pawtucket Red Sox, the team's AAA affiliate. I recommended Don for that job, and he stayed there from 1996 through 2000. When the New England Sports Network job opened up for the 2001 season, Don was hired to do the Red Sox games on TV which NESN broadcast. Don had applied for big league broadcasting jobs in many cities, but he got the job in Boston. He was already familiar with the Red Sox organization, and had occasionally filled in for some Boston games. He did more than 90 games each season for NESN, and I'm proud of him.

Glenn Wilburn is a young man from the Bronx. He grew up a fan of the Yankees, and was a particular fan of Yankees second baseman Willie Randolph. He took my course at Northeastern in 1990. Glenn did not aspire to be on the air, but he wanted to work in baseball. We hired him as our statistician, and he worked with Bob Starr and me in that capacity in 1991 and 1992. (My broadcast partner and I select the interns and WEEI pays them about $25 per game, plus a free meal in the press dining room.) He was very serious about baseball. He worked as in intern in the National League's public relations and operations office doing the waivers wire for four years in New York, then was hired (on our recommendation) by the Red Sox to be the team's assistant public relations director and baseball information director. He was with the team in that position from 1998 to 2002, doing game notes and statistics, and setting up appearances such as players helping out at baseball clinics for youngsters, an after-dinner speaker for a fundraiser, or at the Bosox Club. In December 2002, Glenn left the Red Sox to become assistant player development director for the Montreal Expos. We miss Glenn, who was like a member of our family to Jan, the kids, and me.

The second intern we had in Boston was Jeff Idelson. He did not take my course, as he had already graduated from Connecticut College in New London. Jeff had probably the most intuitive baseball mind I have ever seen in a young person. He could think of things for us to say and find avenues for us to explore that were both interesting and perceptive—anecdotes, odd facts, relations, analogies, and a wealth of other material that we were glad to use. Jeff worked with Ken Coleman and me in 1987 and 1988. Shortly thereafter, during the offseason, I got a call from Harvey Green of the Yankees asking me what I thought about his hiring Jeff as the Yankees assistant public relations director. As I was recommending Jeff, Harvey told me he had another call—George Steinbrenner was on his other line. Harvey had to take the call, of course, as Steinbrenner was upset about something. Harvey called me back about four hours later, and we resumed our conversation about Jeff Idelson. I recommended him for the job, and he was hired. Harvey later thanked me for recommending Jeff. When Harvey left the Yankees a few years later to become the public relations director for the Miami Dolphins, Jeff took over as Yankee public relations director and later for World Cup Soccer. Jeff is now the vice president of public relations at the National Baseball Hall of Fame in Cooperstown. He remains one of the most perceptive baseball minds I have ever encountered. One day, he could run a ballclub as a team president.

Jeff Tagliaferro, who took my course at Northeastern, was an intern and later worked in sales and marketing for the Reading Phillies and the Lowell Spinners in the New York-Penn League, which has sold out every home game for the last few years.

John Ryder was one of our interns who had taken my class. He was very interested in broadcasting and became a sports anchor with Media One, a cable network, a job that my son Duke had held before John.

John also does sports updates for WEEI and has done baseball play-by-play for the Nashua Pride, an independent team in New Hampshire.

Chris DiPierro finished his second year with us in 2002. He was offered a broadcasting job with the Norwich Navigators but took a marketing position at the Fleet Center in Boston. He is now marketing manager for the Boston Bruins.

One of my students was Bonnie Stewart. She now works for Northwest Mobile, a production company first in Seattle and now in Los Angeles. She makes crew assignments (camera crews, tape editors, etc.) for remote sports telecasts, including major league updates.

After taking my class, Corey Massey went on to broadcast for the East Coast Hockey League and now for the Providence Bruins in the American Hockey League.

Michael Haynes was in my first class at Northeastern in 1985. He had already worked as a professional broadcaster, and he went on to become the voice of the Colorado Avalanche in the National Hockey League, where he earned two Stanley Cup rings.

◆ ● ◆

My class at Northeastern usually has about 20 students. In 2002, I had 27. In 2003, I had 30, which was too many. Because it is a performance course, I think the ideal number is about 12. Each student does an interview tape, a sports update audio, a feature or commentary tape, then a TV production in the studio with a professional director. The TV studios at Northeastern and at Franklin Pierce were both primitive by professional standards when I started teaching, but they now are both state of the art. The students work in anchor teams. Grades are based on meeting deadlines—I try to drum into them that as a professional, if you don't meet deadlines, you're fired—natural ability, and improvement over the course of the semester.

◆ ● ◆

Among students from other schools who have taken my course are my son Duke, now a New York sportscaster who was at Stonehill College at the time. Hank Greenwald's son Doug took my course while he was at Boston University. Stonehill allowed Duke to get credit for the course, but Boston University apparently deemed it unworthy for reasons not disclosed and Doug got no college credit but audited the course.

After graduating, Doug has been broadcasting in the minors with stops in Lafayette, Louisiana; Clinton, Iowa; Shreveport, Louisiana; Modesto, California; and the independent Western League. By 2003, he was with the AAA Fresno Grizzlies, the Giants affiliate in the Pacific Coast League.

When I started teaching, I did it to make some extra money, and I did—$1,800 for the first term. I moved up to $2,000 the next term, and that was my salary for the next 15 years or so.

I realized that I was not teaching exclusively for the money. I was teaching to give something back to the kids. I enjoy doing it—as long as it's not my livelihood.

◆ ● ◆

While Northeastern is an urban school in the middle of Boston, Franklin Pierce is completely different. Northeastern has 15,000 undergraduates. The student body at Franklin Pierce is 1,800. It's a wonderful, warm school in Rindge, a tiny town in New Hampshire. It's a pretty, 104-mile ride up Route 2 in the fall. The president of the school, George Hagerty, is a brilliant educator who had an educational research firm in Washington. Before coming to Franklin Pierce, he had been a professor at Stonehill College, his alma mater. In fact, Duke was going to take his course in political science and government when Hagerty became president of Franklin Pierce. He's done a marvelous job of improving the school. The College Board scores of entering students have gone up dramatically, and I have seen a marked improvement in the quality of the students.

President Hagerty has formed a bond with Jerry Colangelo, the owner of the Arizona Diamondbacks and the Phoenix Suns in the NBA, and Mr. Colangelo was the commencement speaker several years ago. He is now a big benefactor of the school. He hosts fundraisers at Bank One Ballpark every year and invites the Franklin Pierce baseball team (the Ravens) to Spring Training every other year.

Another commencement speaker was Marlin Fitzwater, who was press secretary to both Ronald Reagan and George Herbert Walker Bush.

Fitzwater has helped raise funds to create the college's Marlin Fitzwater Communications Center, which opened in May 2002. The dedication of the center was emceed by Sam Donaldson of ABC. A number of former presidential press secretaries, including Mike McCurry, Bill Clinton's press secretary, attended the dedication. The facility occupies the top two floors of the library. A sports administration program will open soon.

I always look for at least one technical student in my class who can run the video and audio equipment. One of my students was a young man named Michael Bua, who later got a job as a camera assistant and message board operator at Fenway Park. He also does on-field video of pregame ceremonies and works for a TV station in New Hampshire as a cinematographer.

Mike Anthony, from one of my early classes, now covers and writes sports, including the Red Sox, for the *Hartford Courant*.

The first several years I drove to Franklin Pierce, Rich Killion, who later managed some gubernatorial campaigns in New Hampshire, and Laura Mitchell, a fundraiser for the school, had a lunch for me every week. They'd bring in people from around the college and the community to raise funds and help increase the profile of the school. Laura, who went to Stonehill with Duke, has since left, and Rich now runs the Fitzwater Center.

I have had a number of guest lecturers at my classes over the years, including pitcher Bob Tewskbury—a New Hampshire native, Don Orsillo, Glenn Wilburn, Joe Morgan, and *Detroit Free Press* baseball writer John Lowe.

Once each semester, I bring both of my classes to the Fleet Center (and previously to the Boston Garden) to work with the Bruins during a practice. They get to see the broadcast facilities and interview a player or a coach. The great hockey players are among the most cooperative professionals in sports. During one of these meetings, Cam Neely asked one of the female students for her phone number. (He was single at the time.) I think it was done tongue-in-cheek.

When he was general manager of the Red Sox, I used to bring Lou Gorman to lunch with selected students and the department chairman at Northeastern in November.

Now, I have reversed the process and I bring a combined group of both classes to Fenway in November. We meet in the 406 Club at Fenway, which has theater-type seats. We have class, and they hear from the general manager; from Dick Bresciani, director of publications; Jim Healey, the former director of broadcasting; Theo Epstein, now the Red Sox general manager; Charles Steinberg, executive vice president for public affairs; Chuck Steedman, senior director of business services including broadcasting; and other front office people. The students have a great time, and many receive internship offers as a direct result of these visits.

Northeastern is a five-year school: students work for one quarter each year. (In fact, Northeastern was recently voted the top cooperative school in the country.) Many of my students and former students wind up working at Fenway on game days, working the message board and in the control room. Many have worked in security, marketing, public relations, tickets, and other parts of Fenway.

◆ ◆ ◆

I taught a graduate class at Emerson in the fall of 1997 and the winter of 1998. Ninety percent of my students were from other countries. I had students from Mexico, Saudi Arabia, and Taiwan. Fitzwilliam Yang, one of my students from Taiwan, sends me an e-mail every year telling me that he has nominated me for Teacher of the Year.

I learned a lot from those students. They were intelligent and fast on their feet. Ad libbing on camera was almost a requirement, especially for sports broadcasting, but one of the foreign students pointed out to me that it is difficult to ad lib in your second language. That really opened my eyes, and helped me see how tough it must be for foreign athletes who come to play in the United States. They, too, have to communicate with the media in a second language.

I enjoyed my time at Emerson College. The department chair was Gregory Payne. Emerson alumni in broadcasting include Jay Leno and Morton Dean.

I enjoy teaching, but Jan is the real teacher in our family. She teaches second and third graders, when it really matters. They learn important things, like how to read. I do it mostly for fun and because I find it rewarding. I like showing the students the ins and outs of the profession—how to prepare for a broadcast and to enhance their natural ability. Of course, if they have no natural ability, all the coaching in the world is not going to help—just like baseball.

Jan says I should be a little tougher on the students and that I should not be such an easy grader. If you show up in my class, and get the work done, you'll probably get a B. If you do well, you can get an A. But if you're really serious, we can help you get started in the profession. I remember a student who said, "I may want to get into broadcasting, into television." That didn't sound very confident to me. My last lecture is about how to get a job and how to keep a job in sportscasting.

To get a job in sportscasting, you really have to want it, and usually have to make sacrifices to get it. You have to start out working nights, working weekends, working for low pay, and missing a lot of social life.

About three years later, I took my daughter Kate out for lunch and I saw the same kid. He was our waiter. He was probably about 26 or 27. I asked him what he was doing, and he said he was still thinking about getting into broadcasting. No chance. I didn't think he would ever get a job in the industry, let alone go very far.

I'm happy when my students succeed, and I think the people I work with, including the department chairmen like Pete Eastman, Richard Katula, and David Marshall at Northeastern, appreciate my work.

The people at Franklin Pierce have been sensational. I mention both schools on the air and the schools don't mind the publicity at all. Trup always mentions that I'm an easy grader.

Among the books I require my students to read are *The Art of Sportscasting*, by Tom Hedrick; Ernie Harwell's books *Tuned to Baseball* and *My 60 Years in the Game*, written with Tom Keegan; Hank Greenwald's *This Copyrighted Broadcast*; Herb Carneal's *Hi, Everybody*; Chuck Thompson's *Ain't the Beer Cold!*; Curt Smith's *Voices of the Game* and *The Storytellers*; and Red Barber and Howard Cosell's books. We started with Ken Coleman's book, *So You Want to Be a Sportscaster*. Unfortunately, it is now out of print.

During the fall of 1985, my first year of teaching, Howard Cosell got an award from Northeastern's Center for the Study of Sport and Society.

My class was invited to hear him at the lecture hall in the engineering building. Cosell had just quit *Monday Night Football*. His book, *I Never Played the Game* had just been published. In it, he really ripped his former colleagues Al Michaels, Frank Gifford, and Don Meredith. I met Howard before the class, and told him that I had been listening to him for years, including his pregame broadcasts for the 1962 New York Mets, which he did with "big number thirteen, Ralph Branca." I said, "Howard, I make my students read your book. It's a requirement in my class." His answer was pure Cosell: "As well you should, young man, as well you should!"

I had a lot of respect for Cosell for telling it like it is, standing up for civil rights, and supporting Muhammad Ali, but he had become a parody of himself and a bitter old man.

One of my students, Jay Adams, I think, was a little bit of a wise guy. He was doing an internship at one of the local TV stations. One of the local anchors said, "I'll put you on camera if you ask Cosell a question to get him going." At the end of his talk, Cosell asked if there were any questions. Adams raised his hand and asked, "Why did you stab your friends in the back when you wrote your book?" Wow. The kid got on TV, but Howard's answer was "Did you read the book, young man?" He answered, "Well, I skimmed it." Cosell proceeded to bury the young man. He cut him open and destroyed him with a collection of polysyllabic words. I'm sure that Cosell enjoyed it. I believe that Adams went on to a career on the Home Shopping Network—another professional broadcaster in my class.

I took my first class in 1985 to a New England Patriots practice. I had to ream out one student who went up to Julius Adams, a defensive end for the Patriots in the twilight of a long career, and said, "Hey, Julius, you got any extra tickets for the Miami game this week?" Adams said, "What are you, kidding? Get out of here!" I told the student off in the next class. I told him that an NFL player like Adams gets six or eight tickets to each game. "You don't think he knows anyone better than you to give them to?" I also told him how rude it was to ask people for free tickets.

My students at Northeastern can walk from the school to Fenway Park, and can take the Green Line subway to see the Bruins. But the Patriots stadium in Foxboro was just too far to get to, so we didn't do anything with the Patriots after that first year.

I was very sad when my friend Pete Eastman passed away from a heart attack in 2000. He really knew how to get things done, and how to cut through the university's red tape. He could always cut right to the heart of the matter, and he was the single biggest reason I was at Northeastern.

I formed some great friendships there with a number of other professors, and I broadcast Northeastern's basketball games when they were outstanding in the mid-1980s with Reggie Lewis. Jim Calhoun was the coach. He went on to lead the University of Connecticut to a national championship. Mike Jarvis coached at Boston University, and I broadcast their games on NESN, too. Jarvis went on to coach at George Washington and later at St. John's. We did a Northeastern game against Boston College, where the coach was Gary Williams, who later guided Maryland to the NCAA Championship in 2002. The 1980s was the heyday of college basketball in New England.

I was the first college basketball broadcaster for the New England Sports Network. I had some of the players in my class, then I went and broadcast their games.

My schedule works this way: from September to Christmas, I teach at Franklin Pierce. Northeastern was on a quarter system, from the third week of September to the third week of December, which is much easier. Northeastern switched to semesters in 2003.

In the fall of 2002, I took my class to the Fleet Center to see the Bruins practice. I also brought along one of my good friends, former Red Sox manager Joe Morgan. Morgan and Bruins head coach Robbie Ftorek were the two best high-school hockey players in the Boston area. During the 1940s, Morgan starred at Walpole High School in his hometown, and Ftorek was a star in the late 1960s at Needham High School. Morgan was a hockey All-American at Boston College, and Ftorek played in both the World Hockey Association and the National Hockey League.

As we were talking with Ftorek, I mentioned that I had my classes from Franklin Pierce and Northeastern with me. Robbie asked me, "Do you want me to do a news conference for them?" So for 20 minutes, he answered their questions. It was a rare sight—two hometown guys who had become head coach/manager for their hometown teams.

30

The Jimmy Fund

The Jimmy Fund is the fundraising branch of the Dana-Farber Cancer Institute in Boston, one of the nation's leading pediatric cancer research centers and hospitals. It was started by Dr. Sidney Farber, the father of modern chemotherapy in the late 1940s and the founder of the Children's Cancer Research Foundation. The fund received a great deal of publicity thanks to its first baseball sponsor, the Boston Braves, and the Ralph Edwards radio program, "Truth or Consequences." On May 22, 1948, a number of the Braves were gathered at the hospital bedside of a 12-year-old cancer patient named Jimmy, a patient of Dr. Farber. His last name was not used to protect his privacy. Jimmy had a gregarious personality. Warren Spahn, Johnny Sain, Bob Elliott, and others were there as the program was broadcast from Jimmy's hospital room. Jimmy wanted a TV set so he could watch the Braves win the pennant in 1948.

The national response was overwhelming—charitable donations of $200,000 poured in—a substantial sum in 1948. Jimmy got his television set, and decided that the money should be used to start a fund to fight cancer in kids.

The original 1948 broadcast is available online at www.jimmyfund.org/abo/broad/jimmybroadcast.asp.

Lou Perini, the owner of the Braves, spearheaded the fundraising efforts, making the Jimmy Fund the official charity of the Boston Braves.

When the Braves left Boston in 1953 for Milwaukee, Tom and Jean Yawkey, the owners of the Red Sox, adopted the Jimmy Fund as the official charity of the Red Sox.

Over the years, the Red Sox have helped raise millions of dollars for the Jimmy Fund through the efforts of the team's owners and such players as Ted Williams, Carl Yastrzemski (whose mother was treated at the institute), Mo Vaughn, Bob Stanley, John Valentin, Derek Lowe, and countless others.

I first became aware of the Jimmy Fund when I listened to Curt Gowdy broadcast Red Sox games often mentioning the fund. Red Sox radio and the Jimmy Fund have gone hand in hand since the 1950s. Ken Coleman became a major force in the Jimmy Fund. While he was broadcasting for the Red Sox, he became chairman of the Jimmy Fund. He continued with the Jimmy Fund even when he broadcast for the Cincinnati Reds from 1975 to 1978. The Jimmy Fund had a small staff in the 1970s and even into the 1980s, and Ken was the fund's main man.

When I came to the Red Sox in 1983, Ken introduced me to the Jimmy Fund, and I plunged right in. I worked as a volunteer at golf tournaments and banquets over the winter, hosted events at Fenway, and made hospital visits with the players. It became a part of our routine at the ballpark to help the Jimmy Fund. We promoted the Jimmy Fund on the air.

By the time Ken retired after the 1989 season, he was no longer the chairman of the Jimmy Fund. That role had been acquired in the early 1980s by Mike Andrews, the outstanding Red Sox rookie second baseman on the "Impossible Dream" team of 1967 (which voted the Jimmy Fund a full share of its World Series winnings). The Jimmy Fund has been a labor of love for Mike over many years. Although he is a native Californian, he has stayed in Boston to devote his time to the Jimmy Fund.

When Ken retired, Mike asked me if I would take over Ken's role at Fenway as the paid liaison between the Jimmy Fund, the players, and the staff. I continue to emcee events at the ballpark, visit the clinic, and promote the Jimmy Fund on the air. I represent the Red Sox and the Jimmy Fund at various banquets, and I pick up checks for the fund from various service club events and fundraisers. I have cherished my work with the Jimmy Fund because it is so rewarding and because I have met so many interesting people.

The Red Sox were in Oakland during the 1992 season when Mike Andrews called me about a 12-year-old Little League player named Seth Ketchum. Seth was seriously ill with cancer and had suffered a number of relapses. He lived near Pittsfield, Massachusetts, about three hours from the clinic in Boston. Mike told me that Seth was becoming withdrawn and depressed, no longer speaking with his mother and his grandmother.

Mike asked if I could get some Red Sox players to call Seth from the clubhouse to wish him well and cheer him up.

Jody Reed spoke with Seth and told him that he would try to get a big hit for Seth. I put Roger Clemens on the phone, and he promised Seth that he would try to win the game in his honor. I also got Jeff Reardon to speak with Seth. He told Seth that he would try to record a save for him. Jeff was from the Pittsfield area, too.

Just like in the movies, all three promises happened. Jody Reed did get a big hit that night. Roger Clemens did get the win. Jeff Reardon got the save.

When we got back to Boston, Seth had undergone a miraculous change. He had opened up to his family. He came to Fenway three or four times when he was in Boston for treatment. At the park, he met Jody Reed, Roger Clemens, and Jeff Reardon. They all took a special interest in Seth. Jeff gave him some bats and balls. On a few occasions, Seth brought his mother and his grandmother to Fenway.

Some time later, we found out that he was not doing very well. A short while later, we were informed that Seth had passed away. We mentioned it on the air and did a tribute to Seth during a pregame show. Seth's mother Lucy wrote us a heartwarming letter shortly after her son's death, telling us how much his time at Fenway Park and in the broadcast booth with Bob Starr and me had meant to him. She concluded her letter by telling us, "Seth said on our return from the game, 'Mom, there's something I forgot to tell them. I think the Jimmy Fund is the best charity they could ever have.' "

Seth's story helps us continue to battle cancer, particularly in children.

◆ ● ◆

About two years later, just before the strike of 1994, I made a visit to the clinic with some Red Sox players—Bob Zupcic, Damon Berryhill, and Scott Fletcher. While there, I met a very special young man named Uri Berenguer. He was about 11 years old at the time. I formed an instant bond with Uri. Uri was a very sick little kid with lively dark eyes, who was both intelligent and well spoken. I found out that Uri's uncle was Juan Berenguer, an outstanding pitcher from the late 1970s through the early 1990s. Juan bounced around a little, but he was with the Tigers when they won the World Series in 1984, with the Twins when they won it all in 1987, and with the Braves when they won the National League pennant in 1991. The speed of his fastball earned him the nickname "Señor Smoke."

I got to know Uri and invited him to Fenway a number of times. He sat with us in the broadcast booth. One day our intern was out sick, and we had Uri hand us the drop-in cards with commercials. We became very good friends. He had a great fondness for what we did as broadcasters, and we became very fond of Uri and his family.

Uri and his mother, Daisy, came to Massachusetts from Panama when he was four years old. They arrived in late November when it was snowing—a novel experience for both of them. The doctors in Panama told Uri and his mother they had no choice but to amputate his leg. His mother brought him to the states in an effort to save his leg. They stayed at the Howard Johnson's Motel near Fenway Park their first night in America. He underwent surgery the next day. When he woke up after the operation, he didn't know whether he still had his leg or not. His mother told him that the doctors at the clinic had saved his leg. (When he turned 16, he found out that his mother really didn't know herself—she was guessing when she told him that he still had his leg.)

But Uri was not out of the woods. Over the next several years, Uri had seven relapses as he continued battling cancer. Tumors developed on his head and he needed more surgery, more radiation, and more chemotherapy. He continued to get better, and then he relapsed. He discovered girls around the same time he lost his hair. Eventually he came through it all, but his family still suffered other tribulations. One day as his mother was taking Uri to the clinic, his sister found some sticks in their Brockton neighborhood that looked like match sticks. She lit them and blew off part of her hand. She didn't know they were dynamite. She had reconstructive surgery to reattach part of her hand.

Some time later, Uri's mother was diagnosed with breast cancer. She continues to battle it, having relapsed three times. She is still having radiation and chemotherapy treatments.

During his last remission, Uri took up sports and became a football player and a sprinter for Boston Latin Academy, a school that requires an entrance exam. I saw him tackle a 270-pound fullback in the end zone, even though Uri is only about 5 foot 6 inches, 150 pounds. He's wiry, fast, and strong.

Uri played baseball in the regional Yawkey League where John Harrington, the Red Sox CEO, took a liking to him. John invited Uri to shag flies in the Fenway outfield prior to the 1999 All-Star Game. Uri was running for a ball hit by Ken Griffey Jr. when he knocked over a young boy named Dan Duquette Jr.

Uri and his family live in Randolph, where they own their own home. The Berenguers are a very enterprising family, but they have not yet been granted American citizenship. That's another battle still to be won.

We worked to get Uri a full scholarship at Northeastern through the help of Professor Roger Giese, director of the Environmental Cancer Research Program at Northeastern. He took a special interest in Uri and helped him get a tuition waiver. Unfortunately, he is not eligible for free room and board because he is not an American citizen and therefore not eligible for federal aid even though he has been here for 16 years. We're working on that, trying to make his citizenship retroactive so that he would qualify. During his freshman year, he lived on campus and did very well, but has since moved home for financial reasons.

Professor Michael Woodnick, the Spiritual Life director at Northeastern, has also helped Uri greatly, and Michael Wildeman, the director of financial aid at Northeastern, has been instrumental in securing a tuition waiver for Uri.

They came to America on a medical visa. Uri's father Felix could not leave Panama for some years because he was working in medical supplies to support his family. Uri's grandmother, who lives in Tennessee, is an American citizen, which should help. I helped Uri's family get an immigration lawyer. We all hope that a Green Card and ultimately American citizenship will come along soon. As of now, Felix has to get his temporary visa renewed every year. If he leaves the United States, he cannot return. The immigration lawyer was able to arrange things so Felix could return to Panama briefly to collect his retirement funds. But when Felix's brother died, he could not go to Panama for the funeral because he would not be permitted reentry to the United States. This is an unfortunate and ridiculous situation that we hope to resolve soon. Felix works counseling prostate cancer patients at a clinic that serves mainly Hispanic patients in Chelsea, Massachusetts. Daisy runs a day care center from her home and is a marvelous businesswoman.

Uri was finally pronounced cured by his doctor, Lindsay Fraser, in February 2000. Uri has a great way of articulating his long and successful battle with cancer, and I take him to many events where he can share his battle with others. I encourage him to tell his life story, including his many visits to us at Fenway. He says that his mother doesn't like me any more because, before we met, he wanted to be a doctor. Now, he is a sports broadcaster.

After his senior year of high school, Uri got a job working with the Red Sox Community Relations Office, going out to sandlot fields with players during the day and working at night games with the Spanish broadcasters as producer/engineer working his way into on-the-air performances. In 2002, Uri became a full-time employee, doing pregame and postgame shows and also an inning or two of play-by-play. He filled in occasionally for Luis Tiant, former Red Sox pitching star, who provides color commentary, among the youngest in history.

As of 2003, Uri has an expanded role doing play-by-play with J. P. Villaman. At the age of 21, he's the youngest broadcaster in major league baseball.

The Spanish broadcast rights holder for the Red Sox is Bill Kulik. He owns the network, runs the network, and sells the rights and also works as producer/engineer on the broadcasts. He took a special interest in Uri and put him on the air. Uri works as the producer/engineer when Bill is not there.

The Spanish language broadcasters do not travel with the team all the time. For those road games they do not go to, they broadcast the game from Fenway Park while watching it on television.

In 2002, at the age of 20, Uri Berenguer became both the youngest broadcaster in the major leagues and the first Panamanian broadcaster in the majors. He says that Panamanian Spanish is the closest to Castilian or "pure" Spanish in the Western Hemisphere. His English is totally unaccented. He knows the players, too, and seems to have a special bond with them. His personality is charming.

Although, as I mentioned, he is not yet an American citizen, Uri has become a model citizen—a shining example of how far hard work, determination, and a supportive family can take you in this country. He has become a special friend of my family, and he has a great relationship with my daughter Kate. They became good friends when we took Uri on a road trip to Tampa Bay and Atlanta. He's like the younger brother Kate (the youngest of three) never had. He is three years younger than Kate. The like to tease each other and me. They shared a waverunner off the beach in St. Petersburg. Kate yelled "shark!" and Uri pushed her into the water. They had a great time.

◆ ● ◆

The Jimmy Fund has volunteers who work one day a week. They try to keep them working the same day each week so that the kids get used to seeing the same faces each week coming to play with them. Uri's "play-lady" was Rosemary Lonborg, wife of Red Sox Hall of Famer Dr. Jim Lonborg, now a dentist. When Uri was first with us in the booth, the video screen in centerfield showed pictures of members of the 1967 "Impossible Dream" team. When Jim's picture was shown, Uri said, "Look! There's Rosie's husband!"

Uri goes with me to Jimmy Fund events, but often he goes on his own, both to visit patients in the clinic where he was treated and to attend fundraisers, golf tournaments, and other events to support the Jimmy Fund and Dr. Fraser.

◆ ● ◆

Jason Leader was a young man from a small town outside of Albany. In 1993. I got a call from Mike Andrews, who played for the Red Sox from 1966 to 1970. Mike is now executive director of the Jimmy Fund. We were in Anaheim at the time. Mike told me that Jason was at Boston's Children's Hospital and that he was not doing well. Mike told me that Mo Vaughn was Jason's favorite player. Could I get Mo on the phone to wish Jason a happy tenth birthday? Mo was in the equipment room in the back of the clubhouse at the Big A in Anaheim before a Saturday night game when I asked him to make the call. As a reporter and an eavesdropper, I heard Mo tell him, "Jason, this is Mo Vaughn. Happy Birthday and cheer up! Everything is going to be okay. I will try to hit a home run for you tonight." By the seventh inning, the Red Sox were losing 7-1, and bang! Mo hit a home run. The Sox still lost 7-2.

That was Jerry Trupiano's first year with the Sox and I went on the air and told the story of how Mo Vaughn had promised this kid that he *would try* to hit a home run for him. I also went down to the press box and told the story to the reporters who were there. We went home on Sunday. The papers and the wire services had picked up the story and by the time the Sox returned to Fenway on Tuesday—Monday was an off day—every magazine, writer, TV show, and radio program had a reporter at the park to interview Mo about Jason Leader. The Jimmy Fund arranged for Jason to come to the park, and Mo took him into the clubhouse for a private conversation. Mo gave him a pair of batting gloves, some bats, and balls. Jason's health continued to improve. Mo would invite him in the clubhouse whenever Jason came to Fenway. They became very good friends. Mo sent him a big floral display with baseball cards on his 11th birthday. But by then, Jason was going downhill. Jason was in our broadcast booth with his father and his brothers and sisters. He was trying to be strong. The Yankees were blowing out the Red Sox. After the game, Jason went down to the clubhouse to see his friend Mo. That was the last time I saw Jason.

Some time later we got word that Jason had passed away. I went to his funeral in a tiny church in the little town of Niversville, New York. It looked like the church on the TV show, *Little House on the Prairie*. There were a lot of young children at the church, and of course the whole thing was very sad. Mark Cummings from the Jimmy Fund and I were standing in the back of the church, when in walks Mo Vaughn. It was about a three-and-a-half to four-hour drive from Boston to Niversville. After the services, Mo greeted Jason's parents, brothers, and sisters in the parking lot. The relationship continued. Mo's parents, Leroy and Shirley, became very friendly with the Leaders. Since then they have created the Jason-Mo Friendship Fund at Fenway. For a number of years, Mo's family and the Leaders would walk the route of the Boston Marathon together. The Jimmy Fund Walk raises about $4 million each year.

◆ ● ◆

Another Jimmy Fund patient we have come to admire is Kate Shaughnessy, the daughter of Boston Globe columnist and noted author, Dan Shaughnessy who wrote *Curse of the Bambino* and *At Fenway*. Kate, who was diagnosed with childhood leukemia, became a leading spokesperson for the Jimmy Fund and made a most memorable speech at our inaugural 406 Club event. The 406 Club is a group of what became more than 500 members who pledged to donate $1,000 per year for five years to the Jimmy Fund. Ted Williams was the keynote speaker at our first winter reception and Kate gave a wonderful introductory speech, which included a poem she wrote about number nine.

Kate successfully completed her treatment, became quite a highschool athlete in Newton, and is now playing on the women's softball team at Boston University. Like Uri Berenguer, Kate continues to speak for the Jimmy Fund and lend her support to various fundraisers. She has not only beaten cancer but has developed into a beautiful young student-athlete and an inspiration for today's Jimmy Fund kids.

◆ ● ◆

I travel all around New England for banquets, golf tournaments, and check presentations for the Jimmy Fund. We've done radiothons at many smaller stations in New Hampshire, Connecticut, and such places as Bangor and Calais, Maine (about two hours from Bangor), which is the easternmost outpost of the Red Sox radio network. Calais is just over the border from St. Steven, New Brunswick, Canada and is about as far east as you can go in the United States.

We do one big radiothon each year at WEEI, the Red Sox flagship station. In August 2002, WEEI raised $300,000 for the Jimmy Fund, and in 2003 we more than doubled our goal, raising more than $1.1 million during the radiothon, hosted by the Red Sox at Fenway Park.

I come from a medical family. My father was a dermatologist, as is my brother Frank. My youngest brother, Charlie, is a plastic surgeon. My son Tom is a doctor. My brother-in-law is a neurologist. The Jimmy Fund is my connection with the medical community. Through my work with the Jimmy Fund, I have met some wonderful people—doctors and nurses and the patients and their families. I've also met some great volunteers through the years, including those involved in the Jimmy Fund councils who direct fundraising activities throughout their communities.

One of the great thrills of my connection with the Jimmy Fund was meeting Jimmy himself. Many people thought that Jimmy had passed away after the Ralph Edwards radio program, because "Jimmy" had leukemia, and at the time, it was almost always fatal. But Jimmy lived and had become a self-employed tractor/trailer driver who lived in Maine. Like so many people from Maine, he shunned publicity. Cancer was a word that was rarely mentioned back then. His sister wrote a letter to the Jimmy Fund in 1996, which did some research to verify her claim that her brother was indeed "the Jimmy." He had decided to come forward and shed his anonymity 50 years after the original broadcast when he was in his 60s because he thought it would help the Jimmy

Fund. His name is Einar Gustafson. He was a wonderful guy and exactly what you'd want Jimmy to be—gracious, humble, well spoken, and a blue-collar, salt-of-the-earth guy. He lost his first wife to cancer and here he was in 1997 doing what he could to help the Jimmy Fund.

I have made some great introductions in my career. I introduced Bob Feller to Roger Clemens—oil and water. I introduced Ernie Harwell to Pedro Martinez—most cordial. But I'll never forget introducing Uri Berenguer to Einar Gustafson. Unfortunately, Einar passed away in 2001.

Uri and I went together to the memorial service for Einar at an auditorium at Dana-Farber. Einer had done so much for the Jimmy Fund at its inception and then 50 years later, had done a wonderful job, inspiring others to continue the fight to treat and cure cancer, especially in children.

The zeal and energy of the Jimmy Fund staff is amazing. I have worked with some of the most dedicated people imaginable from executives like Mike Andrews and Suzanne Fountain, who always know how to get things done, to the program coordinators—and especially the volunteers. The Jimmy Fund is truly New England's charity. Cure rates for many forms of cancer have risen dramatically and much of the research that makes that possible can be attributed to the Jimmy Fund. The unique relationship between the Jimmy Fund and the Red Sox, the only one of its kind in professional sports, will continue to flourish. Shortly after taking over control of the Red Sox, new principal owner John Henry and CEO Larry Lucchino pledged to continue the bond between the Red Sox and the Jimmy Fund. Mr. Henry toured the clinic within days after taking over the franchise. Mr. Lucchino needed no introduction. He had been a patient at the Dana-Farber Clinic in Boston during the mid-1980s while undergoing treatment for cancer—of which he was cured.

About the Authors

Joe Castiglione, a native New Englander, is now in his 22nd season as radio broadcaster for the Boston Red Sox. He has broadcast well more than 3,500 Red Sox games including postseason play. Prior to coming to Boston, Joe spent one season broadcasting Milwaukee Brewers cable-TV games and two years as television broadcaster for the Cleveland Indians. He has also broadcast Cleveland Cavaliers basketball on television and New England College basketball.

Joe is a graduate of Colgate University with a master's from Syracuse University. He has taught a sports broadcasting course at Northeastern University in Boston since 1985 and at Franklin Pierce College in New Hampshire since 1997. Joe is now in his 15th year with the Jimmy Fund of the Dana Farber Cancer Institute where he works in fundraising and event projects. Joe has been married to Janice, an elementary school teacher for 32 years and they have three children, Duke, a TV sportscaster at WCBS-TV in New York, Tom, a physician, now in his residency and Kate, who works for a Boston area production company.

Coauthor **Douglas B. Lyons** is the coauthor (with his brother Jeffrey) of two books of baseball history and trivia, *Out of Left Field* and *Curveballs and Screwballs*. He is also the coauthor, with Eddie Feigner, of *From an Orphan to a King*. He is a criminal lawyer in New York City.